D1108323

Man on Horseback

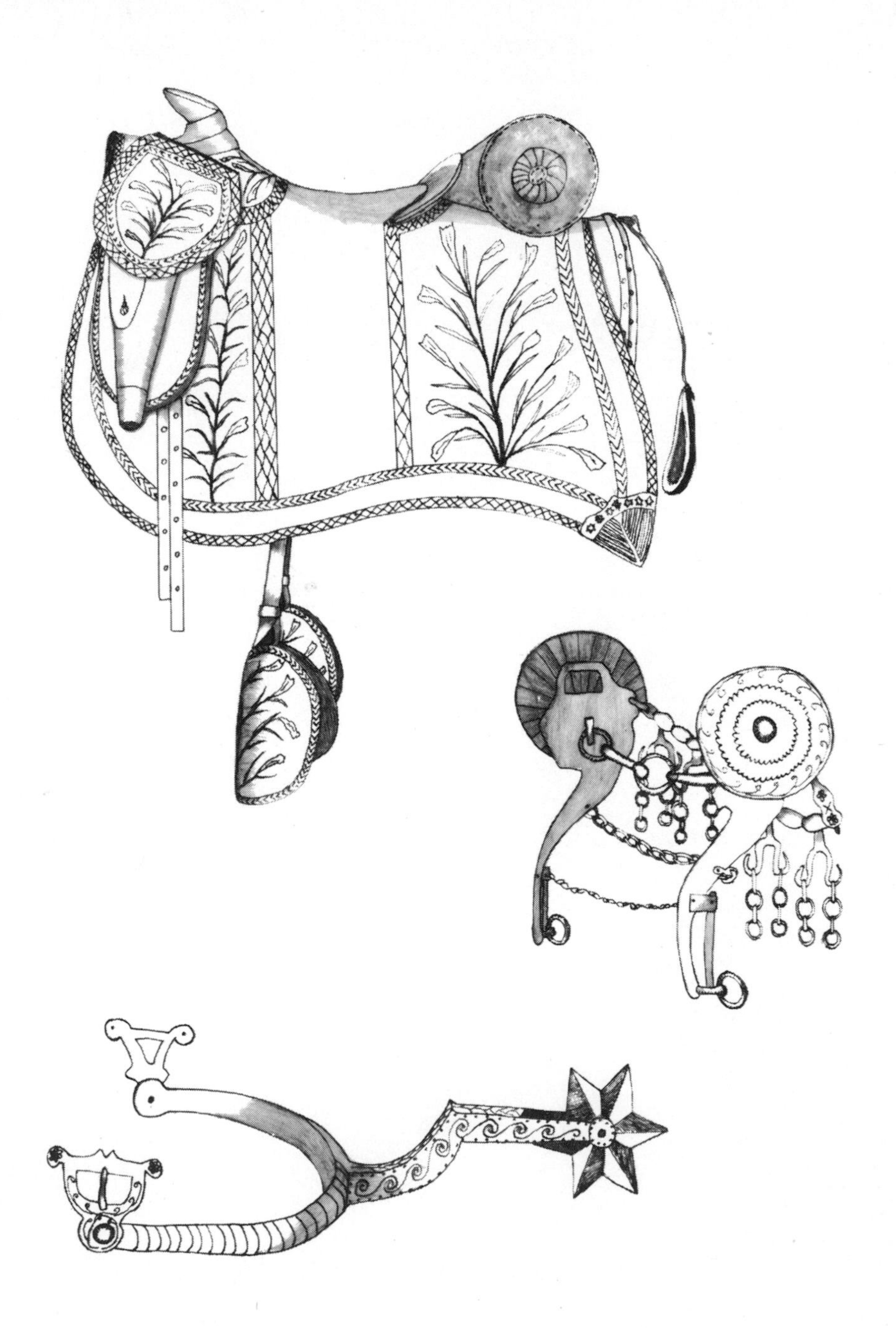

MAN ON HORSEBACK

Glenn R. Vernam

Drawings by the author

HARPER & ROW, PUBLISHERS
NEW YORK, EVANSTON AND LONDON

LIBRARY
NOV 16 1977
UNIVERSITY OF THE PACIFIC
337828
Western
Americana
SF
283
V52
1964

MAN ON HORSEBACK. *Copyright © 1964 by Glenn R. Vernam. Printed in the United States of America. All rights reserved. No part of this book may be used or reproduced in any manner whatsoever without written permission except in the case of brief quotations embodied in critical articles and reviews.* *For information address Harper & Row, Publishers, Incorporated, 49 East 33rd Street, New York 16, N.Y.*

FIRST EDITION

LIBRARY OF CONGRESS CATALOG CARD NUMBER: 64-20544

TO THE MYRIAD LEGIONS OF
HORSEBACK MEN WHOSE BOLD EYES
AND DAUNTLESS BEARING
OVERSHADOWED THEIR EARTH-BOUND
CONTEMPORARIES IN ALL
THE HIGHLIGHTS OF HISTORY
THROUGHOUT THE AGES.

Contents

Foreword

MAN SEATED on a horse's back is history's dominant figure. How the association of man and horse was first formed is one of history's great mysteries. The tracks of the man on horseback are widespread, varied, scattered, often buried under the dust of time, and they extend so far back into the darkness of antiquity that it is difficult to obtain anything like a comprehensive view of man's journey around the world. Man has been using horses for six or eight thousand years, perhaps even longer. But so commonplace has the association always been that he seldom bothered to preserve detailed accounts of everyday activities. What records he did leave were usually confined to the more notable highlights and isolated events. There has been no lack of attention paid to the heroic deeds and general appearance of horseback man. Horses and horsemen appear in every phase of human history.

Even in our own most literate era only a few scattered attempts have been made to record the seeds from which germinated the evolutionary process leading toward modern riding equipment. Both the gear and the knowledgeable men who kept America on horseback fifty or a hundred years ago have vanished into the limbo of forgotten things; and few basic details of the days of Homer, Charlemagne, and Cortez were recorded.

It has been the writer's ambition to gather and preserve as much as possible of the background developments in the horseback world in all past eras. This book has been compiled from a multitude of sources, chiefly in bits and pieces, but all, so far as careful research has been able to determine, the most authentic available. If the reader finds an occasional mistake or omission, may he also find indulgence for one who was frequently lost in the wilderness of uncertainty and had to make out with what looked like the best choice of conflicting decisions. In the hope that the result will provide most of the answers to the many questions horseback folk always like to argue about, and that it will be of general interest to the uninitiated as well, I offer it to all those who have a weakness for fine horseflesh and the smell of good leather.

GLENN R. VERNAM

Man on Horseback

—1—

The Horse in Antiquity

HORSES ARE among the earth's older animals. They started their long march of evolution some fifty million years ago, in company with the tapirs, giant ground sloths, hairy mammoths, and titanotheres. These original horses were only twelve or fourteen inches high, about the size of a fox terrier. They had four toes on their forefeet and three on their hind feet. They were forest-dwelling creatures who lived in the timbered regions of both Europe and North America during the Lower Eocene period. In the course of some thirty million years they evolved into animals about the size of sheep.

Around thirty million years ago, it is thought, the land bridge between America and Europe was severed. Along about that time the horse died out in Europe. As South America was not connected with North America until later, the latter continent was the sole home of the horse for an extended period.

These North American horses gradually developed until, during Miocene times, ten to twenty million years ago, they became something like small ponies. During this later period they migrated across some sort of a land bridge to Asia. It is believed that such a connecting link between the two continents existed across what is now the Bering Strait. This migration allowed the Miocene horse to repropagate in Asia, spreading across to western Europe.

But again horses failed to survive in the Eastern world. They died out completely after a few million years, for some unknown reason. The same thing happened a second time, later on, after the still larger American horse of the Pliocene period had again spread across Asia. It was not until Pleistocene times that a third influx of American horses managed to make a permanent stand in Eurasia.

South America suffered much the same difficulty. It was not until after geological upheavals created the isthmus between the two American continents, in Pliocene times, that horses found a way of moving into the southern lands. And like those first migrations into Asia, these early South American horses eventually became extinct. In the later centuries of the Pleistocene period a second migration of still larger and more highly developed animals moved down into the southern continent, spreading over the entire area.

Of all the earth's lands Australia alone shows no evidence of ever having had an equine population in prehistoric times.

During these formative ages various strains of horses flourished for certain periods and then faded out of the picture to give way to more highly developed animals. As the land masses were uplifted to form high, grassy plains, the horse evolved into a single-toed, grass-eating, running animal. He eventually reached a stature fairly comparable to our modern horses. And it was on the open grasslands of the world that he reached his highest development.

However, despite the fact that horses had lived continuously in North America throughout the ages, and repeatedly restocked the rest of the earth, they finally vanished from both this continent and its neighbor to the south. Why or exactly when is still one of nature's unsolved mysteries. It is quite evident they were abundant here as late as 20,000–15,000 B.C. America's early man was certainly associated with them, though probably only in the role of hunter and hunted. But like their human contemporaries of that little-known era, American horses had long since vanished from their old stamping grounds before the first white man arrived here.

On the other hand, Eurasia's final importation of horses continued to survive and spread. When man arrived on the scene, the animals were in plentiful supply throughout the continent. This was in a very early period. Science has slowly advanced man's age into the past until it now stands at well beyond a million years. The future may well disclose earlier evidence. But whatever the date of man's advent on earth, it is only reasonable to suppose the horse was one of his closest neighbors.

In the beginning, man apparently considered the animals as a food source. Cro-Magnon man, who lived in Europe thirty to forty thousand years ago, hunted wild horses as well as mammoths, bison, reindeer, and aurochs. That these people were great eaters of horseflesh is evidenced by the fact that horse bones are one of the most prominent features of their refuse dumps. At one of their most noted camp sites, near Lyons, France, there are bones of some 100,000 horses among those of reindeer, bison, and mammoths. The Solutré caves in the same region are stacked with the bones of thousands of horses. The fact that most of these bones were from young horses and had been completely dismembered is proof they had been used as food. Additional evidence is to be found in the

FIG. 1. The caveman's horses as pictured in French caves.

20,000-year-old clay models of horses bearing javelin thrusts discovered in the Grotte de Montespan in France.

The Fond-de-Gaume cave in France has fifteen drawings of horses on its walls. In the tunnel of Les Combarelles, 750 feet underground, are 116 drawings of undersized, long-haired horses among those of various other animals. Fig. 1 shows typical examples of ancient drawings and bone carvings found throughout Europe and credited to the 30,000–20,000 B.C. period.

Judging by fossil remains and neolithic cave art, these wild herds which roamed over Europe and Asia at that time were of two distinct types. On one hand, there was the forest-dwelling Nordic horse of northern Europe; on the other, was the open-country steppes animal of central Asia. The Nordic animal was a rather coarse, heavily built, big-headed horse ranging from the Baltic region west to the British Isles. The Norwegian dun was no doubt a member of this family, indigenous to the Scandinavian peninsula. The original Celtic ponies of Ireland, as well as those of Iceland, were probably descendants of this breed brought there by early Norsemen. The Norwegian dun was apparently closely related to the ancient tarpan, which was in all likelihood the common ancestor of both the Nordic and steppes horse.

The tarpan, which existed in Asia until fairly recent times, has been traced back to geological ages. It closely resembles the horse of ancient man's cave paintings and bone carvings. These animals seem to have been a sort of cross between the horse, kiang, and onager. They were small, long-haired, moose-nosed creatures with big heads, long ears, protuberant foreheads, short legs, and stiffly erect manes. Their hair was more like fur, and they carried the black stripe and leg markings present in the Norwegian dun. Their color was mostly dun or gray and they had mulelike tails, only the lower half of which had long hair.

Very similar is the Przhevalski horse of today, named for the Russian explorer who first identified and classified it. This animal is the only true primitive horse of modern times. It is an undersized, reddish-brown, stockily built beast whose descendants are sometimes found ranging in small bands in Mongolia.

The original steppes horse was probably much like the tarpan. Smaller and more neatly built than the Nordic, it still retained the ugly head and furry body. However, it was more fleet of foot and better adapted to the chase. It developed into the sturdy and durable horse which later carried historical man over most of Asia.

—2—

Man Meets the Horse

AFTER THE CLOSE of the Neolithic age, the Nordic horse of Europe appears to have received little attention from early man. Europeans of that period were mostly cattlemen. They preferred beef to horseflesh and, as a general rule, used the ox as their beast of burden. It was not until the later centuries of the pre-Christian Era that they began domesticating the horse.

Thus we find the steppes animal as the one which figured most prominently in early human destiny. He appears first among the Vase Painters of Anau, a sedentary race of agricultural village dwellers who inhabited southern Turkestan between the Caspian Sea and the Oxus River during the 8000–6000 B.C. period. Discoveries in that section strongly indicate that these people were acquainted with horses.

A similar race of village-dwelling agriculturists, recently discovered in the Kurdish hills of the Jarmo district in northern Iraq, stand in much the same light. Relics excavated there reveal the existence of domesticated dogs, goats, sheep, cattle, and horses. Radiocarbon tests date this find as a going concern in 7000 B.C., making it fairly contemporaneous with the Vase Painters farther east.

The legendary Cimmerians, who followed the Vase Painters, were in turn displaced by the Scythians, perhaps as early as 6000 B.C. Both had domestic horses. It was the latter who introduced the animals into the lands of the Iranian Plateau. Some of their tribes, such as the Kassites, who conquered Babylonia, and the Mitanni, who took over the upper Euphrates Valley, spread horses throughout Persia. From there, they moved westward into Cappadocia and Syria. Another branch fanned out to the Indus and Ganges valleys, giving the latter section a horse culture before 1000 B.C.

It was during this period, around 1730 B.C., that the Syrian Hyksos, or Shepherd kings, brought horses to Egypt. Mythology and legendary evidence lead us to believe these Egyptian horses later were taken to Greece.

It was somewhere along in this period that those famous seafarers, the Phoenician traders, discovered a growing market for horses in the lands bordering the Mediterranean. This trade was well established by 1000 B.C. Trading their four-footed stock from Cappadocia and Syria for local commodities of other countries, the Phoenicians inaugurated or added to horse culture all along the coasts of Africa and Europe to the Strait of Gibraltar. Most authorities contend that their commerce eventually led them up the west European coast to the British Isles.

When Caesar invaded Britain in 55 B.C. he found the natives using a strain of small, hardy horses which ran in small droves without care or special feeding. An experienced horseman himself, he thought that many of the better animals showed strong evidence of having been crossed with eastern desert breeds. He attributed this to early importations by Phoenician traders. It is a logical conclusion.

In view of the fact that Britain was using horses several centuries before the Christian Era, we must presume that its domestic horse culture started at a fairly early date. All indications are that it stemmed from the Norwegian dun. The northern horses were heavier and stockier than those of the south. Also, those of northern Europe always were and still are trotters and pacers, whereas the gait of those from the Mediterranean countries is the gallop.

Unlike the Britons, the Germanic Goths had no domestic horses in ancient times. They were introduced to horse culture by the Scythians and Sarmatians. The latter had moved in from the east to crowd the Scythians out of the Black Sea region around 200–100 B.C. By the first part of the Christian Era they had spread across southwestern Russia and over into southeastern Europe. About A.D. 200 the Germanic tribes moved down from the Baltic to settle between the Danube and Don rivers. By the time they had crowded out the Scythians and Sarmatians, a hundred years or so later, they had become a recognized horse people themselves.

Turning back to the East, we find the curious fact that the northern Hunnish tribes, living near where the horse undoubtedly originated, were still fighting on foot as late as 541 B.C. They were, however, well equipped with horses by 300 B.C. Their stock consisted of the tough, shaggy, undersized Mongolian ponies.

Neighboring China, on the other hand, had domestic horses obtained from Chinese Turkestan at a much earlier date. They were similar to the Mongolian ponies, perhaps being the latter's foundation stock.

Manchuria and Korea had no horses until after 300 B.C. Both these countries were supplied with Chinese animals after being conquered by China in 108 B.C. Everything also points to China as the source of Japanese horses.

The ass, man's other beast of burden, is also one of the world's oldest riding animals. Whether or not its lineage extends as far back as the horse, its appearance as a domestic animal is equally obscure. The claim that it originated in Abyssinia is no doubt valid, as the original wild ass is known to have been found nowhere except in North Africa. There is no evidence that it ever crossed the Mediterranean or Red Sea until transported there by man.

All asses and donkeys evidently evolved from those wild North African herds. And their domestication must have taken place at a time most remote. The Egyptians knew them in the early centuries of their civilization. On Ti's tomb at Memphis, asses are pictured in the "Procession of Servants." They were in use as riding animals throughout the East in very ancient times, often serving as popular mounts before horses became common. Herds of asses were often maintained for milk during Bible times. All through history they have been the poor man's horse. Early desert sheiks bred a special strain of white asses which were highly prized.

The large white asses of Damascus and Baghdad are still greatly valued for their color and speed, as they have been for centuries. Syrian asses are noted for their fine qualities as saddle animals. Syria has developed four distinct breeds very popular throughout the East. They consist of a heavy muscular strain used chiefly for agriculture; the big Damascus ass noted for the extreme length of its body and ears; a light, graceful, easy-gaited type preferred by the ladies; and the Arab breed, a generally popular saddle beast. Arabia's Al-Hasa donkeys are universally famous.

The soft gray color of the original wild ass is most prevalent in the East. In France and Spain, on the other hand, the animals run heavily to darker colors. It was from these that North and South America inherited their burro population.

Had not the burro come from Spain to Mexico and America's Southwest with the Spanish conquerors, both territories would have been sadly retarded in their development. Used under the saddle or in harness, he has been the poor man's all-purpose work beast for four centuries throughout a land where feed and water is scarce and the terrain difficult for less durable animals.

The Southwest's Spanish mule, product of a mustang mare bred to a burro jack, is an American development designed to add size and strength to the burro's indestructible body. The result gives a remarkably sturdy and active breed of small mules which takes the place of both burros and horses in many quarters.

There is nothing new, however, about mule breeding. Man has used mules for thousands of years. In the thirty-sixth chapter of Genesis we read about Anah finding mules in the wilderness. That was around 1800 B.C. As only asses crossed with horses can produce mules, we must conclude that Esau's people must have started producing the new breed shortly after horses first appeared in that country. Eight hundred years later, II Sam. 18:9 tells us, Absalom was riding a mule when he got his hair caught in a tree and hanged himself.

The new hybrid apparently captured the public fancy. Homer, writing around 800 B.C., made considerable mention of mules. The Roman emperors were fond of them for both riding and drawing chariots. Mohammed liked them so well for riding that he started importing them into Arabia from Egypt in the seventh century. Spanish riders developed such a marked preference for mules in the fifteenth century that the country suffered a serious decline in the raising of horses. This shortsighted trend became so acute that Ferdinand and Isabella passed a law which made it a capital offense to ride mules without a special government permit, thus forcing the average would-be rider to equip himself with a horse.

It was this Spanish stock which first set America's eastern states up in the mule business. Although some mules did come into the Southwest by way of Mexico, the industry as a whole sprang from the jennets and a couple of jackasses presented to George Washington by the king of Spain and the Marquis de Lafayette in 1783. Washington's successful breeding experiments at Mount Vernon made the nation highly conscious of the superior work animal.

—3—

The Mounted Man Appears

HISTORY, TRADITION, and legends of all peoples link the man with the horse since earliest times. In all such accounts the animal's potentialities as an aid to humanity have been well recognized. Even people who were most primitive, who had little idea of improvement or the better things of life, saw and understood the merit inherent in this noble creature. To them, as to all who followed in their footsteps, an animal possessing such strength, docility, courage, intelligence, speed, and companionability could inspire nothing less than the highest admiration.

We have no way of knowing who was the first man to mount a horse, or when it happened. He was already up and going when the farthermost curtains of antiquity were parted. Of only one thing can we be certain: he was a nomad and a disciple of freedom. Sedentary villagers and agriculturists the world around never showed the initiative which carried the horseman to new lands and legendary conquests.

The various achievements known to have been accomplished by ancient man all attest to much constructive thought and manual dexterity. With such a background, it is easy to visualize one of those early Cro-Magnon youths courting acclaim by throwing himself astride a wounded animal or escaping colt. And, after that first wonderful moment of being borne through the air on the wings of speed, surely only death could stop him from being henceforth a man on horseback.

Many students of the subject are inclined to believe the nomadic tribes of 10,000 to 20,000 years ago traveled on horseback in hunting and war. Several drawings left by the Cro-Magnons show marks that strongly suggest halters or bridles on horse heads. One in particular has what appears to be a rope of some twisted material about the animal's neck. Scientists tell us that neolithic man of that period did not eat horses, some suggesting he had by then already found better use for them.

Nevertheless, the first act in the pageant of horsemanship has never been revealed. Antiquarians have pretty well determined when man first learned other useful arts and crafts. The birth of weaving, masonry construction, religious beliefs, marriage forms, and seagoing boats have all been roughly tabulated on the calendar of time. But no delver in antiquities has yet found a definite answer to the question of when horseback riding actually began.

Several treatises on horsemanship and the animal itself are among the world's oldest literature, written several centuries before the Christian Era. Wherever man has moved in story, fable, or song, his horse is seldom absent from the picture. Yet none of even the most ancient historians of any land mention the animal's domestication. One and all slide over this particular feature as though it did not exist, or had been so long an accepted fact that mention is unnecessary. We have a fairly comprehensive record of man's activities back to 6000–5000 B.C. If his association with the horse was so commonplace as to escape comment even at that early date, who is to say neolithic man was not using a select steed, raised from a colt, to round up the wild herds for mounting his tribal friends?

Greek mythology has a pretty story about the horse Pegasus being the first of his kind and Bellerophon being the first man to ride him. This animal, so the legend goes, was born out of the blood soaking into the ground where Perseus cut off Medusa's head. The goddess Minerva saw possibilities in the new animal, so she caught and tamed him.

When Bellerophon set out to kill the Chimera, he first called on the wise Minerva for a few pointers on dragon slaying. She directed his attention toward the winged steed drinking at the Well of Pirene and told him a successful conquest would be his if he tackled the job on the back of this animal. She then gave him a golden bridle, presumably of her own invention, and sent him on his way with a bit of advice about mounted warfare. Bellerophon thereupon sallied forth to win the first horseback victory in combat. Moreover, his example opened up a whole new concept for men of skill and courage.

Unfortunately, we have no knowledge of whether Bellerophon was originally a Grecian figure or whether this tale was based on some legend stemming from an earlier people. Many Greek myths were derived from ancient Chaldean folklore or other fables from still more remote times. As all such legends must grow from factual germs, we have to give the storied rider credit for being an actuality in some capacity. Such a conception might well have been born when some owl-eyed cave man looked up from his pot of fermented blackberry juice to catch his first sight of a mounted man loping across the countryside, the skirts of his robe or blanket flapping against the horse's sides. Perhaps seen through an early-morning haze and a certain amount of blackberry fumes, the winglike garment rising and falling with the speeding animal's movements could easily contribute to a fleeting impression of some birdlike creature in flight. Neighborhood gossip would soon supply additional details.

Other legends combined with certain archeological explorations lead to the certainty that men of the Russian steppes were riding horses at a time long lost in the darkness of antiquity. Setting aside the Vase Painters, who had horses but may not have used them for riding, we get our first glimpse of the true mounted man in a largely unidentified race known as the Cimmerians. The Assyrians called them the Gimirrai. These were an Asian people who ranged south as far as the Black Sea. They seem to have displaced the Vase Painters northeast of the Black Sea around 8000–6000 B.C. Very little is known about them except that they were nomadic horsemen. They disappeared before the invading Scythians, whose fierce mounted warriors swept into that territory from northern Turkestan perhaps as early as 6000 B.C.

—4—

The Horseman Rides South

MOST OF THE BRIGHT luster of history would be missing if the mounted man had not ridden through its pages, leaving a passage marked by the glint of bold, free eyes and shining armor. In all ages civilization's stirring deeds have centered around him. Be he barbarian, warrior, crusader, knight, conquistador, cowboy, or cavalryman, it was the man on horseback who created the sagas of valor and carried the banner of romance throughout the world. His is the figure that has excited the admiration of footmen for a hundred centuries; he it is to whom the man on foot has always instinctively lifted his eyes, both physically and spiritually.

This is perhaps why mention of the word Scythian, even after six thousand years, still brings an atavistic surge to hearts not completely drugged by a mechanical civilization. Those wild, free nomads who moved as the wind across their untamed wilderness and disdained allegiance to any overlords stand as a great shining blade between the subservience of monarchical serfs and the romance of freedom. Proudly they rode, seeming one with their mounts and looking up to no man, as with flashing spears and strung bows they swept down past the Caspian Sea into the dawn of history. Then, as since, they lifted the gaze of oppressed soil tillers and village dwellers to a life bounded only by the farthest horizons.

The Scythians were a Caucasian people who ranged through northern Turkestan and southern Russia. The earliest of historical writers speak of their prowess on horseback. They were highly accomplished in the riding art and possessed a superior breed of horses when we first glimpse them around 5000–4000 B.C. That they were riding long before that is shown by scraps of their riding gear unearthed from their most ancient tombs.

Somewhere around 4000 B.C. they were well established in history, ranging from the Black Sea to northwestern China. During this period they overran their neighbors to the south and spread their horse culture out onto the Iranian Plateau.

The Scythians considered their horses of highest importance. Riding was universal among them. Only the lowest menial would work or travel on foot. In later centuries they were noted for their vast herds of horses, cattle, and sheep. But always the horse came first, standing as the supreme domestic animal in their eyes. Its meat was rated a great delicacy, its bones provided material for spear and arrow points, and mare's milk was a favorite food. The milk was used both in the raw state and as a fermented drink which the Greeks called *oxygala,* and later Asians knew as *kumis*. They preferred mares for riding. Pliny the Elder (A.D. 23–79) wrote that mares were so chosen because of being less given to delay while urinating during battle. Other writers claimed it was because mares were less likely to betray their presence during surprise attacks on the enemy.

In the beginning we can only suppose these people rode bareback, with nose- or jaw-cords for bridles, as have all primitive races in the infancy of their horsemanship. Archeological discoveries, however, show that the Scythians used crude bits at a very early date. It is quite possible that they devised the first actual bridle bits. Various historians think so. One researcher has found cause to believe the Scythians also developed some sort of a saddle around 700–600 B.C. Perhaps they did use blankets or hide pads bound to the horses' backs—Assyria was using riding cloths as early as 650 B.C.—but it is doubtful if they had anything resembling a real saddle at that time. All the best evidence points to the fact that saddles as such did not appear until several centuries later.

An old Greek vase of the seventh century B.C. carries some pictures of a group of Scythians shoeing, handling, and perhaps breaking horses to ride. There is, however, nothing in the pictures to indicate saddles. Hippocrates wrote about 400 B.C. that the Scythians were much afflicted by swellings and discomfort in their legs from riding, a fairly common complaint among bareback riders all through the pre-saddle era.

We know from various old drawings that the Sarmatians, who superseded the Scythians, rode bareback, bridles and bits being their only accouterments. They surely wouldn't have overlooked any improvements the earlier people might have had.

The Sarmatians came from Kashgaria in Chinese Turkestan, somewhere around 300 B.C. They are thought to have been relatives of the Scythians. At any rate, they moved in like part of the family and, in the course of a couple of hundred years, crowded the latter on west as far as Hungary and Romania. By A.D. 100 they had not only completely ousted the Scythians from their former territory, but had gone on to assume lordship over their new holdings on the Hungarian plains.

They were fierce nomadic fighters and famous horsemen from the time they first appeared. They always fought on horseback and were notably adept at cavalry tactics. They were famed for their wealth in horses, and used the meat extensively as food. Vergil (70–19 B.C.) wrote that they also sacrificed horses as offerings to the gods, as well as eating the flesh and drinking the blood.

Judging by existing pictures left by ancient artists, however, their horses would appear to have been on the small side. Most of them might be classed as ponies. Though they habitually rode mares, Strabo (54 B.C.–A.D. 21) wrote that they alone, of all Asian people, practiced gelding of horses to some extent.

The Sarmatians were the first people definitely known to have used body and horse armor, though their invention of it remains an open question. This was a sort of scale armor made from the hoofs of dead or slain horses, the hoofs being steamed and straightened and then cut into small oblong pieces. The pieces were perforated at one end, by means of which they were laced in overlapping fashion to clothing and horse trappings with sinew cords. They were often made to cover the entire horse and rider, as in Fig. 2. The resemblance of these horn plates to dragon scales was supposed to give them special invulnerability, as well as stirring a certain amount of superstitious dread among the enemy. Pictures on Trajan's Column in Rome, built in A.D. 114, show some of these warriors with both themselves and their mounts almost entirely covered with such armor.

Certain bits of evidence, however, indicate a much earlier appearance of this type of gear. A case in point is a battle scene of around 1000 B.C. between Saul and the Ammonites pictured in a thirteenth century Bible now in the Pierpont Morgan Library in New York. This illustration shows the mounted warriors wearing some sort of scale or chain armor that covers almost their entire bodies. This could have been artistic license, of course. But when we consider the fact that the Scythians were the foremost exponents of horsemanship and mounted warfare during this period, setting the pattern for their neighbors in most mounted combat activities, it is only logical to believe the Sarmatians and other neighboring peoples simply adopted an unrecorded creation that saw birth farther north several centuries earlier.

Here is an interesting fact: Throughout the Russian steppes and Turkestan, where the horse first enters history as a domesticated animal, man used him for riding centuries before putting him into the harness. There oxen were the universal draft animals employed for drawing tent carts, farm implements, and the like. Conversely, in all other nations, including adjoining China, oxen and buffalo were the original riding animals. The horse was reserved for harnessing to chariots long before any attempt was made to ride him. Moreover, most men in these countries considered the horse too noble a beast to be used for pleasure during their early association with the animal.

This attitude toward horses was no doubt due to the temperament and background of the people involved. There was a vast difference between the free-ranging horse-nomads of Asia and the slow-moving agriculturists of Europe. The latter went in for cattle almost exclusively.

They preferred beef to horse meat and developed domestic bovine herds for food, draft purposes, and burden bearing. When they finally acquired horses, their only thought was for the speedier locomotion of war chariots. Throughout those early ages in the West, the horse appears almost entirely as a chariot animal, used principally for war.

And over most of Europe it was the Asian breed which introduced the first real horse culture. True, the clumsy Nordic horse was domesticated to some extent in Britain and the Scandinavian countries, but its use was limited and no effort seems to have been made in early times to encourage its spread into southern Europe. The ox held sway throughout most of the West until the Cappadocian and Syrian horses moved across the Mediterranean.

The Cappadocians of Asia Minor, the Hyksos of Syria, the Assyrians of the Tigris Valley and their Parthian neighbors to the east were contemporaries of the Scythians. Like the latter, they all appear on the scene sometime prior to 4000 B.C. And all are presumed to have received their apprenticeship in horse culture from the Scythians as a prelude to their fame as warriors noted for their horses and horsemanship.

The Parthians were a nomadic Turanian race from central Asia. They drifted down across the Iranian Plateau some time before 2000 B.C., eventually overflowing most of the country between the Assyrian Empire, the Oxus River, and the Caspian Sea. Their main product was a superior breed of horses, apparently much larger and better built than the earlier Sarmatian stock. They were especially noted for their horsemanship and fighting skill in mounted warfare. Fig. 3, from an old print, is supposed to be a typical specimen mounted in the usual bareback manner and using a jaw-strap bridle.

A unique method of fighting on horseback was used by these people. Whenever misfortune caused them to be pursued by enemy forces, they would immediately take flight at a calculated speed, as if hoping to escape. Then, with the enemy at their heels, and without slackening the speed of their mounts, they would suddenly turn themselves to face backward over their horses' rumps and drive a flight of arrows into the faces of the surprised pursuers. As no other people were known to use such tactics, this method came to be known as "Parthian shooting" or the "Parthian shot." Today we use the expression as a common idiom when we speak of closing an argument with a "parting shot."

The name Parthian, incidentally, is said to come from *Parthus,* which in turn derives from an old Chaldean word signifying horsemen. By the same token, it is thought that Persia derives its name from the word *paras,* which is an ancient name for horse.

Berjeau corroborates this by saying that the names of nations particularly noted for their horsemanship, such as the Persians, Parthians, and probably the Prussians, are derived from *paras,* the original word for horse. The Germanic name for horse, *Pserd, Perd* or *Paerd,* is not far removed from the ancient *paras.* The Ethiopian *fars,* the Arabian *feres,* and the Saxon *Hors* show a similar etymology. The word *presh* is used in most Slavic countries as a command for halting horses.

Ancient Iran's Zoroastrian Bible, the Avesta, was first composed

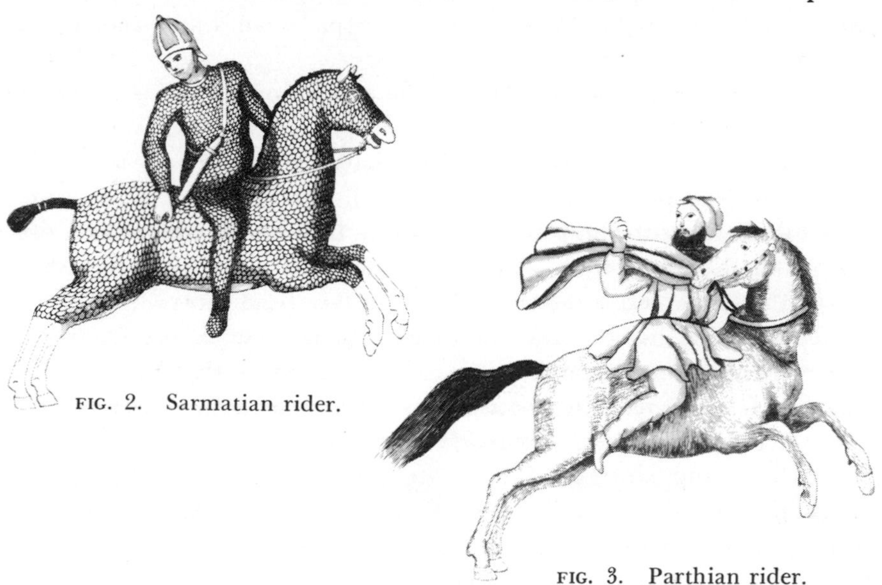

FIG. 2. Sarmatian rider.

FIG. 3. Parthian rider.

somewhere between 1000 and 600 B.C. It contains many references to horses. Their word *Aspa* for the animals was often used in the formation of names for kings. For example, *Arvat-Aspa* meant "Master of Warlike Horses," while *Hu-Aspa* stood for "having good horses."

Buxtorf (1564–1626) claims the original Hebrew word *parash,* meaning horsemen, is derived from the Hebrew root signifying to prick or spur; the spurrer, or rider, was so designated because he pricked or spurred the horse. Ebra goes on to say the horseman was so called from wearing spurs on his heels. Such a connection would suggest the appearance of spurs earlier than is commonly supposed. We shall return to this later.

The Cappadocians, who ranged through Asia Minor from Turkey to Assyria, and their Hittite neighbors in southern Turkey and Syria, were noted for their excellent horse culture in very early times. All the ancient writers extolled the superior qualities of their animals; they seem to have been the most popular mounts all through the Mediterranean area at that time. This strongly supports the belief that Cappadocia and Syria were the main sources of supply for the Phoenician traders.

The riders of these countries were no less famous as horsemen. They carried on an immense amount of trade and communication from one end of the country to the other.

It was from this region that the Hyksos, or Shepherd kings, took the first horses to Egypt. When they invaded that empire in 1730 B.C. their horses were a most important factor in deciding many victories.

The Egyptians, who had never before met any mounted men, were frequently put to flight at the mere sight of such fearsome, half-human, half-animal monsters. Besides the use of horses, the invaders also introduced the chariot and body armor into the Nile Valley. Apparently these innovations were speedily adopted. The oldest existing Egyptian records describe horse chariots. Horses are also important figures in ancient fresco paintings and bas-reliefs. In the forty seventh chapter of Genesis we read that Joseph gave the Egyptians bread in exchange for horses. This would have been around 1700 B.C., only some thirty years after the Hyksos invasion. Exodus contains a description of the flight of the Israelites from Egypt a short while later, telling how they were pursued by six hundred chariots and companies of mounted horsemen. Solomon is recorded as having employed cavalry in warfare and hunting around 965 B.C. His bringing horses out of Egypt during the same period is recorded in I Kings 10:28. The Book of Job says, in speaking of the ostrich, "she lifteth herself on high, she scorns the horse and the rider." Horsemanship in Egypt had thus evidently advanced to the state of mounted warfare and hunting ostriches perhaps as early as 1600–1500 B.C.

Bas-reliefs and carvings indicate that these Syrian-Egyptian horses were smaller than their counterparts farther east. Examples showing a comparison of their size with that of chariot and driver appear in Figs. 4 and 5. The Lycian animals on the frieze of a seventeenth century B.C. tomb at the Acropolis of Lycia, are rather chunky but still undersized. The Egyptian team, on a fresco painting on a tomb at

Thebes, is equally small and even more lightly built. Though the latter animals are thought to be of Nubian stock, they are no doubt fairly typical of that time and place. In color, they ran chiefly to bays and blacks, with occasional piebalds. Some historians believe them to have been the ancestors of the Barbs.

There appears a strong probability that Egypt had two distinct types of horses during its early era. Berenger says the ancient lower Nile Delta horse was a bulky, muscular animal, somewhat like the modern Dutch

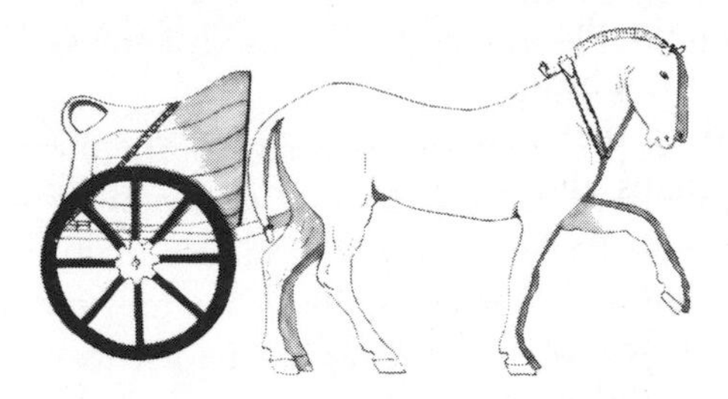

FIG. 4. From Lycia, seventeenth century B.C.

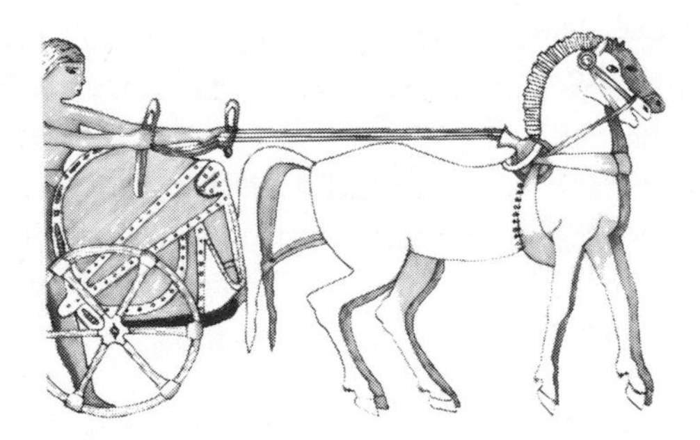

FIG. 5. From Egypt, seventeenth century B.C.

horse. Quite opposite was the nervy, swift, and durable type raised in harsher surroundings farther up the Nile. He attributed the difference to soft ground, rich pasturage, and less activity of the lower country.

James Bruce (1730–1794) wrote that the Numidian horse of upper Egypt was of good size and strength, nervous, agile, and of great endurance. In contrast, Burckhardt wrote that the old Egyptian horse of lower Egypt was of the cart-horse variety, ugly and coarse with a thick neck and thin, short legs. It was clumsy, stood fatigue poorly, and was good only for heavy cavalry. All this leaves little doubt that Egypt had two types of horses, though both might have originated from the same source, leaving environment and breeding to do the rest.

If Greece received its first horses from Egypt, as many legends and early writings indicate, it was quite likely the Nile Delta animal. This would account for the coarse, short-legged and often runty build which various early writers credited to the original Grecian steeds.

Greece might also have received some of the Lycian horses brought by Phoenician traders or others. They were of a similar type. Furthermore, the Greeks must have learned something about horses, if they didn't actually obtain the animals themselves, from the Thracian barbarians to the north. Thrace was conveniently close and it had a horse culture adopted from the Scythians and Sarmatians at a very early date.

Thrace was perhaps the legendary source of the mythological Centaurs, Fig. 6. Centaur, or Hippocentaur, is derived from a Greek word meaning bull fighting by men on horseback. When the ancient Greeks first saw mounted riders, they marveled at the strange half-human, half-animal creatures, as did the Egyptians at sight of the Hyksos. The account of the battles between the Centaurs and Lapithae of ancient Thessaly helps confirm this chapter of Greek mythology.

However, evidence leads us to believe it was the Egyptian horse which first reached the Hellenic peninsula. Herodotus (485–425 B.C.) wrote that it was the Libyans of Africa who first taught the Greeks how to hitch horses to chariots. He also described the Libyans as superior horsemen who always fought on horseback. As Greek mercenaries fought with the Libyans in the latter's war against their eastern neighbors, the Egyptians, it would have been only natural for them to take home knowledge of horse usage.

Greek mythology says that Erichthonius, legendary king of Athens, came to Greece from Egypt. Aristides, Servius, and other early writers claim it was he who introduced into Greece the art of driving horses to wheeled vehicles, riding, and horseback fighting. Further confirmation comes from De Berbe's research, published in 1762, which found the name, Erichthonius, derives from a Greek source meaning inventor, or author, of the horse.

Another legend has it that Neptune and Athena once had a dispute over which could confer the greatest benefit upon man. To settle the contest, Athena gave the olive tree and Neptune gave the horse.

Several ancient writers say the names Neptune and Erichthonius were synonymous. Plutarch and Sophocles both mention Neptune, or Erichthonius, as having first brought the horse to Greece and taught its use. Homer credits both horsemanship and navigation to Neptune. The ancients believed Neptune was the creator of the horse; Pampbus calls him the "Giver of Horses." Equitation was the symbol of navigation at that time. Neptune was supposed to have stabled his horses in a cave under the sea between the Greek islands of Tenedos and Imbros. Demeter, the Greek goddess of fertility, was sometimes depicted as a woman with the head and mane of a horse. Tradition has it that she assumed this form to escape the unwelcome attentions of Neptune.

Further legends say Erichthonius was transported to the heavens

FIG. 6. A centaur.

upon his death, giving us the constellation known as the Charioteer. This ties in with Persian mythology, which has Jupiter drawn by eight white horses. Freret thought the winged horse Pegasus signified a ship given to Bellerophon by Neptune. Various Greek navigation terms were the same as those used in horsemanship. Pindar (about 500 B.C.) calls a bridle an anchor. Homer calls ships horses of the sea and the pilot a coachman. Suidas, writing in the tenth century, says the word *keles,* denoting a runner, applies to both light sailing ships and horses. A further suggestion that the Trojan Horse might have been a shipload of soldiers is contained in one of Plautus' poems, which says, "You are carried over the sky-colored roads [waves?] upon a wooden horse." An early Mycenaean seal shows a horse of immense size standing in a boat and is supposed to represent the importation of horses into Crete.

It is hard to sort the right thread from such a tangled web. The true meanings of many words and phrases have been lost in the confusion of different tongues, different periods, and different colorings of legend. For instance, long after accepting a literal translation of a quotation in the Book of Job, which says, "This animal's neck is clothed with thunder," it was found that the Hebrew word signifying thunder was the same as that for a horse's mane. Perhaps the Neptune-Erichthonius stories could be as easily resolved if we had the right key.

At any rate, so much linking of the sea with horses makes it fairly evident that horse culture reached Greece from that direction. And if Erichthonius was from Egypt, as legendary history suggests, we must conclude that early Grecian horses were an offshoot from those of the Nile.

But however horses arrived, there is no doubt about their eminent position in Greek history. There, as in other Mediterranean countries, they started out as chariot horses before being employed as riding animals. Xenophon (C.434–C.355 B.C.) and Quintus Curtius both wrote of two-wheeled vehicles drawn by one horse, the horse led by footmen. Examples of such rigs are to be found carved on the temple ruins of Persepolis in Persia. Darius and Cyrus used chariots of this kind. Such practices would indicate that the Greek riders had not learned how to handle and control a horse at that time.

On the other hand, this may have been merely a sectional peculiarity or some royal idiosyncrasy. We know Thracians rode horses while still in the barbarian stage. In Lacedaemon, Macedonia, and Thessaly men were riding at a very early period.

Thessaly claimed that Pelethronius of that country invented saddles and bridles. Thessalians were famed throughout Greece for their skill at breaking horses; ancient writers credit them with being the first Greeks to practice that art. They also won considerable renown for their prowess in fighting wild bulls with javelins from horseback. An old proverb boasted that Thessalian horses, like Thessalian women, were the noblest in existence.

Incidentally, Thessalian bullfighting is thought to be the origin of Spanish bullfighting, which later found its way to Spain from Rome. Pliny says Julius Caesar imported it from Greece as an arena spectacle.

While Homer did considerable writing about horsemanship, he failed to give us any details on how or when the practice started in Greece. He treats the subject very casually, as one might any old, familiar custom too commonplace to merit special attention. Even his description of the style of riding in which a man used four horses, jumping from one to another as he traveled, is more in the nature of an incidental observation than an attempt to record an everyday practice.

The Greeks had a class of warrior riders who used two horses, vaulting from one to the other as need arose. Another class was limited to single horses. The third class fought both on horseback and afoot, having servants hold their horses in readiness when they dismounted.

A carving on a Greek sarcophagus shows a battle between Greek horsemen and the mythical Amazons. Xenophon says these legendary females were the Sarmatian women, who hunted and fought on horseback in the same manner as did the men. All this would seem to put at least some of the Greeks on horseback well back in ancient times, although the practice did not assume much importance until they began to appear as mounted soldiers in the army during the seventh century B.C.

Perhaps copied from the Greeks, though they may have come from Asia, were the special warrior cavalry of ancient Gaul, called the *Trimarkisia.* Their riding alternated between the three horses used by each man on mounted forays. Allotting several horses to a rider was an ancient custom among the Russian steppes tribes. And the early Gauls had perhaps more contact with the East than with the civilizations to the south.

There is some obscurity surrounding the Gauls of antiquity. They first appear along the south side of the lower Danube, having apparently migrated into that country from the East. It was the pressure of the Thracians on the south, Germanic tribes on the north, and Scythians on the east which forced them to journey westward about 400 B.C. Since they had lived for an extended period adjacent to, and were crowded out by, such pronounced horsemen as the Scythians and Thracians, it is reasonable to think they had absorbed all the current arts of horsemanship before their advent into Europe. Yet they could have drawn all or part of it from Greece.

As old as mounted warfare, and probably antedating it, was that premier sport of mankind, horse racing. Like a lot of other things, this pastime had its beginning in the dim days of antiquity. Perhaps it started when the first mounted man succeeded in outdistancing some attacking wild stallion. When other village hopefuls got themselves on horseback there was no doubt a race to see which one had captured the best animal. And who is to say the ancient barbarian was not as much given to boasting about his mount's qualities, and perhaps wagering a few choice stone arrowpoints on his judgment, as any twentieth century jockey in a silk jacket?

Though horse racing was popular among all the Asiatics and Africans, we find no mention of it in Greek history until well into the seventh century B.C. This may be due to the fact that most of Greece's early history was written by more advanced men of the southern states, while the horses of that section were still chiefly of the coarse and clumsy stock from the Egyptian delta. Moreover, history indicates that horses were few and expensive to keep or own in much of Greece during early times. Only the wealthy class could afford them. This led to the forming of an organization in Sparta and Athens designed to encourage horse ownership and breeding among the middle-class citizens. It was similar to the later association of Equites in Rome and the Knights of Europe.

Such an influence was bound to bring results. Greece soon claimed one of the finest and most extensive horse cultures in the Mediterranean area, their horses and horsemen occupying a foremost place in literature, art, and sculpture.

In the records of the twenty-third Olympiad, in 684 B.C., we find the horse race for the first time recognized as an established sport. It became extremely popular. The race course was four miles, or a little longer.

It was at one of these earlier Olympic games that we find the first mention in history of a starting barrier being used in horse races. The Romans later adopted the Grecian barrier for use in their chariot races.

In the course of time, Greek admiration for skill and physical prowess led to the introduction of various innovations in horse racing. One of these was a race in which all contestants started with four bareback horses. At designated points they would abandon the ridden mount, vault to the next, and ride on without slackening speed. Coming in on the home stretch, with the last of the four horses, the riders would leap to the ground and make the last half mile on foot beside the horses. Some of these races were run with the riders standing erect on the animals' backs throughout the course.

Existing sculptures and drawings portray Grecian horses of this period as first-class animals. Figs. 7 and 8 show them to be of good size, with clean lines and fine body structure. Roaching of manes was a standard practice. Bareback riding seems to have been the mode through these centuries, although sarcophagus carvings of the battle between the Greeks and the Amazons show some of the mounted warriors riding on a sort of saddle cloth held in place by a breast-collar arrangement.

The Athenian cavalry is said to have adopted the saddle cloth after it first showed up in Greece, about the fifth century B.C. Rolls or pads were often added to the cloths for comfort and security. These saddle cloths were of woven fabric, dressed leather, or skins, sometimes quilted or padded. They were commonly embellished with gold, silver, ivory, gems, bells, tassels, and fancy breast collars.

The Etruscans of neighboring Italy were closely associated with the Greeks during this period. Antiquities show their horses to be a larger, heavier breed than those of the Greeks. The latter were quite similar to the Arabians in build, though usually smaller in size.

The figures on the Parthenon frieze at the Acropolis in Athens are, in comparison with the riders, very similar to the early Sarmatian and Cappadocian ponies in size (Fig. 9). These figures were carved by Phidias about 440 B.C. They are presumed to be typical of that period. The horses originally wore bridles and reins of bronze, but these were removed at some time in the past. Only rivet holes in the animals' mouths and heads remain to mark their former position. Whether any bits were represented, we do not know.

Xenophon mentions spurs being used in ancient Greece, though the quirtlike thonged whip (Fig. 25) was more common. These spurs were undoubtedly the earliest type of single-spike goads, similar to those in Fig. 24, which first showed up about 700 B.C. A form of leg covering that suggests a sort of boot also appears during this period.

As these people had no stirrups, mounting was done by jumping, vaulting with spears, using horse blocks, or teaching horses to kneel. Some even used a rope ladder thrown over the horse and discarded after mounting. Old Greek fresco paintings sometimes show a rider stepping onto his horse from the bent back of a slave.

During the early days of riding it was the duty of highway superintendents to keep piles of stones along the roads in suitable form for use as mounting blocks. The ancients and primitive peoples commonly mounted from the right side of the horse. It was the most natural ap-

FIG. 7. From Rhodes, fourth century B.C.

FIG. 8. Greek-Etruscan rider, fourth century B.C.

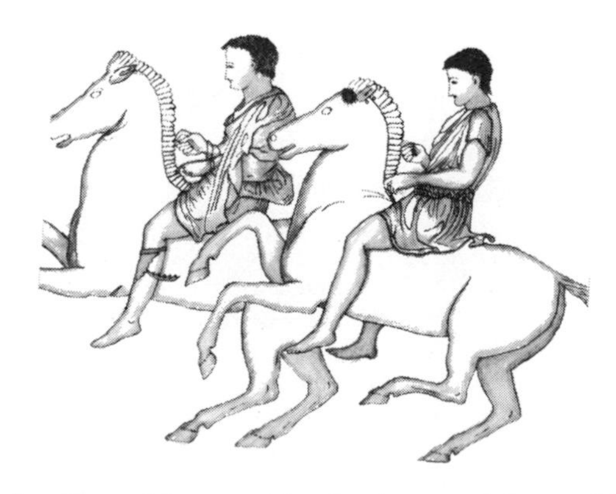

FIG. 9. From frieze on the Parthenon, Athens, 440 B.C.

proach for anyone not trained differently. Offside mounting continued throughout most of the East until the carrying of sabers and swords instituted a change for the sake of convenience. Xenophon, however, indicates that at least some of the Greeks of his day mounted from the near side. If so, they must have been unique among their neighbors. He goes on to say he recommended offside mounting for spearmen as it allowed them to mount from the spear and still have the weapon in its proper right-hand position immediately upon being seated.

The lance used for mounting had a hook or loop fastened to the shaft some distance above the butt. The rider planted his lance butt beside the horse, put his foot into the attachment, and threw the other leg over the horse's back, all in one motion (Fig. 15).

The universal custom of using the left hand for the reins was a practice developed and handed down by ancient warriors. Man is predominantly right-handed. In battle, work, or play, he wanted free and untrammeled use of his good right arm for weapons or other implements; the less dexterous left hand could easily serve as a guiding agent. As it was mounted invaders who invariably introduced horses into the various new lands, their customs set the pattern for all who would aspire to the higher estate.

—5—

Hoofbeat History— Persians, Romans, the East

HORSEBACK MEN

The horseback men were the freest men,
From the days of the big ice pack,
When they first crawled out of their musty den,
To follow a horse's track.
The cave man crouched in the dark and died;
But his son found out that the world was wide,
When he climbed on a horse's back.

Horseback men, oh, horseback men,
Bowlegged, brave old crew!
Here's to your kin where the free stars spin—
Cowpuncher, Cossack and Bedouin,
Gaucho, Mongol and Sioux.

The bold Goth spurred into ancient Rome;
Great Genghis loped with his force;
Our Westerner fought for his wide, new home—
Bestriding a bronc, of course.
New lands, new freedoms, or just the deuce—
Whenever the spirit of man broke loose
He went and saddled a horse.

Horseback men, oh, horseback men,
The weak hide under their roofs,
But only the strong to the tribe belong;
So history's mostly a horseback song,
And set to the thud of hoofs.

But the sword bows down to the monkey wrench,
And the saddle fades from the scene,
For the warrior squats in his miry trench
And charges by gasoline—
And grim time, quitting its one-horse jog,
Whirrs us forward into the fog
On the wings of a swift machine.

Horseback men, oh, horseback men,
Your long day dies at last,
But your fame will climb to a myth sublime,
From the horse tracks thick on the trail of time,
And the echo of hoofs from the past.
—Badger Clark, *Sky Lines and Wood Smoke*

THERE IS NO denying that most of the world's history has been created by horseback men, written to the tune of pounding hoofs. Though many human beings lived for centuries in all corners of the globe before acquiring horses, almost none of them left any lasting achievements. It was those who got up off the ground who went places and did things.

Thus it is that India, lacking a dramatic horseback class throughout most of its existence, has been the only important Eastern nation to show no notably active leadership in historical times. True, it had a horse culture from 1000 B.C. It had its chariots and it learned to ride long before many other nations acquired the art. Yet the few outstanding horsemen who have appeared within its borders from time to time have been transplanted foreigners from horseback countries. India as a whole never displaced its bullocks and buffaloes as riding animals. Horses, as a general thing, have always been reserved for the royalty and ceremonial affairs.

The Assyrians, on the other hand, were quick to answer opportunity's knock. They had accomplished little of note until after the northern nomads introduced horses into their country. From then on, they rose in stature very rapidly. It was as horsemen that we find them coming out of their mud huts along the Tigris River to emblazon their stirring deeds on the early pages of history. Thanks to the horse, they were able to override all opposition during the fourteen hundred years between 2000 and 600 B.C., establishing one of civilization's most fabulous empires.

A bas-relief on the monument of the Assyrian ruler, Ashurbanipal (668–626 B.C.), shows the kind of horses which carried this nation to its golden age. The animal's accouterments are no less imposing (Fig. 10). The saddle cloth was of rich fabric decorated with tasseled fringe and held in place by a cinch and gem-studded breast collar. The protective neck guard, carved and bejeweled headstall, and braided leather neckband hung with small bells were all equally elaborate. Tail wrappings were a customary embellishment.

Much the same may be said for the Persians. Confined for centuries to a small area along the east side of the Persian Gulf, they lifted their eyes to the new four-legged marvels from the north and saw visions. The visions grew as their mounted numbers increased, until they controlled a kingdom extending from India to the Mediterranean.

All ancient writers pay tribute to the horses which carried Persia to her greatest glory. Herodotus says they were famous for their speed, beauty, and quality. Vegetius gives much the same description. They appear to have been somewhat leggy and rather small of body, but neatly built, spirited, durable and capable of keeping the same pace—presumably a gallop—for twenty-five to thirty miles at a stretch.

The Persian name for horse was "wind foot." Horses were held in great esteem by everyone in Persia, high or low. The number of horses a man had was, in fact, the badge of his social standing. The desire to own a quantity of them was equal to a modern American's dream of a four-car garage. The ruler of one small province was said to have maintained a herd of five thousand. Conversely, to be without a mount was the hallmark of inferiority. Persons reduced to riding asses and oxen might get by in sort of a poor-boy, underprivileged way, but having to travel on foot branded one as the lowest of menials. At one time there was even a national law which penalized any horse owner for appearing on foot. Respectable people thought it an essential duty to see that their children were taught to ride properly by the time they were five years old.

Like other Eastern nations, except China, Persia did not geld its horses. This held true even up to modern times. Mares were their favorite mounts, while stallions were groomed principally for export trade. The roaching of manes was customary, as it was among their contemporaries, the Armenians, who were even more famous than the

FIG. 10. From Assyria, seventh century B.C.

Persians for the quality and training of their horses in the pre-Christian Era.

Both nations used the same style of mane trimming. Upper-class horsemen seemed to prefer manes cut in an arched form or notched to resemble battlements. A less pretentious style, and one quite popular with run-of-the-mill riders and common soldiers, was to cut the left side of the mane short, allowing the right side to hang full length. This long hair was usually braided or knotted as an aid to mounting. Riders of that period always mounted from the right side. The knotted mane furnished a convenient handhold.

Another widespread practice throughout this region was that of carefully drying and powdering horse manure for use as stall bedding.

It was thought to be beneficial to the health of the horses and to impart a beautiful gloss and luster to their coats.

To Persia goes credit for originating the cavalry picket line—by the practice of tying their mounts to a long rope. To prevent fighting among the horses—a possibility consistently overlooked by many later cavalrymen—a cord with loops at each end was used to hobble the hind feet, allowing room enough for the horse to get up and down and rest comfortably, but restraining his kicking ability. Xenophon says this custom was in use even before the time of Cyrus (546–527 B.C.). The Persians also made use of nose bags for feeding grain and chopped roughage.

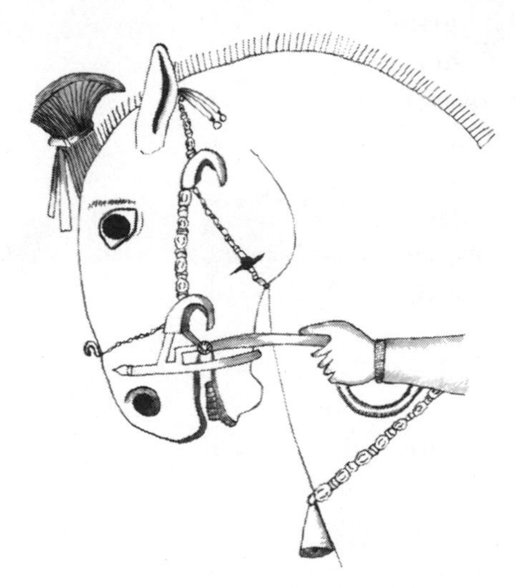

FIG. 11. From Persia, 600–500 B.C.

Persian riding gear ran to rather elaborate headstalls and saddle cloths, which were made of several thicknesses of rich fabric profusely decorated with gems, silk tassels, and fancy embroidery. Heavily decorated breast collars and cruppers held the cloths in position. Bits were of the snaffle variety, some with horizontal or crescent-shaped sidebars. The sidebars occasionally extended around under the jaw to serve as a curb (Fig. 11). Some riders preferred a simple noseband set with small metal barbs on its inner surface. Spurs were not used by the early Persians.

While it is very likely that the Hittites of a thousand years earlier, and perhaps the Assyrians, had some system of pony express riders linking their kingdoms together, the first such enterprise of which we have definite record was instituted during the reign of Darius in Persia (522–548 B.C.). Under his rule, post roads, provided with ferries, bridges, milestones, and inns, formed a nationwide network from India to the Caucasus Mountains. Corps of express riders were maintained by the government throughout the land, working on regular schedules to carry official dispatches and private mail. Royal post stations were located at stated intervals along the highways; and fresh mounts were always kept in readiness for instant use at all stations.

Bokhara horses were apparently favored for relay mounts there. Riders no doubt formed a motley assemblage of Armenians, Cappadocians, Syrians, Medes, Phrygians, Lydians, Cilicians, Parthians, Persians, and Babylonians, master horsemen all. Their most important route was the run of something over 1,500 miles from Susa to Sardis. Fast mail was carried over this route in as little as six days.

A comprehensive account of this organization comes down to us from Herodotus. It was in describing those long-ago pony riders that he wrote, "neither snow, nor rain, nor heat, nor darkness are permitted to obstruct their speed," a quotation which is still used with little change as the motto of our twentieth century postal service in America.

Many elaborate and detailed carvings at the ancient Persian city of Persepolis, some thirty-five miles northeast of Shiras, depict the horses and equipment used during Darius' time. An example is shown in Fig. 12. One of the most imposing of the carvings of armed and mounted riders is the gigantic figure of a horseman at the tomb of Persia's ancient hero Rustam. He is completely armed and accoutered for war. One footman kneels in supplication before him, while another reaches for his hand, a symbolic representation in any land. Some authorities attribute this work to a period antedating Darius' reign. However that may be, such an extensive display of current illustrations leaves us in little doubt about what the well-rigged horseman wore and used during that era.

Though none of these figures shows the use of armor, Quintus Curtius wrote that the horses in Darius' time wore an armor of small metal plates joined together. This sounds like a later development of the old Sarmatian bone-scale armor, and might well have been.

Unfortunately, as so often happens in the march of events, the vigor of these people declined under increased progress and prosperity. Athenaeus, writing in A.D. 200, said the later Persians paid more attention to the luxuriousness of their equipment and the comfort of their sitting ease than to the practice of riding and fighting.

Horses also grew soft under disuse as the cavalry was allowed to melt away in favor of more easily disciplined foot soldiers. However, when Darius marched his army of 600,000 infantrymen against the Scythians in 513 B.C. he was put to bloody rout. The Scythians were still fighting in their old nomadic style. Unencumbered by extra equipment and well mounted on their swift, hardy horses, they evaded pitched battle and resorted to hit-and-run slashes at the Persian flanks. This enabled them to pick off stragglers, prevent foraging, and make slashing attacks on unwary infantry detachments. Their mobility made the defeat of the foot soldiers inevitable.

This type of hit-and-run fighting with light cavalry was always death to foot soldiery unless they overwhelmed in numbers. And it was

FIG. 12. Persian rider, 600–500 B.C

hard to overwhelm a band of desert horsemen in their own territory. In the early days many nations rode to power on the back of a horse; and they bred horses for war long before they knew of any other use. In fact for several centuries horses were raised in many countries for military purposes alone before they became plentiful enough for private ownership. Moreover, the horse was often considered too noble an animal for ordinary tasks.

The rise of war horses was rapid. Atop his mount, the rider was in a position to look down on the plodding horde of lowly infantrymen. This brought quick realization that the mounted warrior was more threatening in aspect and more deadly with lance or arrow. To strike down upon a foe was greatly preferable to meeting him in hand-to-hand combat. In addition, the speed and power of the spirited horse, responsive to his slightest command, gave him a fine sense of kingliness. All this carried with it a mark of prestige and authority.

Armed with his short, heavy Asiatic horn bow, the mounted warrior was one to attract notice. The bow was a formidable weapon in horseback fighting. It had a very flat trajectory and remarkable range. In the hands of skirmishing horsemen few could stand against it.

The bow was the weapon of ancient foot soldiers. It had been almost discarded by most nations after the advent of metal arms, but when the mounted hordes swept down out of northwest Asia they brought the bow back into popular use with a vengeance. Along with the lance, it was soon the chief fighting tool of all horsemen.

Backed by the legendary exploits of the ancient Cimmerians and Scythians, mounted warriors moved into recorded history from all lands. They made it possible for the Hyksos to overrun Egypt. When Aram, grandson of Noah, was fighting the Medes and Cappadocians, both sides employed cavalry to the number of five thousand. Saul was using cavalry when he defeated the Ammonites around 1000 B.C. The Lycians had a strong cavalry force, mounted on a superior breed of horses, when they fought the Persians in 550 B.C. At the time of his attack on Greece in 490 B.C., Darius had transport ships specially built to carry his cavalry across the Mediterranean.

In North Africa at the dawn of history the Libyans appear as horseback fighters. Numidia, Mauretania, and Carthage all had excellent cavalry at a very early date.

A highlight among the royal appendages of glittering Carthage, around 220 B.C., was the court's special Sacred Legion of cavalrymen. This was made up of a select body of Clinabarian nobles mounted on milk-white stallions. The horses had their tails completely denuded of hair, their manes roached, and their ears cropped off close to their heads. Each wore an enormous ivory horn on the center of its forehead, affixed to the jeweled bridle. With their gilded trappings reflected in the warriors' polished armor, in Carthaginian eyes they stood as true manifestations of the gods.

Needless to say, the early cavalry was definitely on the primitive side. It probably bore considerable resemblance to the mounted Indian forces of western America. In fact, Dodge says the early Asiatic bowmen, like the American Indians, often shot from over or under their horses' necks while riding concealed, their bodies suspended against the sides of their mounts by means of an arm thrust through a loop of cord or knotted mane. All these people rode bareback or with simple saddle cloths, in many cases without even a bridle.

In Jacques Louis David's famous painting of the battle between the Romans and legendary Sabines, about 745 B.C., the mounted soldiers are shown riding horses without any riding gear in the heat of the fray. One animal alone wears a plain headstall with snaffle bit. While this picture was not painted until 1799, David is said to have made most exhaustive research into ancient records in the effort to give an accurate picture in every detail.

Livy (59 B.C.–A.D. 17), as well as Ansonius, wrote that the Carthaginiians, Numidians, and Mauretanians rode without either saddles or bridles. Their horses, thought to be Barbs, were guided by voice or by light wands in the hands of the riders. The animal was tapped on the side of the face with the wand to turn him in the opposite direction and on the nose to stop him.

Silius Italicus (A.D. 25–101) represents the Numidians as superb horsemen but as riders who were totally ignorant of bits or reins. Some of these are shown on Trajan's Column in Rome (Fig. 13). The 10,000 horsemen which comprised Hannibal's cavalry forces in his campaign against the Romans in 218 B.C. were mostly Numidians. They must have made a fearsome array, bearing down like a stampeding herd of uncontrolled beasts. No wonder they won fame as foes to dread.

Ansonius goes on to attribute the bridleless riding to the fact that these people had little suitable material for constructing equipment.

In "Pictures of Attila at Rome" (A.D. 451) Raphael shows the Huns riding after the fashion of their country: "The devil of a bit of bridle had they—nothing but a strap around their horses' necks, which they held in their hands." Well into the Middle Ages the Arabs are said to have followed the same method. It was apparently a universal style that cropped up from time to time among superior horsemen using superior strains of horses.

Dodge tells us that ancient cavalry was of two classes. The first or heavy cavalry used bridles; the light or irregular troops rode without bridles, guiding their mounts by voice, legs, or wands. Various early cavalry figures pictured on Trajan's Column are shown riding without bridles or bits; others have them. Bridles seem to have been optional equipment with various groups in many lands over a very long period.

The Ethiopians must have been rather notable fighters on horseback. Herodotus speaks of them as a nation of cavalrymen who aided Xerxes on his expedition against Greece in 480 B.C.

The Thessalians were a similar brand of mercenaries. It was they who were used by Pyrrhus of Epirus in routing the Romans at Heraclea and Ausculum in 280 B.C.

There was an ancient semiaboriginal people in Spain, called the Celtiberi, who were important as horseback fighters in the B.C. period. It is thought they acquired their horses from the Phoenicians at an early date, later established a reputation as outstanding warriors. Unfortunately, they were too few to stand up against Roman might. They were conquered in the second century B.C., after which they disappeared as a distinctive race, although they left a heritage in Spain.

Philip of Macedonia is credited with having originated massed cavalry charges in formation when he was fighting the Greeks in 340 B.C. His son, Alexander the Great, was probably the first to train mounted troops through drill practice. His Companion Cavalry became one of the ancient world's finest cavalry bodies. With this army he conquered most of the old Persian Empire. His methods of troop training were later allowed to decline until they were eventually forgotten. This was reflected in the mediocrity of Greek and Roman cavalry in later centuries.

A statue of Alexander made by Lysippus after the battle of Granicus in 334 B.C. shows the horse wearing a saddle-cloth held by a surcingle and breast collar. The plain bridle has what appears to be a snaffle bit.

The Romans were among the earliest nations to have cavalry, probably dating back to 1500–1000 B.C. At least some of their original horses are supposed to have come from the Phoenicians. Some may have been obtained from Egypt and Libya. But all indications are that the Romans received the bulk of their foundation stock, as well as the secrets of horsemanship, from Greece. A typical second century cavalryman, as depicted on Trajan's Column, appears in Fig. 14.

Most of the practices common to Rome were adapted from the earlier Greek methods. The styles of mounting were identical, even to the loop on a lance butt (Fig. 15). Vegetius wrote of wooden models built by the Romans for the neophyte to use in learning to mount horses properly. Plutarch (A.D. 46–125) described the pyramidal piles of stones required by Rome at stated intervals along all the roads, similar to those used in Greece. Woe betide the highway superintendent who allowed these mounting blocks to get out of order, especially if some dignitary found himself set afoot in the neighborhood.

Rome adopted the Greek style of riding two horses with one foot on each while standing erect. This type can still be seen in rodeo circuits of the twentieth century under the name of Roman riding.

FIG. 13. Numidian captured by a Roman, third century B.C.

FIG. 14. Roman cavalryman, 114 A.D.

FIG. 15. Roman soldier, second century B.C.

The Greek way of leaping from horse to horse in a two-to-four-horse group at certain intervals without slackening speed was also copied by Rome. Both nations had similar rules for riding and chariot races; and both preferred broad-backed riding horses whose "backbones did not rise about the flesh on either side." As bareback riders, they definitely had a point there.

Apparently Greece and Rome began using saddle cloths about the same time—in the fifth century B.C. They were secured by cinch, breast collar, and crupper. However, the Romans were never so skilled in horsemanship as the Greeks and the desert nomads farther east. They seem to have been rather a heavy-handed race, inclined to cruelty toward their mounts. Perhaps that was why the bulk of their cavalry was made up of mercenaries from other nations.

Still, the Romans did take considerable interest in their horses, both in sport and war. Suetonius (A.D. 70–140) wrote that in the Rome of Julius Caesar's time an ignorance of riding was considered as much of a disgrace as being unable to read and write.

Romans called a riding horse a *singularis* because it was used alone, in contrast to chariot horses, which worked in pairs. Other horses were *itinerarii* for traveling; *sarcinarii* for packing; *celes* for racing; *tolutarii* or *gradarii* were gaited horses; *cantherii* were geldings. Since the later Romans came to prefer geldings for riding, and their favorite gait was a slow, easy gallop, it is thought that their name for gelding gave us the word "canter."

It was during the reign of Romulus, founder of Rome in 725 B.C. that the Order of Equites was established. This was another revival, copied from the old Greek society for the development of horses. The Roman version was chiefly a military organization. The Equites, a forerunner of the Knights of Europe, formed the army's cavalry division. According to Livy, Romulus started the order by selecting 300 individuals from the country's three principal tribes. He named them the *Celeres*. This force was later increased to 1,800. They remained a select group, accorded many special privileges and honors. Seats were reserved for them at the circus and theaters; they were first in line for state offices and positions of rank. Their insignia consisted of a gold ring and a tunic with two narrow purple stripes. The striped tunic gave rise to our modern expression "being in the purple." While the order was open to plebeians as well as patricians, there were certain requirements, such as the ownership of $17,000 worth of property.

In the beginning, the state furnished each member of the society with two horses—one for himself and one for his servant—plus the necessary funds to equip and maintain them. This practice was discontinued around 400 B.C. The privileges that went with the order were so many and so desirable that more and more of the wealthy and would-be important citizens flocked to join the group. With so many able to furnish their own outfits and seeking honor more than service, the state was prompted to let them foot the bill.

Nevertheless, the Equites was a worthy society. It furnished the foundation stone for Rome's later excellent cavalry legions. These legions numbered 300 men each, as against 6,000 men in the infantry legions. One horseman to twenty infantrymen was a significant ratio, if it meant anything in fighting strength. And it most likely did. The old Romans were a pretty canny lot when it came to shaping up the conquests which won them half the known world. And there is no question but what, as an adjunct to the main army, the Equites performed yeoman's service in creating the far-flung Roman Empire.

No less notable were the activities of the early horsemen of Chinese and Mongol lands to the northeast. And here we come upon another odd factor. Though the Asiatic barbarians of Chinese Turkestan had been riding for several thousand years, it was fairly late in the pre-Christian Era before horse culture showed up among the wild tribesmen of the north. Neither were the Chinese of antiquity a riding nation.

It is uncertain just when China adopted a horse culture. That it was at a fairly early date, we know, but considerably later than their neighbors to the west. Then, like the southern nations, they confined their use of the horse to chariots well up into the fourth century B.C. What riding they may have done was of a limited nature and individual practice. Neither a mounted populace nor a Chinese cavalry appears in any degree until 325 B.C.

China's neighbors on the northwest were the barbarian Huns. These people were no doubt descendants of the ancient tribal group known as the Hien-Yün or Hün-Yu, whom Chinese tradition traces back to before 1600 B.C. Various admixtures of Chinese blood through female captives during the centuries had developed a distinct race, a branch of which came to be known as the Mongols.

Somewhere in the 450–400 B.C. period they were introduced to horses. The animals apparently came from the Russian steppes or Turkestan.

From then on the Mongols rose rapidly as a nation of raiding aggressors. Riding bareback with bow and spear, they became a serious threat to the slower moving Chinese by the middle of the fourth century B.C.

It remained for a Chinese feudal lord by the name of Wu Ling to take a leaf from the Hunnish book and turn the tables on the barbarians. Wu Ling had control of a principality in the kingdom of Jao, in what is now Shensi province. He had been putting up a stiff fight against the raiding Huns, but his foot soldiers and war chariots were no match for the slashing attacks of elusive warriors on nimble-footed horses. He finally decided to meet the devil with his own fire, so he fitted out his army in enemy costumes and drilled them in the Huns' style of fighting on horseback. With loose robes discarded for trousers and boots, and their force practiced in cavalry tactics, the celestial troops went forth to win a string of signal victories. This was in 325 B.C.

Immediately following Wu Ling's success, the overlord of the principality adjoining him on the west adopted the same idea. The two then joined hands in clearing their borders of the troublesome Huns. This worked so well that they went on to conquer considerable adjacent territory. They wound up by eventually taking over the whole of China and establishing the Tsin dynasty. Thanks to their discovery of mounted soldiery, they maintained the solidarity of China until 202 B.C. when a weak emperor allowed a soldier of fortune named Liu Bang to take over the kingdom.

Liu Bang was either a poor student of warfare or a man with his mind on other things. At any rate, after setting up what became the Han dynasty, he permitted his army to slip back into its old order of chariots and infantry. The rulers who followed did no better. As might be expected, with the decline of Chinese fighting power the Huns came back and the Chinese found themselves again forced to pay annual tribute.

It was during this period that the scattered Hunnish-Mongol tribes, descendants of the ancient Hün-Yu, joined forces in a union known as the Hiungnu. The man who conceived the federation and set himself up as the leader referred to himself as "Lord of All Those Who Shoot Bows from Horseback." His neighbors, the eastern barbarians, were a similar nomadic Mongol race called the Dunghu. Both were skilled horsemen and fierce fighters given to swooping down in wild raids on the ineffectual Chinese whenever they wanted to increase their herds, harems, or home furnishings. It was not until a clear-sighted military leader by the name of Ho Kü-Bing acquired command of the army in 124 B.C. that the dismounted celestials had a chance to resume the offensive. Ho Kü-Bing immediately put the army back on horses and successfully revived the old Hunnish style of fighting. Between 124 and 119 B.C. the remounted Chinese drove the enemy out of the region and went on to capture a vast stretch of country to the north and northwest.

The only reason they didn't extend their victories farther was that they ran out of horses. Horse breeding had not been extensively practiced in China during the Han period, and there was a limited supply of mounts. The five-year campaign against the Huns had cost them 110,000 animals out of the 140,000 they started with. Altogether, it made a halt in conquest necessary. Their gains, however, were an established thing, making it possible for China to stand again as the foremost Eastern nation after a century of subjugation.

According to Chinese history, the best horses in the world were raised in the province of Da-yüan (later Farghana or Kokand), lying in the upper Jaxartes River Valley west of the Pamir Mountains, in northern Iran. These horses were so famous that the Chinese emperor began to cast covetous eyes on them. When the Da-yüans refused to part with them peaceably, in 130 B.C., he raised an army of 10,000 men to take them by force; but his men met defeat at the hands of the hard-riding Da-yüan cavalry. The emperor raised a second army of the same size, which eventually managed to conquer the country and appropriate the horses. This was probably the highest price ever paid for a start in choice horseflesh, but it may have been worth it. Later Chinese history speaks of these animals as "the blood-sweating Celestial steeds."

Even into the first centuries of the Christian Era the Turkestan-Iranian horses were considered far superior to the native Hunnish-Mongolian mounts. Who is to say that Chinese history might well have been written to a different pattern these last two thousand years had fate allowed it to rest on the backs of different horses?

But even the best of horses must have the right riders. Around 50 B.C. a succession of weak rulers, factional intrigue, and tribal dissension caused the old Hunnish Empire in Mongolia to start breaking up. Conquests by the Dunghu, or eastern barbarians, and growing aggression by the now well-mounted Chinese contributed to further disintegration of the Mongol regime. Many of the conquered began turning their faces toward new lands in the West.

By A.D. 100 the Dunghu and the Sienbi of Manchuria had pretty well taken over Mongolia and the Gobi Desert. The Hunnish tribes that refused to submit to their rule or Chinese overlordship moved west into Zungaria and northern Turkestan. This was the country of the Alani. It was a land rich in fine horses and grazing herds. While the semiagricultural inhabitants were doughty fighters, overpowering numbers forced them to submit to the Huns. It was the same old story of all the world's complacent, well-fed civilizations crumbling before the onslaughts of tough and hungry nomadic horsemen.

By A.D. 374 the Huns had exterminated most of the Alani. The remainder had fled west into the Caucasus Mountains, where some of them became the Casetes and others moved in with the German Goths.

And still the wild-riding barbarians were not satisfied. Soon after 374 they crossed the Don River and began treating the Goths as they had the Alani. This forced the Goths and Suevis, who had been occupying the Hungarian plains since 200, to move into the Balkans, from whence they reached southwestern Europe.

The Huns controlled all the Russian steppes and Hungarian plains by 400, when they began invading Romania. They started raiding Roman territory eight years later, reaching the Rhine about 412. Their Mongolian hoofs thundered down on Greece in 422–426, and had taken over what is now Jugoslavia by 434. By 440 they controlled everything from the Baltic to the Roman Empire and from Kashgaria to eastern France. They invaded Gaul in 451 and Italy the following year. It was only after they became bloated with success and good living that they were driven back to the Russian steppes.

The migration of these peoples gives a rough chronology of the spread of Asian horses and riding customs throughout most of Europe. This did more to disseminate horse culture and the art of horsemanship in central Europe than anything that had happened in all the preceding six thousand years. The Western nations were soon on the way to a civilization such as they had never known.

Emblazoned on the pages of horseback history, this pageant of conquest and migration was unique in breadth and scope. Covering Eurasia from Gobi's windswept plains to the balmy shores of Portugal, it provided the world's greatest spectacle of man and horse against the forces of nature. Without the horse, such an epic could never have been possible.

—6—

The Horse in Sports, Literature, Art, and Religion

Here's to that bundle of sentient nerves, with the heart of a woman, the eye of a gazelle, the courage of a gladiator, the strength of an ox, the docility of a slave, the proud carriage of a king, the blind obedience of a soldier; the companion of mountain, desert or plain—one that turns the moist furrow in spring in order that all the world may have an abundant harvest; that furnishes the sport of kings; that with blazing eye and distended nostril fearlessly leads our greatest generals through carnage and renown; whose blood forms the ingredients that go to make the ink in which all history is written; and one, who finally, in black trappings, pulls the proudest and the humblest of us all to the newly sodded threshold of eternity.

—*Author unknown*

IT MUST NOT BE CONCLUDED that the horse was dedicated primarily to warfare. As a companion in sport he rose to glory in all lands. Hunting and racing probably started when the first mounted man found his horse would bring him within shooting distance of desired game or permit him to overtake a fleeing enemy on a less speedy animal. It is easy to believe the early Scythians and Sarmatians spent more time in testing their horses against each other or the fleetness of game than in pursuit of neighboring foemen.

Old Persian and Egyptian carvings, back to early centuries B.C., depict the use of horses in hunting. The Book of Job alludes to their use in ostrich chases. Xenophon wrote that the Amazons hunted on horseback with their husbands, the Sarmatians. He also made mention of Cyrus hunting on horseback. Herodotus tells of hunting on horseback as a sport practiced in the time of Darius, who once fell off his horse and dislocated his heel. All desert nomads are recorded as hunters of note, while many a civilized king's tomb bears stories of the chase.

Equally important among all these peoples was the racing of horses. It combined the pleasures of a thrilling sport with the testing of mounts for better qualities. As a further incentive to the development of both horses and warriors, there arose the game now known as polo.

We have no certain knowledge of where polo first appeared. The people of Hunza, on the upper Indus River in Karakorum, claim it originated among their most remote ancestors, and has continued as a leading sport in their country to this day. It is played in a rough form, little changed from ancient times, using horses that are said to have descended from Alexander's Bucephalus. This legend finds support in Marco Polo's mention of seeing such a game, called *bouskasshis,* being played in that region.

Turning back to duly recorded history, we first sight the game in Persia, where it was played by ten or twelve men using headless sticks. From there, it spread west to Constantinople, north into Mongolia, and east to India and China. The Chinese were playing it with a light wooden ball around A.D. 600. It was a favorite sport among the Arabs after being introduced from Persia about A.D. 650, during the height of Arabia's power. The game followed their conquests westward across Africa.

In all the old Persian territory, polo continued to be popular until it died out in the 1500s. Not much was heard of it again until after its revival in Bengal in 1854. The native princes of India thereupon took it up with so much enthusiasm that it was quickly restored to its former high position throughout that country. It was they who introduced it to the English soldiery stationed there. The British, in turn, found it so much to their liking that they carried it home to England and Ireland in 1869, where it received immediate acceptance as a top-flight sport among the horseback fraternity.

The first modern match was played in England in 1871. The first organized tournament took place at Hurlingham, England, five years later. That same year James Gordon Bennett brought it to the United States, where it became so popular the American Polo Association was formed in 1890. Polo has been played longer than any other game known to man.

The horse has been an inspiration to men of words and artistic ability since time immemorial. As primitive man felt moved to perpetuate its likeness on the walls of his smoky cave, so have all ages of men since then endeavored to do justice to this prince of the animal world.

Literature was a scarce commodity during many periods of the world's history. Yet in whatever was written or pictured we find the horse holding a prominent place. Even as far back as the ancient Hittites, a *Handbook for the Treatment of Horses* was inscribed on six clay tablets dated around 1360 B.C. The Bible speaks frequently of horses back to two thousand years before Christ. The Zoroastrian Bible of ancient Iran, the Avesta, composed during the 1000–600 B.C. period, contains many references to horses. Homer describes a chariot race in his *Iliad,* written about 800 B.C. He also wrote to a considerable extent about horses and horsemanship in general. Xenophon's *Hippike* of 365 B.C. was a complete treatise on horsemanship, and its precepts hold as true today as when they were written. Xenophon, however, makes no claim to originality for much of his work. He quotes frequently from an earlier book written by Simonedes 135 years previously. Xenophon is, nevertheless, considered the patron saint of modern horsemen, chiefly because his book is excellent in concept and the oldest to survive.

He had many followers. Education flourished in the golden age of Greece. Her scholars explored all the byways of knowledge. Most of those who wrote found occasion to speak of horsemanship in greater or less degree. In prose, poetry, and song we find a medley of plaudits directed toward the horseman and his mount. As other countries rose to the level of articulate expression, their creative artists, too, celebrated the horse.

Roman literature is full of tributes to the equestrian world. Among the early Arabian writings on the science of zoology, advanced study of the horse was developed to a high degree. Numerous special monographs on the animal described its various characteristics, qualities, habits, colors, varieties, and the like.

One of the first books printed in England was *Properties and Medeycines for an Horfs,* written by Wynkyn de Worde about A.D. 1500. Frederigo Grisone, in 1532, applied most of Xenophon's principles in his *Ordini di Cavalcare.* Antoine de Pluevinel, Master of the Horse to the King of France, wrote his *Manege du Roi* in 1623. The English Duke of Newcastle published his *Art of Horsemanship* in 1657. M. de la Guerimiere, Master of the Horse to Louis XIV, published *Ecole de Cavalerie* in 1733. In 1771 Richard Berenger brought out *The History and Art of Horsemanship,* a large section of which is a reprint of Xenophon's original book. The last two centuries have seen a variety of similar works presented to modern readers in assorted languages.

And along with these special treatises have come a multitude of other literary tributes to the horse and its rider, for horse stories have ever captured the imagination of man. They range all the way from the *Anabasis* of ancient Greece to Will James's *Smoky* and *My Friend Flicka.* by Mary O'Hara.

One of the old legends so dear to romanticists and horse lovers—and one which might well have been basically true—concerns the famed knight Rinaldo and his horse Bayard. The story goes that Rinaldo once fell into disfavor at the court of Charlemagne, king of the Franks. The king deprived Rinaldo of his horse. That was about the worst thing short of imprisonment that could happen to a man in those days. Rinaldo felt his disgrace keenly. Desperate for a way out, he finally decided to try using Charlemagne's superstitious beliefs about horses to his own advantage.

Accordingly, Rinaldo disguised himself as a blind beggar and sought audience with the king. No one recognized him so he petitioned the king to let him mount Bayard, claiming knowledge that the animal possessed supernatural powers which would restore his sight if he were allowed to sit on its back. The king was intrigued. Much study of ancient folklore had convinced him that horses were more or less emissaries of the gods and so might have unsuspected qualities. What an occasion it would be if he should discover such a phenomenon in Bayard through this ragged beggar! He therefore gave orders that man and horse be brought together at once.

Rinaldo was jubilant under his rags, but he knew he must keep his wits. When the groom brought out the horse, Rinaldo lost no time mounting. For a moment he sat still, pretending to be a blind person having a supernatural experience while at the same time shaking the reins free and making sure the road ahead was clear. Then he abruptly shouted, "I can see! I can see!" Bayard immediately recognized his master's voice and, no doubt encouraged by a familiar hard heel in his flank, dashed off down the road.

Charlemagne was too surprised and delighted to think of anything but the miracle he had witnessed. To commemorate the event, he ordered a great celebration, complete with a procession carrying banners and crosses. And thus was inaugurated the first public fete in Brussels, Belgium.

Throughout the history of man there have been three things he has never tired of talking or hearing about—God, love, and horses. In many cases, the horse was the means for carrying out all the activities of life and of love. Wars, migrations, explorations, knightly romances, and stories of the chase would all be dry reading indeed were they without the horses which lift them into flashing pageantry.

In the field of art, the same situation prevails. Horses are the only subject that can compare with women in popularity. Nothing else has the horse's grace, beauty, symmetry, fluidity, and poetry in motion. From the caves of France to the China Sea, the horse has served as a model in man's struggle to express the ultimate in art, sculpture, and decorative design. Painters, sculptors, carvers, designers, and tapestry weavers have recognized horses, women, and the sublimities of nature as examples of perfection. The horse especially has always been selected as a symbol of beauty of form, color, intelligence, and restrained power.

Most of our knowledge of antiquity's horses and horsemen comes from the imperishable work of bygone artists and sculptors on the masonry of the remains of cities. Early man was often portrayed mounted on a favorite horse on tombs or imposing monuments.

Greeks of antiquity showed a preference for equestrian decorations for their vases and urns. Much of the fine Persian glassware of the A.D. 700–1000 period was decorated with horses and horsemen engaged in various pursuits. The same motifs showed up through later periods in Rome, Spain, France, England, and America. As a decorative device for buildings, places of amusement, temples, and courtyard walls, the horse has no rival.

Members of the nobility have been horsemen all. Frequently the peer's personal seal pictured him on horseback, and his portrait on his favorite mount hung in the entrance hall of the manor.

When the coining of money started, the various emperors and certain provincial lords simply transferred the figures on their seals to the new coins. We find such a likeness of a horse on an old Corinthian silver piece of 700–500 B.C. A chariot team appears on a 500 B.C. tetradrachm of Syracuse, as well as the decadrachms of 413 B.C. Early Iberian coins of the B.C. period unearthed in Spain's Ebro Valley carry horse pictures. The Ephthalites, or White Huns, of western Turkestan used a coin bearing a mounted warrior on its face. Through the ages there were various other coins with similar pictures, including the New Jersey copper cent of 1786.

In our time leather work, jewelry, silverware, coppers, bronzes, woven fabrics, dishes, desk lamps, neck scarfs, den furniture, the wallpaper on

Junior's room and what have you—all come emblazoned with the same equine designs old grandfather Og carved into his spear shaft with a flint knife.

Horse pictures in plenty hang in the art galleries of the world. Most of the memorial statues around the globe would be sorry things indeed if the horse was not there to lend stature to the hero. What schoolboy is not familiar with that storied first horse ridden by man, the mythical Pegasus? How many higher classmen would be able to recognize history's array of knights, kings, generals, conquerors, and national leaders without their equally famous horses?

Napoleon is just a little man trying to look important when not mounted on his favorite steed Marengo. Buffalo Bill Cody without his white stallion Muson would be just another westerner. Even George Washington loses stature when dismounted from his gray Arabian Magnolia. It is the horse Rienzi, later renamed Winchester, which captures the imagination far more than does its rider, General Phil Sheridan, as they race over field and meadow toward the Winchester battlefield.

Among the many equally famous pairs identified as often by horse as by rider, we might mention General Robert E. Lee and Traveler; Caligula and Incitatus; General William Sherman and Lexington; the Duke of Wellington and Copenhagen; General Zachery Taylor and Old Whitey; Lord Roberts and Colonel; General J. E. B. Stuart and Highfly, General Stonewall Jackson and Old Sorrel; Charlemagne and Tencendur; General Ulysses Grant and Cincinnati; Teddy Roosevelt and Rodan; Roy Rogers and Trigger; Adraslus the Greek and Arion; the knight Roland and Veilantif; Phidolas the Corinthian, and Aura, the great mare which won the Olympic race without a rider; Achilles and his two horses Balios and Xanthos, the latter being the fabled steed that purportedly could talk with a human voice; Captain Miles Keogh and Comanche, the horse that was the only survivor of Custer's ill-fated battle of the Little Big Horn. Comanche, incidentally, was decorated with military honors and lived to the age of twenty-eight. Upon his death he received the special honor of having his remains mounted in a natural pose at the Kansas State University.

The first large memorial to be cast in metal in the United States was an equestrian statue of General Andrew Jackson, done by Clark Mills, the American sculptor, in 1848. This was before there was any foundry in this country equipped for large metal casting. So successful was the result that Mills was commissioned to make a colossal statue of George Washington on horseback at the battle of Princeton. The unveiling of this second statue in Washington on the hero's birthday in 1860 introduced the general casting of statues great and small throughout America.

As in life the horse was ever in close association with his master, so from time immemorial he has been an important part of his master's funeral procession, accompanying him on his last journey. The more notable the man, the more attention would be paid to having his riderless horse properly caparisoned for the occasion.

Homer, Vergil, and various others described the parades and processions of olden times in which the horse of the deceased was led at the head of the funeral procession. Even today the practice is sometimes followed in a military or state funeral.

Many historical personages had their horses buried with them when they died. Others, when they lost a favorite mount, had the animal buried with full honors in a tomb of its own with special memorial carvings. Alexander the Great even built a city over the grave of his horse Bucephalus. The fact that Bucephalus means "bull-headed" was no reflection on the horse. The word comes from the small ears and big, wide poll which was the mark of fine quality among Greek horses. According to Plutarch, Alexander bought the animal for thirty talents from an owner who had difficulty in handling him. The horse immediately took a liking to his new master. From that time on, Bucephalus was the only horse Alexander ever rode in his campaigns of conquest. The horse, in turn, never allowed anyone else to ride him during the entire thirty years of his life. It is uncertain whether he died naturally or was killed during the victorious battle with Indian King Porus on the Hydaspes River in 326 B.C. However, Alexander had the animal entombed on the bank of the stream where he died near Jhelum, in West Pakistan. The city he built at the spot was named Bucephalus as a memorial to the horse that had served him so long and well. This was the greatest monument ever erected in honor of an animal.

The Parthenon frieze at Athens, which portrays numerous horsemen, is claimed by many to be the world's most wonderful pictorial representation of sculpture in low relief. When Emperor Trajan built his monumental 127-foot Column in Rome, in A.D. 114, he honored the horses as much as he did the men in selecting the 2,500 figures to be carved on it in commemoration of his many campaigns. Artists paid extravagant tribute to the horse at the ancient city of Persepolis, in Persia. There, the massive stone temple walls hold a profusion of equine sculptures showing the horse in all manner of forms and employment. Even the great flight of steps leading up to the building appear to have been designed for the ascent of mounted horsemen. Various authorities are inclined to believe the whole structure was designed to accommodate some sort of horse worship. Perhaps it was. Horses have been linked with the spiritual world ever since the first man found himself borne through the air on the wings of speed. Every race of people around the globe has myths, legends, and present-day beliefs which put the horse on a plane with the gods.

In the Book of Kings, the Bible tells us the kings of Judah dedicated horses to the sun. That was around 900 B.C. Vergil, the Roman poet, said the Sarmatian tribes of Goloni and Massagete sacrificed horses to the sun. Xenophon said the same thing about the Assyrians and Persians. Figures of such horses being led to the sacrifice are to be found on the ruins of the temple at Persepolis. Ancient Greece made an annual sacrifice of four horses and a chariot to the sun. They also sacrificed one horse each year to their corn-spirit god Virbius in a ceremony to insure good crops. The Spartans made a similar offering each year from the summit of Mount Taygetus.

Mars was an ancient god of fertility before he became the Roman god of war. In his earlier role he was greatly reverenced by the people and propitiated each year by an offering to insure good crops. On October 15 as part of the autumn festival a chariot race was held on the Field of Mars. At the end of the race, the right-hand horse of the winning team was speared to death as a sacrifice. Its head and tail were immediately cut off, and as much blood as possible was caught in a sacred vessel. The head was decorated with loaves of bread and hung in a tower, while the still-bleeding tail was rushed to the king's residence. Whatever blood dripped on the royal floor was supposed to further enhance the charm. The blood caught in the vessel was stored away in a safe place until the following April 17. At that time the vestal virgins mixed it with blood from unborn calves and gave it to the shepherds to protect their flocks from disease.

Until 1870, Japanese horses were held as something sacred, worshiped, and kept in temple stalls as divinities. While they were used for riding under certain conditions, the thought of expecting them to pull in harness was too degrading to be considered.

White horses were symbolic of victory among most peoples throughout the ages. They were also thought to bring general good luck to their owners. Therefore when men began rising to superior positions among their fellows they acquired white horses.

Kublai Khan kept ten thousand horses in his private herd, each animal without a blemish. Of these, one thousand were snow white and were maintained for use in parades and ceremonies, never being employed for war or ordinary riding. They were considered semidivine and were bred exclusively for the emperor. His subjects were forbidden to own such horses.

Herodotus wrote of the Sicilians paying an annual tribute of 350 white horses to Darius, king of Persia. The ceremonial rites in sacrificing white horses among the Kalmucks included a rule that no one could participate without first bathing and putting on a clean shirt. Tamerlane's Tartars sealed all alliances with foreign nations in a ceremony that included sacrificing a white horse. A similar ceremony was conducted when Tamerlane reviewed his mounted troops. The ancient Germans had certain white horses which were consecrated to the gods, exempt from all labor except drawing the sacred chariot on solemn occasions. Livy expressly points out how white horses were on a par with the purple robe, the armed guard, and the diadem as insignia of royalty in Rome.

Dionysius always rode behind four white horses. There were three hundred white horses in a cavalcade which attended the conqueror of Agrigentum. Nero made his entry into Naples in a chariot drawn by four white horses managed by a specially skilled driver. Christian princes later followed the same practice; and royalty continued the custom well into the seventeenth century. A reflection of this is found in the figure of a white horse used by the Germans as an emblem for their standards.

Persian mythology has Jupiter drawn by eight white horses, white being a fitting representation of that god's purity and brightness. In contrast, the horses of Pluto were black. The sun was represented by animals of a rosy color, while those of the moon were one each of white and black.

The Buraq was the winged horse with a woman's face and a peacock's tail on which Mohammed journeyed to the Seventh Heaven.

China has a legend that when Ch'in Shih Huang Ti built the Great Wall of China in 219–204 B.C., a white horse appeared mysteriously on the scene, taking up its position shortly ahead of the builders. There it remained, moving just ahead as the workers progressed. The men finally concluded it was a magic horse sent to guide them along their route of construction. Accordingly, it was allowed to wander at will, all men being forbidden to interfere with its actions. The animal continued to move on ahead of the builders as they advanced, often going up hill and down where only a supernatural beast could find a foothold. The course of the wall was made to conform to the trail of the horse.

At one place along the line, one of China's fierce dust storms suddenly fogged down out of the northwest to blanket the countryside with an impenetrable curtain. This naturally caused the workers to lose sight of the horse; even its tracks were obliterated. While the storm continued, they could only go on building in the direction they figured the horse had gone. They completed some ten miles of the wall in this manner.

Then, when the storm ceased as suddenly as it had begun and the blinding dust cleared away, they discovered the animal off to the southwest, headed in an altogether different direction from that taken by the wall. That, of course, left nothing to do but abandon the recently completed piece of construction and go back and start over. Accordingly they returned to the proper place and started a new line of wall toward the horse. Any skeptics who doubt this legend may still see the offshooting length of wall, abandoned because it failed to follow the route of the magic white horse.

When Ho Kü-Bing, the famous Chinese general, died in 117 B.C., his friends erected over his tomb the statue of a horse stamping on a Hunnish warrior. This statue, discovered not long before World War II by some French archeologists, is claimed to be the first Chinese attempt at sculpturing a horse.

In Cambodia, Gautama Buddha rode the great white horse, Kanthaka, when he left his home and family to start preaching his faith in 534 B.C. The priests, or *bonzes,* of that country still memorialize the horse along with its rider when teaching Buddhism to their neophytes, or *chelas.* The lessons are given from a pulpit built in the shape of a horse. The carved wooden horse, painted in colors and with decorative bands on its neck and legs, carries a sort of platform on its back. The priest sits on the platform while instructing his students.

Equitation even entered the Vatican in Rome at one time. Among the most valued treasures kept there is the great diamond-studded chalice of Pope Pius IX. This sacred vessel, famous for its beauty, was made in 1854 to commemorate the proclamation of the dogma of the Immaculate Conception. It was made from a golden bridle bit and a jeweled saddle once given to the Pope by the Sultan of Turkey.

Then there was the horse which actually became a god. This was Morzillo, the favorite big black mount of Hernando Cortez. The year was 1524. Cortez was on his way from Mexico City to Honduras. He had with him a small party of Spaniards, and was riding Morzillo.

They reached a large lake near what is now Remedios, in eastern Guatemala. The region was inhabited by a Mayan tribe called Petén-Itzá, who had a large and very fine city on an island in the lake. The city, called Tayasal, had many white-walled buildings laid out in a beautiful setting against the green slopes of the valley. These people worshiped deer as beneficial spirits and allowed them to roam unmolested about the shores of the lake. There were great numbers of the animals, all very tame. When Cortez' party arrived and saw all the tame deer, they went wild, chasing and killing them in a hunters' orgy.

It was an extremely hot day, and the horses evidently were not conditioned to such strenuous activity. At any rate, many of them became overheated and collapsed. The mount of Palacios Rubio died of sunstroke immediately after the chase. Cortez' Morzillo was one of the animals badly injured by the heat and he became quite sick. He also got a splinter in his foot, which made things worse.

Meanwhile, the natives had been terribly awed and shocked by the strange beings who had the audacity to chase the sacred deer and slay them with great blasts of what appeared to be thunder and lightning. They thought the strangers must surely be gods or demons and, probably not wanting to go the way of the deer, they assumed friendship toward the Spaniards and invited them to visit the city. Taking a bodyguard of twenty men to guard against treachery, and riding Morzillo, Cortez accepted the invitation. The natives, however, remained friendly, offering their best to the bearded white men with due reverence.

By the time the Spaniards had finished their visit and feasting, poor Morzillo was in such bad shape that Cortez saw it was useless to attempt to ride him any farther. As the natives had evinced no hostility, he showed his good-fellowship by asking permission to leave the horse with them until he returned. To a people who could conceive such a remarkable animal as being nothing less than a kind of god, this was something of an honor. It was also a rather frightening responsibility. But the chief finally consented to accept the trust. The people accordingly stabled the beast in the city's main temple, decorated him with garlands of flowers, and brought him chickens, fruit, and other fine foods to eat. The best was none too good for a god.

But it was a losing battle. Whether from his injuries or from starvation, Morzillo soon died. The Indians, still trying to do the best they could for everybody concerned, then carved a stone image of the horse sitting on its haunches with braced forefeet (Fig. 16). This they installed in the center of their main temple, where it received all the attention formerly accorded Morzillo and eventually became an object of worship.

Cortez ran into trouble on his way back to Mexico City, which prevented his return to Tayasal, and it was not until 1697, 172 years later,

FIG. 16. El Morzillo, the horse that was a god.

that the natives saw any more white men. This was the year Ursua reached their city, coming over the old trail Cortez had used on his way to conquer Yucatan. Great was his surprise when he found the stone image of Morzillo still standing in the center of Tayasal's main temple and still being venerated as a god. The story of its origin, as gathered from the Indians, coincided perfectly with the records of the Cortez expedition.

Ursua had two Franciscan padres, Orbieta and Fuensalida, attached to his army. The first move of these priests was, quite naturally, to put on a conversion campaign and stop the worship of the stone idol. But the Petén-Itzás were not interested. They chose to stick with Morzillo and other time-tested gods in preference to experimenting with visionary beliefs. In retaliation for such obstinacy, the priests rounded up a few stalwarts of Ursua's company and destroyed everything they could find in the temples and about the city. Poor old Morzillo went with the rest.

The more primitive natives of that section will tell you that to this day the stone horse god may be seen in the bottom of the lake on moonlit nights, still receiving the worship of the vanished Petén-Itzás while awaiting the return of Cortez.

—7—

The Saddle Is Born

THE HORSEMAN'S DREAM

The horseman looked at the sweaty back
And sides of his grime-stained horse,
Then felt of the seat of his leather pants,
And what was beneath, of course;
From harsh-rubbed thighs and bowed, cramped knees,
Which came with the bareback miles,
There rose a fair dream of a thing that would
Do much to improve his style.

With fork of oak and a raw sheepskin
And thongs and some leather, tanned,
He fashioned together a strange device
Unknown to the world of man;
Two bent wood strips for the feet, so he
Could rise to the homage due
To lords of the realm, who had ever known
Respect from the earthbound crew.

Well built for ease of the human form,
He fitted its shape exact—
A throne for a king and a royal dress
To cover a horse's back.
Then came the urge of the artist's touch
On cantle and skirt and horn;
He carved it deep and with jewels trimmed
The fruit of a dream thus born.

—Glenn R. Vernam

THE EXACT ORIGIN of the saddle is one of the best-kept secrets of antiquity. There is no definite record as to who invented it, or when, or where. The subject has brought out almost as confusing an array of opinions from authoritative historians as it has from the myriad guesses of lesser investigators. About all we know for certain is that it took shape in the picture after some six or eight thousand years of bareback riding, and has remained one of the chief implements of civilized progress ever since.

A reference to saddling an ass, somewhere around 1000 B.C., is found in the Bible, II Sam. 17:23. But with translations made through the centuries, this passage is no doubt merely speaking of whatever rigging they used at that time for horseback riding. It would most likely boil down to a blanket pad at best, if not simply an untanned sheepskin.

Ancient Egypt and Greece had a sort of saddle that fit over the withers of chariot horses, where the pole-yoke rested, but there is no evidence of anything but saddle cloths for riding. Both Jack Bishop and Dr. Maddox suggest that the Romans may have used light wooden-framed saddles before the dawn of the Christian Era. Dodge says the ancient Gauls also used saddles built on trees. In his *History and Art of Horsemanship,* Berenger gives a picture of a pad saddle supposed to have belonged to the King of Quadi (Fig. 17) in the second century. It appears to be simply a stirrupless pad fastened on by a cinch, although it might possibly be built on a light tree. In either event, it shows considerable improvement over the saddle cloths used by the Mediterranean nations until several centuries later.

The Quadi were an ancient Germanic people living along the Oder and the Danube. They were a very progressive nation during the second and third centuries. Their proximity to the Gauls might be construed as a significant link in this phase of early saddle development. An additional possibility is that the modern saddle gradually evolved from the type shown on a funeral monument in the Museum of Roman-German Antiquities at Mainz, Germany. This relic, which gives some indication of both pommel and cantle, is said to have been carved during the time of Drusus Senior (38–9 B.C.), the general who brought the Roman armies north to conquer the German tribes. The fact that Mainz was founded on the site of Drusus' old Roman camp lends some weight to the conjecture. Nevertheless, we cannot get around the overall picture, which shows everyone riding bareback until much later.

There are records of early Roman race riders who occasionally adopted the dangerous practice of tying themselves to their saddlecloth girths as a precaution against being unhorsed during the race. However, Trajan's

Column, profusely decorated with horsemen, shows only saddleless riders; and old writings and drawings picture nothing more than saddle cloths until well into our era.

Galen, writing about the Roman cavalry around 170, said these horsemen were often subject to pains and swellings in their legs for want of foot support while riding. That was almost exactly what Hippocrates wrote about the Scythians of five centuries before. While it is possible that certain leading figures had some primitive form of saddle, like the one accredited to Drusus' time, it is evident that the Romans of that age were, as a whole, as lacking in saddles as were their ancient brethren.

FIG. 17. Quadi saddle, second century A.D.

The first writer to make specific mention of a saddle was the historian Zonaras. This is contained in his account of Constantine II being thrown out of the saddle while fighting with Constantius, his brother in A.D. 340.

The oldest representation of a true saddle is found on the column of Theodosius II at Constantinople, carved in the fifth century. It shows a rather high-forked rig, without stirrups, being used with elaborate saddle blankets (Fig. 18).

From these sketchy beginnings the saddle industry must have progressed rapidly. In the Theodosian Code, written around A.D. 440, is a rule which limits the weight of saddles, including the bridle, to not over sixty pounds. As a sixty-pound saddle would be a pretty substantial outfit in any man's country, the makers must have been doing a very complete job with the best of materials at that time. The regulations go on to state that the weight of the cloak bags in which travelers carried their baggage—probably something on the order of modern saddlebags—should not exceed thirty-five pounds. Any infringement on the rule was to incur the penalty of having the cloak bags confiscated and the saddle broken into pieces.

Some writers attribute saddle invention to a tribe of early Franks called the Salii. They base their assumption on the idea that the word *sella,* which is a Latin term for saddle, is derived from the name of these people. *Sella* also indicates anything to sit on: a chair, bench, or stool.

FIG. 18. Byzantine rider, fifth century A.D.

It is quite possible that our word "saddle" stems from the Latin *sella,* but to say the Latins based their word of many uses on one certain object devised by the Salii is somewhat far-fetched. This idea becomes more doubtful when we consider that the early Franks are described as a rather primitive people.

On the other hand, we have Dodge's statement that the ancient Gauls used saddles built on trees. The Gauls preceded the Franks in western Europe. If Dodge was referring to these pre-Frankish Gauls, who were overthrown by the Franks in the third and fourth centuries, it would have been only natural for the latter to appropriate their victims' riding method. If that was the case, though, no honor could be extended the Franks for the invention.

Furthermore, there is the question of whether the Gauls actually used tree saddles before the Franks came. We know the Gauls had considerable intercourse with the Romans before and after the dawn of the Christian Era. If the Gauls had possessed such rigs, it would seem that such a horse-riding nation as Rome would have adopted the principle long before the fourth century, when saddles first began to show up there. Greek horsemen, too, were among the most enlightened people of that period. They would surely have copied any riding improvement existing in southern Europe. Yet, like the Romans, they were without saddles until the fourth century.

Much may be found to favor the belief that the first saddles came out of the region bordering the Black and Caspian seas. Here were born the earliest horsemen, whose experience in horsemanship and supplying the needs of the mounted man far antedated that of any other lands. To these experts most likely belongs the credit for devising headstalls, bits, reins, saddle cloths and scale armor. Why not the saddle? It seems only natural that a people so long experienced in a given art would be the first to work out such an improvement for the comfort and security of its devotees.

Unfortunately, that brings up another pertinent question: If these people did invent the saddle, why did such an outstanding development not spread to the east and north as well as to the southwest? So far as history reveals, Rome, Greece, and Asia Minor were using saddles for a long period before they showed up elsewhere. All the wild hordes to the north, who had practically lived on horseback for centuries and whom logic would dictate as the first to welcome any improvement, were still riding bareback long after saddles had become fairly common in the south. Mention has already been made of Attila's Huns riding without saddles or bridles when they swept down on Europe in the fifth century. Thus, we may ask: If central or southwest Asia was first to devise saddles, why did the Western nations alone adopt the creation?

So let us take a look at the arguments put forth by advocates of the Hungarian plains as the birthplace of saddles. The Goths, Scythians, Sarmatians, and Alani who inhabited this region in the early centuries of our era were among the world's foremost horsemen. They were in a stage somewhat advanced from that of the old nomadic barbarians and are known to have introduced various practices unknown to earlier races. Whatever intercourse they may have had with other nations was pretty well limited by geographical and linguistic factors to their neighbors on the south.

Add to this the fact that the ancient Hungarian saddle dates back to a time that no man knows. Perhaps it sprang from that unidentified Gaulish saddle previously mentioned. Or consider its possible relation to the Quadi saddle. The latter people were fairly close neighbors of the Hungarians and much like them in everyday pursuits.

At any rate, the old Hungarian saddle was very ancient and very primitive in form—quite on a par with the native saddle of the North American Indians. It could be constructed from materials everywhere available in the natural state and required no metal parts. It had the basic form of all saddle construction used in later times throughout the world.

The earliest known representation of the Hungarian saddle is much the same as our American McClellan rig, of which it was an ancestor. See Fig. 83 for a more modern example and for construction details, all of which are only superficial improvements on the original design. We shall return to this saddle for further discussion.

History shows the Romans using frame saddles of this type as early as A.D. 385. As Roman influence extended well toward Hungary and Roman horsemen were the first Mediterranean people to adopt the saddle idea, a link between the two would appear obvious.

However, there are other factors to confuse the picture. In the first place, we learn that the Germanic tribes of that period thought such sissified contraptions as saddles were unfit for real men. They despised the Romans for succumbing to such luxuries and called them babies and old women. That would seem a strange attitude to take if such a worthwhile creation had been developed among their own cousins on the Hungarian plains.

In the second place, this same type of saddle makes its appearance in far-distant Mongolia. When Dr. Roy Chapman Andrews' archeological expedition was exploring Mongolia in 1926, it chanced to uncover the grave of an ancient Mongol horseman. The man had been entombed fully dressed and with his head lying on his saddle. Though all archeological evidence dated the man's burial as not later than 900—and probably much earlier—the extreme dryness of that region had preserved both the ancient's saddle and dress in first-class condition. Dr. Andrews reported that the saddle was an almost exact replica of our modern McClellans, which, in turn, originated from the Hungarian saddle. This type of rig is totally unlike anything used in Mongolia in later times.

As existing pictures and carvings of ancient Mongol and Chinese saddles show styles more in keeping with later Mongol outfits, it would appear that Dr. Andrews' warrior had been using a saddle brought back from Europe sometime prior to 900. If he had ridden west with his companions in the customary bareback fashion, it would have been natural for him to equip himself with such a worthwhile prize captured from some enemy. On the other hand, we cannot overlook the possibility that this might have been a Mongolian creation in its own right, a development not commonly in use by the rank and file of the barbarians and later discarded for the typical Mongol design.

McGovern leads us further into this possibility when he tells us there exists an old Chinese drawing, supposed to be of the 250–150 B.C. period, which pictures a mounted Mongolian emperor, or *shanyu,* riding with a saddle. Though the saddle itself is mostly concealed by the rider, it appears to have a rather wide, flat horn, a low, sloping cantle, and big rounded skirts that cover most of the horse's sides. It is equipped with a single cinch, breast collar, and crupper and is mounted on a decorated saddle blanket. The bridle is of conventional design with narrow headstall. Altogether, it bears a great similarity to Chinese outfits in use several centuries later.

If there actually were saddles in China two centuries before Christ, they must have been original creations. The rest of the world was still without them at that time. Granting for the moment that such things did exist, we might picture a connection between them and the problematical saddle of the eastern Gauls. This could easily be extended to cover the 38–9 B.C. monument of the saddle at Mainz. Such a conception would have the saddle moving westward across Asia from the Orient, reaching the Mediterranean countries from the north.

But this again brings up the question of why, if the Mongolians invented the saddle, all the nomadic horsemen between the Gobi and Greece continued to ride bareback for the next five hundred years? Wars, raids, and invasions always disseminate knowledge of better equipment, especially if it proves an aid to conquest. These various barbarian races were continually shifting about and overrunning each other's territories. Yet nowhere does the saddle appear among them before the fourth century.

Much the same question applies to China. Assuming that this pre-Christian Era saddle was one of China's numerous inventions instead of Mongolia's, why did its use not spread to adjoining countries? The Chinese were using cavalry and did much horseback riding after 325 B.C.

If they had possessed such a boon to horsemen, surely someone would have copied it.

Warwick's description of the Buddha statues in Chinese caves lends weight to the idea that China had saddles no earlier than anyone else. Buddha, as we know, left his wife and home in 534 B.C. to start riding hither and yon, teaching the doctrine of his faith. In the caves of Yun Kang, near Tatung, in North Shansi province, is a carved statue of Buddha departing on horseback from his sleeping wife. The figure shows the horse Kanthaka accoutered with only a saddle cloth. It is said to have been carved by the Toba Tartars between A.D. 386 and 532.

A later carving at the Shih Chia Fo cave pictures Kanthaka licking the foot of Maitreya, the Buddha of the Future. In this presentation the horse is wearing a crude form of saddle over a decorated blanket. Still another carving of Buddha shows him riding forth to view the sorrows of the world, a ceremonial umbrella held over himself and the horse.

All this would seem to indicate that China was riding bareback until 386 or later. Had the Tartars, who carved the likeness, known anything about saddles at that time, we might think they would have included full equipment with such an important personage. The fact that the saddle is shown on the other and later carvings, when such rigs were definitely in use, should have some significance.

Or should it? Perhaps the Toba Tartars were only being intentionally realistic in their work. It could be that the artists knew there were no saddles when Buddha started his career in 534 B.C. and so chose to be honest in their depiction, though they themselves were familiar with the article of the later era in which they lived. In that case, we might judge the saddles on the other figures, carved by less conscientious workmen, to be fictional representations. In order for Buddha to have had a saddle, even in his later years, they had to have been in use in China by around 500 B.C. This is very doubtful, as it was another two centuries before the Chinese started riding to any extent.

Of course, there are always possibilities. The Chinese were great inventors. They might have devised something in the saddle line in ancient times, its use being limited to a few upper-class individuals whose disinterest allowed it to fade out of the picture. Buddha might have acquired something of this nature during his later pilgrimages. The same possibility might apply to the previously mentioned Mongolian emperor of 200 B.C. But if such was the case, it still offers no explanation as to why the idea failed to spread westward among the horseback nomads. The whole proposition makes a wonderful guessing game.

A similar problem involves the use of stirrups. There is no certain evidence that stirrups preceded saddles, though many historians believe them to be an earlier invention. In either case, the first saddles to find their way into history were without stirrups.

Stong tells us the stirrup was an ancient Oriental invention first mentioned in old Chinese literature. That lends color to the idea of saddle development in early China. McGovern thinks stirrups originated among the Sarmatians of central Asia around 300 B.C. If McGovern is right, they must have simply attached bent wood or leather loops to blanket pads. History shows no frame saddles among the Sarmatians of so early a period. Those pictured on Trajan's Column are all bareback riders, though a few have saddle cloths.

Incidentally, some of the Magyars were still using stirrups attached by narrow leather straps to a piece of heavy woolen rug well into the twentieth century. No cinch was used. The rig was merely thrown over the horse and held in place by the rider's weight. This was a very old method employed by various peoples in the infancy of saddle use. It was frequently found among the early pad saddles of the American Indians, of which more will be said later. Some authorities think a pair of stirrups hitched to a pad may have been the forerunner of the real saddle.

But if such was the case, why is there no mention of stirrups by any of the ancient writers? And why did the saddle appear in the Mediterranean region 250 years before anybody thought to put stirrups on it? There, as has been noted, saddles of a sort were in evidence about A.D. 340; yet it was in the neighborhood of 600 before we find any stirrups.

Waterer puts the date in the middle 600s. Dwyer says they showed up in southern Europe during the time of the Roman emperor Maurice, around 602. Stong says the same thing. The latter thinks the central Asian nomads brought them from the Orient, where they originated. One unidentified writer believes they were introduced into Rome by the Franks. His contention is that the Franks got them from the invading barbarians.

St. Jerome (A.D. 340–420) has been noted as the first writer to mention stirrups, but this is open to question. Pitiscus wrote that the name for stirrups originates from *strator,* a Latin term for anything by which a person mounts or dismounts from a horse. As this would likely be a holdover from the old horse block, it denotes little in the way of time. There is record of a poem from a very early Roman period which tells of a man being dragged to death by having a foot hung in the stirrup. The consensus of most historians is that Rome was the first of the Western nations to use stirrups. Roman cavalry instituted the practice in the seventh century as the first practical method of alleviating the painful swelling of legs and feet so common among riders forced to let their legs hang unsupported during continuous riding. This is logical reasoning, but there isn't much logic in the time it took them to figure out the remedy.

Stirrups, however, were destined to provide much more than a support for swollen limbs and an easy means of mounting. But for them, the glamour of knighthood would no doubt have shaped a different chapter in history. Those were the days of lances and battle-axes. In mounted warfare, a man was only as good as his seat in the saddle. Few of the feats that build legends would attach themselves to men easily removed from loose saddle seats by spear thrusts or blows from a mace. It is hard to imagine Richard the Lion-Hearted or Barbarossa as such shining figures etched against the sky had they lacked the means of rising high above the backs of their mounts in attacks on the enemy.

It was the invention of stirrups that made all the difference. They furnished the means whereby the medieval horseman, for the first time, could lift himself to full height, his feet planted solidly on a firm support, when striking down at a foe. Stirrups also allowed him to duck, dodge, and bend in any direction without losing his seat when facing a similarly equipped adversary. Furthermore, with feet firmly planted in stirrups, his body could more easily absorb the shock of heavy weapons driving against his shield. Even in more peaceful pursuits, it was the addition of stirrups that made the saddle a secure and wholly serviceable creation.

This was well recognized by the Order of Equites, when that body came into being in the 700s. They soon found that, well seated in their deep saddles, the extra purchase offered by stirrups made them virtually one with the horse. In jousting tournaments or open warfare, such an advantage was comparable to the later advent of gunpowder against bows and arrows. Stirrups, in fact, might be called the stepping stone to knighthood and the foundation of European feudalism.

It was the Roman cavalry, during Vespasian's time, which started us on the way to mounting from the near side of the horse. All bareback riders of antiquity, as well as the early civilized nations and American Indians, mounted from the right side. This is a most natural method for predominantly right-handed humans. The same practice continued through the early days of saddles. It remained for the Roman cavalry to change the style. They were armed with heavy and somewhat cumbersome swords slung on the left hip for convenient right-hand use. This proved awkward when mounting the horse from the off side. In consequence, mounting was shifted to the left side so the sword could follow the rider aboard instead of barring his way. And like so many customs established by the early Romans, this practice continued through all later centuries of civilized man.

The best evidence indicates that these early Romans used a single-rig saddle of the McClellan type, with iron or bronze stirrups. It was built on a wooden sidebar tree, usually leather-covered. Some of the more elaborate ones seem to have run to quilted fabric coverings.

This was the basic form of all saddles ever devised. High cantles and forks, swells, rolls, pads, horns, and the like were simply superstructures built on the standard base. And it was from this base that the two distinct types of saddles familiar to modern eyes sprang. On one hand we have the old Hungarian-McClellan style, with low fork and cantle, rather light in weight and usually minus a horn. On the other hand we have the high-forked rig with a very distinct horn, high form-fitting cantle, large skirts and, in many cases, swells or knee pads on either side of the fork. The saddle of the medieval knight and American cowboy evolved from the latter type. In the former we find the bulk of European riding saddles, along with some from the Orient and Africa. The English pad saddle is the only deviation from the original built-up-tree design, which found little acceptance outside of its home country and eastern North America.

—8—

Bits, Spurs, and Horseshoes

WHEN WE THINK OF SADDLES, we naturally think of bits and spurs to go with them. And when we look for the origin of the latter, we find it as obscure as the history of saddles.

Circumstantial evidence points strongly toward the wild tribes of the Kirghiz steppes of southern Scythia as having been the first to devise actual bridle bits. While this seems reasonable, what is believed to be the oldest specimen ever found is a stone bit taken from the ancient lake dwellings at Robenhausen, near Zurich, Switzerland. These dwellings date back to neolithic times, though the bit itself could have been left by a later people. It is of worked stone, made in elongated, slightly curved form, with double knobs at both ends. It is deeply grooved between the knobs as if designed to accommodate some sort of headstall.

It is safe to assume that the first bits were of wood, horn, bone, stone, or twisted rawhide thongs. Only those of stone would have been durable enough to survive the ravages of time and the elements. And we have only one undated example of these to speculate on. Thus it remains a matter of conjecture as to what went on in the realm of horse bits before the ages of iron and bronze left us permanent samples of ancient creations.

According to Greek mythology, the goddess Athena invented the first bridle while helping Bellerophon master the winged horse Pegasus. Another legend says that Pelethronius of Thessaly was the first man to attach leather to a horse. As there is no way of telling how far back in antiquity these tales were born or from what country they originated, we can still only guess at the conception of the age-old idea.

The weight of opinion leans toward the Scythians as being at least among the first to attach guiding devices to horses' headstalls. Bits from the early Iron Age have been found in Scythian tombs. It is reasonable to think that such a simple and useful device would be developed by confirmed horsemen before too many generations had passed. And we do know the Scythians had bits in earliest recorded times. Trajan's Column shows bits in use by their successors, the Sarmatians, in the first century (Fig. 2).

Assyrians and Babylonians received their introduction to horses from the Scythians, who were using horses to draw their chariots as early as 4000 B.C., and probably for some time before. An Assyrian shell cylinder of the 4000 B.C. period, now in the Metropolitan Museum of Art, New York City, carries pictures of horses and chariots in battle. The ancient Chaldean city of Ur, representative of the same era, produced the earliest description of a chariot we have. It is written on a plaque now in the University of Pennsylvania Museum at Philadelphia. Various harness ornaments of the 4000–3000 B.C. period have also been found in the royal tombs of Ur.

If the Chaldeans acquired their horses from the Scythians, no doubt the animals were equipped with whatever devices the former owners had used to guide and control them. However, through all those ages many horsemen raced with unbridled mounts. Others used some sort of hackamore-style rigs or plain nosebands of cord or leather. Nosebands that were studded on the inside with spikes would serve almost as effectively as bits. Various old carvings show this kind of bridle. Xenophon described them as being used in Greece around 400 B.C. The first ones were undoubtedly of the simplest bar-mouthpiece variety.

The fourth century Greek rider in Fig. 8 is still using the primitive jaw-strap bridle, yet chariot horses of the same period and region are often shown wearing metal guiding devices. This suggests there was considerable overlapping of styles in any given period. And the variation of practices would be more pronounced on an international scale. Bitted bridles popular in an early age in one region might have been totally unknown for centuries in another. Other peoples may have used bits at an early period and then allowed them to go out of fashion for several generations. It all narrows down to the fact that bits were known and used in many places before 4000 B.C., perhaps back in neolithic times, but were not adopted by all peoples as a standard adjunct to horseback riding until almost the dawn of the Christian Era.

One contrivance for controlling horses used by most of the Mediterranean nations during their early years of horse culture was a headstall fitted with metal plates whose corners carried sharp points that pulled into the sides of a horse's mouth. This was probably the first improvement over the spike-studded nosepiece. Diamond- or sickle-shaped sideplates were favorites.

This type of headstall appears to have been a favorite during the early ages. Many reflected the artistic temperament of their owners. Some described by Homer were decorated with purple-stained ivory plates, examples of which have been found at ancient Troy.

Many ancient Greek and Persian vases of Homer's time, and earlier, were decorated with horses wearing bridles and bits. The horses on the Parthenon frieze (Fig. 9) were originally fitted with bridles and reins; and bits are definitely suggested. Various antique bits similar to those in Fig. 19 have been discovered in that country.

Old Greek writers are fond of crediting the invention of snaffle bits to their own country. This might well be so. It is not out of the way to think the Greeks might have devised the first improvement over the simple straight bars of earlier times.

Xenophon left us a description of the two kinds of bits in current use during his time. One which he called the easy bit was of snaffle design with a thick bar similar to a mouthing bit. The other was the wolf bit, whose mouthpiece was studded with sharp little iron spikes ranged along its length like animal teeth. It was designed for a particular breed of Greek horses called the *lycospades.* These animals, which ranged in a wolf-infested mountain area, were especially vicious and hard-mouthed. The more severe bit was necessary to control them.

Both straight and jointed bits have been found at the site of Troy. Snaffle bits were used by the ancient Gauls. It is anybody's guess whether the Gauls adopted the principle of bits from Asia or Greece. On the other hand, it is not improbable that the Gauls' natural inventiveness created a strictly Gaulish product. Or it could have been an outgrowth of the old stone bit of Switzerland.

In the second century Arrian, a later Greek, wrote that the Persians used sort of a halter with a bar mouthpiece. A Persepolis carving (Fig. 11) shows a type such as Arrian might have referred to. The leverlike construction of sidebars and iron-bar curb gives proof of severe bits in use prior to 500 B.C., when Persepolis was built. A specimen of the sixth century B.C. (Fig. 12) is shown with long, curved sidebars suggestive of a curb.

The illustration in a thirteenth century Old Testament at the Pierpont Morgan Library in New York mentioned earlier shows curb bits on horses in the battle scene between Saul and the Ammonites. Whether

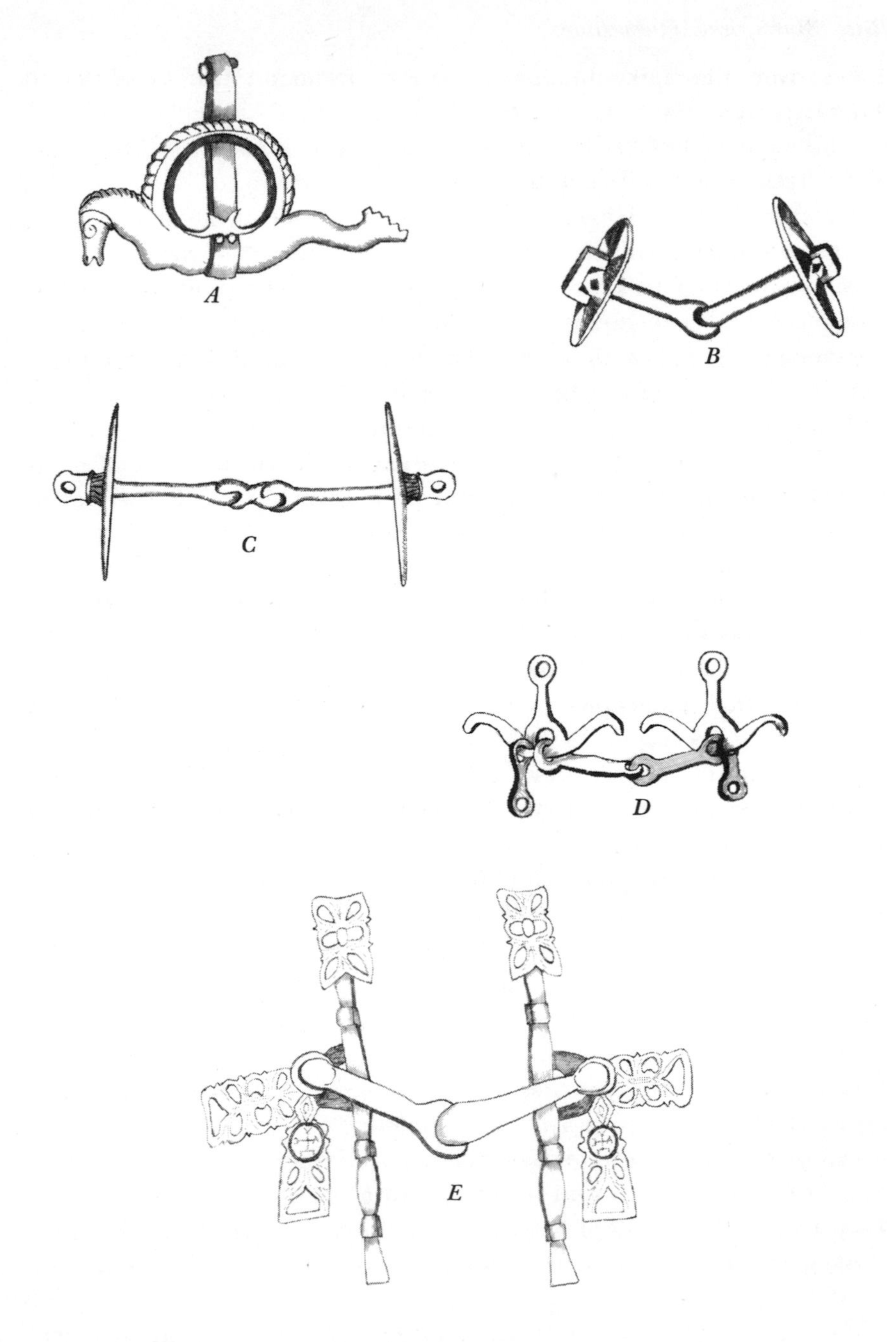

FIG. 19. Bits: *A* ancient Greek, Neptune design; *B* and *C* early Greek; *D* English, King Coel's bit third century; *E* Visigothic, seventh century.

this picture is supposed to show the actual equipment used some thousand years before Christ or merely an artistic conception of that period we have no way of knowing, but its authenticity cannot be entirely discounted.

The best evidence available leads us to believe curb bits appeared on the scene somewhere around 1000 B.C. Xenophon mentions them in one of his writings as being in use in Greece. Berjeau says the Sarmatians were using both straight and curb bits before the Christian Era. Persia was using them to some extent, as various carvings of that period indicate.

Farshler gives the Romans credit for originating the curb, but this is questionable. If it is true, it must have been at a very early period. The Romans acquired most of their innovations from Greece; and, backed by Xenophon's statement and the undoubted practice farther east in ancient times, it looks as if Rome merely adopted a bit someone else had invented a good while earlier.

At any rate, curb bits were neither very plentiful nor widely used by anyone before the first century. All history depicts them as decidedly in the minority with snaffles and bar mouthpieces until after the first thousand years of our era.

An old snaffle-type bit from an ancient burial ground in England was found between Bath and London in what is believed to have been the grave of the third century King Coel (Fig. 19). It is equally possible, however, that this was the grave of some Roman invader. In such case, the bit might easily date to before the Christian Era.

One somewhat similar bit came from an old battlefield in Andalusia. This is thought to have belonged to Witiza, king of the Visigoths around 675. (See Fig. 19.)

Another ancient relic of snaffle pattern is ornamented with bosses of horses' heads. A fairly late bronze bit was found at Pompeii. It has a twisted-bar mouthpiece and plain curved bar curb. No doubt the curb bits mentioned by Xenophon and Berjeau were somewhat on this order. Bar bits with sidebars instead of rings and fitted with solid bar curbs seem to have been a preferred style. Some may have had ports on the mouthpiece. Later Greeks and medieval Europe used a bit of this nature having a post roller-port and curb.

Martingales to further control the head action of spirited horses came along in this early period. They are said to have been invented by a certain *Evangalista,* an eminent horseman of Milan, Italy.

Another item much in use as a control measure during those times was the horse muzzle used on stallion war horses. These were big, heavy affairs made of iron and often artistically designed (Fig. 20).

One of the reasons most of the ancients and the knights of the Middle Ages rode ungelded horses was that stallions were more or less inclined to viciousness. Especially in the excitement of battle, they would often create more havoc than their riders. But such propensities were not so

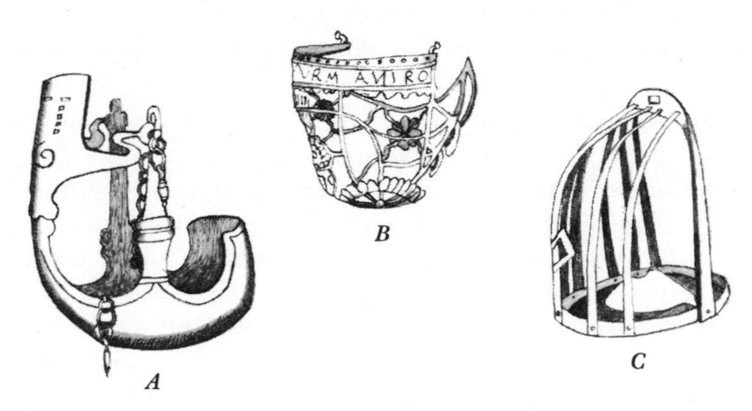

FIG. 20. Horse muzzles: *A* Greek, fifth century; *B* German, twelfth century *C* German, seventeenth century.

welcome at home, where peaceable association with stable boys and other horses was to be desired. Grooms were often compelled to wear a special mailed glove to lead or hold their masters' mounts. This also created problems when riding with friends or cavalry companions. To prevent accidents, it was a common practice to muzzle the animals.

There is no way of knowing when this innovation came into being. The Persians and Greeks were using muzzles before the fifth century B.C. A muzzled horse is among the figures carved before 500 B.C. on the temple at Persepolis. The use of muzzles was continued all through Europe until gunpowder put the hand-to-hand fighting of riders on armored horses out of business.

All the simpler forms of bits and bit substitutes held sway until the era of metal armor got under way. It was not until the Middle Ages that bits evolved into the extravagant creations we have come to associate with mailed knights and noble gentry of Europe. From then on for several centuries bits ran to the wildest extremes. Some were truly strange contrivances. They were often so absurd, whimsical, or monstrous that some of the horse's teeth had to be pulled to accommodate them. Ornamentation too reached elaborate heights and bizarre shapes prevailed. Examples of such bits appear in Figs. 21–23.

It was during the knighthood period that bit chains appeared on the scene. Cutting a rider's reins was a favorite trick of enemies in battle, thus putting the opponent's horse out of control. To help prevent such mishaps, riders started attaching hinged metal plates, or rein guards, to the reins in the 1400s.

Rein guards were heavy and cumbersome, however, both in the rider's hands and on the horse's bit. When some bright mind discovered that lightweight chains would serve the purpose with half the bother, bit chains blossomed into immediate popularity. Various advantages of lesser nature have perpetuated the use of these sweetly tinkling chains down to the present day. The soft notes of bit chains are soothing to both horse and rider. They are equaled only by the musical jingle of spur rowels on the rider's heels.

It was not the jingle of rowels, however, which first induced their acceptance by horsemen. Spurs had no rowels in the beginning. The earliest ones were simply goadlike, single-prong affairs of a strictly utilitarian nature.

Who invented such a widely used aid to horse control is uncertain. Some historians credit the origin of spurs to the early Scythians or Sarmatians. There is no evidence of this among ancient sculptures, however. Too, if they were a product of the early nomads, it seems queer they did not show up among the Persians. Persia was one of the first nations to adopt the customs of the northern horsemen; yet, the old writers find agreement in stating that the early Persians did not use spurs, nor did their descendants until a rather late date. Even then, most writers speak of the few there were as being mostly small brads set into boot heels.

Stone says the early goad spurs first appeared in history about 700 B.C. The originals were no doubt little more than crude spikes of wood, bone, or metal, fastened to the foot by thongs. Such insecure anchorage as the soft boots or foot wrappings in use by most peoples at that time would have necessitated the spurs being small and short.

Fig. 24 shows some of the earliest examples left to us. Perhaps one of the first designs made to actually fit the foot was something like the ancient Byzantine model shown. It was some five hundred years before they developed into the long shanks set into fitted heelplates like

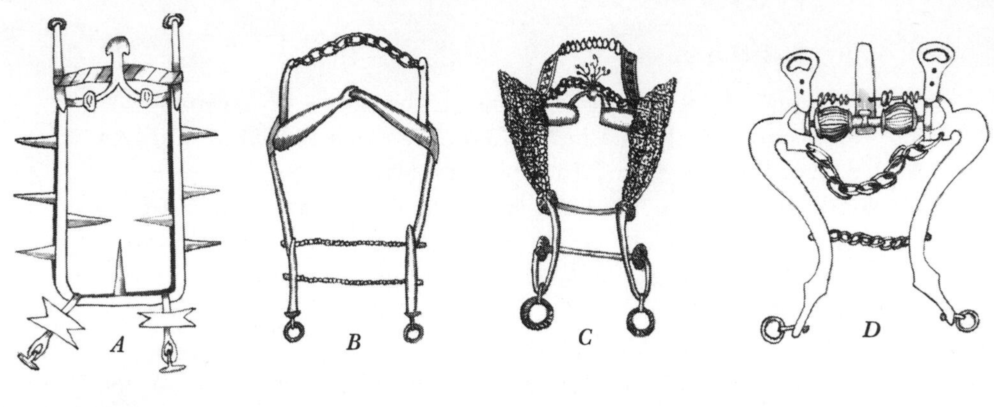

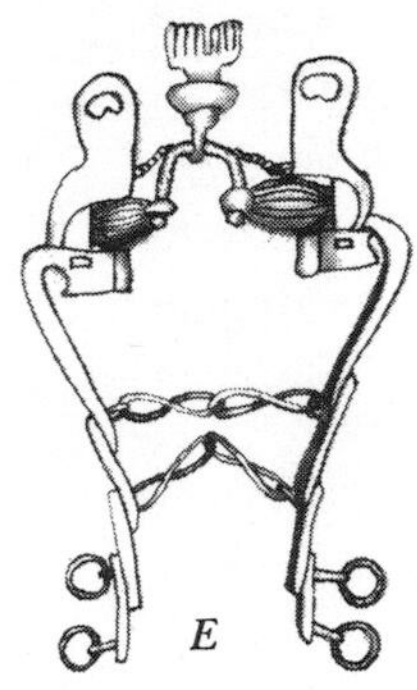

FIG. 21. Bits: *A-C* French, sixteenth century; *D* Spanish, seventeenth century; *E* French, eighteenth century.

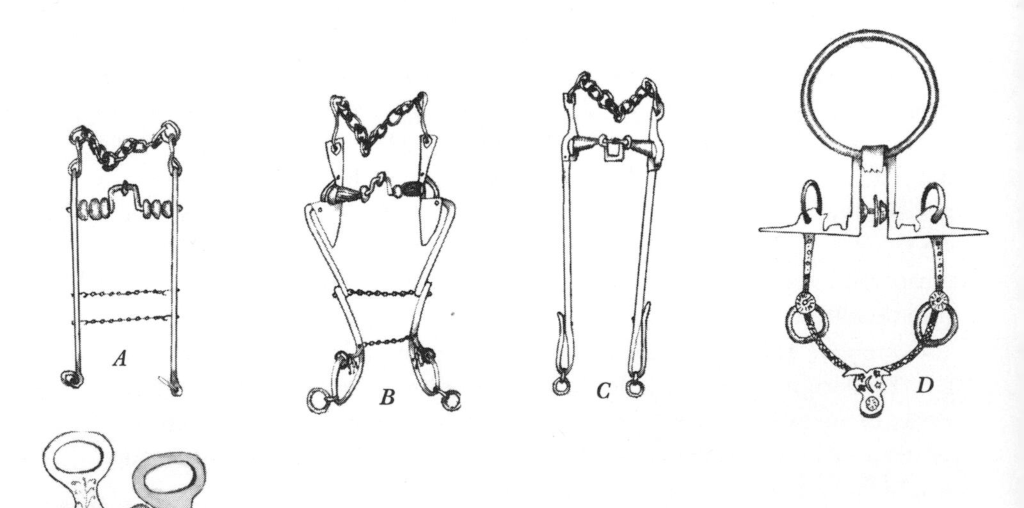

E

FIG. 22. Bits: *A* German jousting bit, sixteenth century; *B* German, sixteenth century; *C* German, eighteenth century; *D* Arabian, eighteenth century; *E* Spanish 1800.

FIG. 23. French bits, eighteenth century.

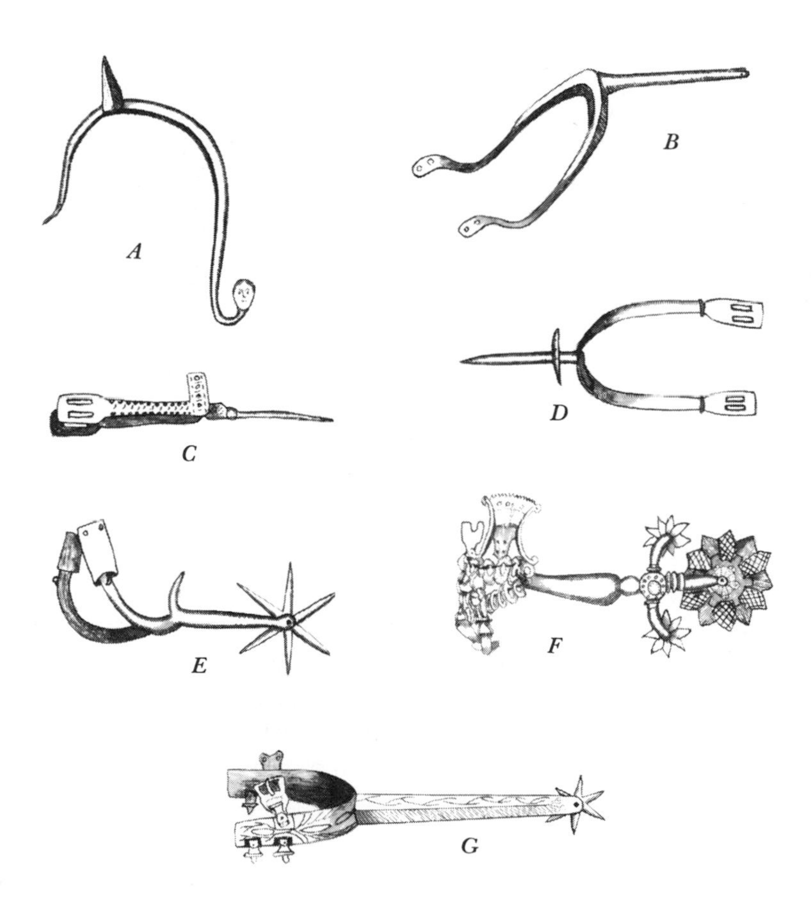

FIG. 24. Goads and spurs: *A* ancient Byzantine; *B* King Coel's goad, English, third century; *C* Arabian; *D* Moroccan; *E* French, fourteenth century; *F* French, fifteenth century; *G* Italian, fifteenth century.

the Arabian goad. These gradually grew larger and longer until about A.D. 1100, when stops had to be put on them to preserve the horse's inner unmentionables. These were similar to the Moroccan goads, and had spread to most of the horseback nations.

This Moroccan style is still a favorite among the Arabic peoples and a few other Eastern nations. They are often handsomely decorated with chased-silver plates set with coral. The straps may be covered with velvet and set with precious stones.

Arabic lands also use a sort of lazy man's version of the old boot-heel goad in stirrup form. The stirrup has a jutting spur prong built into it on the side next the horse. (See Fig. 55.)

In Greece, the quirtlike, thonged whip (Fig. 25) was a favorite per-

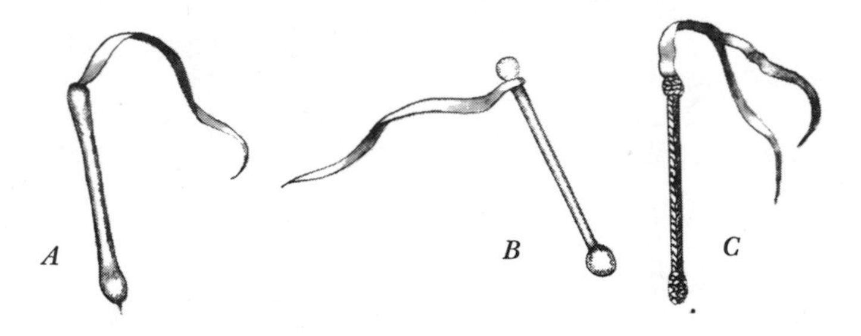

FIG. 25. *A* Roman goad whip; *B* and *C* Greek whips.

suader, though spurs were also used. As Xenophon tells of them, they must have been in use there as early as 400 B.C.

Xenophon also speaks of a leg covering for riders that suggests a sort of boot. If boot it was, it was probably the one brought by the Hunnish invaders. In any event, we would not be too far wrong in crediting the birth of substantial footwear to the horseman's spur.

Rome evidently got their spurs from Greece. Vergil, the Roman poet, mentions spurs in his poem on the "Warrior Horse." The Equites were spur users in the early part of the Christian Era. The Romans even had a spur, or brad, set in the butt of one style of whip (Fig. 25). They called it a *scorpio* because of its resemblance to a scorpion's tail.

The old single-prong goad spur continued in use in Europe until about 1200. The early Norman knights are commonly pictured using this type. We find them so shown on the Bayeux Tapestry of the ninth century (Fig. 57), as well as in various other contemporary illustrations. A Spanish manuscript of the eleventh century mentions them. They also appear in eleventh century European history. A stained glass window in the cathedral of Chartres, in France, shows goad spurs in the thirteenth century picture of the French crusader Thibaut VI, Earl of Blois. The monument of Don Rodrigo de Lauria in Aragon, Spain, depicts the don as wearing goad spurs in 1342. They were apparently about the only type used throughout Europe during this era.

The first suggestion of rowels does not occur until about 1200; then it was usually a case of attaching stars or rosettes to the ends of the old goads. What look like rowel spurs are shown on the French hunters in the manuscript of the *Livre du Roi Modus* of the thirteenth century. Similar styles appear on the thirteenth century horsemen in the French manuscript of the Apocalypse (Fig. 75), the fourteenth century knight from the *Roman de Tristan* manuscript (Fig. 60), and a fourteenth century Italian fresco painting by Andrea Orgagna at the Campo Santo di Pisa (Fig. 61).

One authority states that regular loose rowels were not used until the early 1400s; Stone says the 1300s. The best evidence seems to favor the latter.

An old shanked spur found in England was thought to have been from the third century or earlier; this gave every indication of having carried a rowel or at least a fixed rosette now missing. At any rate it was definitely not of the goad type (see Fig. 24). It came from the same burial ground as the old bit thought to have belonged to King Coel or a Roman of still earlier days. If this spur is as ancient as believed, it must have been a unique development, born ahead of its time. Nevertheless, it was around 1400 before loose rowels came into general use. And they were about the only style in favor throughout Europe from then on.

This was the age of chivalry, of the cavalier, the *caballero,* the knight, the chevalier, and the royal man-at-arms. The spur was his mark of rank, the symbol of romance and adventure. Only he was allowed to wear this shining badge of knighthood, earned by acts of valor and awarded only by the king or feudal lord.

The expression "winning your spurs" is still used to signify the attainment of a chosen goal. For the armored knight it meant final achievement after many tests. Wandering troubadours sang of his deeds while feminine eyes brightened at the sight and sound of the tinkling golden spurs.

Even in modern times the wearing of spurs lends an aura of romance, and imitation spurs were worn by swivel-chair army colonels well into the twentieth century.

During the knighthood period, armor for both horse and rider was considered essential. Armor for the horse often extended down its sides to the stirrups or below, interfering with the rider's spurs. This was especially true when he wore short-shanked spurs. The obvious remedy was to lengthen the shanks. The result was that the armored knight's spur shanks grew longer and longer until they often reached the length of twelve or fourteen inches.

At this time the love of pomp and show fomented a surge of elaboration which ran to fantastic lengths after the early 1400s. For the next two hundred years, spurs grew steadily in size and ornamentation. It was much like the bit styles of the time; everyone was trying to outdo his neighbor. And the spur makers entered into the spirit of the thing with enthusiasm. (See Fig. 26.) There was even a folding type. Its heel-plates were of ornamented openwork in silver-plated steel, while the engraved shanks carried 5/8 inch rowels.

Big rowels were the style at this time. Starting fairly small in the early 1400s, they increased in diameter as shanks grew longer. By 1600, they were enormous. It was during the late 1400s and 1500s that the fad for multiple rowels reached its peak; two rowels to a spur became commonplace, and some had as many as six.

The following century brought with it a gradual decline in all such extravagances. Shanks grew shorter and rowels smaller until, with gunpowder finally grounding the armored knights, spurs eventually tapered off into more conventional designs.

A Frenchman by the name of Guermiehe, equerry to Louis XIV, brought out a design in 1768 which was remarkably like the American cowboy spur of a century later. It was quite popular in southern Europe for some time. Spain was about the only country to cling to the big, elaborate spurs in later years.

The shoeing of horses is a very old art, yet it was essentially a practice of civilized nations. The ancient nomads rode unshod horses for the most part because the half-wild horses of the Asian deserts seldom needed shoes. Horses born and raised in any open country, and allowed to run at will over the dry, rocky terrain of mountains and desert, develop a hardness of hoof that requires little attention. So it was with the animals that spread south and west out of Turkestan and the steppes. Most of the ancient writers specially mentioned the great durability found in the feet of those Eastern breeds. It was only after civilized man began confining his mounts to stables and soft pasturelands that foot protection became generally necessary.

The first attempts at shoeing employed that old stand-by, rawhide.

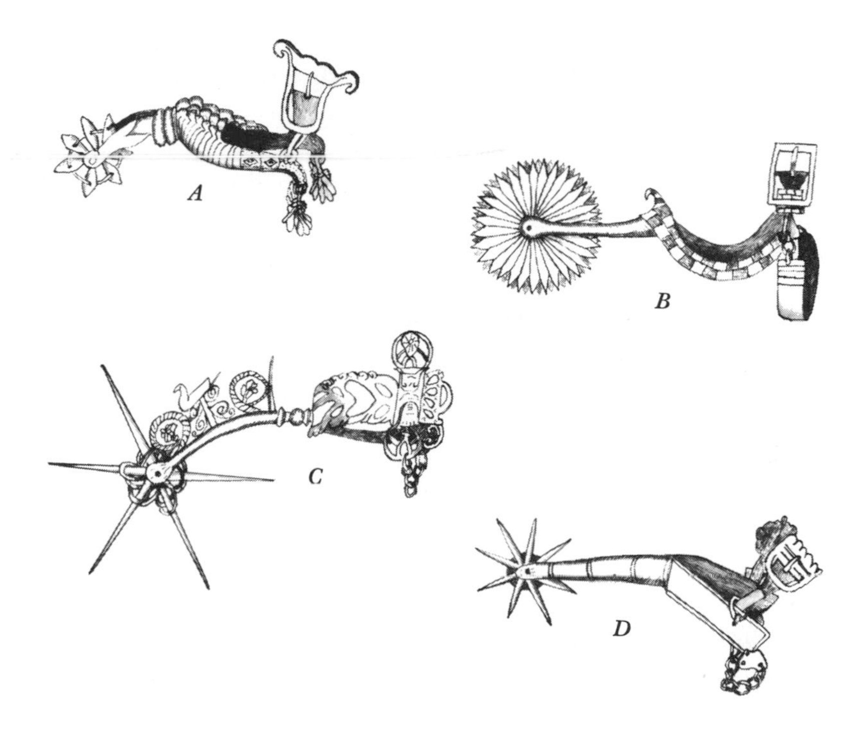

FIG. 26. Spurs: *A* French, sixteenth century; *B* French double rowel, sixteenth century; *C* German, sixteenth century; *D* Spanish seventeenth century.

A circular piece of hide was cut to the proper dimensions, with a series of holes punched around the edge. When soaked soft it could be drawn snugly around the hoof with a drawstring and then allowed to harden to shape.

The Tartars, Kalmucks, and Turks used this method on what few horses they found it necessary to shoe. Those rawhide foot coverings also appeared from time to time in many sections of the world. They wore surprisingly well, as anyone familiar with rawhide will testify.

Arrian of Nicomedia wrote that Alexander's Macedonian cavalry shod their horses in this manner.

Hoof coverings of plaited straw were used in a few sections of the Orient. Such shoes could not have been very durable, but they were economical and could be easily replaced. Moreover, they seldom appeared among people who did much extensive riding. The Japanese used these straw boots until modern times.

Catullus, Pliny, Xenophon, and other early writers made considerable mention of horseshoes, but those of that period were a sort of leather boot fastened onto the horse's foot with straps or cords. In the course of time metal plates were attached to the bottom of the boots for greater durability. The upper-class Greeks often decorated these hoof coverings with gold and silver trim.

The early Romans used the same type of metal-plated leather boots, evidently copied from the Greeks. It is believed they introduced such hoof boots into England in 55 B.C. Some historians credit the Romans with having originated the conventional nail-on horseshoe, but this is largely guesswork. Nero is said to have shod his horses with silver, while his wife used gold for hers, but these were probably merely the old leather boots with silver and gold bases instead of iron. There is no definite record of all-metal shoes during Nero's activities in the first century.

While certain researches have indicated that all-metal shoes may have been in use as early as 320 B.C., the first authoritative appearance was around A.D. 481. A shoe taken from the tomb of the French knight Childeric (Fig. 27), is quite modern in design. If it did belong to that early knight, its similarity to later shoes would indicate it was an adaptation from an earlier type rather than an original. Even horseshoes must have a trial-and-error period of evolution. To find such a finished example in Childeric's time suggests that experimental models must have appeared many years previously. However, horseshoes did not become common in Europe until around 900. Their use was almost simultaneous with the rise of mailed knights.

The old Egyptians and Arabians probably learned horseshoeing from the Greeks or Romans. Horseshoes showed up on both sides of the Red Sea somewhat earlier than they did in Europe. They were different, though, from those used farther north, being flat, oval plates with small holes in the center, instead of the typical rimlike style. The toes of the shoes were almost square.

When the Spaniards got hold of those Arab-Moorish shoes, they rounded off the toes and often turned up the heels to double back against the hoof. They favored a thin, flat style in general, though they made extensive use of both the Arabian plates and the continental rimmed type.

Incidentally, a flat-plate, fully rimmed shoe with open center saw some use in colonial America for horses used on tread-power machines. These had a strong resemblance to the old Arabian shoes.

When the conquistadors came to America, they immediately found themselves faced by a dearth of iron to shoe their most essential horses. During their early years in Mexico they tried using the abundant silver for horseshoes but found it too soft to make a suitable substitute for more durable material. As they had no other metal, they reverted to the ancient method of covering their horses' hoofs with rawhide.

The Indians of the Southwest, who got their horses from the Spaniards,

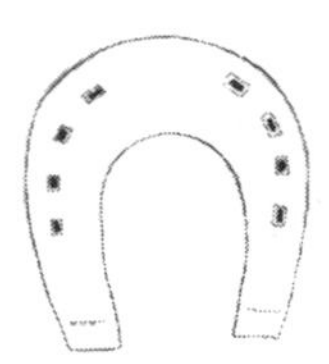

FIG. 27. French horseshoe from Childeric's tomb, fifth century.

adopted this method of rawhide shoeing whenever protection of their mounts became necessary. They passed it on to the Indians farther north until it became a common practice with all the American tribes.

Down in Honduras, the early Spanish colonists found gold so much more plentiful than any other metal that they used it extensively for horseshoes. It wore away quickly but was in good supply and easily worked.

When Jerry Lynch of Virginia City, Nevada, took a fortune out of the Lady Brian mine, around 1870, he kept his favorite mount shod with silver shoes. This, however, was more a show of wealth than a utilitarian measure.

Big wooden shoes have been used occasionally for horses working in deep snow or on boggy ground. Wrapping their horses' feet heavily in burlap was a trick often used by outlaws who hoped to hide their trail from pursuing trackers. Pressed and enameled paper has been made into very serviceable horseshoes. Aluminum has come into some popularity in later years for lightweight shoes used chiefly in racing. A nifty little number in unbreakable plastic is the latest addition to the long line of materials man has put to use for protecting the indispensable hoofs of his mount.

As long as we have horses and horsemen, however, it is doubtful if we will ever have anything better than the age-old crescent of iron to cover the rim of the hoof. It is easily shaped to the animal's foot and can be made in a variety of weights and designs for assorted purposes; it lends itself to odd shapes and styles for correcting hoof troubles and undesirable leg actions; it is cheap in cost, easily replaceable and most durable in service; it is, as it has been for two thousand years, the basic requirement for all men whose successful ventures depend on the feet of a horse.

The horseshoe also has a long history as a symbol of good luck. Back in the first century Pliny the Elder recommended it as a shield against unforeseen dangers. Men of all ages have considered the finding of a horseshoe a harbinger of good fortune.

The shoe, however, must be hung with the open end up. This enables it to catch and hold good luck for its finder, while barring the intrusion of a devil from without. A horseshoe-shaped charm is considered to have almost as much power.

The origin of this superstition is lost in antiquity. Perhaps it is connected with the godlike qualities man attributed to the horse. A horseshoe's resemblance to the rainbow and the new moon might have fostered such beliefs. Both the crescent moon and the rainbow have been omens of good luck since the beginning of human history. Extending the idea to horseshoes would have been a logical development well in line with the idea of similarly shaped halos around the heads of pictured saints and angels. But whatever the foundation, faith in the luck of horseshoes outranks that of all other mystic charms man has adopted.

Even the untaught American Indian instinctively took the horseshoe crescent as one of his favorite symbols. When the white man first came into the virgin wilderness he found the Indian painting this age-old mark on his tepee, horses, and accouterments, always as a token of good fortune.

The Apache horse thief even painted it on his leg to commemorate a successful raid. It was also useful as a warning. If painted in a reverse position on an enemy's war post or tepee flap, it would strike terror to his heart. To the white man who found such an inverted horse track painted on his doorstep or the gate of an empty corral, there was no doubt about its significance.

Legend has it that St. Dunstan, a bishop of great skill as a horseshoer, once recognized the Devil in a horse he was shoeing. With the animal securely tied and its hoofs pared down, the saint managed to extract a promise from his satanic majesty that he would never enter or disturb a building on which a horseshoe had been hung. Ever since that day, a horseshoe over the door has been a symbol of security.

Thus we find the horseshoe motif as a decoration for bits, spurs, saddles, boots, belts, desk ornaments, and den furniture. It is quite possible we would all be as well off without such talismans. On the other hand, it is doubtful whether you could fire a shotgun into a crowd without hitting at least one staunch believer in the efficacy of the horseshoe, though you would probably have to use the other barrel on him to make him admit it.

—9—

Eastern Horsemen— Invaders and Stay-at-Homes

It was the mounted warriors of barbarian nomads who overran and conquered most of the well-fed, more sedentary nations of western Asia and eastern Europe. Need of pasturage or desire for loot ever urged these foot-loose wanderers toward new fields; and along with their rape, pillage, and murder, they invariably brought to the invaded regions new skills, crafts, and customs from other lands. In turn they tended to adopt the better regional practices of their victims for the enrichment of their own people. Thus it was the barbarians who did more then anyone else to spread culture in the ancient world. And, as the invading barbarian was always a horseman, most of civilization's early progress sprang up in the tracks of his horse.

Genghis Khan wrought destruction over half of Asia in the early thirteenth century, but in so doing he spread new knowledge from Mongolia to the Caspian Sea, knowledge that would have required centuries to pass from village to village. This great barbarian's fabulous empire would probably never have risen above the nomadic stage had he not brought back the craftsmen and customs of the many lands he raided so ruthlessly.

In the fourteenth century Tamerlane's Tartars carried the culture of Turkestan to the Mediterranean, of the Mediterranean to Persia and India, and of these countries to northern Russia. In return, they absorbed all the finest in architectural and constructional ideas, economic and agricultural practices, dress, food, crafts, arts, and decorative schemes for the embellishment of their beautiful capital city of Samarkand.

Had it not been for Attila's Huns of the fifth century and the ancient Gauls, men might still be wearing wrap-around robes and felt slippers. In sophisticated societies there was little difference between men's skirts and robes and those of the women all through the early centuries of this era. It took the barbarians to put man in distinctive clothes of his own.

Some sort of leather or skin trousers and boots of felt or leather were in use by the Asiatic horsemen from ancient times. They were likely one of the first innovations designed for more comfortable riding by a strictly horseback people. They evidently found their way down through the Scythian tribes and then west into the land of the Gauls, who became the first Western nation to use them and introduce them to the rest of Europe.

The leather trousers were no doubt the ancestors of the leather pants still worn in some sections of Central Europe. The Gauls called these *braccae,* from which we get the word "breeches." As these people migrated slowly down the Danube into Europe, they made the acquaintance of the Romans, who called them the *Gallia braccata* or "trouser-wearing Gauls." But these harsh leather pants and boots looked pretty wild and barbarous to the civilized gentry around the Mediterranean. Most of the Romans were still driving chariots, particularly in battle, so flapping robes were no great handicap. Their horsemen were making out fairly well with the socially more acceptable short skirts and sandals with ankle wrappings.

It was the same in China. The celestials never wore trousers until they began to copy the dress of the raiding barbarians. In Rome and Greece, the elite clung to their robes until Attila's hordes swooped down on them in the fifth century. Their lumbering chariots and naked or robe-draped cavalry showed to poor advantage against the more suitably clothed barbarians.

Ammianus Marcellinus, the son of a Roman Equite, wrote thus of the invaders:

> Their heads are covered with round caps and their hairy legs are covered with goatskins [skin trousers]. . . . Their shoes are not so well fitted for the infantry. But on the other hand, they are almost one with their horses, which are poorly shaped but hardy. . . . In truth, they can remain on horseback day and night. On horseback they buy and sell; they eat and drink; bowed over the narrow necks of their steeds, they even sleep and dream on horseback.

In much of southeastern Europe the Huns compelled men of the conquered lands to wear pants. Neighboring nations soon realized that the Eastern garb was far superior to unwieldy robes in cavalry fighting. And cavalry fighting was swiftly dooming the old war chariots. It was only a matter of time until everyone was trousered. It might thus be said that the man on horseback was responsible for the style of dress which sets the male half of the world apart from its female members.

India, Germany, and the British Isles were the last to give up their robes and chariots and take to riding their horses, and in appropriate outfits. The Celts, a branch of the old Gauls, held out longest of all. A remnant of their old costume is still to be found in the Scottish kilt.

Similar conditions existed in the Far East. India clung to its robes and chariots until long after most other nations were on horseback. In fact, Indians, Siamese, and Burmese, of all the world's peoples, never figured prominently as horsemen. What little cavalry they had in early times was mostly composed of horsemen from Cathay, who rode undersized but tough, active ponies with short stirrups and loose reins; and they fought well with their seven-to-eight-foot spears.

Indian saddles were rather crude, hard, wooden affairs built quite high in fork and cantle. The skirts were two large circular leather flaps that hung low over the horse's sides. These skirts were painted or gilded according to the social status of the rider. They seem to be fairly typical of the rigs in China and Tibet shown in Figs. 32 and 39.

The civil population of India rode mostly donkeys and bullocks, as they still do. A ring in the bullock's nose served as a bridle. They had horses, a rather small, chunky breed with good stamina and intelligence, but few people became good horsemen. They had a custom of spotting their horses with red paint and dyeing their tails green.

Saddles were chiefly of the hard, wooden type decorated with lacquer, somewhat resembling those of the Chinese. Those of the wealthy often had the seats covered with leather or velvet. The fork, horn, and cantle were commonly inlaid with pearl shell or embossed silver, as in Fig. 28. In later years they turned to the flat English style imported

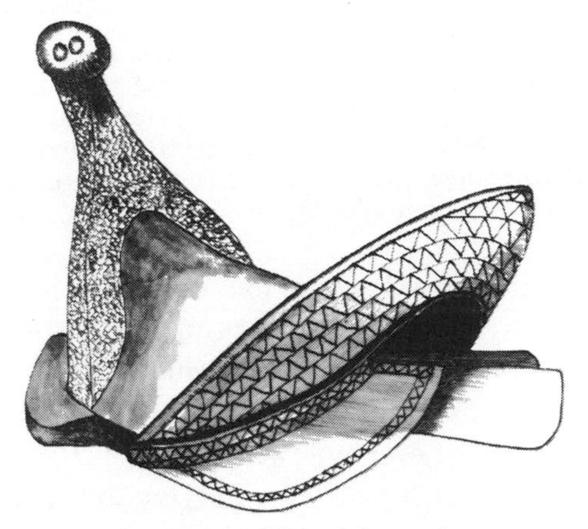

FIG. 28. Indian saddle, eighteenth century.

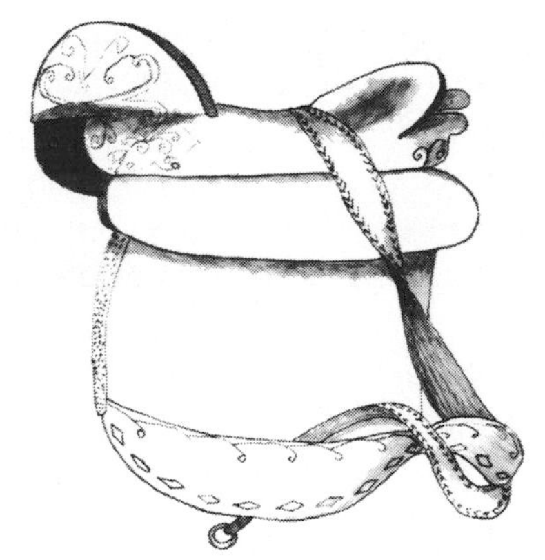

FIG. 29. Burmese saddle, nineteenth century.

by the British. They often covered these with a cotton slip cover or a bedquilt tied in place.

Figure 30 shows some Indian stirrups. The most common, especially in the olden days, were of wood in conventional design, but very light in construction, like *A*. Plain iron ones were in use quite early, mostly with wide, low bows and rectangular treads. Fancy cast brass *B* began to show up in the seventeenth century. Lances were a favorite weapon in this country, requiring the fitting of cavalry stirrups with lance rests. *D* is equipped with loops to which a lance bucket is fastened. *E* has a built-in lug containing a socket in which the lance butt rests.

Fancy cloth martingales and breast collars were fairly common, usually decorated with bells and tassels. Bridles consisted of narrow headstalls and light reins. Bits were chiefly of the snaffle variety.

Later saddles of the upper class in the Benares region ran to plain wood trees covered with heavily padded and quilted woolen fabrics stitched in red and yellow patterns. This covering extended over pommel, seat, and cantle, completely enveloping the tree. A sort of ornamental crupper was formed with half a dozen colored ropes fastened to the back of the saddle and extending fanlike to the root of the horse's tail, where they were tied together. Other long colored cords were also braided into the animal's mane, their ends being looped over the saddle fork. Under all this went a wide padded blanket, usually in colors.

The bridle was quite comparable, being of fancy design in red or yellow and fitted with a double-ring chain bit. A wide strip of red cotton cloth with flowing ends served as a martingale.

In contrast to this colorful outfit, the rider was more than likely to be found bundled up in a nondescript blanket or quilted robe that resembled a bedquilt.

In many places in India they say the Hindu always rides once in his lifetime—on his wedding day. On such an outstanding occasion, the ritualistic highlight of the wedding is a procession through the city. The bride leads the parade, being borne on a palanquin. Following her, comes the groom on horseback. He is dressed in all his finery. The horse is no less resplendent, decked out with a plume on its head, its neck covered with gold brocade hung with tassels. The saddle, usually a padlike affair, is covered with a gold-brocaded blanket which extends back over the animal's rump and down to its hocks. It is also heavily trimmed with tassels.

The rider himself is as much a fixture as the rest of the outfit. He has nothing to do with handling the horse. Oh, no! It must be led by a couple of friends, one on each side, while he sits aloof in regal splendor. Other members of the party fan both him and the horse as they move along, while still others keep them protectively shadowed by a big sunshade.

In Kashmir we find two types of saddles, both built on wood trees.

One type has the fork and cantle made very much alike, both rather high and curved up and outward. It has a leather covering. The other type has a moderately low fork and cantle and is covered with an embroidered silk cushion, similar to Persian saddles. Both styles use iron stirrups, plain stirrup straps, and single cinch.

A curious custom of mounting prevailed in this valley in bygone

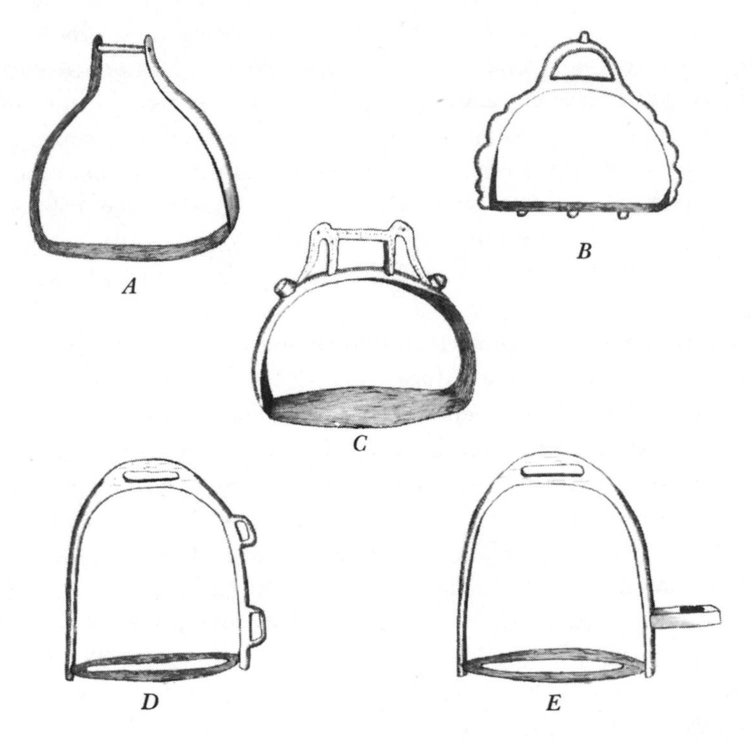

FIG. 30. Stirrups: *A* light wood, India, seventeenth century; *B* cast brass, India, seventeenth and eighteenth centuries. *C* brass, Java, eighteenth century; *D* and *E* Indian trooper stirrups for lance bucket and lance lug socket.

times, whereby the Mussulmen always mounted their horses from the right side while the pandits mounted from the left.

The hard, wooden saddle was also used in Burma, Siam, and Java. There it was usually covered with cloth embroidered in colors. The lower part of the sidebars was commonly left uncovered. It had no built-in rigging, being held in place by a surcingle cinch that went over the seat. Fig. 29 is a typical example.

Stirrups were of wood, iron, or cast brass. They were similar to those of India, though usually made with oval treads. Fig. 30, *C*, is typical. A knot in a rope-end to fit between the rider's toes often served for a stirrup in many parts of the Orient. The Javanese were still using this method well into this century.

The Siamese were said to have been very poor horsemen. Not many of them owned horses. What few they had were generally imported from Batavia. These belonged mostly to army officers, about the only ones able to afford such luxuries. And luxuries they must have been indeed; the utility value of the horses couldn't have been much, according to one eighteenth century visitor to that country. He wrote that they were unable to ride the beasts in a proper manner, stating that "an officer never goes on horseback but what he takes two slaves along, one on each side, to prevent his falling off."

They would undoubtedly have been as well off had they emulated the Pacific-islanders, who never made any pretense at being horsemen. Horses arrived in the islands very late. Most of the inhabitants simply kept on riding bullocks with rings in their noses and paid little attention to the more suitable animals.

It was not until circumstances forced the Chinese to copy the dress and fighting methods of mounted invaders in the fourth century B.C. that they were won over to the more practical attire. Even then, the wearing of trousers was pretty well confined to the military. It did not become a national costume until the seventh century A.D.

It was likewise the influence of the barbarian horsemen which created a general interest in horsemanship among the Chinese populace. Their men on horseback not only drove the enemy beyond their country's borders, but also helped extend those borders into heretofore forbidden lands. With better knowledge of riding came more ease of communication and better transportation within the empire. It also simplified life for the herdsman, the wandering trader, and the agriculturist far removed from main trade routes.

Nor did this apply only to the men. Chinese women, as we know, have ever since had a predilection for trousers and jackets. Whether or not this had anything to do with Shi Hu's selection of a bodyguard is open to argument, but it is rather doubtful if he would have set up an army of women in dresses to police his city.

Shi Hu was the old war lord who took over North China in A.D. 334–

349. One of his first acts as the new emperor was to form a company of 10,000 mounted women to serve as guards for his imperial capital city of Ye. The trousered women were uniformed in brocaded silk garments and purple headdresses. They were meticulously trained as expert equestrians and first-class archers. They must have been as formidable a body as the Huns whom they emulated. At any rate, they did a good job of protecting the emperor. Not only did they guard the city, but they served as mounted escorts when Shi Hu went abroad. And when they were not on guard duty, they were kept busy fanning and entertaining his majesty with music and dancing while he reclined at ease in his palace. A nice arrangement all around.

Perhaps it was the descendants of this imperial guard which kept the Chinese war-lord principle in business for the next 1,500 years. Those provincial tribes were all horsemen, maintaining the old traditions as horsemen did everywhere. Their mounts were inclined to be a coarse, long-haired, runty breed in later years, but they were extremely tough and hardy.

The Chinese saddles were quite similar to those of Mongolia, though the former were more addicted to padded seats. The one carved on the old roof tile (Fig. 31) reflects the typical Mongol style in pommel and seat back.

The saddle in Fig. 32 is distinctly Chinese in design. It has a rather short seat. The exposed portions of its crude sidebar tree are inlaid with bone. The pommel is heavily padded. Seat and flaps are a quilted silk pad embroidered in colors. The big skirts are also embroidered in colored designs. The saddle blanket is a blue rug with white trim, an outsize style generally used in China and Mongolia for decorative effects and to protect the rider's clothing.

Another type of saddle dispensed with the cantle entirely, having an extra-long, flat seat. Otherwise, it was very similar to Fig. 32.

Metal stirrups of the European type were used for the most part, though they were ordinarily of a larger and bulkier style than those found in most places. Wide, flat treads predominated, like those of Tibet (Fig. 39). The stirrups were often lined with cork to prevent the foot from slipping. Cloisonné decoration was frequently added. Many were carved and inlaid with gold, silver, ivory, or bone. The plain iron ones were usually gilded for added effect.

Bridles, cruppers, and breast collars were similarly decorated as a rule. The headstall and matching crupper (Fig. 39) had cloisonné trim.

Pierced and gilded metal set with turquoise and carnelians was used extensively for such purposes. Bridle plumes were quite common. Headstalls were chiefly of the narrow variety. Bits ran mostly to the snaffle type, though curbs were sometimes seen.

The island of Quemoy had a two-passenger saddle, if saddle it could be called. It looked more like a hayrack and was equally good for carrying people and bulk cargo (Fig. 33). In use until the present century, this saddle was built entirely of wood save for the sling ropes. The outrigger sides were said to be quite comfortable when padded with

FIG. 31. Chinese roof tile, Ming Dynasty, 1368–1633.

blankets. But mounting and dismounting obviously called for considerable ingenuity.

The Japanese and Koreans, who evidently adopted Chinese *bagu,* or horse trappings, along with Chinese horses in the third or fourth century B.C., rode much the same sort of saddles as the celestials. Fig. 34 pictures the Japanese version. *A* is simply a wood frame lacquered in gold. Probably a padded quilt was cinched over it for riding comfort. The forks of some of these lacked the big pommels, being more like a two-pronged fork with the tines spread out and the stub of a handle sticking up. The cantle was about the same, although made a

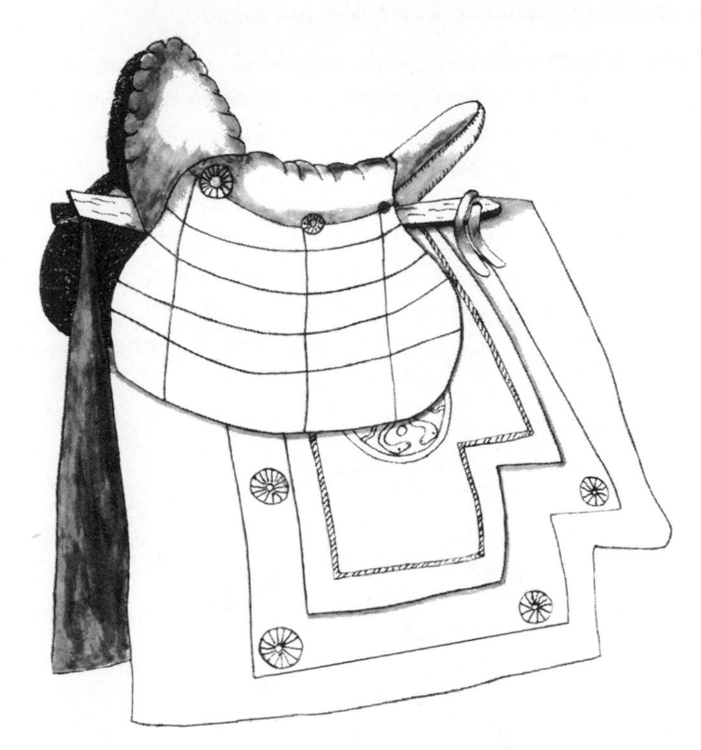

FIG. 32. Chinese saddle, seventeenth century.

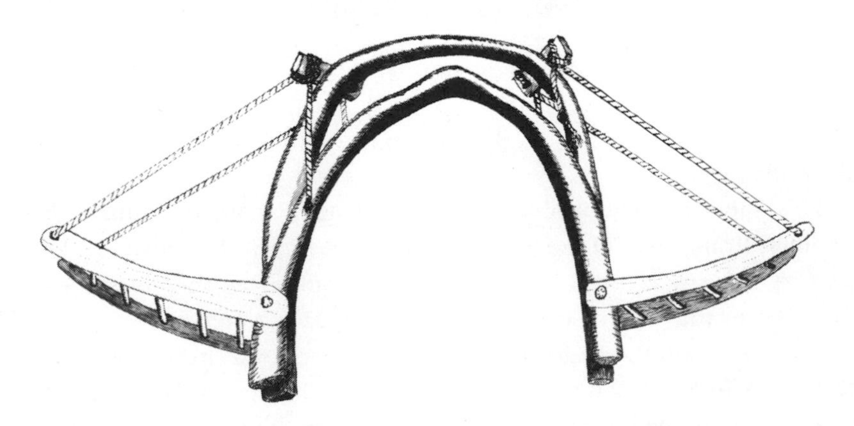

FIG. 33. Quemoy two-passenger saddle, twentieth century.

little wider. These forks were lashed together and fastened to the sidebars with colored cords. Straps were looped over the sidebars for attaching the single *harubi,* or cinch, as in *C.* It made a rather insecure outfit and was far from durable.

B is a more substantial *kuru,* or saddle, but shows little improvement in design. By the 1800s the Japanese had gotten around to putting deco-

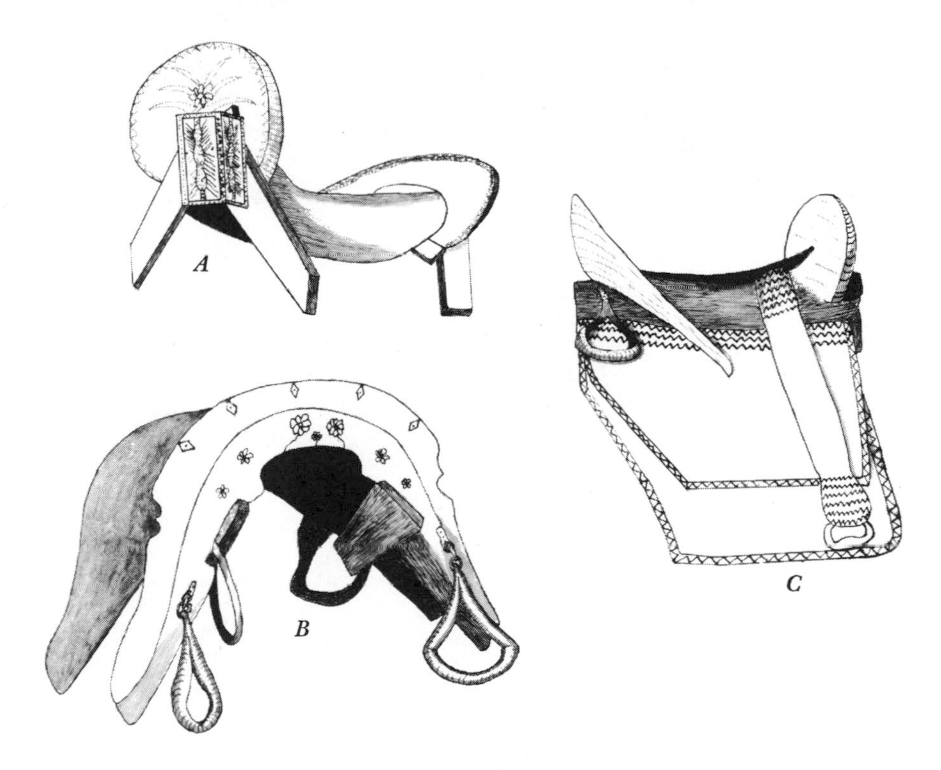

FIG. 34. Japanese saddles: *A* seventeenth century; *B* eighteenth century; *C* nineteenth century.

rated skirts on saddles, as in *C,* but the old gold-lacquered saddle body was about the same.

It was with their stirrups, called *abumi,* that these people really outdid themselves (Fig. 35). Some of these weighed as much as ten pounds each. They were often delicately decorated with inlaid silver and colored with red lacquer.

The earliest style, *A,* was fairly short and had hooded toes. Some of these were eventually made with long footplates like the more modern ones. Around 1700 a later style, *B,* was developed. These had perforated footplates to let the water escape when crossing streams and were called *suiba abumi,* or "crossing-the-river-on-horseback stirrups." An

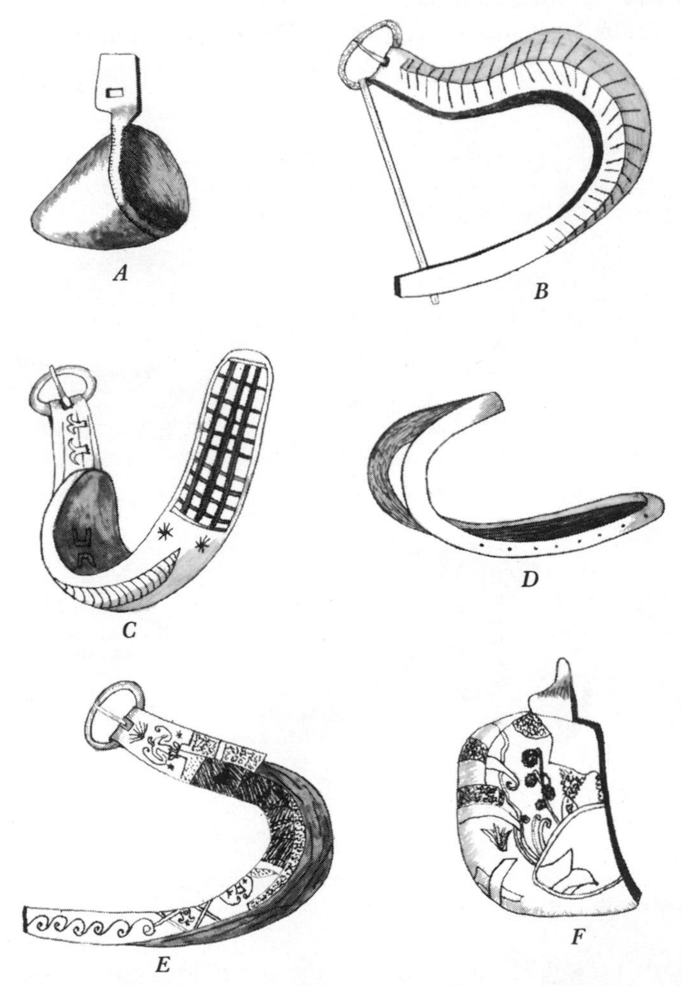

FIG. 35. Japanese stirrups (*abumis*): *A* very early; *B* early with outside foot stay; *C* with perforated tread, eighteenth century; *D* wood tread in iron frame; *E* and *F,* nineteenth century Tokugawa types.

improved design *C* came along a little later. It had an iron rod which came down across the outside past the heel to prevent the foot from slipping out sidewise.

All these footplates were large enough to accommodate the entire foot. They were made of iron, some being inlaid with brass. The front curved up and back to bring the stirrup strap over the instep. Ordinarily, they were made of a single piece of metal. Some, however, were merely iron frames with wooden insets, *D*. More elaborate examples of the *tokugawa* type, *E* and *F*, were often lacquered with gold and carved in fanciful designs. They survived until modern times.

Along with their stirrups, the Japanese used the *abumi zure,* a leather guard on the inside of the ankle as protection from the stirrup. This was commonly attached to the *sune ate,* a metal shin guard lined with padded cloth. Some of these had a continuation which was hinged over the lower portion and extended up over the knee and thigh to serve as a sort of leg armor.

Mounting was done from the off side. All buckles and other fastenings were placed in a corresponding position.

Bridles, or *omoguis,* were of the narrow headstall kind, usually well decorated with lacquered metal plates and gem or silver trimming. Fig. 36 pictures the type of bits (*kutsuwas*) in most common use. Curb bits, *seme kutsuwas,* were much in the minority, though some riders preferred them. Most of the sideplates on bits held to the unique Japanese design.

Japan did not use spurs, *hakusha,* until a very late date. Even then, they assumed so little importance that they failed to attract the attention of most writers.

Neighboring Korea reflects the Japanese pattern in most of its horses and riding equipment. Korean saddles have practically the same wooden frame. A typical example is covered with sharkskin and has the seat lined with deerskin, hair side uppermost. The exposed wood is lacquered in colors and bound with silver. The leather crupper is studded with matching silver plates. The Chinese-type fenders are of carved leather.

This is a fairly representative saddle of the better class. Only the wealthier individuals could own such outfits. Most of the Koreans fortunate enough to enjoy riding horses used little more than a blanket pad tied on with a surcingle.

Horses and horsemen, in fact, have always been something of a rarity among the common people of both Japan and Korea, as they are in China. Only the upper class could afford to own and maintain horses. Moreover, according to Dodge, Far Eastern horses were not of good quality as a rule, and the horsemanship of the Far Eastern riders was equally inferior. Dodge says most of the people gave the impression of being either in awe or afraid of the animals.

Japanese drivers of vehicles often had a man run alongside the rig to help them turn corners and hold the outfit back when going down hill. Riders followed the custom of tying their mount's tail to the cinch on the theory that it would help prevent the animal from acting up. As

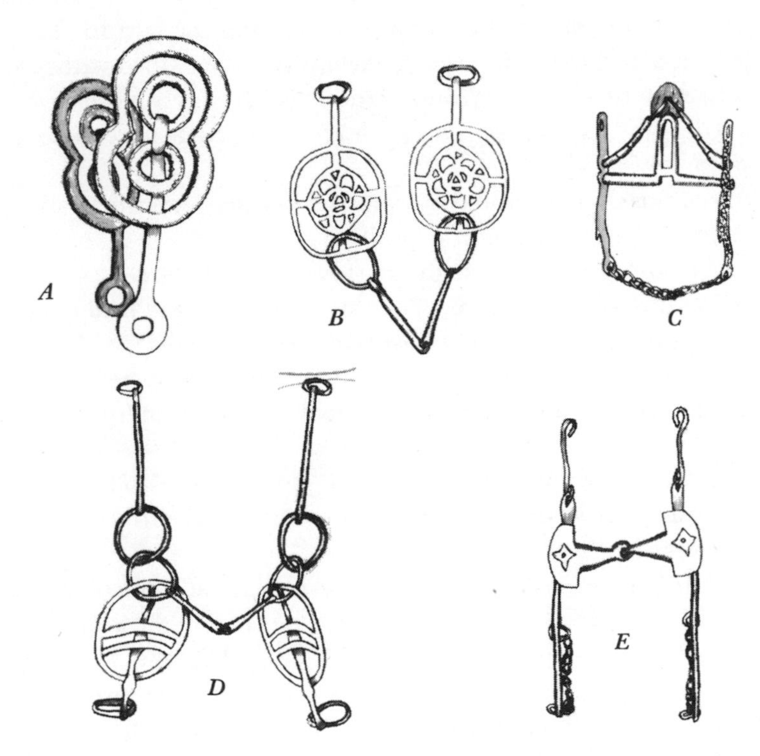

FIG. 36. Japanese bits: *A* sixth century; *B* eighteenth century; *C* and *E* nineteenth century.

a further precaution, they would fasten the horse's chin back to the martingale so tightly that it couldn't move its head up or down or reach ahead. What we must suppose figured as a safeguard against kicking was their habit of backing the horse into the stall. There he would be fed from a tub placed where the manure trough should be, while he cooled his heels against what would be considered the manger in other countries.

With such an attiude toward their steeds, it is little wonder that these people remained isolated and provincial for so many centuries. Men on foot seldom stray far from home or see the visions which draw their more mobile brothers toward far horizons. They are also more amenable to the decrees of overlords whose tax collectors' success depends on the subjects' immobility.

In vivid contrast were the mounted inhabitants of neighboring Manchuria and Mongolia. There the horseman was king and his horse a royal throne. These were free men in the broadest sense of the word. They claimed allegiance to no one save the strongest horseman in their territory; and he was merely a leader allowed to command by virtue of his courage and ability to hold them together.

From the Arctic Circle to the Caspian Sea, this man moved in a world where the boundaries of his ambition were limited only by his stamina on horseback and control of his steed. As an infant, he was slung to the saddle at his mother's knee. For the rest of his life his horse was his constant companion in traveling, fighting, hunting, courting. On horseback he tended his flocks of cattle and sheep; on horseback he followed the seasons north and south, feasting his eyes on new lands and peoples; on horseback he lived his life as lord of all he surveyed. Rude and unlettered barbarian though he was, all civilized men paid homage to him as a free spirit.

To see a company of these people on the march must have been a wonderful and moving experience. Imagine, if you can, 150,000 riders with 500,000 horses and perhaps half that many cattle and sheep moving across the prairies in a mass ten miles wide and twenty miles long. Ox-drawn tent-carts and baggage wagons rock through the dust like the spinal column of some great undulating monster. Brightly caparisoned warriors and herdsmen weave vivid patterns back and forth through the throng. The bright garments of women flutter in the wind to add a touch of family stability to the wild assemblage.

At first sight, the company seems to lie like a long, low cloud along the horizon. Then, with each passing moment, the cloud rises higher against the sky, its gently rolling surface reflecting glints and flashes of shifting colors from the low-hanging sun. Up front flies the chief's big banner decorated with nine yak tails. A forest of tall, pointed hats, which might have passed for Mexican sombreros two thousand years later, ride above the bulky figures in felt or padded coats. Long barbed lances and small round shields highlight the suits of lacquered leather armor or metal plates tied together with leather thongs. Short Asiatic bows hang at saddle forks, while broad belts of red or blue leather hold scimitars and short swords of Chinese design. Some of the horses also wear protective hard-leather breastplates, many of which include projections back over the necks and down the legs of the animals. Such armor was heat-shrunken to extreme toughness.

Publius Cornelius Tacitus, the noted Roman historian (A.D. 55–117) left us a good descriptive account of these barbarians who raided southeastern Europe in the first century A.D. He wrote:

> In the onset of cavalry, they are irresistible. Their weapons are long spears and swords of enormous size, which they wield with both hands from the backs of their horses. Their chiefs wear coats of mail formed of tough hides of animals, or plates of iron fastened to leather garments.

The latter was evidently one of the earliest forms of metal armor, apparently an improved version of the old Sarmatian bone-scale armor. As this historian was the son of a Roman Equite, he was no doubt a reliable authority on current military subjects.

The horses of these people were inclined to be small and shaggy and not much to look at, but they were, like their masters, the next thing to indestructible. Bred through the centuries for toughness and durability, they had developed unbelievable stamina. These animals, which were never shod, were able to cover three or four hundred miles in a three-day journey.

On raids against other nations, each of the invaders would have a string of three or four horses, each being ridden in turn for suitable periods. In this manner they would travel secretly until near the enemy territory. There, they would hide out for a few days to rest men and horses. When all were properly refreshed, they would set out swiftly, riding steadily day and night into the enemy country to the depth of 100 to 250 miles. All this would be accomplished with as little disturbance as possible. Then, at the appointed time, they would all turn toward home, raiding as they went.

The main body—perhaps two-thirds of the company—would move as a wide central force, with the rest fanned out in wings to thirty or forty miles on either side. Whatever loot they captured—livestock, commodities, valuables, captives to be sold as slaves, and the like—would be brought back to the main band as raiding groups alternated to and from the outflung wings. All the captured goods would be carried along intact to the home camp, where they were divided according to tribal rules. The Great Khan received one-tenth of the whole as his due. The rest was apportioned equally among the lesser lords. They, in turn, were each allowed one-tenth of their individual allotments, the balance being divided equally among all who took part in the affair. Horse stealing within the tribe was punished by cutting the thief in two with a sword.

All these people were trained to go for many nights without sleep and travel for days with only a minimum of food. This they would counterbalance during leisure periods, when they might sleep forty-eight hours at a stretch and eat three or four meals in one. They enjoyed feasting and drinking to great excess on suitable occasions, but remained sober and abstemious at all other times.

Marco Polo, who visited Mongolia in 1275, wrote that Kublai Khan's warriors could ride for ten days without lighting a fire or cooking a meal. Their traveling rations consisted of dried milk, which they had processed by skimming, boiling to proper consistency, and drying in the sun. It then had been beaten into a powder and stored in skin bags—the original powdered milk.

Ten pounds of this ancient soldier's K-ration were allotted to each man as a food supply for long journeys. Each morning the man would put one-half pound of the milk powder and the proper amount of water into a leather bottle. Tied to his saddle, it would be churned to a thin porridge for the evening meal.

When Genghis Khan established his control over the major part of Asia, around 1200, he knit his fabulous empire together with one of the world's greatest pony express systems. His riders, or *yams,* numbered into the thousands, using in the neighborhood of 300,000 horses. Each relay station maintained from two hundred to four hundred mounts, half of which were always kept ready for instant service. Stations were eighteen miles apart in the settled sections and about forty miles apart in the desert regions. The men were required to ride day and night, covering two to three hundred miles at a stretch. Bells on the horses announced their passage, besides serving as sort of a royal badge of identification. They carried regular mail, an early version of parcel post, special delivery letters, and the khan's governmental dispatches. It was said the khan thus received daily communications from all his governors and army commanders throughout the far-flung kingdom. The service was also used to bring special foods and dainties to the capital from all parts of the empire. The riders commonly bound their heads, chests, and stomachs with tight bandages to help withstand the terrific pounding of swift and relentless riding.

Kublai Khan maintained much the same sort of widespread courier service during his reign. According to Marco Polo, it was even more elaborate and extensive than the one developed by Genghis Khan. This probably came about through increased wealth and more attention to horse breeding when the better stabilized empire demanded less in the way of warfare.

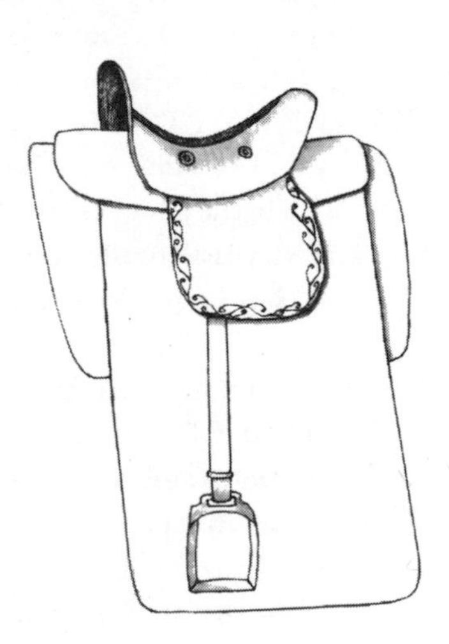

FIG. 37. Mongolian saddle, nineteenth century.

FIG. 38. Mongolian saddle, 1929.

Following the old days of bareback riding, most of these people equipped themselves with the typical Mongol saddle (Figs. 37, 38). Its style has changed very little in succeeding centuries. It had a somewhat crude, wooden sidebar tree. Some of them were simply lacquered and gilded in decorative designs. Others were covered with leather, sheepskin, or padded quilt. The high, round-topped forks were almost duplicated by the cantles. They were single-rig affairs, with big, extra-long skirts. The latter frequently were lavishly decorated in gold. Floral designs were much favored. The saddle blankets were leather, quilted silk, bearskin, or heavy rugs, usually quite ornate and reaching well down over the horse's sides.

Breast collars were often used, but cruppers only occasionally. They, as well as the bridles, resembled those of the Chinese. Snaffle bits predominated, though curbs were often seen.

Mongolian stirrups were large and square with big, flat footplates. Bronze was a favorite stirrup material, though the use of iron was more common. Many were elaborately decorated with pierced or carved designs, silver inlays, and red lacquer.

Farther south, among the Kalmucks, a wooden tree without any covering was the usual saddle. This was also a single-rig outfit with the Mongolian-type, high, tapered, round-topped fork that fairly well matched the cantle. The fork was often reinforced with a leather patch but had no regular covering.

Up around the Aral Sea was a sort of meeting ground where the leather-covered and bare-wood trees overlapped. The uncovered ones were usually carved and painted in bright colors. Many riders eased their surfaces with straw-stuffed leather pillows. They rode with short stirrups, the knees well bent.

The Cossacks of the steppes also rode with very short stirrups. This helped them rise even higher when striking down at an enemy. In later years they acquired good leather-covered rigs which resembled western American saddles more than the Mongol type. They also differed from the Mongols in using more curb and other severe bits. This was no doubt a European influence filtering east from the Spanish and Hungarian territories.

The Cossacks have always been world-famous for their horsemanship. They were most adept at all the mounted-nomad tricks of horseback fighting. Riding on the side of a horse, under its belly, standing up, sitting backward, forward, or lying on its back in any position were all part of any horseman's regular training. This training also included the practice of shooting from any position. Firing over or under the mount's neck while hanging to its side, or throwing the horse for use as a protective breastwork in battle was standard procedure with any Cossack. The horses were small but very active, sturdy, and intelligent.

The Circassians, of the Caucasus Mountains bordering the Black Sea, were almost entirely a horseback nation. They were very rich in an extraordinarily tough and hard-footed breed of horses which they never shod. Their army was all cavalry.

These people used a wooden tree which, like the Kurds, they covered with straw. But there the similarity ended. The extremely high fork and cantle, totally unlike the flat Kurdish rig, looked like a somewhat exaggerated version of the Mongol saddle. Also, unlike most Orientals, they rode with long stirrups, legs almost straight. A rope hackamore usually served as a bridle.

Many Mongolian peoples also used camels as mounts to a considerable extent, chiefly the Bactrian two-humped species common to central and southern Asia. Saddles used on them were crude felt affairs made to fit between the animal's humps. In most cases a rope attached to a nose pin served as a bridle.

A section of Chinese Turkestan practiced the rather peculiar custom of keeping horses blanketed at all times. The blankets, seven in number, covered the animal from head to tail. The number of blankets was supposed to have religious significance as well as to keep the horse sweated out and in proper condition.

In Tibet we find a curious item: Their stirrups, or *obchens,* were often made like those of the Japanese (Fig. 35). Both appear to have come from the same origin; but why they should have come to rest in two such widely separated and isolated kingdoms is hard to understand. This becomes all the more mystifying when we consider that all the rest of Tibetan riding gear reflects the distinct Chinese pattern.

Tibetan saddles, called *ghas,* are definitely Chinese in style. Some are of carved wood, often encrusted with beaten gold. The example in Fig. 39 is wood-covered with carved, pierced, and gilded steel set with semi-precious stones. The seat is of quilted silk.

The braided silk used for the bridle is decorated with mountings of pierced and gilded iron. It often carries a chain bit, though snaffles predominate. The breast collar may be of leather or colored cotton cloth, and sports a large yak-hair tassel.

A plain leather-covered sidebar tree found among the common and less pretentious riders of that country is shown in Fig. 40, A. It was used over a large embroidered blanket and employed both crupper and breast collar.

A more elaborate type (Fig. 40, B) consists of a pair of stuffed pads attached to a wide backband and surmounted by a short leather seat. The seat leather continues downward to form a kind of short fender. The pads are of leather or fabric, decorated in colors. Breast collars and cruppers are generally used by all riders in this mountainous land.

A more modern style came into use in later years. This saddle has a solid wooden tree with mortised sidebars. The fork is straight, carrying a conventional-shaped wooden horn. The cantle is wide and flaring, and sloped back at a generous angle. The horn is often capped with leather. Stirrup straps run through holes in the sidebars. The whole tree is covered with thin leather painted in colorful designs and glued to the wooden tree.

By the time the old Mongolian Empire had run its course and had begun to fall apart, the Tartars of south Central Asia had built themselves up to take over command of the East. The Tartars were de-

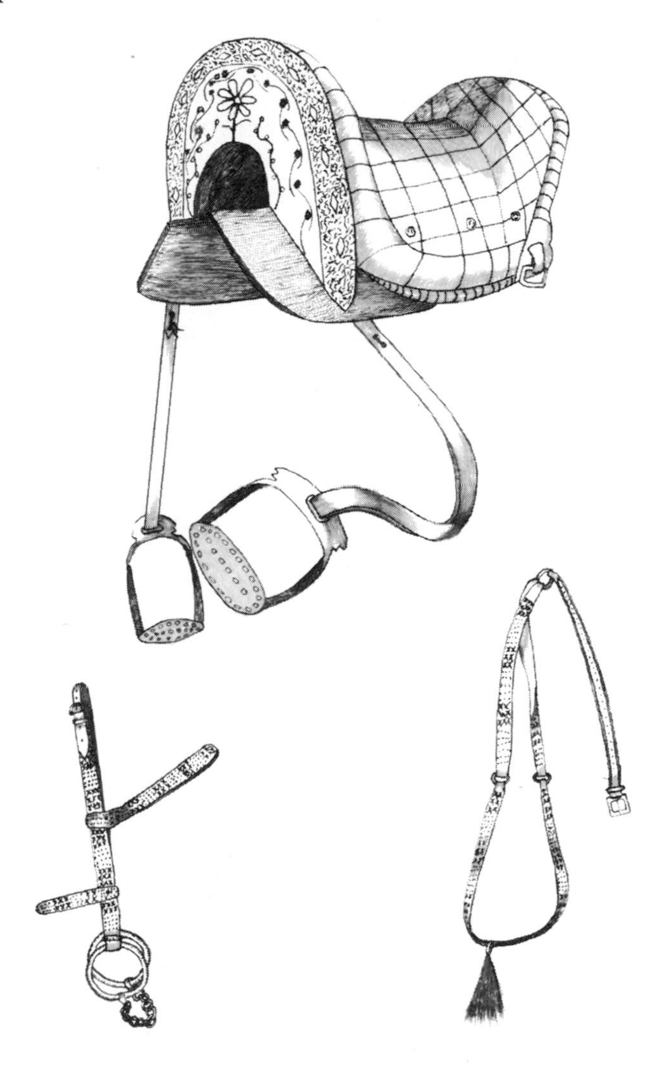

FIG. 39. Tibetan equipment, seventeenth century.

scendants of Genghis Khan's tribesmen and endowed with the same temperament. They had inherited all the horseback skills of their ancestors. Under the leadership of Tamerlane (1336–1405), in particular, they won control of that vast territory between Syria and the Ganges River and north to the Arctic Circle. It was they who raised ancient Samarkand to its epitome of richness and beauty. Under their reign,

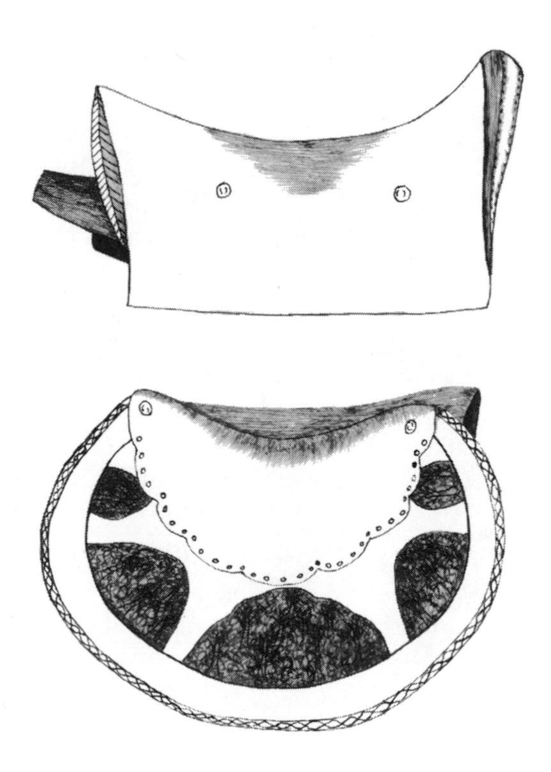

FIG. 40. Tibetan saddles.

Tabriz, situated at the crossing of the great Korhassan Road and the equally famous north-and-south travel route, was (with its million souls) the largest city outside China.

As early as 600, Turkestan and Afghanistan had a civilization that was comparable to anything Europe could boast of seven hundred years later. A collection of wall paintings of the A.D. 600 period, removed to Berlin from Turkestan, pictured costumes and riding equipment similar to that used in France and Germany in the 1300s. All the wealth, skilled handicrafters, and trained artisans of the East were theirs, either by capture or inducements.

And they won it all on horseback. It was the old story of the mounted nomads, starved for the better things of life, seizing the riches of people grown soft under fancied security. They were an easy prey for the mounted bowmen from the steppes, a land of countless wild horses and hordes of equally wild men, where people hunted with falcons, always went fully armed, ate horse meat, fought on horseback, and made their homes wherever night found them. Their women were no less hardy. These large, well-built, and beautiful Amazons often accompanied their men to war, riding and fighting in the same manner as had their ancestors of six thousand years before.

The Tartars always took three horses to a man when going on raids or war expeditions. Each man had his mounts trained so the two extras would follow, without use of lead ropes, the one being ridden. Thus they would travel much as had the earlier Mongols, riding night and day without ever lighting a fire to betray their presence to the enemy. At times, they would cover six to eight hundred miles in this manner, changing mounts frequently and halting every hour for fifteen minutes of rest and grazing.

For food, each would take a sack of rye meal, some biscuits, and salt. Whenever a horse gave out, they would immediately cut its throat, drink its blood, and divide the meat among the company. The choicest meat would be cut into one-inch slices and placed under the saddle next to the horse. After half a day's ride, these slices were taken out and as much horse sweat as possible rubbed into them, after which they were turned over and re-placed under the saddle. By the time the day's ride was finished, the well-salted and pounded meat was considered ready for a tasty evening repast.

Their horses were inclined to be lean and leggy and of poor appearance. Yet they were strong, swift, and very durable. Though they were for the most part rather hard riding animals, they were excellent for the rough usage demanded by warfare and desert raiding.

Tamerlane revived Genghis Khan's old pony express system for use throughout his vast territory. Roads and bridges were built, while post stations were set up at suitable intervals along all the highways. The roads were maintained in first-class condition, well leveled and with loose stones removed. In winter, they were kept clear of snow and open to traffic. Mileage posts were erected at stated distances along all the main roads. All post stations were well supplied with horse herds and provisions for travelers. Some of the stations had fountains that were packed with ice during the hot season for the refreshment of wayfarers.

Mail riders were scheduled for fifty to seventy miles a day. In case of accident to a mount, the rider was empowered to appropriate the horse of any traveler on the road. This ruling did not exempt even the mounts of merchants, lords, or ambassadors. Refusal to comply would cost the objector his head.

The old Mongolian-style saddle was the principal rig used by the Tartars, especially in the north. Farther south, the painted-wood type showed up to a fair extent. Jenkinson said Russian saddles were an important trade item brought to Samarkand by the Muscovites in 1557. His account suggests they were of the Cossack type, quite possibly an outgrowth of the old Hungarian saddles.

Bridles, bits, and stirrups differed little from those used by the Mongolians. Snaffle bits predominated, likely owing to the old Persian influence in the south. Big, decorated saddle blankets were preferred, both for display and as a nomad horseman's bed. The almost universal Eastern custom of riding with short stirrups was standard practice.

—10—

The Stockman Through the Years

Since the days when Lot and Abram
Split the Jordan range in halves,
Just to fix it so the punchers wouldn't fight;
Since old Jacob skinned his dad-in-law
Of six years' crop of calves,
Then hit the trail for Canaan in the night,
There has been a taste for battle
'Mongst the men who follow cattle,
And a way of doing things that's wild and strange,
And the warmth of Laban's words,
When he missed his speckled herds,
Still is useful in the language of the range.
From the poem, "From Town," by Badger Clark

THE RAISING OF LIVESTOCK is one of man's oldest occupations. The nomads of Turkestan and the Kirghiz steppes were running herds of horses, cattle, and sheep at least five or six thousand years before Christ was born. When the old wandering horseman of antiquity rode into the first gray dawn of history, his flocks and herds were already well formed and he was trained in their upkeep. No doubt the domestication of meat animals and their maintenance in private or community bands started back in the early Stone Age when man first discovered the advantage of home supplies as a stable food economy.

By 4000 B.C., all the nomadic tribes of the East were trailing their herds wherever they went. Later, the more civilized nations adopted the idea of a perpetual food supply which reseeded itself and flourished unto harvest without the sweat of human toil, then transported itself to the storage vaults or market place on its own feet.

By the time Lot and Abram came along to leave (in the Book of Genesis) our first written record of the cattle industry, range problems were already beginning to show their craggy heads. We all know how these two Chaldeans from over in the Ur district were forced to divide up the country in the interest of profitable returns from their herds. That was somewhere around 1960 B.C. The ensuing selective-breeding program conceived by Abram's grandson, Jacob, while managing Laban's herds, has been the basic pattern for all progressive stockmen ever since.

News of Jacob's coup might have been what induced the early Egyptians to start some sort of selective breeding. Old sculptures and inscriptions show that these people were raising cattle before 2000 B.C. These animals are shown to have been first-class stock. Their sacred bulls, in particular, were undoubtedly products of planning and forethought.

All the way up through Persia, Asia Minor, and Turkestan the stock raisers were working for improvement in their herds early in the B.C. period. Horses and cattle were the backbone of their economy. The man who could come up with a superior strain stood to win a leading place in his region.

Among the nomads we find fierce independence and distaste for oppressive authority. They would ride headfirst into threatening trouble or fight to the death in defense of their own rights or the interests of an employer. They would freeze, starve, or stay in the saddle twenty-four hours a day rather than bow their heads to overlordship or accept menial work on foot. Careless of money, they would spend their last shekel for personal adornment or wild, carefree amusement, or to help a friend in trouble; but woe to the individual who would wantonly cheat them or steal so much as a suckling calf. And among all of them hospitality was ever the freest of uncalculated generosity. Stockmen east or west, past or present, have always lived by a creed of fraternal openhandedness and man-to-man equality that no tradesman or sedentary worker ever knew.

Among the Cossacks and early Hungarians, where absolute nomadism had given way to sort of a semisettled society, the ancient stockman was little different from his cousin of later centuries in the Western world. He had the same dark-faced, hard-bitten, level-eyed look; the same slender, sinewy body and bowed legs which disdained contact with the ground. Though scorched by summer suns, frozen in winter blasts, and worn to rawhide leanness by dawn-to-dark riding, he moved through his world with an omnipotent bearing that bespoke a sense of self-assurance not given to men denied the advantages of his life. Mounted on his favorite stallion, resplendent in fringed-leather pants, red-embroidered white coat, huge black sombrero, and well-furbished weapons, he was of a race apart, a happy, carefree god of the saddle, ready for fight, fun, or fiercest contest with nature. Men who valued their lives avoided asking him to drink with a shepherd or milker of cows.

He was equally skillful at roping a critter, burning a brand of ownership, or pitting his riding ability against any untamed horse in his herd. Nine months of the year would find him happy and contented, riding the vast ranges to tend his thousands of horses and cattle. The remaining months would be spent with his wife and family, replenishing his equipment, breaking horses, and working off accumulated high spirits in company with his friends.

The ancient Hungarians, like most of their contemporaries, thought it disgraceful to ride mares or geldings. They would use only stallions. In later times, however, they were one of the first Western nations to institute the custom of gelding horses. Some historians believe they originated the practice.

While the gelding of horses may have been brought to Hungary from some Eastern nation, the evidence is all against it. Strabo wrote that the Sarmatians did some gelding around the dawn of the Christian Era, but there is no indication that it found much favor at home or among any other early peoples.

There is a certain significance, however, in the fact that the French called geldings "Hungarian horses" at one time. Moreover, Hungarians were particularly recognized as castrators of horses during the Middle

Ages. Many of them followed this as a profession until the late 1700s, traveling all over Europe in pursuit of their trade.

The German name of wallack, as applied to geldings, is thought to have come from a Turkish-Hungarian tribe of similar name. The Polish name for gelding is *oghier,* which indicates a relationship with the Oghurs, one of the ancient Hunnish tribes from the East.

Roping and branding were not confined to the Cossacks and Hungarians in ancient times. It was more or less a universal practice among all early stockmen. Egyptian inscriptions dating back to 2000 B.C. indicate that the pharaohs branded both their slaves and their cattle. The early Greeks and Romans marked their horses with letters, figures, and picture brands. They also branded bondsmen and robbers on the cheeks. French galley slaves were branded as late as 1830. Even the pious New Englanders preserved a token of this quaint custom by branding a scarlet A on defenseless women whom they judged to be less worthy than themselves.

The word "branding," as might be supposed, derives from the Germanic name of a live coal or burning piece of wood. The latter undoubtedly served as the original branding iron.

Marking with identifying brands seems to have spread from Egypt through Arabia and the Moorish lands of Africa. The Egyptians probably got it from Turkestan by way of Asia Minor. From Africa, it was only a step across to Spain, where the Spanish dons were using big, elaborate replicas of their coats of arms as livestock brands at a very early date. The rest of Europe picked up the custom from both south and east in the early centuries of this era. British history mentions branding horses and cattle in the 700s.

The oldest ropers on record were a company of Persians with Xerxes' army in 480 B.C.; and the Sarmatians were noted for practicing both roping and branding in 200 B.C.

Lariats were used by gladiators at Rome in Vespasian's time. Such fighters were called *laqueators.* Perhaps the Romans had learned the roping art from wandering foreigners. Such a wanderer was Bebrix, from Asia Minor, employed by Caligula around A.D. 38 as the emperor's chief bring-'em-back-alive hunter in North Africa. Bebrix supplied wild beasts for the gory spectacles in the Roman amphitheaters. He was an expert roper, habitually capturing animals on the plains from horseback or dropping his loop over those cornered in the brush by native helpers.

Bebrix undoubtedly brought the craft from his native land as a practice long established.

Kublai Khan's followers introduced roping and branding into China. The Huns, Mongols, and Tartars were all familiar with ropes and brands from ancient times. The Mongols had a unique way of roping in which a snarelike noose was carried on the end of a pole. Two riders would maneuver on either side of the prospective victim until the one with the noose was able to toss it over the animal's head.

Genghis Khan's warriors used ropes in battle, as had the ancient Persians. And the ropes made good weapons; a noosed enemy was usually worse off than one attacked by a sword. The roping of livestock was also a common practice with them.

The Finns too had an odd way of roping reindeer in early times. Instead of throwing just the loop over the animal's head, as other ropers do, they threw the whole coil, loop and all, retaining only the rope end in the hand. The idea was to entangle as much of the rope as possible in the branched antlers of the reindeer. They used braided rawhide ropes.

It was the European stockmen who developed the big war horses used in the knighthood era, as well as the fine breeds of draft horses that did the world's heavy work for so many centuries. They already had the coarse and heavy, big-footed Nordic horse, less desirable than the ox for work, but they wanted something more active and amenable than these ungainly, big-headed creatures. When the Arabian and Barb horses began filtering into Europe, the stockmen there awoke to a vision of an animal that combined the intelligence and action of the southern breed with the weight and steadiness of the big Nordic. By dint of skillful cross-breeding and selection of sires, there soon arose among these horse raisers a heavy-duty but active animal which eventually developed through the old Flemish draft horse into the modern Belgian. Further work of the same kind created such special purpose animals as the Norman and Percheron of France, England's Shire and the Clydesdale of Scotland, as well as assorted varieties of less import. Thus it is not unreasonable to say the chief motive power for centuries of civilized progress came into being through supplying the needs of medieval horseback men.

An odd link connecting the stockmen of antiquity with those of today still exists in the Camargue district of southern France. Both the men and women of this section have been ardent cowfolk since very ancient times. Their horses are of a unique breed not found elsewhere. They are smallish, strong, and of great endurance, but inclined to be wild and unruly, not unlike American broncos. It is thought they are either descendants of Nubian horses brought to France by the Romans or of Saracen animals from farther east. They bear much resemblance to the long-haired horses of Tibet and Mongolia.

Camargue cattle, too, are of ancient origin. They are apparently related to the old Asiatic breed. They are small, active, rough, and wild. All that can be certain about them, as about the people and horses, is that they date back to beyond the memory of present man.

These people are proud to keep their heritage alive. Their stockman traditions have perpetuated their unharassed way of life through the centuries of monarchial greed, economic wars, and tumbling civilizations in surrounding regions. The annual spring roundup and branding, called *ferrade,* assumes more the aspect of a social event than necessary work. Everyone from the oldest to the youngest attends in holiday mood. Races, riding and roping contests, and other sports are interspersed with dances, games, and homey features to enliven the task of gathering, sorting, and branding the wild herds, or *manados.* As a whole, the Camargue folk exhibit the age-old characteristics of cattlemen the world over. Their every move bespeaks courage, chivalry, determination, endurance, individuality, and self-reliance.

Their cowboys, known as *gardians,* may wear wooden shoes and work their cattle with tridents, but no one who has ever seen a cowboy could mistake them for anything but what they are. A reflection of American chaps is seen in the thigh-length leather leggings tied to a belt. Hackamores are used for breaking green horses. Curb bits with long, curved sidebars are used with rather plain black leather bridles on working animals. Short-shanked spurs with small rowels are most common, though some riders prefer a long-shanked type with narrow heel plates and large-spoked rowels similar to those of the old Norman knights. Most Camargue cowboys, however, use only a single spur, doubtless figuring that the other side of the horse will keep up without any special attention.

They usually brand with the initial or family heraldic emblem, most of which are as old as the land itself. They have a sort of cowboy association, called *Nacioun Gardiano,* whose chief function is to maintain traditional sports, crafts, pride, and customs of their people.

It is their lariats and tridents which provide the most distinctive touch. The tridents, or *ficheirouns,* have iron heads made in half-moon shape, with sharp horns and a spike in the center. The heads are set on the ends of seven-foot wood shafts. When viewed in relation to some of the old Greek legends of Neptune, these tridents make one pause to wonder if perhaps the Camargue cowboy did not find his beginning in the age of fable at the other end of the Mediterranean. But however

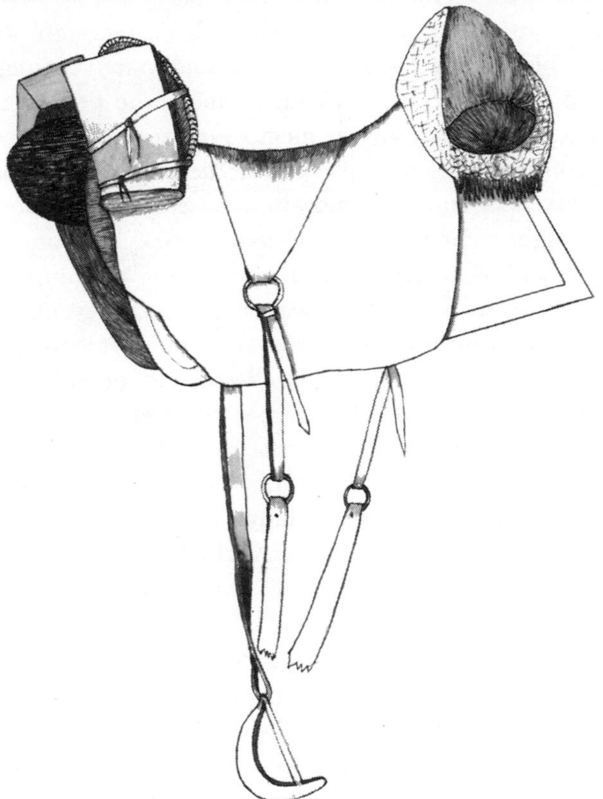

FIG. 41. French Camargue saddle, 1922.

that may be, the trident in his hands is a most efficient tool for working stock.

He does correspondingly well with his rope. It is commonly of twisted horsehair in various colored patterns and up to thirty-six feet long. Though it is too light for successful throwing on horseback, he exhibits fine proficiency with it on foot or in corral work. He usually carries it in sort of a knapsack slung over his shoulder instead of tied to the saddle.

The Camargue saddle (Fig. 41) has been described as looking something like an embroidered easy chair set on a wide cowhide skirt. The high cantle is heavily padded and trimmed with brass nails. The wide, curved, hornless pommel is padded and tufted like the cantle. It carries double rigging, the back cinch angling forward to almost meet the front one under the horse's belly. Long stirrup straps are without fenders. The large wrought-iron stirrups have curved bars across the front to keep the rider's heelless wooden shoes from slipping forward. Two leather saddlebags are attached to the pommel. These are frequently supplemented by a pair of bright-colored cloth bags, called *saquetouns,* tied to the back of the saddle. Cruppers and breast collars are commonly used.

As already mentioned, Camargue womenfolk take a companionable interest in all range work. In earlier periods they rode behind the men on blankets fastened to the cruppers behind the saddle. Changing times, however, led the women to use the more modern style of individual saddles, dressing and riding astride like the men. This vigorous outdoor life, incidentally, has made the Camargue women widely famous for their beauty.

—11—

The Horseman Rides West

MOUNTED MEN OF the Western world have quite lost relationship with those of the Far East, though it was the Easterners who first gave us the horse and most of its accouterments.

The dividing line between the two great groups might be considered to run along the east shores of the Black and Caspian seas, then angle southeast to the Indian Ocean. Though the Asiatic horse gradually moved south across Persia and Arabia, and thence westward, the Asiatic rider stayed with his northern steppes and mountains. Through the ages, his customs, riding equipment, and horses naturally developed along purely Asiatic lines.

South of the Black Sea, the environment, needs, and natural idiosyncrasies of the desert peoples, while fundamentally the same as those of the northerners, had certain uniquely southern characteristics. It was from these southern races that we of the West received most of the basic patterns of our horseback culture. For Arabians, riding west through Africa and into southwestern Europe—as Persians had ventured into Arabia at an earlier period—brought the arts of horsemanship with them.

The Kurds, who occupied the region south of old Media, were not content with the plain, hard, wooden saddles of central Asia. At an early date they began building their trees quite flat on top and covering them with plaited straw. This was topped off with a heavy blanket. It made for much more comfort in riding. Unfortunately, they seemed to think more of their own comfort than that of the horse. They never removed the saddle from a horse's back except to dry it out occasionally. The animal was kept saddled day and night the year round.

Whatever their blindness to the needs of their mounts, the Kurds were not lacking in fortitude and courage. Though peaceably inclined when unmolested, they were almost unconquerable when provoked. They always fought on horseback, with bows and arrows and curved scimitars. As horsemen and cavalry experts they had few equals.

Their horses were small, but tough, swift, and durable, requiring little care—the ideal type for the slashing attacks of desert cavalry. And there were quantities of horses available. In the 1600s, one chief alone was able to mount 20,000 cavalrymen. Most of the riders used severe bits and rode with short stirrups.

As late as 1786, Franklin said the Persians traveled only on horse or mule back. Wheeled vehicles were unknown.

Even state visits between dignitaries were conducted on horseback, according to Della Valle, when he was in Persia in 1617. He mentioned seeing the Turkish ambassador meet with the Persian king in the public square amidst a crowd of onlookers. Both men were on horseback, where they remained mounted while exchanging greetings and offering homage to each other. Of course, they took care of the social amenities later in the palace, but they seemed to think the saddle was the place for handling matters of importance. That this was the standard method of procedure was demonstrated when this same king met with a company of visiting Uzbek Tartars in a similar manner shortly afterward.

In Persian weddings it was part of the ceremony for the bride to ride on horseback to her husband's house. The horse was always richly decorated and led in the procession by a woman friend of the bride.

As Persia was the middle ground between East and West, it was only natural there should be some overlapping of riding gear. The old Tartar saddle, with high fork and cantle and padded seat, was much in evidence. Opposite it was the type more common to Arabia and North Africa. The latter were built on unpadded wood trees and covered with leather or velvet. Some were only partly covered (Fig. 42), the rest being lacquered.

Among the elite, both saddles and bridles were usually decorated lavishly. Saddle skirts were often so large as to nearly cover the rump of the horse. Fancy breast collars were the rule. The whole rig might be almost entirely covered with silver and gold embroidery in fancy stitched designs. Some were encrusted with silver or gold and set with carnelians and mosaics of turquoise. Buckles and rings were often of gold. All leatherwork was of the finely tanned Turkey leather, so called by Europeans because they obtained it from the Turkish traders. It was in reality a Persian product.

Riders wore beautifully worked boots of yellow leather painted in floral designs. They used snaffle bits and rode with short stirrups.

Turkish outfits were much the same as Persian. Their common saddles were said to have been large and cumbersome, cinched on with a single girth which encircled both horse and saddle. Bridles were clumsy and ill made though much decorated, including blue beads to keep off the evil eye. These riders were so adept at managing their mounts with voice and knee pressure that whips and spurs were seldom used. Dumont said they rode with such short stirrups that their knees were almost at right angles.

The better saddles (Fig. 43) were quite ornate affairs. Elaborately embroidered red leather or velvet coverings were the rule, or in some cases a woven fabric that resembled a Persian rug, with fringed skirts and cantle. The cantle was semicircular, shaped to fit the rider. The horn, often ball-shaped, might be of metal or jewel-studded wood.

Stirrups were designed to complement the saddle. A popular type, made of iron inlaid with gold is shown in Fig. 44, C. This measured 14½ inches long by 5 inches wide in the center. Both ends flared out from the center to a width of 8½ inches, making it reversible. A somewhat similar stirrup in shape, though shorter and more compact, is shown in Fig. 44, D. It is of gilded brass pierced and chased in elaborate design.

Pommel holsters for the big flintlock horse pistols were of leather covered with heavily embroidered velvet. Fringed edges were common,

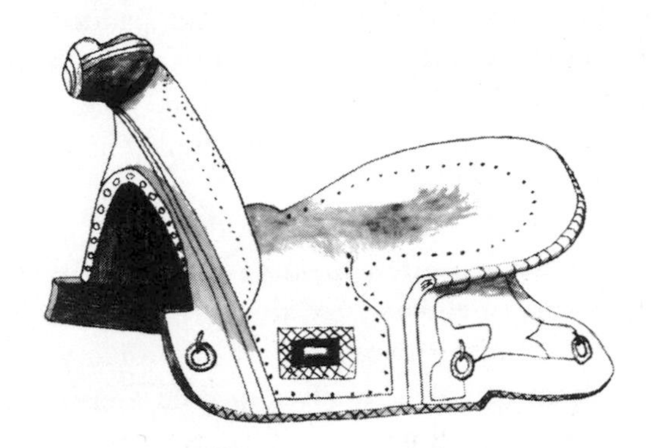

FIG. 42. Persian saddle, eighteenth century.

FIG. 43. Turkish saddle, 1760

and red was a favorite color. The whole thing would average in size about 6 by 15 inches.

A description of one such outfit brought to England is found in John Evelyn's diary of December 17, 1684:

> The furniture, consisting of embroidery on the saddle, housing, quiver, bow, arrows, scymiter, mace; the Bashaw's velvet mantle furred with the most perfect ermine I ever beheld; all which, ironwork in common furniture being here of silver, curiously wrought and double gilt to an incredible value.
>
> Such and so extraordinary was the embroidery that I never saw anything to approach it. The reins and headstall were of crimson silk, covered with chains of silver gilt . . . it [the horse] was shod with iron made round and closed at the heel, with a hole in the middle about as wide as a shilling.

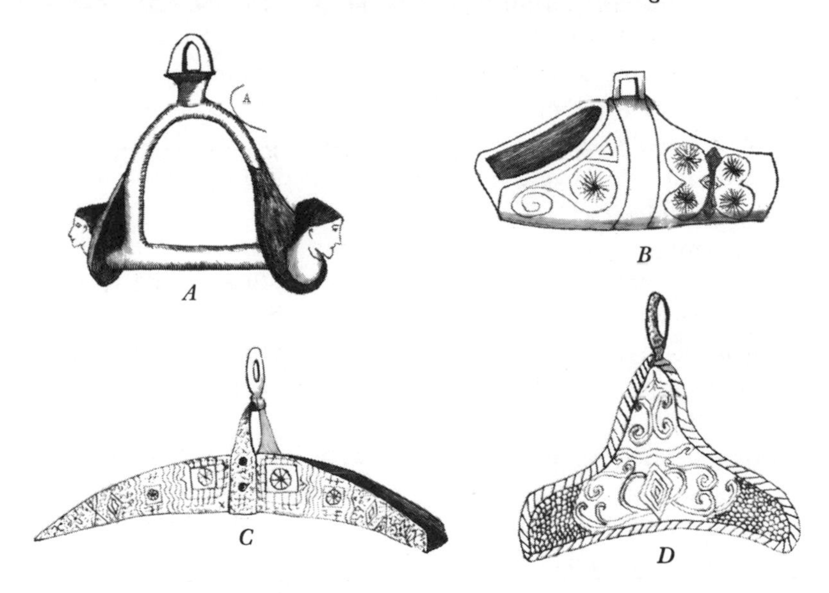

FIG. 44. Stirrups: *A* ancient Greek; *B* ancient oriental, carved wood; *C* Turkish, sixteenth and seventeenth centuries; *D* Turkish, eighteenth century.

Fig. 45 is a more modern saddle, showing Western influence. Most Asia Minor saddles of later years tended to copy the style of European military rigs. They had half-covered leather seats and semicircular cantles. The pommels were rather wide.

Syria followed the Persian style. In later years Syrian saddles were patterned after English saddles to a considerable extent. These were often almost completely covered with sheepskin. Belled and tasseled breast collars and other fancy trappings were common. Bridles were heavily decorated with shell work, pierced brass, silver mountings, and silk tassels. Narrow headstalls and ring bits were much favored. The Syrians rode with short stirrups and well-bent knees.

In the horseback days of antiquity, the Greeks were foremost among the civilized nations in promoting improvements and advancements in the horseman's world. Following the arrival of the saddle, however, they seem to have allowed progress to slow to a halt. After the eighth century little is heard of them as horsemen, while their saddlery represented nothing of note. Most examples resembled pack saddles more than anything else. In fact, a form of pack saddle was often used indiscriminately for either riding or packing. And for some unknown reason the saddle, which extended only to the middle of the horse's back, was built so that the rider had to sit over the mount's withers, his legs hanging down in front of the animal's shoulders. It is hard to understand how a people who once represented the epitome of horsemanship could fall so far behind in their thinking as to devise a rig so unsuitable for both man and horse.

Their neighbors on the island of Sardinia were evidently more progressive. They used a single-rig, tapering round-fork saddle of medium weight. It was covered with colored leather of very artistic design and usually carried a pair of outsize saddlebags made from coarse-woven wool. It was far more comfortable and practical than either the Greek or Egyptian outfits.

Egyptian saddles, while fairly comfortable for riding, were odd. The seat was shaped like a section of half-round tile, its open side down over the horse. A two-inch square projection, set perpendicularly on the front fork, served as a pommel. The cantle was quite high with a generous slope, having a scooped-out shape that resembled a huge oyster shell. Large, square fenders covered the stirrup straps.

A simpler saddle was favored on the upper Nile. This was a rawhide-covered sidebar tree with low pommel and cantle made very much alike. The seat and cantle were left open in the center, giving the appearance of an unfinished Whitman tree. Light in weight, it used a single cinch and had the stirrups hung well forward. A rug or blanket was usually thrown over the seat.

Breast collars and bridles expressed the usual Oriental love for lavish decorations. Colored saddle blankets in fanciful designs completed the ensemble.

Egyptian ass saddles have suffered little change through the passage of time. These differ from those used in most of the East in having extremely high and bulky pommels instead of being merely flat pads. Fig. 46 shows a typical model.

This pommel affair is built full and almost round. It is ordinarily covered with leather. The main purpose is to provide an anchor post for the rider. Very short stirrups are used, drawing the feet up under the thighs. This throws the body forward where, with the knees drawn up high and thrust forward, riding is done mostly by balance, the knees gripping the big padded pommel on either side.

The seat and stirrups are usually covered with a colorful ruglike fabric. A single cinch and breeching are used, mounted on a fancy embroidered blanket. A string of beads and brass coins around the animal's neck, plus some jingling rings and bangles on the bit and reins, complete the outfit.

Syria and Palestine have an ass saddle which is practically the same, except for long stirrups. The more common rig is a pad with a pair of joined stirrups thrown across it, similar to Fig. 47. This type dates back to the days of Moses.

Many Oriental donkey riders use only a blanket tied on the animal's back, dispensing with stirrups altogether. On this they may sit sidewise, well back on the beast's rump, their feet hanging down over its flank. This has the advantage of lazy convenience. And owing to the slow, patient gait of the little animals, there is seldom need for the more secure seat of a regular saddle.

All the various phases of horsemanship and equipment of the Near and Middle East tended to funnel through Arabia as that nation expanded into prominence and moved west across Africa in the seventh century. Some items were rejected; others were changed or modified; entirely new factors were incorporated in many instances. But in the main, the patterns born in the ancient Persian lands moved with the desert Arabs into western Europe.

The one notable exception was the Arab's horse. There is no clear evidence that this animal ever entered the Persian scene; it seems to have had no connection with any of the ancients. Despite the assumption common in some quarters that the Arabian horse was more or less synonymous with the original Eastern animals, the breed is in reality a rather latecomer in the equine world. Authorities are in considerable disagreement as to just when it did appear, and they are equally uncertain as to its source. All we can be sure of is that it was an offshoot from some desert mixture that came into being well on in the Christian Era.

In close relationship to the Asiatic Arabian stands the Barb horse of the Arabs in North Africa. Many authorities think the two breeds are parallel branches stemming from the same source. They are very much alike. Both have only five segments in their vertebrae and sixteen in their tails, where all other horses have six-segment backbones and eighteen in the tail. They have the same short bodies, fabulous staying qualities, nobility, courage, and companionability toward man. Their shank bones have the southern characteristics, being smaller and more solid than those of northern horses, and are proportionately stronger and more flexible.

One factor that set the two breeds somewhat apart, an entirely human feature, was that the Asiatic Arabs marketed their stallions and rode mares, whereas those of Africa rode stallions and reserved the mares for breeding.

The Libyan desert might be loosely defined as the dividing line separating the Arabian horses from the Barbs. The former extended east through Arabia, the Barbs holding sway from Libya on west.

One old Bedouin legend has it that the Arabian horse came from the original wild horses which Ishmael caught in the Nufred desert in ancient times. The old ones called them the *Kuhaylan,* or black-skinned antelopes, because of the black rim around their eyes, which made them look as though they had been painted with kuhl (antimony).

Another tradition deals with the origin of the African Barb. It tells how an Arab chief of West Africa once left a wounded mare at a small, isolated oasis. This water hole was at a spot where no other horses ever ranged and where fellow tribesmen did not go. One year later, this particular chief, being in the vicinity, was moved by curiosity to visit the oasis and see if his mare had by any chance survived. Much to his surprise, he found her still there and fully recovered. And what was more astounding, the mare was with foal. The Arab took her home with him, happy over regaining his mare and full of wonder about her pregnancy.

When the colt was born it proved to be a very promising specimen. It was believed to be the get of one of the wild asses which inhabited that region. The native name for these asses was Hamar-el-Omaknen, and they called the colt Haymour. It eventually grew into a decidedly unusual animal of unprecedented qualities. Being a mare and of such outstanding superiority, it was kept for selective breeding. From it developed the famous desert breed called Haymours.

There is a good possibility that this legend may be more fact than fable. The original home of the wild ass was in West and North Africa. The jennet, a colt from a female ass and a stallion, has five lumbar vertebrae like the Arabian horse. Jennets, ordinarily sterile, have been known to breed on occasion. It is not illogical to think that one of these creatures roaming the wilderness might have come upon the wounded mare left unattended. At any rate, among the three breeds of Arabian horses coming from west Sudan, the Haymour, the Bou-ghareb, and the Meizque, the Haymour has always stood supreme.

Over in the Arabian Desert we also find three principal breeds of horses. The finest and most beautiful are the Saqlawi, or Seglawi. A more muscular, primeval strain is called the *Kuhaylan* or Kohlan. The Maneghi, or Mu'nique, is a longer-bodied, running type.

Here we meet another legend. While Mohammed was fighting his way to greatness, he once had occasion to lead 20,000 of his cavalrymen over a waterless route for three days. Both men and horses were weak for lack of water when, upon topping a last dry ridge, they suddenly saw a sparkling river below them. Reaching the foot of the ridge and a desirable camping spot, the troopers dismounted and turned their mounts loose. The herd immediately stampeded for the river.

At that moment someone raised the cry, "Enemies!" The bugle sounded "To horse!" in a frantic effort to call back the released mounts. But the horse herd was too greedy for water to heed a bugle. Only five mares out of the 20,000 animals answered the call. Eyes wild, parched muzzles quivering, these five halted in the rush for water and returned to their masters.

The warning proved a false alarm, but when Mohammed saw how the love, spirit, and obedience of those five mares overcame their natural instincts and consuming thirst, he decided to keep them for selective breeders. And from them came the superior strain of all that is finest in Arabian horses.

But regardless of how and where this famous breed originated, the fact remains that the Arabian horse made a belated appearance. Strabo, the Greek historian who traveled over most of the East from Russia to Nubia between 24 and 20 B.C., stated that there were no horses in Arabia at that time. He said the Arabs rode camels, calling themselves cameleers instead of cavaliers. As Strabo was a close friend of Aelius Gallus, the Roman general who invaded Arabia in 24 B.C., he was in an excellent position to learn the facts about anything he had not seen in person.

Arabian history tells us that all early records of the Egyptians, Assyrians, Babylonians, and Persians refer to the Arabs as cameleers. When the Assyrian ruler Shalmaneser III was fighting the king of Damascus in 854 B.C., the latter had as his allies the forces of the Arabian sheiks Ahab and Jundub. Following the Assyrian victory, Shalmaneser had inscriptions carved depicting his destruction of Karkar, the royal city of Damascus, along with its 1,200 cavalry, 1,200 chariots, 20,000 infantry soldiers—and 1,000 camels of the Arabians.

Even after the advent of the horse, camels were an important method of transportation. Arabs frequently rode them to war, leading their unencumbered horses tied to the camel-saddle cinch. Upon arriving near the scene of action, they would leap from their camels to the backs of the saddled mares and take off for the expected fray. Racing camels were commonly used for this sort of business.

Most camel-riding saddles had pommels and cantles like the later Tuareg outfit in Fig. 48. Some were leather-covered and skirted, others were padded with leather cushions and sheepskins. Common adjuncts were big goatskin saddlebags decorated with long rows of tassels and braided fringes that reached below the animal's belly. A blue bead tied to the hair of the camel's withers was supposed to thwart the evil eye.

In olden times the women of this region rode in pairs on camels. A couple of wooden boxes some three feet square and large enough to sit down in were slung on the camel, one on each side. A woman rode in each box for balance.

Among the later Bedouins an individual camel-riding tent was often seen. This was the carriage of affluent dignitaries or, on occasion, of a favorite woman. It was a boxlike affair with either overhead bows or four widely curved horns at the corners to support the tentlike canopy. The interior was adorned with silks and cashmeres, the seat padded with rugs and cushions.

The single-humped racing camels, known as *dhaluls,* were the favorite riding camels. No bridles were used. Instead, a halter of multicolored wool served for leading and tying the beast; guiding was done by tapping the camel on the shoulder with a camel stick.

Even in modern times, the Bedouins commonly refer to themselves as Ahl al-ba 'ir, or the People of the Camel. Arabia is still the world's chief breeding center for Uman dromedaries.

Our best authorities on the subject believe that horses began to take the place of camels in Arabia during the early part of the Christian Era. Syria seems the most likely source of the equine replacements. One record, the oldest definite one, is the account of Constantine's sending two hundred Cappadocian horses to Felix (Yemen), the prince of Arabia in A.D. 356. The gift was a gesture of good will which Constantine hoped would serve as an opening wedge in introducing the prince to Christianity.

The superb Arabian horse, developed into a distinct breed, taught the Arab what the horse could do for him. It also created a horseman who raised Islam to the zenith of its glory.

During the seventh century, the Arabs established an empire that extended from the Indus River Basin to Tangier in Africa. This vast territory was conquered almost solely by mounted troops. They called themselves the *fursan* (cavalry), as opposed to the *harbiyah* (infantry) and *ramiyah* (archers).

It was during this period that Abd-al-Malik, Arabian emperor between 685 and 705, put into operation a pony express system. Perhaps he based his idea on the mounted mail service Darius established in Persia a thousand years previously; or it might have been an original creation. In any case, it was a first-class setup. It provided a regular postal service, or *barid,* throughout the kingdom, using relays of express riders. Designed principally for carrying government dispatches between Damascus and the various provincial capitals, it was eventually extended to include private mail and provide transportation for travelers. Established routes connected the imperial capital with all the leading centers of population. There were hundreds of these routes. Regular postmasters were employed at the various stations, which provided hostlers, relay mounts, inns, and the like. The riders used horses and mules in Persia and camels in Syria and Arabia.

Wars and a crumbling empire eventually abolished this fine system, but it was revived some five and a half centuries later by the Arabian sultan Baybars during his reign (1260–1277).

As a general rule, the Arabs from Asia went to war on horseback, raising colts as they went along on extended journeys. They contended, as they still do, that mares endured hunger, thirst, and fatigue better than stallions, were gentler, more willing, and less likely to betray their presence in enemy territory, as mentioned earlier. Most riding was done without bridles in early times, the horses being trained to obey a rider's voice and knee pressure. One early writer claimed the horses of Balascia were trained to do entirely without bridles and had feet so tough and firm that horseshoes were a useless encumbrance.

FIG. 45. *A* Turkish saddle; *B* headstall, 1925.

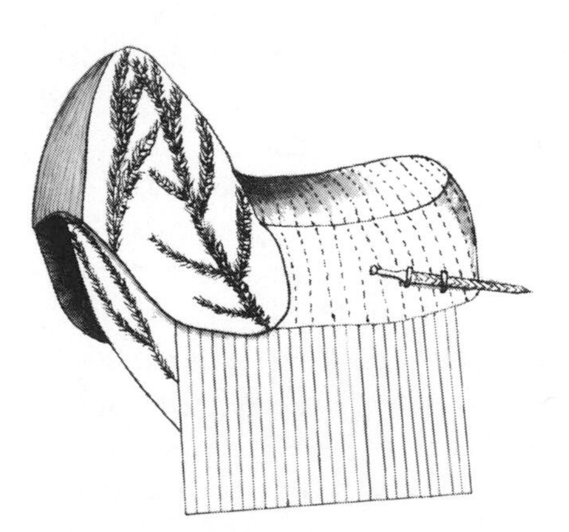

FIG. 46. Egyptian ass saddle, 1890.

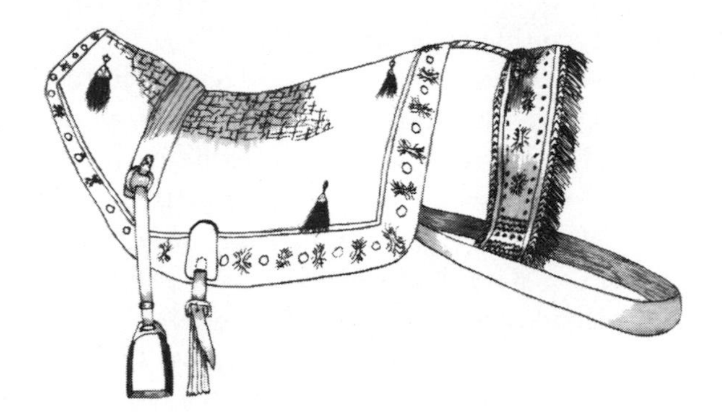

FIG. 47. Donkey saddle, Palestine, 1935 .

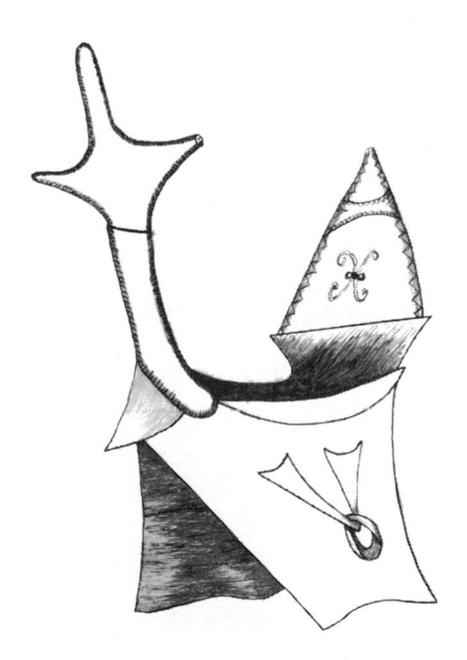

FIG. 48. Tuareg camel saddle, nineteenth century.

It was this hard-riding Arabian cavalry which routed the great army of Heraclius, the Byzantine emperor, in 636.

But Arabian horsemanship was not directed entirely toward war. Sports claimed a goodly amount of their attention, as it has among all horseback people. Racing and polo were favorite pastimes. Al-Waldi was one of the caliphs foremost in promoting and patronizing race meets. At one of these affairs, in 710, an assemblage of 4,000 race horses was present. Such contests were designed to further interest in horse breeding, as in all other lands, past and present.

Breeding became a fine art among the Arabs. Only examplary skill could have developed such a superior and long-lasting strain of riding animals. The Arabian horse of today has the same characteristics as his ancestor of fifteen hundred years ago: the dished face, full forehead, wide jaws, big windpipe, short body, great lungs, large eyes, outstanding intelligence, and definite color formation. Color, incidentally, was apparently considered of signal importance by early Arab breeders. The good and bad influence of certain markings are ever highly emphasized in Arabic horse literature.

This tells us not to look with favor on a black horse, though it may excel in spirit. On the other hand, white is a most desirable color. Both black and white, however, are on the rare side, the breed running about 35 per cent bay, 30 per cent gray, 20 per cent brown, and 15 per cent chestnut. There are no pintos, yellows, roans, or piebalds as there are among the Barbs. The occasional whites usually have blackish-blue points. White feet are fairly common; an old Arab jingle cautions the horseman: "If you have a horse with four white legs, keep him not a day. If you have a horse with three white legs, send him far away. If you have a horse with two white legs, sell him to a friend. If you have a horse with one white leg, keep him to the end."

A dark chestnut is supposed to be good, but a light chestnut with white mane and tail is of doubtful quality, besides being unlucky. Another warning of ill luck is a white ring around the fetlock. This latter animal will be a stumbler, a quitter, and inclined to weakness. If you want a lucky horse, pick one with both near feet white. Four white feet, plus a star in the face, is also good, as are white hind feet and a star in the face. A horse with two white forefeet and near hind foot white might do in a pinch, but fight shy of one showing the off hind foot and one forefoot white. Dark colors with dark legs indicate quality horses, while grays show a weakness under extreme heat.

Who is to say these ancient superstitions were without merit? All horsemen recognize the physical potentialities in certain off-color horses of today. We know human complexions often reflect the basic characteristics of mankind. Should it be any more surprising to find the same thing in horses? And the Arab, who virtually lived with his horses for centuries, unquestionably learned many things about the animals which people less closely associated with them would never discover.

For instance, the Arab would measure the length of a newborn colt's shank from the center of the knee to the hairline of its hoof and tell you exactly how tall it would be when it matured. He says four times the shank length will be the grown animal's height at the withers. Or he will look at the worn-down teeth of an old horse, whose tooth cups no longer reveal its years, and arrive at a definite age by examining a tiny vertical groove in the enamel of one eye tooth.

However we look at such beliefs, the fact remains that the Arab horse has stood the test of time. Aside from its docility, spirit, beauty, and tractability, it is unparalleled in its power to carry weight and maintain its speed over long distances—also to travel incredible distances without food, water, or rest. Such horses have been known to cover a distance of three hundred miles burdened by a rider and without rest. Arabians will carry up to a fourth of their own weight without noticeable discomfort. Races up to three hundred miles in length are not unusual.

It was on the Arabian and his cousin, the Barb, that the famous line of English Thoroughbreds was founded. By virtue of descent, the American Saddle Horse shares in the same ancient desert blood. The unparalleled qualities of our own western horses show an equally proud inheritance transmitted through the horses the conquistadors bred from Arabian immigrants in Spain.

And if the Arab's horse was distinctive, his saddle was fully as much so. This was the saddle which eventually changed riding style throughout Europe and laid the foundation for present-day gear in the Western world.

The Arabs originally had several types of saddles. Those of the African tribes differed considerably from those used by the Arabian Bedouins, while there were local variations in both regions.

The early ones in Arabia were similar to the old Persian and Byzantine rigs of the A.D. 750 period. Some silver trimming was used. In fact, silver was the only metal chosen for saddle decoration until the Arabian caliph Al-Mu'tazz fitted himself out with a suit of gilded armor and a golden saddle somewhere between 866 and 869. After that, all kinds of gems, pearls, and gold were used with silver.

The Bedouin outfit in Fig. 49 is a continuation of this old type. It enjoyed considerable popularity in the East even until modern times. The padded seat was usually covered with colored velvet and was exceptionally wide. The elaborate breast collar and fancy bridle, trimmed with a wealth of fringe and tassels, well reflected the spirit of those desert wanderers. Panther and gazelle skins were often employed as

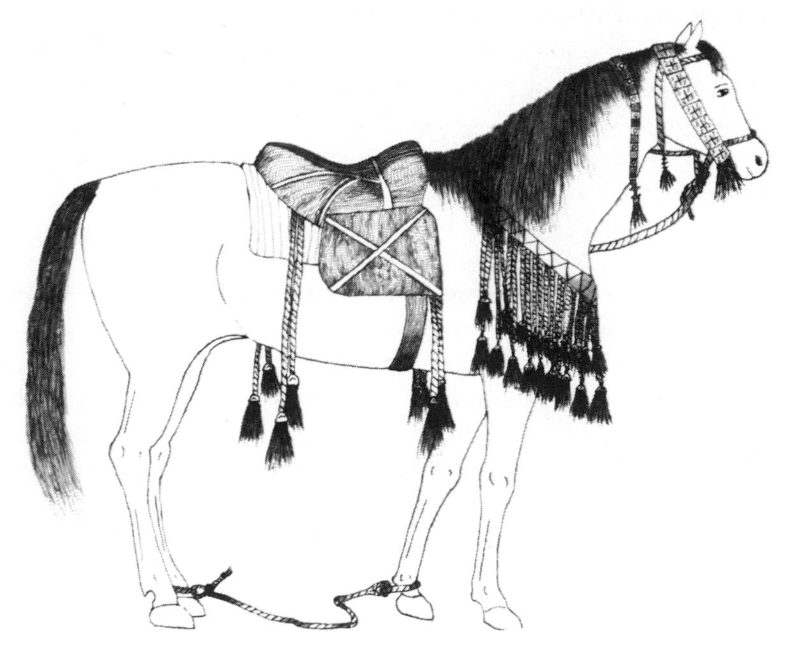

FIG. 49. Arabian Bedouin outfit, 1906.

saddle blankets. Hunters usually spread a sheepskin over the mount's rump when they went hunting.

Bitless bridles were common among the Bedouins. Unlike their African cousins, who always used bits, they relied chiefly on a light headstall made something like a hackamore. It was often profusely decorated with silver, gold, and pearls and had a crown piece of gay-colored wool.

Hasselquist, who visited the Bedouins in 1749, mentions a saddle then in use which had "a cantle so high it reaches more than halfway up a rider's back." He goes on to say, "With this saddle they never use a girth, which makes it very difficult to mount and keep their seat. The Arabian understands the *équilibre* and keeps the body in just counterpoise, a most dexterous feat." The stirrups were of the flat Turkish style which contained the whole foot. This style of stirrup is shown in Fig. 44 *C*.

Though Hasselquist does not give much information about the rest of the saddle, it was undoubtedly on the order of the one in Fig. 50. That was the type which, transmitted through the Moors, evolved into the Spanish saddle. It had most of the better features that would appeal to the working rider. The fork, seat, and cantle were all covered with leather. The carved silver plates and silver edgings furnished a decorative design that would be most attractive in any man's country.

One elaborate saddle owned by an Arab sultan was built on the modern pattern, covered with leather, and set with pearls and other jewels at a cost of $60,000. As these were 1906 dollars, it was perhaps one of the world's costliest examples of saddlery.

While this is an extreme example, the Bedouin is well known for seeing that his riding gear reflects his wealth and position. His is a vivid life: His horse is always saddled for immediate action; his spear stuck in the ground beside the picketed animal; his rug-floored tent furnished with copper and brass utensils and silken cushions; his flowing robe flicking about boots of red morocco leather with turned-up toes and wrought-iron heels; his lithe, pantherlike movements and the fierce light in the eyes of the strong, dark face—all bespeak the kaleidoscope of color that is his everyday existence. Having all his possessions in keeping with his station in life is his ambition and pride. It is his working equipment, the foundation stone of his life.

He is a prideful man. Though he may live in a tent and eat with his fingers, he has a sense of superiority, politeness, and good breeding that denotes a born gentleman. The careless grace with which he swings his robe, the touch of individual artistry in his gestures and movements, the independent air which marks his approach to any given subject proclaims the fact that he is his own man. His whole bearing reflects a highly tempered core, keenness, and tough courage. That he is always ready to ride, hunt, fight, visit, or care for his herds without thought for his own ease or comfort is quite lost sight of by earth-bound people in the light of his refusal to do manual labor on foot. In short, he has been the embodiment of the man on horseback since time immemorial.

It is a matter of record that the saddle was a mark of status in early

FIG. 50. Arabian saddle, 1760.

FIG. 51. Moorish saddle, sixteenth century.

Arabian history. Under Caliph Umar II (717–720), one of the various penalties for professing Christianity was that of being forced to ride without a saddle. Under Harun al-Rashid, some sixty or seventy years later, Christians and Jews were permitted to use plain wooden saddles marked with two pomegranatelike balls on the cantle, but were restricted to mules and asses as mounts.

When the Arabs moved west to conquer Africa, their horses and equipment quickly won approval throughout the captive territories. The North Africans were a kindred race whose temperament and ac-

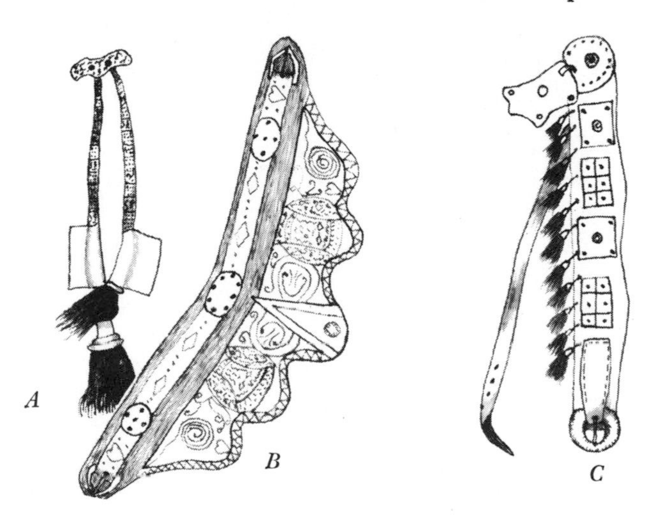

FIG. 52. *A* Moorish amulet and *B* breast collar, eighteenth century; *C* Sudanese breast collar, nineteenth century.

tivities were well suited to the Eastern infusion. It was only a matter of time till all the North African nations were using copies or variations of Arabian riding gear. This spread down into the Sudan and French Cameroons, where the natives still use the old-style ring bits and wear spurs. Their Oriental-type saddles are covered with colored leather and decorated most handsomely. They are excellent horsemen, taking pride in their fine stock.

It was the Moors, however, who were most instrumental in introducing Arabian horsemanship and saddles into Europe. Fig. 51 shows one of their saddles. It had a rawhide seat covered in the center with a patch of embroidered black velvet. Heavily engraved silver covered the pommel. The cantle back was covered with black velvet, as were the jockeys and skirts. The latter was embroidered in elaborate designs. The neck strap and breast collar (Fig. 52) were of red cloth embroidered in gold, with gold and silver mountings. A Sudanese example is trimmed with gold plates and horsehair tassels. The tassels were often dyed in bright colors. Ring or curb bits were used with elaborate headstalls in matching designs.

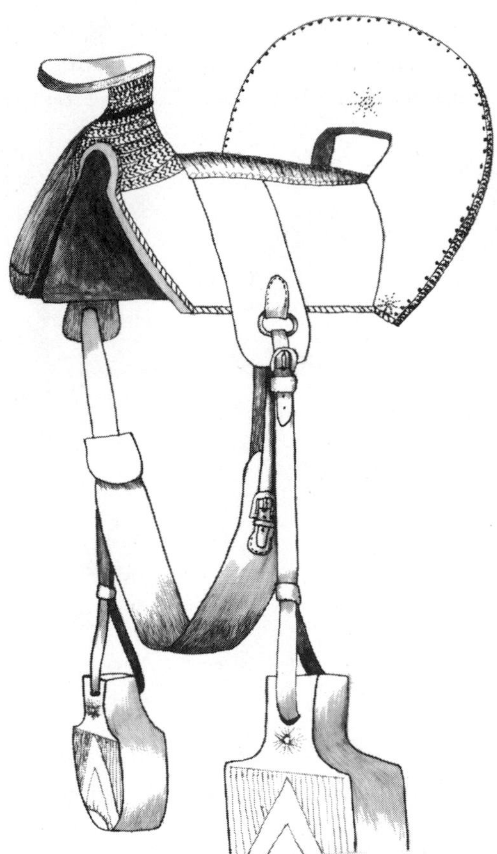

FIG. 53. Moroccan saddle, nineteenth century.

Fig. 53 is a nineteenth century rig of more modern design. It has a plain, rawhide-covered, hardwood tree with horn wrapped in snakeskin. The single web cinch and huge, carved wooden stirrups present a nice blending of East and West.

Moorish spurs were of the long-shanked variety, usually of soft iron embellished with gold and heraldic designs.

The crescent-shaped talisman hung from the browband was an ancient good luck charm which the Moors introduced into Spain. This same amulet journeyed with the Spaniards to America, where it is still often seen in use among the Navajo Indians.

In Tunisia, the horns and cantles grew even higher than the Moorish,

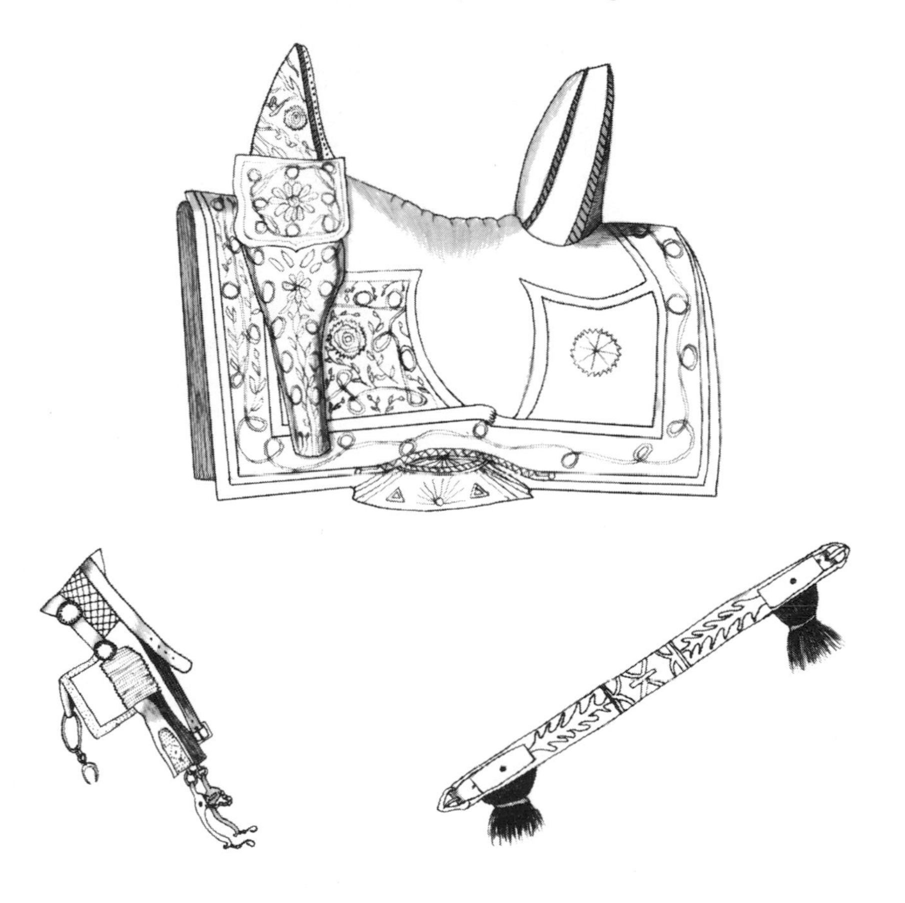

FIG. 54. Tunisian equipment, seventeenth century.

assuming extravagant proportions. But they still retained the old red-velvet cover embroidered in gold (Fig. 54). The pistol holster was of matching design. Bridle and breast collar were also of embroidered red velvet trimmed with engraved silver mountings.

Among the poorer class of Tunisians, pad saddles were more the rule. Some were used without stirrups; others had a pair of stirrups hung on

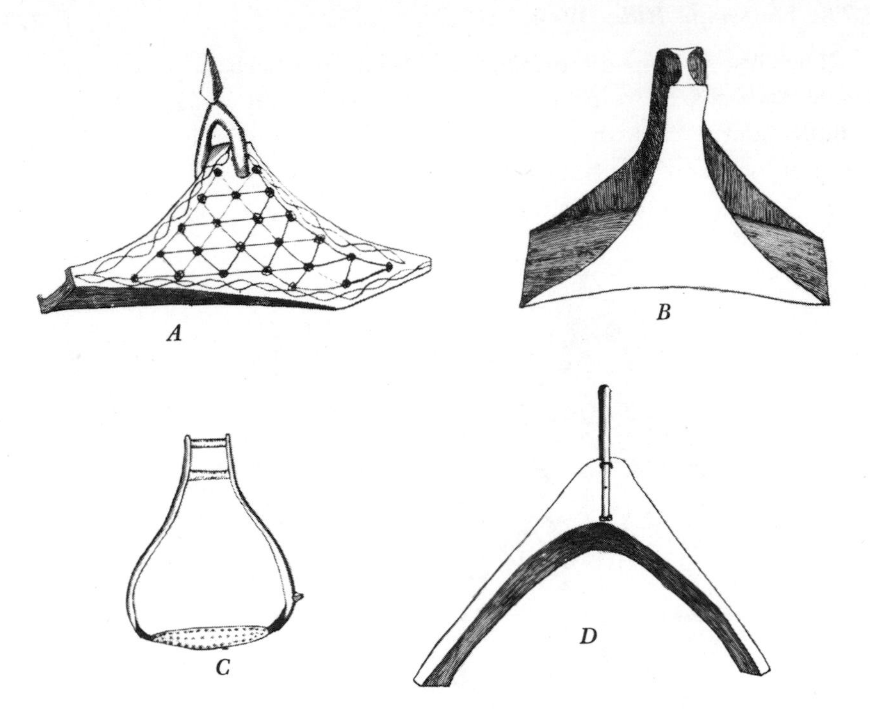

FIG. 55. Stirrups: *A* Moroccan brass; *B* Moroccan iron; *C* Turkish stirrup with spur; *D* Haussa brass.

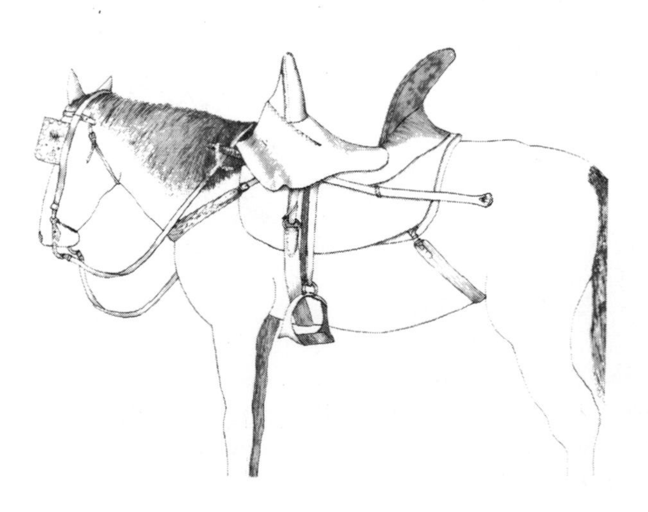

FIG. 56. Algerian Spahi outfit, nineteenth century.

either end of a strap thrown loosely across the pad. The pads were also occasionally used without a cinch; perhaps this was a hangover from the ancient ass saddles.

The old Turkish and Moorish type of stirrups were most popular (Fig. 55). Some slipper stirrups of the later Spanish variety (Fig. 69) were used. Brass was a favorite material for stirrups, though iron was also used. With either metal, ordinarily there was an overlay of carved silver or gold.

The Algerian Spahis departed the farthest from the usual pattern in developing saddles. Their rigs had abnormally high pommels and cantles (Fig. 56). The seat was exceptionally long in contrast to the short trees used by the other Arabs. It sloped steeply toward the pommel. The wide, flat pommel, resembling a roughly trimmed ham, rose almost perpendicularly as high as the rider's waist. The cantle reached more than halfway up his back, flaring out like the back of an old-fashioned rocking chair. Plain leather skirts predominated. The leather seat jockey extended down to cover the sword customarily carried under the left leg. This was one of the few double-rigged saddles to appear in history. The rearmost of the two web cinches was set clear back around the horse's flanks. Rather short stirrups were hung from the center of the tree and were without fenders. Big, metal, Turkish-style stirrups with square or rectangular treads were favored. Breast collars were usually well decorated.

These people, like the Klass riders of Tunisia, used blind bridles with rather mediocre headstalls. It gave their mounts a decidedly farm-horse appearance, but seemed to have no effect on their efficiency. Curb and ring bits were the rule.

—12—

When Knights Were Bold

WHY WERE NORTHERN Europeans so slow to begin to ride horseback? All the southern nations, as well as the Asiatics, had been mounted for centuries before Christ was born.

With such an example surrounding them on two sides, it is strange that the Angles, Saxons, Jutes, Danes, and other Teutonic folk did not copy the advanced method of locomotion at least to some extent. The fact remains, however, that they held aloof from riding until it was literally forced upon them. When Caesar invaded England in 55 B.C., he found the natives in possession of horses, but they used them only for chariot driving and the like. And they continued to do so. It was not until the seventh century that riding became general in the north.

Bede, in his eighth-century history of the English people, says it started in 631, when the prelates and some of the nobility began to ride horses. Previously they had all traveled on foot or ridden in carts or chariots. Chariots were used chiefly for war at that time, their main function being to transport infantry soldiers to the battle sectors.

Nevertheless, once impressed by the advantage of being mounted, the English rapidly adopted this new means of transportation. Within the next several hundred years the horseman and his horse were objects of national interest throughout the north. By the middle 800s England was taking her horses seriously; various laws governing their use began to appear. In 876 Howel Dda even established government regulations of prices and dealers. Under his laws a colt less than fourteen days old was priced at 4d., one two weeks to one year old at 24d., one from one to two years of age at 48d., and a three-year-old at 60d. Palfreys, pack horses, and plow or cart horses (presumably broken and ready to work) were figured at 120d.

Along with this, the seller of a horse had to guarantee the animal would be "free of giddiness for three days, a broken wind for three months and a dropsy for one year." Also that "he was not to tire when on a journey with others or loathe either feed or water." If the purchase failed to meet any of these conditions, the seller was required to take the horse back or refund one-third of the price paid.

Among Dda's other laws we find that anyone laming a horse had to forfeit the price of the animal, or for mutilating it, pay one-third of its value. If he cut the hair off the tail of another man's horse, he was obliged to feed and care for the animal until its tail grew out again, meanwhile furnishing the owner with a usable mount free of charge. If he cut the tail of a stallion, it cost him an additional 24d. in cash. The fine for galling a horse was 4d., providing the skin was not rubbed off or the flesh raw. In the latter case, the fine went up to 16d. Anyone suspected of killing a horse, no matter how strong his defense, had to have the sworn oaths of twenty-four reliable persons in his behalf if he would escape incarceration. Even to mount another's horse without permission brought a fine of 4d., plus another 4d for every league it was ridden.

In those days the king's villeins, or serfs, were obliged to furnish him with horses to carry the army's baggage whenever the call to arms came. Those who held land in his domain were subject to call at any time for building camps or fortifications for the army, each equipped with a horse and an ax. The Master of the King's Horse stood alone as sort of a privileged character. He got his lands rent free, plus a double portion of corn for his own horse.

Starting with the early baronial days, the petty kings scattered over northern Europe, and all maintained some sort of individual armies or fighting forces to help insure their life, liberty, and whatever kind of happiness they thought suitable. After discovering the advantage horsemen had over foot soldiers, they began mounting some of their serfs in time of war. By the eleventh century they had shaped up a set of feudal laws which made certain tenants and all landowners subject to call for military duty in the lord's service, mounted on horseback and wearing a coat of mail. Though this enforced service applied only to the heads of families or to the eldest son if the father was dead or unable to serve, many of the younger sons also volunteered.

Service as a mounted knight, with its attendant chances for glory, gold, and romance, was the one bright star in the horizon for most young men of vision. In an age when the bulk of the population was little more than an unidentified mass of humanity, the horseman alone was able to gain recognition as an individual. A great part of medieval history is written around those who appeared on horseback. A common attitude toward foot soldiers of that period is found in *The Minstrel of the Legendary Host*. It describes the company's forces as being "60,000 knights, not counting foot soldiers, of whom no account was taken." As might be expected, such conditions provided a powerful inducement for the wide-awake to look toward knighthood as a profession.

Though a shift upward in class was frowned upon by the upper class as a general thing, the gates to knighthood did occasionally open to pages and horsemen's servants whose skill or bravery won them promotions. There were even cases of infantrymen being elevated to the saddle.

Exceptional bravery, courage, or a gift for horsemanship shown by his foot soldier would on occasion so impress a superior that he would find means to give the fellow his just dues by promoting him to mounted service. History records several such enterprising individuals who rose from feet to fame by this method. One such underling won his spurs by leading a victorious charge on his master's horse after the latter had fallen, wounded in battle.

Along with this, well-trained horses were an essential part of the national welfare. Men who were skillful at breaking and managing horses received special favors from their superiors and frequently won promotion into the higher ranks. Such distinction set them apart from the mob, earning them titles of quality and respect and various extra privileges. Not infrequently this led to an honored position among the chivalric fraternity.

Of course the great majority of knights were members of the nobility or wealthier landowners. They were invariably horsemen to begin with. They considered appearing in public on foot as tantamount to working in the fields with the serfs. Horsemanship stood in their estimation as "the foremost way to employ the mind, form the body and add grace and strength to activity." Furthermore, they were the ones better able to own good horses and the accouterments suitable to a knight, as well as having leisure to practice their profession. It was only natural that such men should, as a rule, be of higher intellect and more inclined toward adventure than those of coarser mold.

Thus it was that the elite of all nations were the men on horseback. It was they who carried the shining banner of gallantry and glamour in society as well as in warfare. And, as might be supposed, it was they who ultimately found themselves at the king's side in troubled times or fair. The king, in turn, was ever interested in maintaining quality and dependability among the men in whom he placed so much trust. Such selective discrimination could only lead to a distinctive fraternity of those chosen for representation.

Perhaps founded on the principles of the ancient Roman Order of Equites, the English, French, and German knights were drawn from the loose associations of mounted warriors in their respective countries during the eighth century. The church, which largely controlled national affairs at that time, saw in the new association a favorable avenue for expanded operations, and was quick to bring them into its own field. Churchmen instituted rules and regulations to hold the wilder spirits in check and forward the cause of Christianity through such influential citizens. The net result was a sort of closed corporation into which neophytes could enter only after confessing their sins before a priest and going through a pious ritual. None but priests were allowed to administer the rites and raise a man to the status of a knight, or *caballarii* as he was then called.

From *caballarii,* incidentally, comes the English "cavalier," the French *chevalier,* the Spanish *caballero,* and the modern "cavalry." The word "knight" is derived from the Anglo-Saxon *cniht,* meaning a servant, one who serves, a person subservient to a lord or king.

It was not until the dawn of the tenth century that conferring the Order of Knighthood became the function of the king. Athelstan, the first Saxon king of England, was the first monarch to create a knight. This occurred in the year 924.

FIG. 57. French saddle, Normandy, ninth century.

FIG. 58. Norman saddle, 1000 A.D.

The knights of this period used outfits similar to the one shown in Fig. 57. This is the Norman version of the 800s as pictured somewhat crudely on the Bayeux Tapestry of France. The rider wears the conical metal helmet and outer garment of chain mail. The curb bit, goad spurs, and iron stirrups are representative of that era.

Fig. 58 is a later style Norman saddle made on the same pattern and in use about 1000. It has a cloth-covered, padded seat and stuffed rolls in front and back. Otherwise, it shows little improvement over the earlier model.

But the fighting knight needed a more secure seat than these early saddles offered. An unhorsed man had little chance of survival in battle; and in a meeting of spears or battleaxes it was all too easy to be unhorsed. Saddles of this type also promised little help in staying aboard during the favorite sport of tilting. As mounted warfare and combative games were about the only route to fame and fortune, the rider naturally looked toward any improvement in his main item of equipment.

By the middle 1000s he had evolved a saddle that at least lessened the chances of his being pushed back over the horse's tail. The model of 1050 (Fig. 59) would call for nothing less than a pry pole to lift the

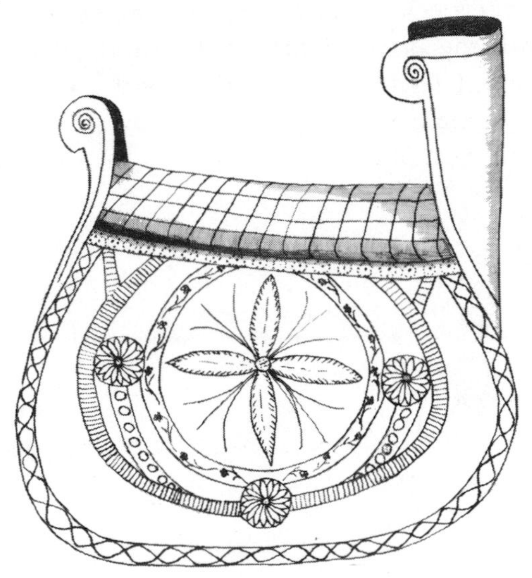

FIG. 59. English saddle, 1050 A.D.

rider clear of the arm-chair cantle. The seat was padded for comfort, while the skirts were of richly embroidered velvet.

The long-seated, low-horned type was, however, used more for ordinary riding than for outfitting knights. The saddles of the knights usually had high forks with winglike projections built up to protect the thighs and groin of the rider. They also often had extra padded rolls for leg grips. Horns as we know them were not used.

A saddle of this style, found pictured in the *Roman de Tristran* manuscript (Fig. 60), is shown in use by a Norman knight of the fourteenth century. Its short tree and boxlike construction gave the rider a maximum of anchorage. Many were faced with armor for added protection, some having forks and cantle made of metal. Both French and English knights used them to a considerable extent. The Norman style of riding up over the horse's withers may have had certain advantages in combat, but it was hard on the horse and inclined to hamper its action.

Subsequent types generally popular are found in Figs. 61–64. Most of these appeared along with the development of heavier armor and more elaborate embellishments. They were very heavy, built on rigid wooden trees with swell forks similar to our modern western saddles, in most cases. Metal plating was used on them very often. Many ran to extremes in design and decorative features. Most were fairly comfortable for both horse and rider, as well as being practical for the purpose intended.

Breast collars and single cinches seem to have been standard rigging

FIG. 60. Norman knight, fourteenth century.

with European saddles from earliest times. Cruppers did not show up to any extent until about 1300. Plain iron stirrups were the rule among the earlier horsemen, but these gave way to more artistic creations after the advent of horse armor.

Through the earlier centuries most of northern Europe's saddles were covered with fabrics of one kind or another. Colored velvet was a most popular material for this purpose. Although in early times some leather was doubtless used as well, carved wood and well-embroidered velvet remained in favor until supplies of good leather and the skill of experienced craftsmen combined to make leather saddles more desirable.

Leathermaking is an old art. Homer's *Iliad* describes a tanning method in use around 1200 B.C. The Persians and Turks were turning out excellent leather in very ancient times. Other nations in the East practiced

FIG. 61. Italian knight, fourteenth century.

FIG. 62. French knight, fifteenth century.

the craft to a considerable degree all through the ages, while it was found to some extent in southern Europe. The north, on the other hand, made little progress in developing a good product during the early period. The oldest historical reference to the Cordwainers' (leather workers) Guild in London is given as 1087. Even then, the workers were using an imported product for the most part.

The English also imported the name (which they corrupted) for their craftsmen in this field. The word "cordwainer" comes from cordovan, the Spanish leather with which they worked. The cordwainers were naturally closely associated with the early saddlers, a fairly contemporaneous organization. First-class leather was something of a rarity in northern Europe until after the Moors introduced Eastern tanning methods into Spain in the eighth century. Cordoba subsequently became the chief leathermaking center of that country. Much of this product was exported to neighboring nations, where it soon took on the trade name of *cordobán* or cordovan leather. England, one of the heaviest importers of the Cordoban leather, used so much of it that the Spanish name became more or less synonymous with the material.

When William the Conqueror invaded England in 1066, various London craftsmen were already organized into guilds under control of the king. Some of these associations were then supplying the country's knights with equipment. It is reasonable to suppose the saddlers were one of these. The saddlers themselves make the claim of being the oldest organized guild in London. They have a document attesting to their existence in 1154. Another surviving document, believed to have been written between 1164 and 1174, concerns "The convention between the Gild of Saddlers and the Conventional Church of St. Martin-le-Grand." They received their royal charter from King Edward I in 1272. This was one of the first guild charters granted in England.

The other was for the Loriners' Guild, which made bits, spurs, stirrups, and other metal parts for saddles. It received its charter three years earlier, in 1269, but the best evidence suggests that the guild did not come into being until some time after the saddlers' original organization was in operation. At any rate, the two might be considered mere divisions of the same craft.

One of the oldest English saddles known to exist gives us a glimpse of this venerable guild's early work. Made around 1414 for Henry V, it still hangs over that monarch's tomb in Westminster Abbey. It was built on a heavy oak tree and covered with velvet embroidered in gold.

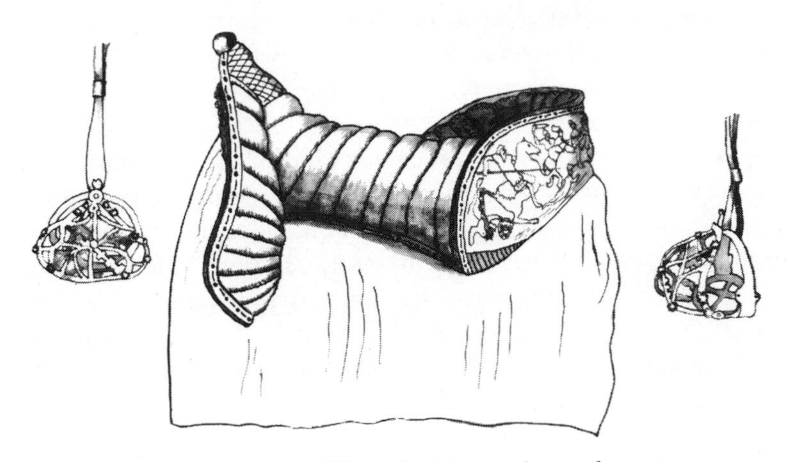

FIG. 63. German saddle and stirrups, sixteenth century.

FIG. 64. Caparisoned horse, England, sixteenth century.

All through the Middle Ages the Saddlers' Guild held the distinction of being the largest, strongest, and most aristocratic union in the world, as well as the oldest. Its art was among the finest in the land, besides being the most lucrative. They were envied by artisans of lesser stature as much as they were admired by those who rode to fame and glory on their skilled handicraft. Important citizens and members of the nobility, even up to the rank of king, often sought honorary membership in the distinguished organization. Acceptance always carried assurance of an enviable position in current society.

The Saddlers' Guild Hall in London, built in the late 1300s, was one of the nation's first guild headquarters. Though the victim of three destructive fires in days gone by, the hall has been rebuilt each time and still stands on the site it has occupied for six hundred yeads.

The leather workers and tanners worked in close conjunction with the saddlers. These crafts comprised 11 of the 111 guild trades listed in London in 1422. Most of the other guilds were created after the pattern established by the saddlers. And it was from these that the trade-union idea spread among working groups in other parts of Britain, then moved east throughout Europe and later to America.

Charles the Sage established the first leather workers' guild in France in 1397. It was controlled by the church. Prospective members had to purchase such a privilege from the king at a cost of 16 sous, besides taking an oath to observe the customs and moral precepts of the trade.

These rules were strict. The European leather craftsmen were the most exacting of any guild in their demand for quality workmanship. In sixteenth century England, for instance, the Assize of Tanners ruled that

> they tanne no Shepis Ledder, Gotis Ledder, Deres Ledder, Horsis Ledder nor Hyndes Ledder; nor that they tanne no Ledder to sell, but if it be thurgh tanned. And if they do to the contrary to any of thees, the Fyne is at every tyme 6S, 8D, and to forfet all that forfetable, and if he will not beware by two Warnyings, the third tyme to be jugyed according unto the statute.

Shoddy work in saddlery got an equally cold reception. In the 1600s the Saddlers' Guild had a law which permitted search for inferior products. Fines, and even imprisonment, were meted out for slighting standards set by the supervisory council.

On September 15, 1608, one George Marr was made to pay a substantial sum for turning out a "sidesaddle very faulty, besides evil workmanship," and as further punishment the same saddle was to be burned at his door. Richard Brighton likewise found himself faced with a fine on October 31, 1648. He was convicted of trying to slip "two naughtie strapps" on a saddle.

One of the prisons for debt and minor offenses of that period happened to be located on the east side of Wood Street near the Saddlers' Guild Hall. One contemporary wrote that the prison's convenient location made it the logical place to receive "those offending and recalcitrant members of the (Saddlers) Company and all contumacious makers of bad saddles." As late as 1822, the guild brought action against a trader in Holborn and succeeded in destroying the defective saddles he had for sale.

This code extended even into the arts. Thirteenth century painters operated under laws for protection of the public. Those who exercised their craft on saddlery, especially, were held strictly in line. One of the earliest known laws governing painters was a ruling of 1283 which decreed that

> no one shall put any but good and fine colours on gold or silver—a good blue, good simple, good green, good vermillion or other good colours tempered with oil and not brazil, indigo of Baghdad or other bad colour, no silver rough or partly old on saddles. No one shall use tinfoil or plaster on saddle bows nor any other thing except to be applied with a brush. Any false work found is to be burnt, and he who made it shall suffer the penalty of the court.

There was just no fooling around when a person set out to rig up a saddle. He either did it right, or else. In some other respects, though, the saddlers showed a far more liberal attitude than did men of other professions. In that day and age, when women were quite generally considered as beneath notice, this guild seems to have been the first to accept them along with the men on the basis of merit.

In the London Guild records for 1537 we find that "the good wife Coupir, the good wife Pounde, and the good wife Yong" were taken into the association. The guild made a point of encouraging saddlers' widows to continue their deceased husbands' trade under its protection. It required several centuries of enlightenment for such a progressive attitude to penetrate other trades.

Packsaddle making, a business in itself all through the early ages, was also under control of the saddlers. When harness makers came into prominence along with the advent of coaches and carriages, they operated more or less in conjunction with the saddlers. The latter, however, remained the aristocrats of the trade and carried the most prestige.

At least they did until the coach and harness makers began to cut the ground from under them. When the harness makers got their charter in 1677, they joined up with the coach makers to work in opposition to the saddlers. The latter put up a stiff fight against the innovation, along with the cordwainers and packsaddle makers, trying to abolish the growing threat to their trade, but the march of time was against them. Although they petitioned the king for a decree forbidding the use of coaches, and even went so far as to introduce bills in Parliament to abolish all coaches and passenger vehicles on the ground that they infringed on rights granted by the charter previously given them by the Crown, the saddlers were unable to halt progress.

Coaches had been unknown in England until Walter Rippen demonstrated their practibility by building one in 1555. Until then, wheeled transport had consisted of crude, two-wheeled carts and chariots. A sort of wheeled litter, called a whirlicote, had been developed during the reign of Richard II, but it was of little consequence to the general public. Most people walked or rode horseback. Even after the coach proved itself, it was viewed with considerable skepticism for some time, much as the automobile was to be later regarded by horse-and-buggy drivers. A coach was built for the queen's use in 1556, but the traveling public did not see much of coaches until Henry Fitzalan, twelfth Earl of Arundel, began using them in 1580. That was when their effect was really brought home to the saddle makers.

As vehicles increased in England, the growing threat to their livelihood caused many members of the London Saddlers' Guild to emigrate to Germany, Russia, France, and Spain. Fate, of course, was destined to catch up with them there, also; but in the meantime, they found temporary respite in lands still dedicated to the man on horseback. They also did much to spread the principles of the guild and the art of making fine saddles.

The influence of coaches was also felt to a certain degree among the armorers. People who could travel in groups inside carriages through dangerous country did not need the protective armor so necessary when riding alone on horseback. The growing use of gunpowder about this time was also having a bad effect on the armor business.

Armor for the protection of horses is even older than saddles. Aside from the ancient bone-scale outfits of the Sarmatians and the metal-scale type said to have been used in Darius' time, we find the Tibetans starting the long parade of horse armor as early as 400 B.C. True, it was not overly effective, being mostly padded quilting laced with metal scales or iron-studded leather, but it offered a certain measure of protection for that vital creature which kept man up out of the ruck of ground battle. The Tibetan example shown in Fig. 65 is typical of such rigs. Thickly padded quilting decorated with silk fringe and hair tassels comprised the main body part. It was edged with iron-studded leather. The head and neck coverings were also of leather studded with iron.

The Chinese had a very similar type. In later times they used small metal plates or rings tied together over quilted silk blankets. By the twelfth century, they had graduated to large metal plates tied or riveted together. Occasional outfits of this style were still to be found in China until the nineteenth century.

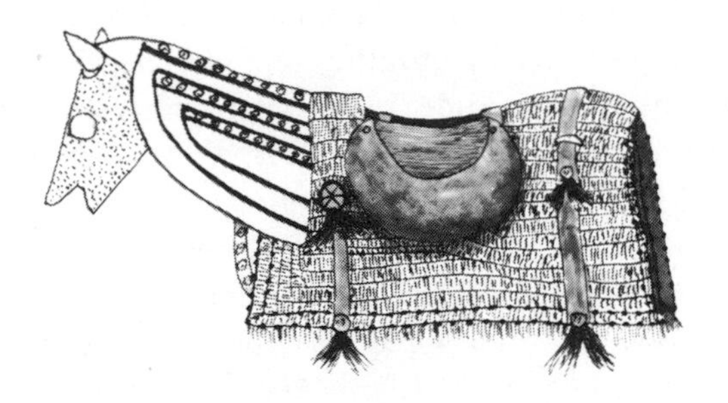

FIG. 65. Ancient Tibetan horse armor.

Japan never had much but pieces of leather sewn onto quilted cloth. Little of the later plate armor reached their island before the days of armored horses were over. Nipponese, moreover, did little horseback fighting at any time. What armor they had was used chiefly for ceremonial and parade purposes, in which case decorated leather served as well as heavy plate.

The Orient as a whole, including Persia, India, and the Mongol territories, made no extensive use of horse armor. Their mounts were mostly small in size, while their style of fighting called for speed and mobility rather than overpowering weight. Carrying heavy loads of metal was a definite handicap in such tactics. Furthermore, the intense heat common to much of this region was murderous to horses cased in steel overcoats. The Turks were about the only ones who used it in any quantity.

Europe was the principal arena for armor all through the Middle Ages. As in the Orient, armor began with padded cloth and leather. Little else was used until around 900. Yet those old leather bardings, as horse armor was called, were pretty sturdy affairs. The Salzburg outfit was said to have been up to two inches thick in its heavier parts.

The leather was boiled in resin and glue and then pounded into shape. It was almost as impenetrable as iron. In addition, metal plates were often riveted over the more vital sections.

Though there has been mention of the ancient Assyrians using chain mail in early times, there is no good evidence of its existence in a true form until it showed up in Europe well on in the Christian Era. The Assyrians undoubtedly did use some type of metal armor, as depicted in various carvings and some fragments found at Nineveh. But this was probably something of the scale variety fastened to a cloth or leather base rather than linked chain.

Marcus Varro, the Roman historian (116–27 B.C.), write that chain armor originated among the Gauls. Other writers attribute its invention to the southern Germanic tribes of ancient times. That the Gauls did use some kind of armored cuirass is substantiated by the second century B.C. Gaulish trophies appearing in relief at Pergamon, in ancient Mysia. A flexible cuirass of scale or chain armor was also used by the Roman Equites in the first century A.D. The best evidence suggests that the chain type was used contemporaneously with the old scale armor for a considerable period, both being introduced into Spain by the Visigoth invasion of the fifth century. In any event, whatever those ancient creations may have been, they were undoubtedly a far cry from the finely worked product we have come to recognize as regular chain mail, which appeared in its true form in the early 900s.

It became a great favorite among the knights. They continued to wear it to a large extent even after the more protective plate armor arrived on the scene.

Constructed of double or triple links of fine steel chain carefully annealed, and worn as a long-sleeved shirt falling below the knees, its light weight and flexibility allowed the wearer to leap onto a horse or get up from a fall to fight on foot without difficulty. Such an advantage over the heavy plate armor, which demanded help or a winch to get a dismounted man into action again, was quite obvious, overshadowing its lesser strength. Both types had their advocates all through the Middle Ages.

Chain mail helmets were usually conical in shape and had only nasal protectors in front; the rest of the face was left unguarded. One of these helmets is shown on the knight in Fig. 57. They were more comfortable than the casque type of heavy metal (Fig. 60), but lacked some of the boxlike protection found in the latter. Contemporary illustrations picture both styles in use through most of the knighthood era.

Horses, on the other hand, were made to wear the more burdensome plate almost exclusively after its introduction in the 1200s. Such horse armor became very elaborate all over Europe until it reached its zenith in the sixteenth century.

An outfit made in 1514 for Charles V of Germany by the Augsburg armorer, Daniel Hopfer, had all component parts gilded and etched in overlapping festoons in an openwork design. Further etchings depicted cherubim striking with sparkling flint bars, and roses surrounded by pomegranates in each of the festoons. The whole rig weighed about eighty pounds.

Another German-made barding was created for Charles V in 1518. Its chamfron, or head covering, carried a two-headed eagle on the crown flanked by ear coverings made to resemble ram horns. The breast collar, or poitrel, was of steel scales. Pearls, pendants, and Biblical figures carved in relief covered the croupiere which went back over the horse's rump. Further decorations of pearls and engraved pendants graced the flanchards, which extended down over the horse's sides. The various parts were joined together by embossed hinges in the shape of lion heads.

Fig. 66 shows a less elaborate outfit made by Hopfer in 1521, for Charles V of Spain. It was designed for tilting rather than the more strenuous work of actual warfare. It was mounted over a rich blanket that covered most of the horse, plus a saddlecloth with fringed and decorated edges.

A barding made for Charles V in 1541 was perhaps one of the finest examples of the armorer's art. It was of steel, scalloped at the edges and lined with silk. Its surface was almost entirely covered with heroic figures carved in relief. On the right side was Hercules battling serpents, subduing the bull, slaying the Hydra, and wrestling with Antaeus. The left side pictured Samson tearing down the temple of Dagon, carrying away the gates of Gaza, fighting the lion, and receiving a haircut from Delilah. Embossing on the chamfron showed Samson as a child, while a dolphin's head surmounted the croupiere above the horse's tail. The whole affair was a magnificent creation.

Charles also had an elaborately engraved iron war saddle to complete his iron-clad outfit (Fig. 71).

Most chamfrons were similar to the designs in Figs. 62, 64, and 66. A lighter type consisting of only a narrow face plate was occasionally used. It was hinged at the crown where it connected with the crinet (crinière), or mainfare (mainferre), which covered the animal's neck. Some were studded with sharp spikes. A horse dressed up in one of these must have presented a rather awesome appearance coming head-on, especially if the customary mad stallion.

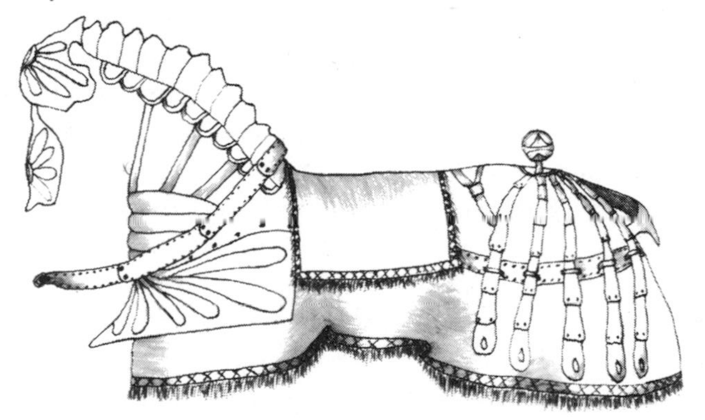

FIG. 66. Horse armor of Charles V of Spain, 1521.

Such armor also extended to the bridle reins. Plain leather reins sufficed in the early days of crude weapons. Time, however, taught the danger of having one's reins chopped off by an opponent's sword or battleax in the moment of conflict. This led to the disaster of being adrift on an unmanageable horse. Special rein cutters were later affixed to the backs of halberds.

As a defensive measure, scraps of metal were first riveted to the leather reins. The improved armor of the sixteenth century, however, brought with it the better-designed rein guards of steel plates hinged together and hung the length of the reins. These, like the bits, spurs, and stirrups of that period, were usually engraved or embossed with attractive figures designed to match the rest of the armor. The heavy curb bits and stirrups in particular were often magnificent creations encrusted with gold, silver, and precious stones.

Altogether, horse armor was a rich and beautiful thing, unexcelled for the purpose intended and a masterpiece of the craftsman's art. Through its crusaders, artisans, and wandering knights, western Europe spread its influence throughout the civilized world. It took the advent of gunpowder to send it the way of a good but no longer useful servant. When matchlocks and snaphances began flinging leaden pellets through the plated fronts of slow-moving knights with disastrous results, the mounted warriors started shucking their cumbersome trappings for the sake of easier movability.

Yet horse armor did serve a great purpose, and really more than one. During its period of use, it did much to develop better horses throughout Europe. The undersized, lightly built native animals did not stand up well when compelled to carry the weight of battle armor on forced marches. They also lacked the weight so essential in crashing attacks against infantry battalions or in charging mounted enemies. As knighthood grew in prominence, the cry for bigger and stronger horses became correspondingly louder.

Fifteenth century England even went so far as to pass laws governing all horse breeding in the interest of better stock. Among these regulations we find that in 1540 the breeding of any mares of less than fourteen hands in height was prohibited. Another law commanded every duke and archbishop to keep seven stoned (stud) trotting horses for the saddle, none under fourteen hands tall. Nor were lesser individuals exempt. The ruling went on to state that "any layman who receives 100 pounds yearly, or whose wife shall wear any French hood or bonnet of velvet, is obliged under penalty of 20 pounds to keep a stoned trotting horse for the saddle." Other classes of citizens were rated accordingly. Anyone who had a park or suitable enclosure was required to keep at least two brood mares.

These larger horses, especially the tall ones, offered a decided advantage to riders in combat. The taller a horse was, the more valuable it was apt to become. As the more affluent knights and members of royalty were best able to afford preferred mounts, the larger horses came to be associated in mens' minds with persons of high quality. The common expression, "to ride a high horse," has thus come down to us from those times as a show of pride, ostentation, or superiority.

As stallions were naturally the largest available animals in most sections, they became the preferred mounts for warfare and knightly ventures. Their size, strength, and spirit were also more in keeping with the pomp and style that attended the world of gallant horsemen. As a matter of fact, it was considered vile and dishonorable for knights to ride mares in the time of King Edward III. All through that era mares were used almost exclusively for draft purposes.

Other types of horses, of course, came in for their share of riding. Even the knights and nobility used lesser animals to a large extent on everyday occasions. The big war horses were commonly reserved for war, ceremonial parades, jousting contests, and individual combat. Geldings and smaller animals were more often used for ordinary riding.

Palfreys were especially favored by the clergy and ladies and as mounts for lackeys. Not a few men preferred them for casual riding. They were quiet and gentle animals of smallish size, much like the Irish ponies. White ones were particularly prized. Most people of any consequence maintained a variety of horses in keeping with their station in life.

An old manuscript entitled *The Regulations and Establishment of the Houshold of Algernon Percy, Fifth Earl of Northumberland, 1512,* gives the following description of a nobleman's stable in England of that period:

> This is the ordre of the chequir roul of the nombre of all the horsys of my lordis and my ladys, that are apoynted to be in the charge of the hors yerely, as to say: gentill hors, palfreys, hobys, naggis, cloth-sek hors, male-hors. First, gentill hors to stand in my lordis stable, six. Palfreys of my ladys, to wit, one for my lady and two for her gentill-women, and oone for her chamberer. Four hobys and naggis for my lordis oone saddle, viz, oone for my lordis to ride, oone to lede for my lorde, and oone to stay at home for my lorde. Item, chariott hors to stand in my lordis stable yerely. Seven great trottynge hors to draw in the chariott, and a nag for the chariott man to ride, eight. Hors for Lord Percy to travel in winter. A great doble trottynge hors, called a curtal, for his lordship to ride on out of townes. Another trottynge gambaldynge hors for his lordship to ride upon when he comes into townes. An amblynge hors for his lordship to journey on dayly. A proper amblynge little nagg for his lordship when he gaeth on hunting or hawking. A great amblynge gelding, or trottynge gelding, to carry his male.

These various horses are classified as follows: Gentill, a superior, better-bred animal. Palfrey, an easy-gaited, gentle and pleasant-mannered horse. Hobys and naggs, small, strong, active descendants of native wild Irish ponies. Cloth-sek, a male horse that carried the rider's cloth-bag or personal baggage. Great double trottynge, a big, awkward beast too unwieldy to gallop. Gambaldynge, a showy parade animal. Curtal, a horse whose tail had been docked.

Docking of horses' tails and cropping their ears, which had been common in medieval times, went out of fashion about 1500. Such practices grew to be considered detrimental, being rated as actual blemishes by the time of Queen Elizabeth's reign. It was in this latter period that certain lofty minds introduced the practice of feeding horses a sort of baked loaf, called horse bread, instead of grain.

Other experts were on hand to advise the uninitiated about selecting desirable horses. Most of them were unanimous in their contention that bay was the most natural and perfect color for a horse; if it had some white hairs above the root of its tail, it was especially good. Dark browns were perhaps the next best. White indicated speed, a good mouth, and luck for the rider. Blacks were equally good for speed, but lacked the good mouths and were inclined toward spookiness and treachery. Hard mouths were supposed to be characteristic of black-headed roans, while poor mouths, timidity, and a propensity for disease tended to show up in piebalds. Dark chestnuts were very desirable, swift, and strong, but often had poor mouths. Creams had most of the good qualities except speed.

Grooming, feeding and riding all received a generous amount of attention from authoritative voices. One English writer of the 1600s advised:

> For getting onto the back of a horse, without knowing what the animal is enabled by nature, art and practice to perform, is not riding. The knowledge and utility of which consists in being able to discern, and dextrous to employ the means by which the horse may be brought to execute what the rider requires of him, with propriety, readiness, and safety; and this knowledge in the man, and obedience in the horse, like soul and body should be so indispensably necessary, that where it is not, there is no meaning between the man and the horse, they talk different languages and all is confusion—while many fatal accidents may ensue; the man may be wedged in the timber, which he strives to rend, and fall the victim of his own ignorance and rashness.

Similar instructions in almost as confusing language paved the way for all prospective horsemen who had the ability and courage to study treatises on the subject. Those who couldn't read no doubt had to learn it the hard way; for the knighthood brethren did not take kindly to any slipshod handling of their mounts.

All in all, horses received more consideration than did most people in old-time England. James III issued a decree about 1475 that any farrier who, through drunkenness or ignorance, pricked a horse's foot while shoeing it was obliged to deposit the value of the animal and furnish the owner with another mount until the injured beast was cured. In case the cure proved unsuccessful, he had to pay the owner in full for the horse.

During the reign of Edward VI, conviction of horse stealing drew penalties comparable to the blackest crimes of sacrilege, murder, and housebreaking. It also meant forfeiting all the benefits of clergy.

These and other laws pertaining to the breeding, care, and welfare of horses prevailed throughout most of early-day Europe. Horses meant power in any country. The development of better stock for the homeland and the correction of any abuses was of major importance to all nations. There were few which did not prohibit the export of breeding stock prior to 1600.

Conversely, all were eager to obtain Arabian and Barb blood to improve their own native breeds. The admixture of the desert strain gave them some of the speed, action, and durability so sadly lacking in the northern animals. But it was a slow business; distances were great; international traffic was difficult; and the Arabs were as averse to parting with their better horses as anyone else. Most of those obtained in the early years came from the Moors, after they moved into Spain in the eighth century; and occasional mounts were brought back from the East by returning crusaders. But few though they were, it was the Arabians who did most to give Europe the superior grade of horses which carried her horsemen to conquest and romance for over six hundred years. And it was the blood of Arabian and Barb studs imported into Europe which laid the foundation for our great line of Thoroughbreds.

An importation of this type is said to have given English-speaking youngsters the Shetland pony. Originally, the ponies of the Shetland Islands were a small, tough, grubby strain, no doubt related to those of Ireland and Iceland, and probably an offshoot from the ancient native horse of Britain. Climatic, forage, and survival problems had sacrificed size and looks for durability.

When the admiral of the Spanish Armada attempted to conquer England in 1588, he brought with him some of his choice horses for use after the victory. Unfortunately for him, things did not go as planned. The armada was put to rout. Among the scattered ships which escaped to the north was the one carrying the admiral's horses. It ran aground on the Shetland Islands; and in order to float it the Spaniards were forced to lighten the ship by putting the horses ashore.

It is believed that those which survived the harsh environment were crossed with the native ponies to produce a strain combining the finer qualities of the southern animals with the size and hardiness of the islanders. Ensuing centuries of scanty fare and inclement surroundings developed this superior miniature breed.

It was evidently a similar situation to that which created the band of dwarf horses found in a cliff-walled cul-de-sac near America's Grand Canyon of the Colorado in the 1940s. Apparently animals had been marooned there by some strange act of God or an early traveler in ages past. Food scarcity, time, and the determination of nature to perpetuate the species had diminished the stature of the horses to the height of a card table while retaining their conformity to that of normal horses in all other respects.

—13—

Age of the Cavalier

THE DEVELOPMENT OF firearms is usually credited with sounding the death knell of armor and the golden age of knighthood. Yet there was another cause, often overlooked, which probably did as much as all the guns in Europe to change the outlook of the man on horseback. And this cause, as it had in all the great epochs of civilization, revolved around the Eastern horse and its rider.

When the Moors invaded Spain from 710 to 750 they brought with them their Arabian and Barb horses, as well as their native riding gear. This was a leading factor in their successful conquests in Spain and later in France. At that time, the French and Spanish were riding big, slow horses with the heavy, cumbersome, boxlike, wooden saddles in favor with all the European knights. The Moors, on the other hand, had their swift, nimble horses and lightweight saddles which permitted extreme flexibility of action. Practicing their old hit-and-run desert tactics, they were able to ride rings around their slower adversaries and cut them to pieces in swift, slashing attacks or pick off the smaller detachments of Spaniards in lightninglike surprise raids.

The old European style of riding in high-peaked saddles with body-encircling cantles and long stirrups was called riding *à la brida* by the Spaniards. There were three main variations in *la brida* saddles. One, the *silla de croata,* was a rather plain wooden rig used for common every-day riding and ordinary cavalry units. Of better design was the *silla de estradiota.* Its fork and cantle were made of metal, being shaped to pretty well enclose the thighs of the rider. With this, a light horse armor was used. The man also wore some armor. The important fighting men usually rode the *silla de armas,* which was specially adapted to the heaviest horse armor and knights clad in full mail.

In direct contrast were the Arabian-Moorish saddles. They were the lightweight, well-fitted rigs with high forks and moderately low cantles that had evolved through the centuries among the world's most experienced horsemen. Most of them were built with rolls or slight swells on the fork. Being unencumbered with armor, they were ideal for use with the small, quick-footed mounts. They were also more comfortable riding and easier on the horse than anything Europe had ever known. The short stirrups used brought the rider's knees up snugly under the swells and his body somewhat forward over the horse's withers. This permitted him to stand high in the stirrups when striking down with lance or sword, besides assuring him the maximum of security when seated in the saddle. The Spaniards called this style of horsemanship riding *à la jineta.*

The performance of men who rode *la jineta* style was so much more adept than those of the *la brida* school that *jineta, gineta* or *zeneta,* as variously spelled, came to be known as the common name for superior horsemen in the Spanish territories. Not that this had much effect on the nobility and more ostentatious knights. They clung to their big horses and shining armor, chiefly for its pomp and magnificence, well into the sixteenth century. Ordinary horsemen in the south, however, had pretty well surrendered to the influence of *la jineta* by 900. From there it spread slowly northward. By the time the Moors were driven out of Spain in 1492, practically all of Europe had adopted their style of riding and much of their equipment. Their saddles in particular were generally preferred by the majority.

Much of this was due to the fact that the lighter, less complicated saddles were cheaper and, with small horses socially acceptable, a person could ride whatever kind of mount he happened to have without feeling inferior. After about 1200, pad saddles, hornless saddles, light-frame saddles, padded seats, padded pommels and cantles, and saddles without any cantles whatever began to appear in various sections of the Continent. Armored knights and heavy cavalry were about the only users of the old equipment through this later period.

By the time the influence of Moorish riding gear started to penetrate the north, Spain was turning out an excellent grade of saddle. Spanish tanners and leathermakers were producing the choicest materials on the Continent, while their artisans were doing the same with construction development. By about 1100 the whole of Europe was basing most of its saddle-making precepts on the southern principles.

The ancient kingdom of Galicia, in the northwest corner of Spain, was one such source of fine saddlery during this period. A reference to Galician saddles is found in the *Poema del Cid,* which relates the achievements of the redoubtable Spanish soldier-hero the Cid, Ruy Díaz de Bivar (1040–1099). In speaking of the count of Barcelona's approaching army, it says, "For saddles they have Moorish pads, with slackened girths they ride; our saddles are Galician made, our leggings tough and stout; a hundred of us gentlemen should scatter such a rout."

Down on the southeast coast, the kingdom of Murcia enjoyed a similar reputation. Ibn Said, who was born at Granada in 1214, wrote that in his time Murcia was "renowned for its saddles and harness richly gilt."

Three principal types of *la jineta* saddles were developed in Spain to meet popular demands. The *silla de jineta campo* was an extra-sturdy but rather plain sidebar rig with few decorative embellishments. It was used chiefly for everyday work and mounting common soldiers. The predominating style among most better-class horsemen was the *silla de jineta para caballeros.* While based on the *silla de campo* frame, this saddle was covered with a special black Barbary leather and had highly varnished stirrups. With it went a black bridle and reins, martingale and tie strap, all made from the soft, velvety morocco leather. The bit was a highly polished curb of the Mameluke variety inlaid with gold.

Most elaborate of all among the three styles was the *silla de jineta para fiesta.* This was somewhat comparable to the Spanish-Mexican saddle shown in Fig. 104 and might be considered the oldest ancestor of our modern Western saddle. It sported a rich array of silver mountings, black Barbary leather and velvet skirts delicately embroidered with gold and silver. A heavy sword in its ornate scabbard was commonly slung from the horn. The stirrups were almost entirely covered with engraving and highly embossed relief work.

Stirrups of the period were, in fact, the high point of the designer's art in saddle making. The old triangular iron type had about disappeared by the late 1200s, giving way to more elaborate creations. By the fourteenth century, footplates had become broader and the sides heavier to accommodate more ornamentation. A horse's head was one of the de-

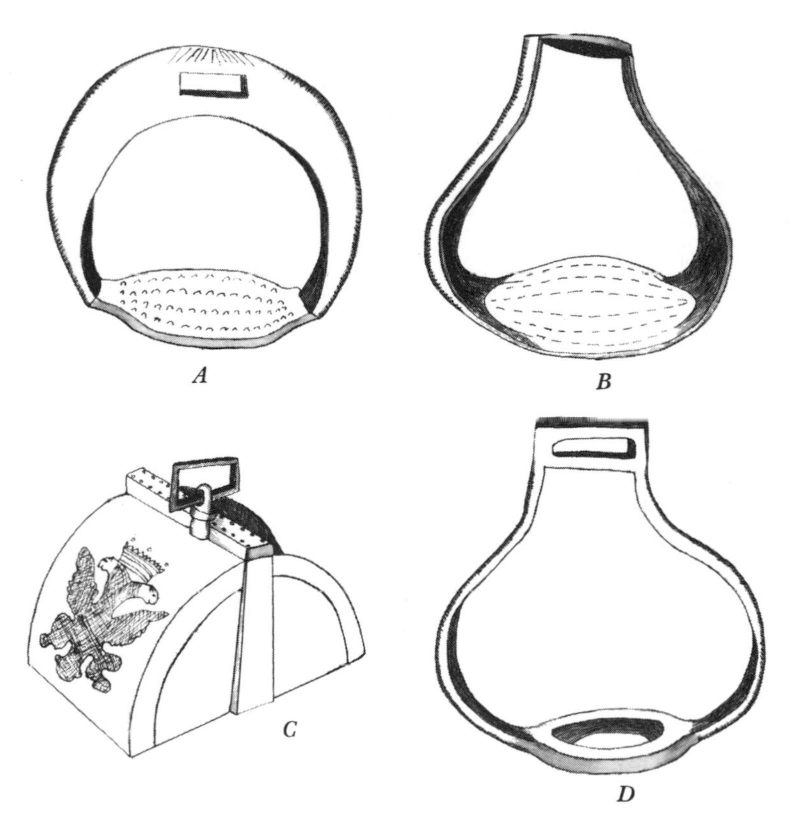

FIG. 67. *A* ancient hand-forged iron stirrup, southern Europe; *B* hand-forged iron, Germany; *C* stirrup of Peter the Great, Russia, 1700; *D* old European army stirrup.

signs most likely to show up in these decorations. Ornamentation reached its height in the seventeenth century, when much metal openwork in fanciful patterns took the place of solid sides. Figs. 67–70 show some typical examples of the fourteenth to eighteenth century designs.

But regardless of design or period, the Old World almost always used some form of metal in stirrup construction. Wide use of wooden stirrups was an American custom.

The sixteenth century Spanish war saddles used by the military were modified versions of the old *la brida* rigs incorporated with *la jineta.* They retained the heavy trees of the former, as well as the metal plating on the outside of pommels and cantles (Figs. 71–72). The cantles on these, however, were considerably lower and only partly encircled the rider. They were also padded on the inside instead of being left bare.

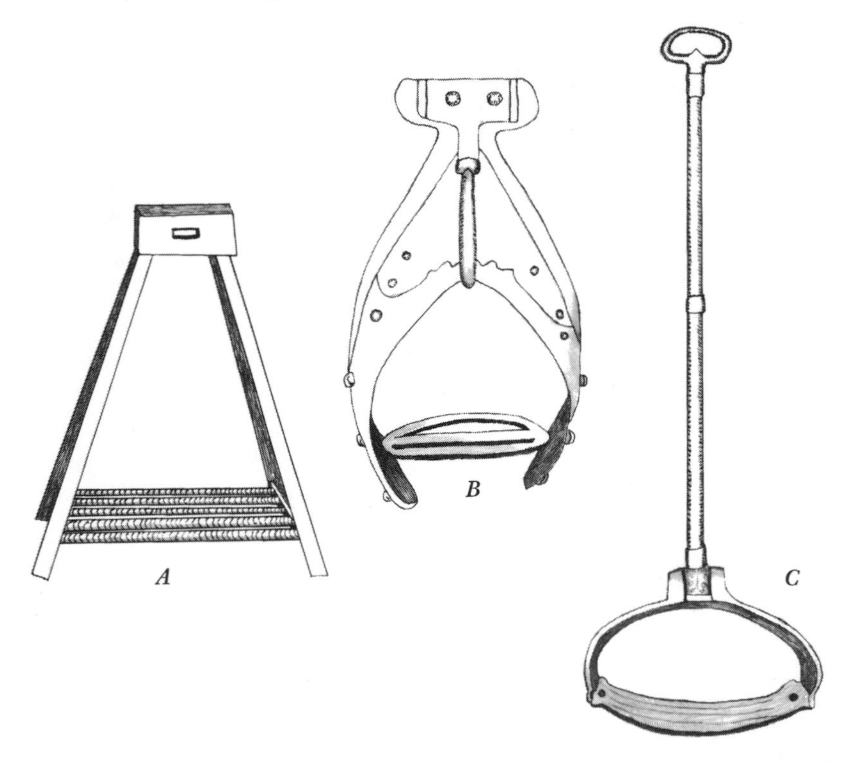

FIG. 68. Stirrups: *A* wood, Italian, fourteenth century; *B* Italian, sixteenth century; *C* ancient European rod stirrup.

Similar padding covered the seat, usually extending up over the inside of the pommel. Heavily embroidered or brocaded skirts of colored velvet predominated. Skirts were lined with woolskins, leather, or velvet. Extra padded rolls for thigh comfort were commonly attached to the upper part of the skirts. All metal work was invariably etched or engraved in fancy designs, Biblical scenes and mythological figures being especially favored for the larger surfaces of cantle backs and pommel fronts. Pommels were of various shapes. Swell forks ranged from winglike projections to true built-in swells. Horns were equally varied, being squarish, ball-shaped, U-shaped, or flat, bladelike projections. Many were set at a definite angle.

This was the type of saddle the conquistadors brought to America. Garcilaso de la Vega, the mixed-blood son of a conquistador and an Inca woman, who later wrote a history of the conquest, stated, "My country

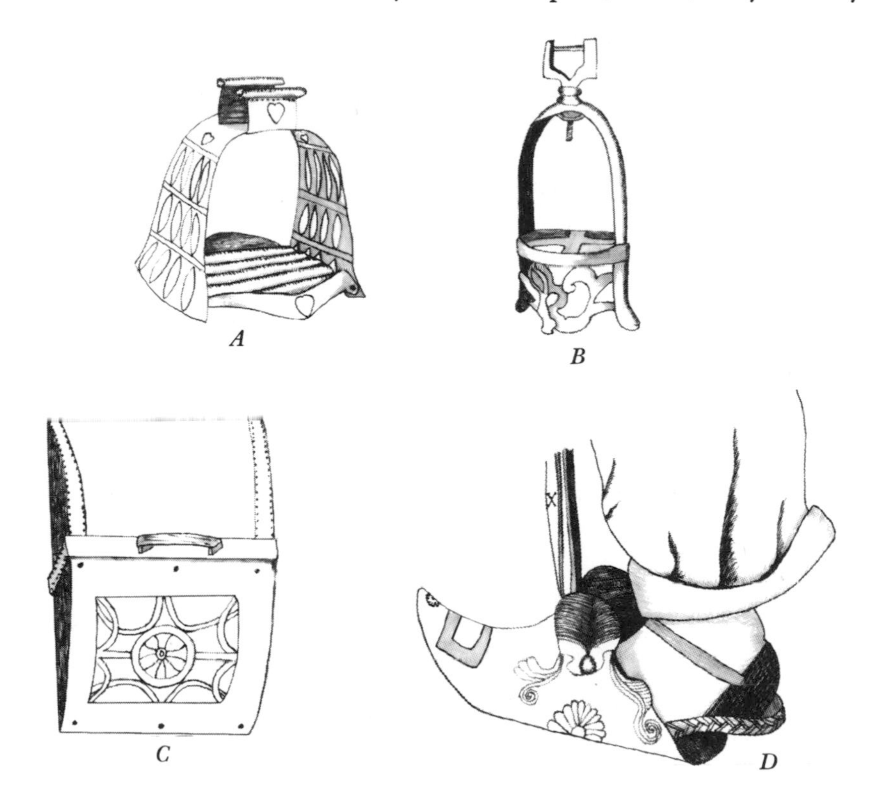

FIG. 69. Spanish stirrups: *A* 1525; *B* seventeenth century; *C* mule stirrup; *D* Spanish-Moorish bronze, eighteenth and nineteenth centuries.

was won *à la gineta;* that is, by men riding in the fashion of the Moors." These saddles all used the customary single cinch and, in most cases, breast collar and crupper.

It was the Moorish influence which gave the individual European his greatest opportunity. The Eastern saddle was much better adapted to everyday use than those of the knights, and was far easier to copy in simple forms. As riding gained in popularity among the civilian population, the ingenuity of saddle makers began to feed the growing need with a variety of styles.

The simplest of these was a type of pad saddle used extensively by the common people of Spain during the sixteenth century. It soon

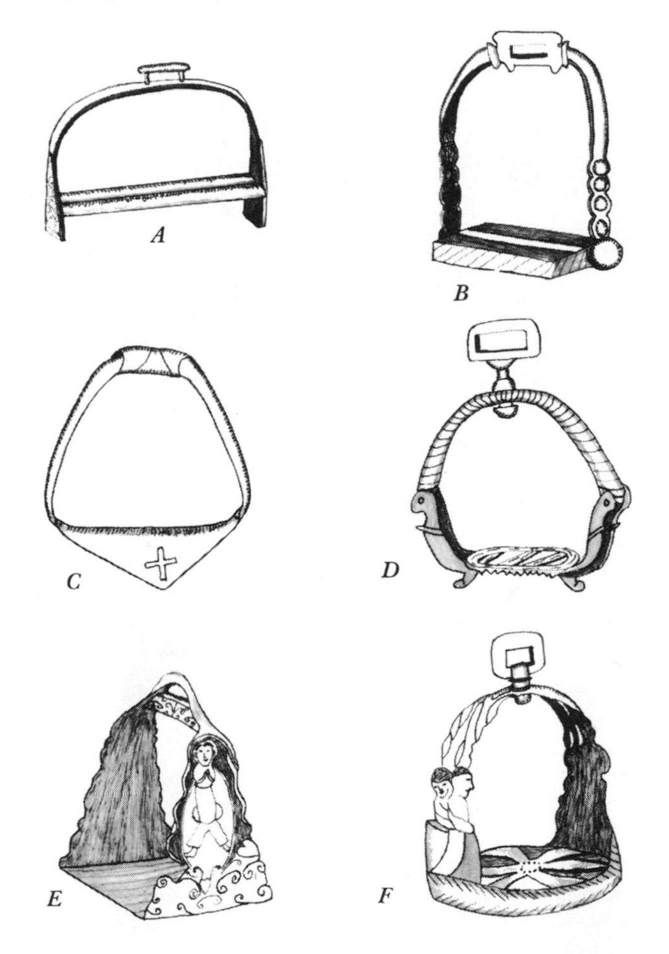

FIG. 70. Italian and French stirrups: *A* and *B* Italy, fourteenth and seventeenth centuries; *C* France, 1425; *D* France, 1675; *E* and *F* France, seventeenth and eighteenth centuries.

moved north into other countries to become the forerunner of the English riding saddle of modern times.

In the Aragon region of Spain there was a rather crude skeletonlike tree, covered with a bright-colored blanket when in use. The whole rig was cinched down by a surcingle that went over the top of the blanket. On festive occasions it was trimmed with a matching serapelike covering having long fringes that extended back over the rump of the horse; the fringes often hung down to the animal's fetlocks. Additional fringes and tassels decorated the breast collar. The matching bridle would frequently carry enough colored tassels to almost hide the animal's head. Outfits of this sort were no doubt the progenitors of the South American Gaucho saddles. Spain continued to use them well into the twentieth century.

Over on the island of Majorca a rather odd type of saddle (Fig. 73) was quite popular in the 1400s. It evidently drew from the combined Spanish, Moorish, and Italian designs, with perhaps a touch of Hungarian added. The suspended seat slung between pommel and cantle strongly suggests Hungarian influence. The low cantle and very short Oriental-type stirrup straps are definitely Moorish. Stirrups closely resemble the Italian design shown in Fig. 68. The fork was covered with rawhide, plain leather being used for seat and skirts. Plush, velvet, or hair-hide covered the cantle.

Another early Spanish saddle was one called the *bur*. It was a sort of combination of the knight's and the Moorish rig. Built to hold the rider very much erect, it had wings out over his knees and used the long stirrups of the knights, but had the Moors' low cantle, padded seat, and small pommel. A somewhat similar saddle, which may have evolved from the *bur,* was used by stockmen of Australia in the early days of "down under."

Further developments up into the sixteenth century gave the Spaniards the style shown on Fig. 74. The long stirrups and small pommel remained, but the fork wings had been discarded and the seat sloped for more comfortable riding. The design was on the crude side, the outside skirts having apparently been hung on as an afterthought, but it denotes sound progress in the development of plain working saddles.

The elite, however, were not so much interested in serviceability as they were in style and comfort. The old utility and war saddles were heavy and cumbersome in appearance. Their structure also had a way of concealing a large portion of the starched and ruffled garments whose splendor was so important. Being stuffed into the close confines of a wrap-around saddle was also woefully detrimental to the pleats, puffs, creases, and silken surfaces of clothing primarily designed for social display.

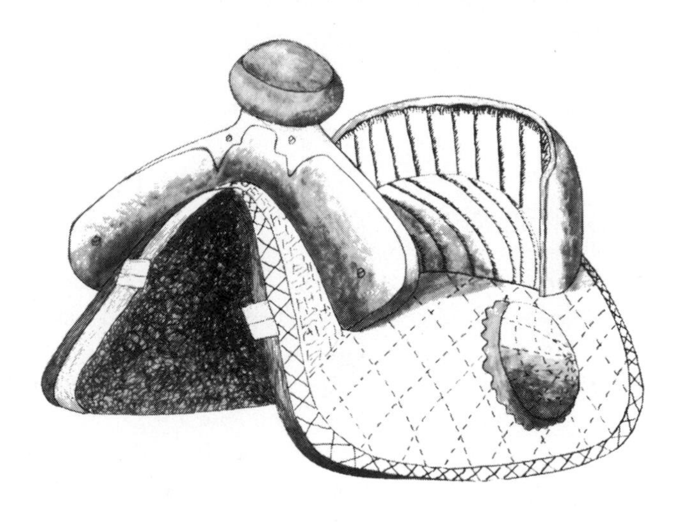

FIG. 71. Two Spanish war saddles. The one above belonged to Charles V, 1540.

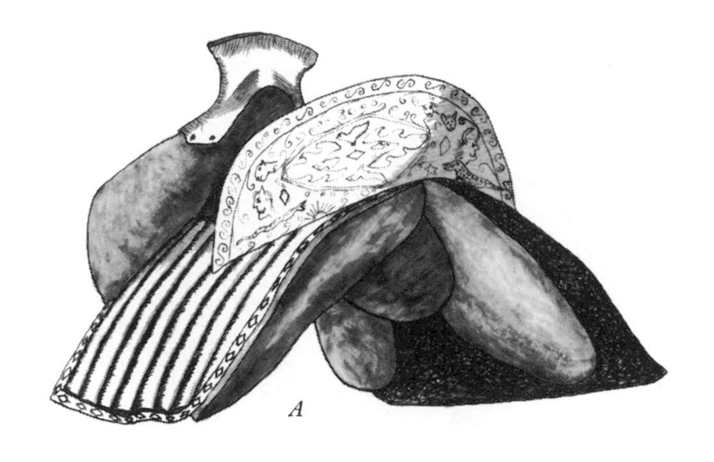

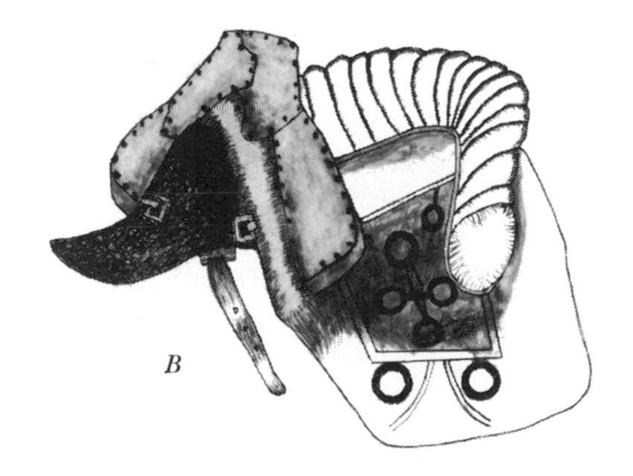

FIG. 72. *A* Italian saddle, 1540; *B* German saddle, sixteenth century.

In consequence, the superstructure of gentlemen's saddles was cut down or eliminated altogether. Many of these saddles were made without cantles, some had no horns, others had both features pared down to where they offered little threat to either delicate garments or courtly muscles. A thirteenth century example is pictured in the French manuscript of the Apocalypse, which shows a horseman receiving a crown from heaven (Fig. 75). It has only a vestige of the old high cantle, while the horn appears to be little more than a metal bar with hooked end. The rest of the outfit is typical of the period.

Another example is the German model painted by Lucas Cranach in 1508 (Fig. 76).

FIG. 73. Majorcan saddle, fifteenth century.

The fourteenth century English saddle (Fig. 77) portrayed in the "Arthur of Little Britain" manuscript shows little improvement over the styles of a hundred years previously. The covering of leather held to the same design as the earlier one of velvet. The richly decorated trappings, curb bit, and triangular stirrups were fairly representative of first-class European equipment before 1350.

A contemporary saddle of plain design was much in favor for casual riding in France during the thirteenth and fourteenth centuries. It was fitted with pommel and cantle that resembled small, half-circular discs, both very much alike. A string of little bells on the crupper was a common embellishment at that time.

A Spanish saddle shown in the Velásquez painting of King Philip

IV's son, in 1629, lacks a horn and most of the cantle. The seat and skirtlike jockeys were covered with what appears to be velvet, under which is a main skirt of rich fabric fringed at the bottom and extending down over the stirrup straps almost to the stirrups themselves. The kneepads, affixed to the forward part of the skirts, are of bucking roll design and about four inches in diameter. They are somewhat flattened on the back side and slanted to fit the rider's legs. The openwork stirrups are of iron with flat treads about two inches wide, reflecting a popular pattern of the 1600s.

To return for a moment to the use of bells on horse trappings, we

FIG. 74. Spanish saddle, sixteenth century.

find them adorning the mounts of all peoples from earliest times. Mention of horse bells may be found in many of the oldest poems, histories, and accounts of antiquity's man on horseback. All the way down from the Mongolian plains to Persia, the Arabian domains, and across the wide expanse of Europe the musical tinkling of horse bells enlivened the myriad trails of horsemen drifting ever westward through the pages of time. Even our American Indians picked up the age-old practice and carried the soothing jingle across another continent.

That bells were considered of signal importance by Europe's medieval riders is evinced by their frequent mention by such eminent authors as Chaucer and Congreve. Bell races in the early 1600s were the most important track event in England. The big prize for the winning horse was

FIG. 74. Spanish saddle, sixteenth century.

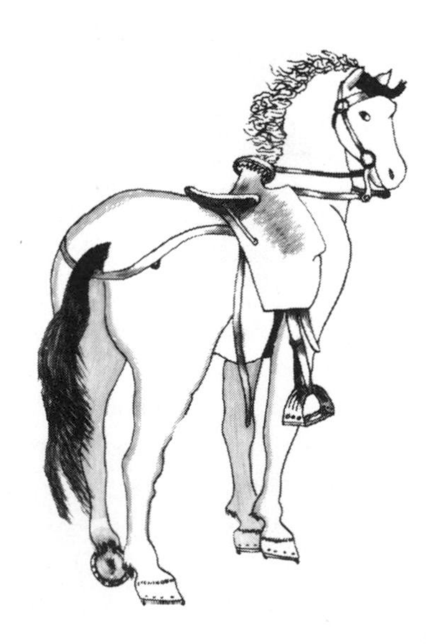

FIG. 75. From France, thirteenth century.

a bell. Old records indicate that the bell was as highly regarded as cash prizes in later years.

The old custom of the prize bell being awarded by the king or lord may have had something to do with racing being called the sport of kings. On the other hand, such a designation might have arisen from the fact that kings and affluent leaders were the only ones able to promote racing to any extent. But however that may be, horse racing as a spectacular event has been one of man's most popular sports since the dawn of history, regardless of station in life.

FIG. 77. English outfit, fourteenth century.

Presenting trophy cups to race winners was another English innovation arising from the old bell races. King Charles I started the practice about 1630, when he began substituting silver cups for the bells formerly used as bell-race prizes. Such appropriate trophies, first used for drinking the health of successful contestants, soon became immensely popular in all forms of competitive games.

Starting as a catch-as-catch-can contest between individuals in the dawn of horse-borne transportation, racing found its first historical recognition as an organized sport in the Olympic games of 684 B.C. It was on this Olympic racecourse that we find mention of the original starting barrier being used. The Romans later installed a copy of the Grecian barrier for their chariot races, continuing its use after horseback racing was introduced.

Siena, Italy, claims to have the world's oldest horse-racing course in continuous use. There has been racing on it since the early 1200s. Their modern Palio race was started in 1605, when its course circled the public square. Races became regularly scheduled events there in 1651.

Though England was to become one of the foremost horse-racing nations on the globe, it got off to a comparatively slow start because all northern horses were trotters by nature. Then, during the long knighthood period, when influential horsemen were breeding for size and strength and the general public was forced to get along with nags and ponies, speed was given little consideration. There was naturally some racing, as is ever present among men on horseback. But it was not until 1510, during the reign of Henry VIII, that the sport as we know it was established in England. Even then, history gives us little to go on until English racing records were started in 1709.

There is mention of their using the old Grecian four-mile course in 1769, but such long races were evidently none too popular as regular features. The shorter courses seem to have become more or less standard about that time. But long or short, the English stand in most minds as the people most enthusiastic about horse racing.

It was they who introduced the sport into America, where it was first established in New York in 1665. It appeared in Virginia soon afterward, whence it spread to the other colonies. It was the South, however, which fostered most of the important racing until after the Civil War.

In those days much of eastern America was covered with timber. Particularly in the North, clearings were small, straight roadways almost nonexistent, and room for racecourses as a rule severely limited. In consequence, most of the racing was done by quarter horses which were bred for short bursts of speed. This led to the development of that strictly American breed which was to loom so prominently in the western horseman's world of later years.

The first Thoroughbred was imported into America in 1730. It was a stud named Bulle Rock, twenty-one years old at the time. His breeding success sparked further importations which, in turn, resulted in the establishment of all-Thoroughbred racing in this country. The first race of this nature was sponsored by Governor Ogle of Annapolis, Maryland, in 1745.

A similar sequence of events emanating from England led to the establishment of Canada's first stake race in 1836.

A question often asked by horsemen is why the Spaniards were the only Europeans to practice neck reining. The most logical opinion suggests it developed through the use of the big curb bits in vogue through the Middle Ages. Moorish and Spanish love for ornate equipment called for bits to match the rest of their outfits. They also valued the severity of harsh bits where severity was needed. Being basically superior horsemen, they simply devised a method of using the severe contrivances in a manner that worked no harm on the animals' mouths under ordinary circumstances. Moreover, with the highly intelligent desert horses, the touch of a rein on his neck was the easiest and most efficient method of guidance in swift action. It all worked out very nicely to give the Spaniard his show of elegance without abusing his horses.

For some unfortunate reason this way of guiding horses was never adopted by any of the heavier-handed northern peoples. Even to this day, most of them still haul their mounts around by pulling on one side of the bit. With the extra-severe bits of the Middle Ages in current use, such practices worked a great hardship on the tender mouths of valuable animals.

Nevertheless, King Charles I issued a decree in 1628 that all snaffle bits in the English army be replaced by curbs. He had decided the latter were more becoming military features and better suited to the general managements of mounts.

The ruling, however, must have been more of a unification measure than a necessity, for Europe as a whole had been curb-bit territory from the start. And it was Europe that went on to develop the weird array of sixteenth century bits which no other age has ever duplicated.

At the same time, many soft-hearted individuals and humane societies raised their voices in growing protest against the big curbs. By the beginning of the 1700s, the reversal to snaffles, bars, and gentle port bits had gained throughout Europe. Even the military, which still cherished old King Charles's opinion about the more suitable appearance of curbs, had modified the bits until they were little harsher than the ordinary civilian models.

The same thing happened with spurs. During the cavalier period they grew to enormous proportions. Then, when conservatism began to lift its drab, cheerless head in the seventeenth century, all of northern Europe started reducing its spurs to bare utilitarian dimensions. Only the Spanish territories held to the big, fancy styles in later years.

Spurs with the Spaniards were something like firearms in the hands of expert gunmen; they knew how to use them properly. And Spaniards seem to have been about the only Europeans capable of displaying their favorite implements in extravagant form without feeling compelled to use them as instruments of assault and mayhem.

Their saddles, too, retained the large, well-fitted patterns long after their neighbors cut down to simple forms better adapted to gentlemanly ease and style. The Andalusian rig, in particular, had evolved through some seven hundred years into a saddle that was designed both for comfort of the horse and the hard, exacting tasks of a working rider. In all these, the ornamentation so dear to Spanish hearts continued to grow and flourish through the years.

This is not to say, however, that decorative features were absent in the north. This was the age of the gay cavalier, the dandified gallant, who lavished his wealth on personal appearance and rode with a dirk in his belt and a short, heavy sword in the scabbard beneath his left knee. His riding gear was the display case of his position in life. He denied himself nothing that might add to its handsomeness and eye appeal. From the saddlers' shops throughout Europe he gathered a glittering array of golden bits, spurs, and stirrups. For his saddles he demanded coverings of blue, red, green, yellow, and other colored leathers, all decorated with mountings of silver, gold, and precious gems, golden embroideries, gilded metal, engraving, etching, and leather carving in most intricate designs.

A choice leather for fancy saddlery of this period was the product called shagreen, made by the Persians. As described by Sir John Chardin, it was made from the rump skins of asses, dressed with lime, and tanned with salt and galls. After the skins were dehaired, scraped, and stretched on a frame, they were covered with goosefoot seed. Then they were moistened and covered with felt, after which pressure was applied to sink the seeds into the skin. Subsequently, they were shaved down to the level of the depressions and then made to swell by soaking. The resultant leather bore a strong resemblance to parchment and had a peculiar granular appearance. After being dyed in attractive colors it made a most handsome material for various articles of riding gear.

One unidentified writer of that period summed it all up in one succinct paragraph:

> Horsemen have a very expensive pastime. A gentleman nowadays must have two headstalls to his bridle, and two reins. To his saddle, two flaps, a crupper, a breastplate, and a martingale with its appendages. The buckles and studs that ornament their trappings—not a bridle but would furnish a dozen silver knives and forks; not a saddle that would not supply a teakettle and a lamp.

There is a strong possibility that this disparaging writer was just envious because he was not able to afford a horse—or maybe could not even ride one. It is a fair chance that he was even the sort who would force his wife to wear drab homespun.

The cavalier, the true horseman, has ever expressed his inherent love for the beautiful in the adornment lavished on his horses—and his women. Conversely, this is likely why soft feminine eyes have such a way of turning toward the silver spurs, jeweled bridles, and carved leatherwork which represent the horseman.

Hand-carving of leather is one of man's oldest decorative crafts. Whether the ancient Assyrians and Persians originated it or learned the art from some earlier people is another problem for antiquarians. We do know, however, that the Persians were practicing it in very early times. They introduced it into Arabia and Egypt, from whence it was passed on to the Numidians and Moors. The latter carried it to Spain. It was from Spain that Europe secured most of the choice carved product during the Middle Ages.

At least one early attempt was made to bring the art to England. In 1579, one Richard Hakluyt sent an experienced dyer and leather worker named Hubblethorn to Persia for the purpose of learning the Eastern secrets of this fine craft. In his letter of instructions to the dyer, Hakluyt wrote in part: "They have cunning artisans in Persia, who make buskins of Spanish leather, design flowers of many kinds in most lively colors . . . to learn which art would do no harm."

How much the Englishman profited from his venture is uncertain, but there is no record of any great falling off in Spain's leather business during succeeding years.

But if northern Europe stayed behind in leather carving, it held unquestioned leadership in designing personal dress for the cavalier. France and England, in particular, outdid themselves in glorifying the genus gentleman. A man's plumed hat, ruffled shirt, satin waistcoat, and outer garments rivaled the plumage of the male wood duck.

And the one thing in all this array of splendor which set the true cavalier apart from his colorful pedestrian companions was his boots.

Boots of many kinds have been worn for many different purposes, but those of the horseman represent one thing only—the mounted man. Wherever you find them, boots stand as his unique mark. They first galloped into the light of history on the feet of the barbarian Huns raiding west into northern Europe early in the Christian Era. Slowly they worked their way down into Persia and through the Mediterranean countries, eventually reaching England via Spain and France in the 1300s. Until then, the Norman and Saxon knights had made out with a buskin-type shoe (Fig. 78). With the advent of the boot, however, the mounted man quickly turned to the innovation which was to symbolize the Western horseman for all future time.

Though there is some uncertainty about the exact time boots first appeared in England, it is known that they crossed the English Channel very soon after their introduction in France. The French knights pictured on the eleventh century Bayeux Tapestry are all shown wearing shoes or slippers. Even as late as 1325, history records only shoes on the feet of European riders. But some fifty years later, we read about the cavaliers' quaint custom of arraying themselves in high boots of colored leather, each boot of a pair in contrasting hue. Thus the improved footgear undoubtedly won a speedy acceptance throughout Europe immediately after its introduction.

The heavy jack boots, so popular in military circles for centuries, originated in Spain for the use of cavalry officers. They went well with the heavy armor coming into vogue and soon won a preferred place among most European cavalrymen. They remained in favor, especially in Germany, well into modern times.

Of similar, but more attractive, design was the English strong boot. These also survived until comparatively recent years. Some made the voyage to America.

Meanwhile, models of a more dashing, swashbuckling type appeared among Europe's civilian horsemen in the late 1500s. Most of these originated in France, later spreading over the continent. They were made of the finest *cordoban* and morocco leathers, their exceedingly wide

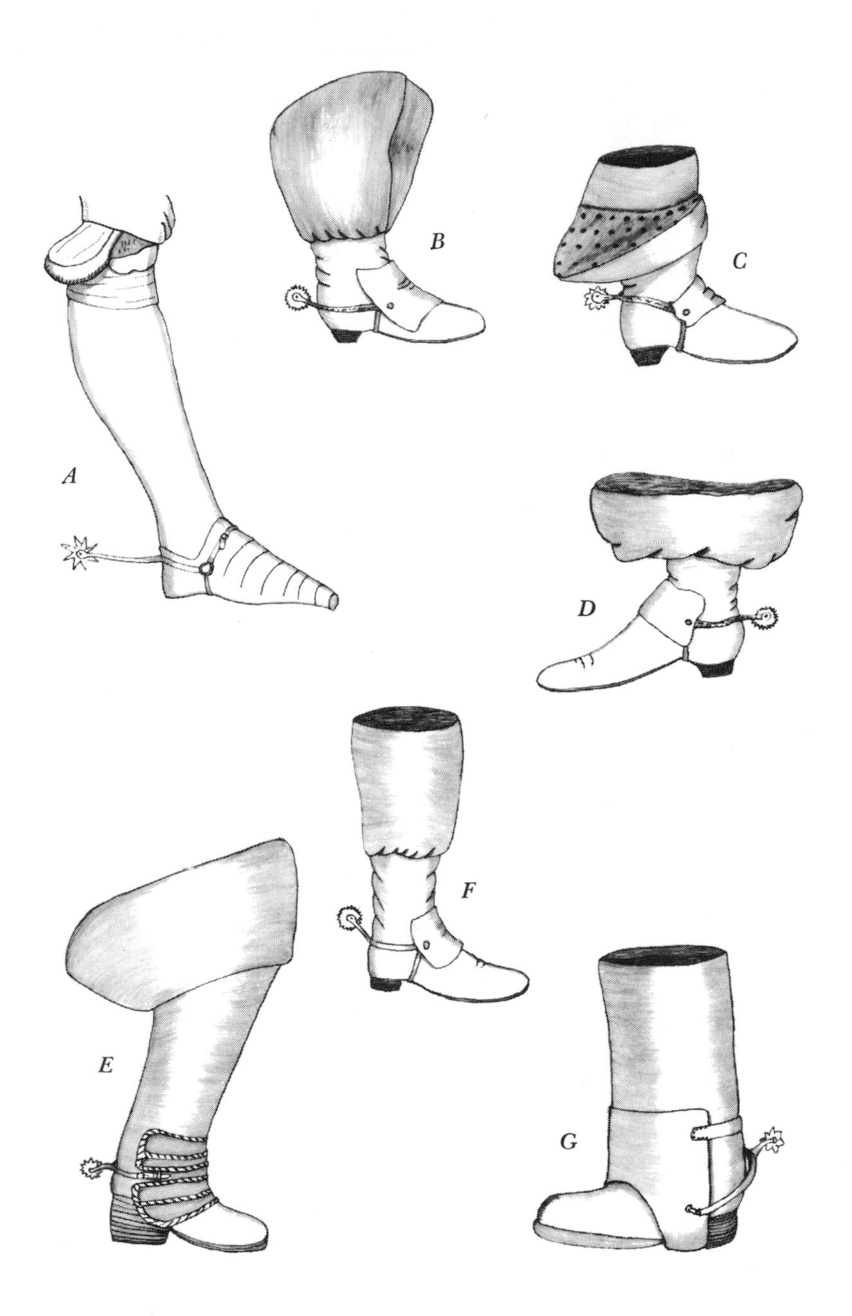

FIG. 78. Boots: *A* Norman-Saxon, 1000–1400; *B* English, 1625; *C* French, 1625; *D* French, 1715; *E* English strong boot; *F* English riding boot, 1635; *G* German jack boot, 1540.

tops often lined with silk or velvet. Worn with silk stockings, jeweled garters, and fancy buckles, they made an imposing appearance, to say the least. And they remained in favor until superseded by the simpler forms of the nineteenth century.

Another ancient symbol of the man on horseback is the gauntlet. Man has worn gloves and mittens of some sort ever since he first learned to clothe himself against nature and the elements, but the gauntlet was strictly a horseman's creation. From the early days of mailed knights to the present, it has stood as a badge of distinction in all civilized lands.

The word "gauntlet" derives from *gantelet,* early French diminutive for *gant* ("glove"). The idea of gauntlets started back in the 1200s, when the knights had the sleeves of their chain-mail hauberks made long enough to extend down over their hands, the ends being closed in mittenlike pouches. Openings in the palms made it possible to slip the hands out when desired. Somewhere around 1300 knights began using plain leather for the part which covered the hands as an aid to more flexibility. These gauntlets usually had scales of metal or bone attached to the back of these coverings for added protection. Then, about 1330, the extra length was cut off the hauberk sleeves and the leather made into a long-cuffed glove. The glove was reinforced by having steel plates riveted onto its back, thus forming a separate piece of armor.

Five years later the armor was extended up over the wrists of the gauntlet. By 1337, the leather was protected from the knuckles to well up the wrist by a single plate shaped to fit the hand. The upper side of the thumb and forefingers was covered with overlapping plates. On some of these the knuckles were additionally armed with spikes or knobs, called "gadlyings." Such gloves were rather formidable weapons in hand-to-hand combat.

The next improvement showed up about 1400. It consisted of smaller plates which were joined by articulated joints at the wrist, knuckles, and finger joints. The fingers in this style were separated, making a true glove. This style remained in favor until around 1433, when wearers reverted to the earlier mitten type, called a "miton." It was of steel with hinged joints. Examples of glove and miton appear in Fig. 79.

The miton was the favored style through the next couple of centuries. It was not until well into the 1600s that the armored glove with separate fingers again came to the fore. Some of these later gauntlets followed the trend of seventeenth century extravagance and reached nearly to the elbow.

This was the era when big gauntlet gloves were standard equipment in any gentleman's wardrobe. As practically all gentlemen were horsemen by right of position, there were always gloves aplenty at hand to bring any personal hostilities to a sudden head. "Throwing down the

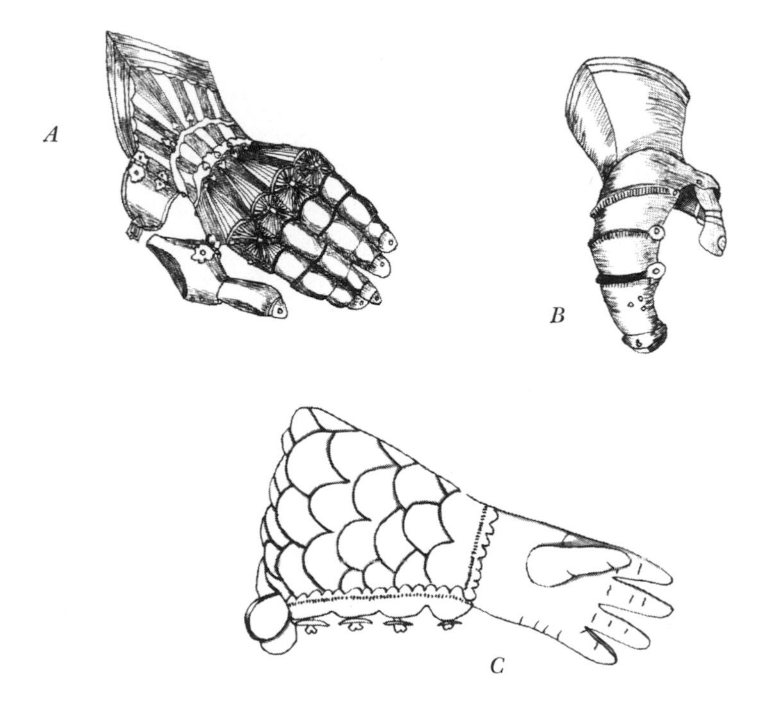

FIG. 79. English gauntlets: *A* fifteenth century armored; *B* miton; *C* seventeenth century leather.

gauntlet," or slapping an opponent's face with one's glove, was the accepted gage of battle or challenge to combat.

During this period there were also several types of single gauntlets for one-handed use. One of these, the manifer, was a heavily armored glove used by hostlers and grooms when leading or holding the unpredictable stallions habitually ridden by knights. For tilting across a barrier with an opponent, the knight wore a sturdier specimen, called a barrier glove, to prevent a possible crushing of his hand against the barrier. Another style was specially constructed for seizing an enemy's sword blade. The tourneying glove had one finger plate long enough to turn down and reach the inside of the wrist piece. The finger plate, after being folded down around the hilt of the sword or jousting lance, was fastened securely to the wrist piece by the turn of a locking pin which slipped through a hole in the finger plate. The vicelike grip locked around the weapon's hilt prevented it being either shoved back through the man's hand or wrenched forward from it.

The wearing of armored gloves in combat quite naturally led to the use of plain leather counterparts in everyday pursuits. With the decline of armor, the big leather gauntlets continued as regular wear. The horseman had too long enjoyed their protection to be without them. As a safeguard against biting horses, slipping ropes, trailside brush, occasional falls, insects, sunburn, and the like, their worth was inestimable. Too, hawking was a favorite sport among the elite in those days. For this, strong gloves were a necessity if one valued the skin of wrists and fingers.

Utility combined with pride led to handsome gauntlets decorated with fringe, embroidery, and buttons. Fig. 79 shows a style popular in the 1600s. These gauntlets were sometimes eighteen inches in over-all length. They were made of scalloped leather in overlapping layers, the outside being left open to button with four fancy buttons.

Similar gloves in styles ranging from very plain to extravagantly elaborate clothed the hands of European horsemen so long as the horse remained a means of locomotion.

The mounting trend toward lavish dress that engulfed Europe all through the Middle Ages was reflected in the rage for greater elaboration in bits, spurs, and other riding gear. It all reached a climax in the 1700s. From then on, there was a gradual reversal to simpler forms. Western Europe was never primarily a land of herdsmen or nomads. With the feudal baronies giving way to a better regulated regime, there was less need for heavy protective equipment. Life was becoming easier and distances were being shortened by better roads and an increase in populated centers. While riding remained the chief means of travel, a growing population of less affluent and more conservative individuals demanded gear better fitted to sober minds and slim purses. The result was an output of simpler saddles and plainer accouterments.

The saddles in Figs 80–81 were typical of this later period. Such rigs commonly used single cinches of webbing or leather and plain stirrup straps without fenders. Plain, narrow iron stirrups were the rule. A good many of these, particularly the English models, came to America in colonial days.

The simpler style evolved into the modern English saddle during the early 1800s. The latter found much favor in western Europe and along America's eastern seaboard, especially as a gentleman's saddle. It is

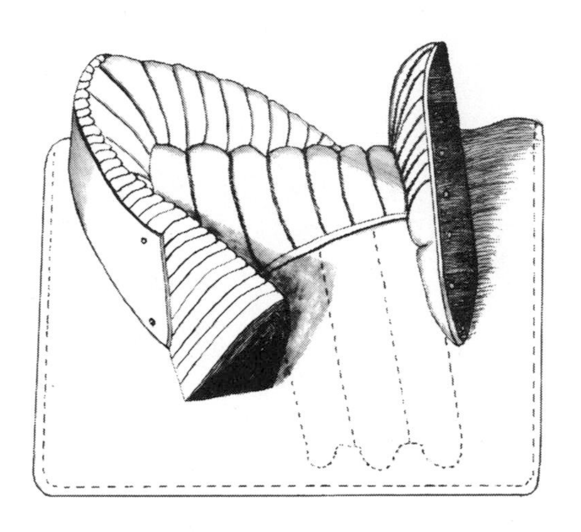

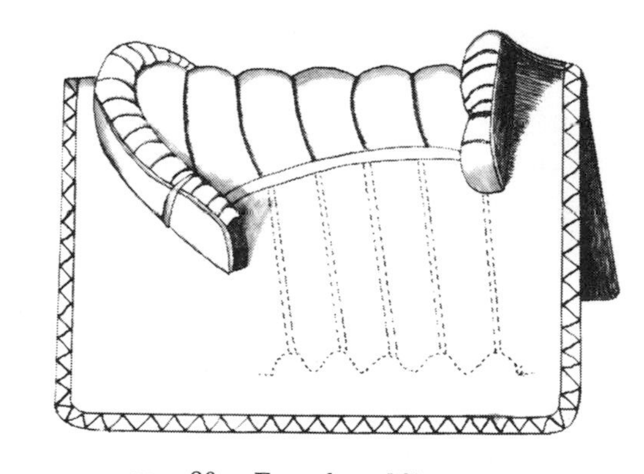

FIG. 80. French saddles, 1750.

still being made on both sides of the Atlantic, built on a plain wooden tree with metal fork of the Somerset or Park type shown in Fig. 109.

In construction, these have heavy webbing stretched across the tree to support the seat. Over the webbing goes a double layer of duck, serge, or light leather enclosing a layer of padding. The whole thing is covered with leather or pigskin. Pigskin is preferred because of its peculiar ability to withstand friction. Cowhide is usually used for skirts and flaps. The latter are ordinarily lined with cloth and often padded. Breast collars and cruppers were commonly used with these saddles in Europe.

English riding instructors of the early 1800s made a practice of having buckskin-covered saddles for their pupils' use. The soft roughness of buckskin was a great aid in helping novice riders hold their seats. Coarse

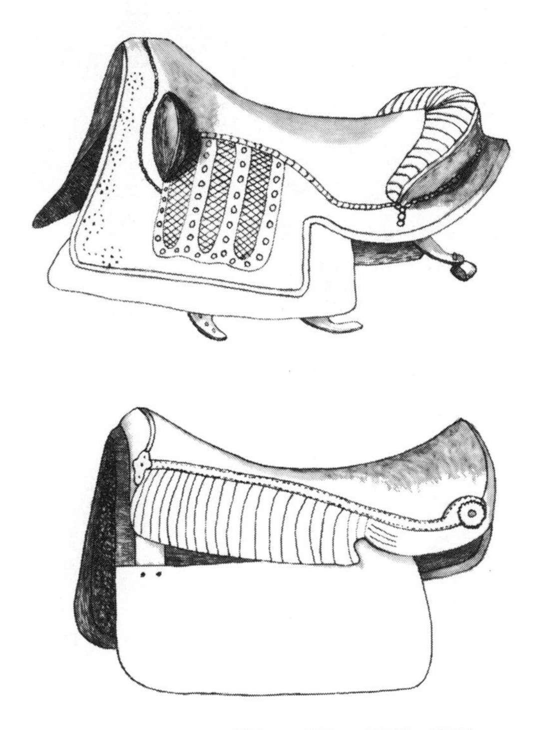

FIG. 81. English saddles, 1760–1775.

rugs or sheepskin with the wool out served the same purpose in the Orient.

Another simple design which appeared in England during the early 1800s was the pilch, or pad saddle, made without a tree. This seems to have been a direct outgrowth from the sixteenth century pad originally developed in Spain. It was of the simplest construction, being merely a treeless pad covered with enameled duck, sheepskin, or pigskin. The seat and skirts were padded and quilted, while a stuffed roll around the back served as â cantle. Cinch and stirrup straps were sewn to a webbing strip which was, in turn, sewn to the underside of the pad. The straps were brought out through holes in the cover to hang down outside the skirts.

Some pilches came equipped with detachable knee horns that could be put on for a lady's use or removed when a man rode. Such horns were of two types: one was made with a screw base which simply screwed into an iron plate sewed into the underside of the pad; the other was built to fit forklike over the front of the saddle, an extra cinch holding it in place. The latter kind often had a base peg that fitted into a hole in the pad for added stability.

Pilches were intended primarily for children, though some less pretentious adults rode them. They saw a limited amount of use among a certain class of riders in the United States and Canada until the late 1800s.

—14—

Military Europe

THE BASIC PATTERN of British cavalry saddles (Fig. 82) was quite similar to their civilian rigs. The pommel was built somewhat higher, while a fantail cantle replaced the flatter broad seat, but it was virtually the same old sidebar tree. The ends of the sidebars were lined with felt padding and covered with leather to prevent their chipping or splitting. The russet leather skirts were screwed onto the sidebars. The sidebars were also fitted with rings fore and aft to secure equipment.

Regular cinches were of broad leather or webbing. Double cinches were often used, one over the top of the other, especially in later years. Russet leather breast collars and cruppers with brass mountings in a design pretty well standardized throughout Europe completed the outfit.

An earlier version of this saddle was built on the Nolan tree, which employed wooden forks. In the early part of this century a change was made to steel forks for both pommel and cantle. The seat was supported from underneath by stretched webbing and covered with russet leather laced to fork and cantle. Leather from American buffalo hides was a standard covering in the 1875–1890 period. The complete saddle weighed twenty one pounds.

The cavalryman usually carried a saber slung to the left side of the cantle. His carbine rode in a full-length scabbard, or "bucket," slung vertically on the right side back of the cantle. If the armament included a horse pistol, it was carried in a 13½-inch holster hung on the right side of the pommel.

After the big, fanciful curb bits of the Middle Ages finally faded from the scene in the 1700s, the military turned chiefly to snaffles and modified curbs with low ports. Cavalry officers and their elite civilian contemporaries had a marked preference for the bridoon type. This was simply a separate low-port curb and a snaffle used together with double headstall and two sets of reins. In use, the snaffle was placed behind the curb. Ordinary enlisted cavalrymen used the English bit shown in Fig. 86 until the twentieth century. This bit was made to accommodate a second set of reins for special occasions. Headstalls, as a rule, ran to the rather plain, narrow variety among both civilians and military.

German cavalrymen used much the same style of outfit. Their saddles were somewhat lighter, weighing around 17½ pounds, but were similarly designed. They used the wooden tree with iron forks. Pommels and cantles were slightly lower and broader than those of the British, but the seat construction was the same. Skirts often had hair-stuffed knee pads as an additional feature, and were screwed to the tree. Breast collars and cruppers were standard until about 1860, after which they were pretty well discarded. Fur-covered saddlebags were also used in the early days, but were changed to the plain leather type soon after the Franco-Prussian War. Web or leather cinches and the conventional iron stirrups with medium treads were used. The carbine boot was like that of the British. Opposite it was the saber. Some troops were armed with 10½-foot lances of hollow steel tubes with four-edged steel blades. Bits were of the extremely low-port variety (Fig. 86) used with narrow headstalls.

In Austria and Hungary we again meet the ancient saddle of the Hungarian plains. Though it has been modernized to a large extent, it is basically the old design (Fig. 83). Originally, it was made entirely of wood tied together with thongs and covered with sheepskin or cow-hide, hair side out. The later models had the wood forks riveted onto the sidebars. The sidebars were lined with felt pads, which were held in place by leather pockets that slipped over the sidebar ends. The center-fire cinch rigging was laced onto the tree through holes in the sidebars. The nigh cinch strap was made to receive the buckle of a wide

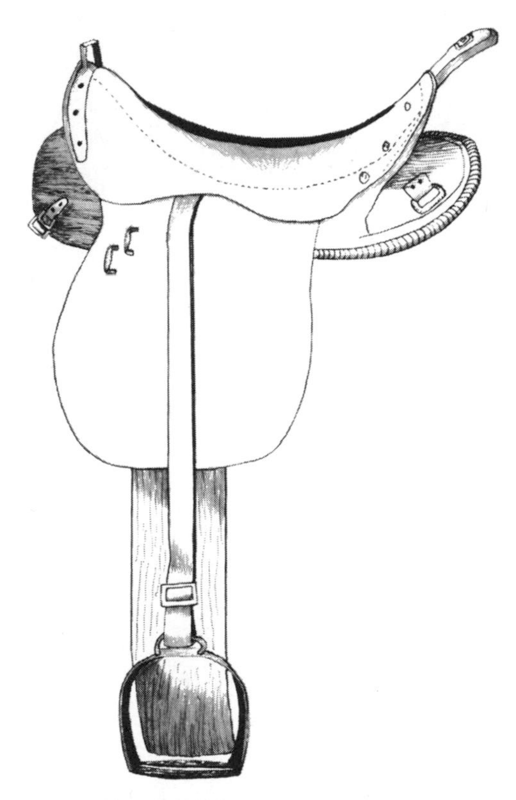

FIG. 82. English cavalry saddle, 1896.

web or leather cinch whose other end was laced onto the opposite side of the tree. Stirrup straps went over the tops of the sidebars and out through slots in the wood. Short stirrup straps were used with the heavy, broad-tread steel stirrups.

It was the construction of the suspended seat, however, which gave this saddle the most distinction. The base for the seat was a wide leather strap suspended between pommel and cantle. In fastening this base strip down to the forks and sidebars, the lacing was adjusted to bring the sitting place forward, backward, or in the middle, as the rider desired. With the foundation properly adjusted, a one-piece cover that included the skirts was placed over it and secured by the cantle-peak loop on the rear and either a buckled strap or thong at the pommel. The stirrup straps coming out through the holes in the skirts further helped to hold

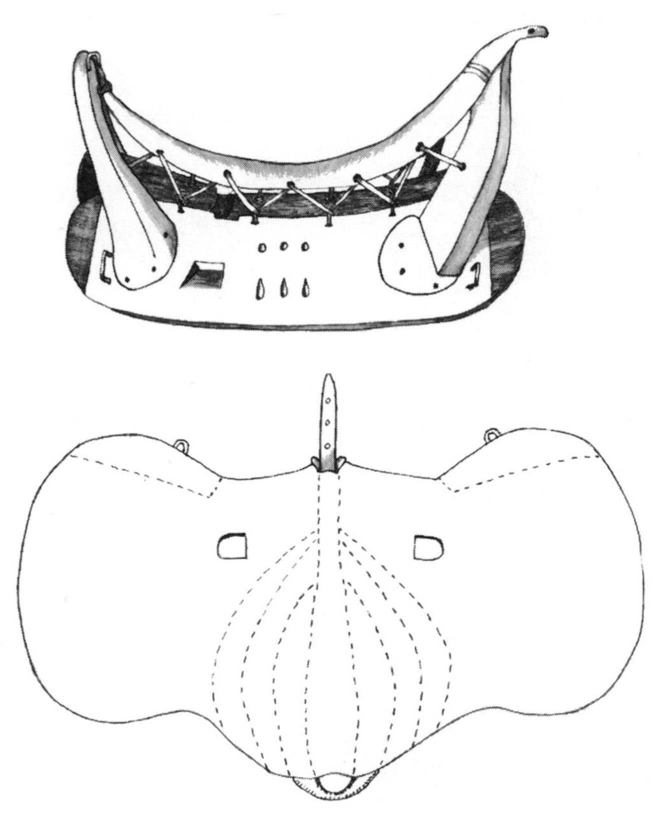

FIG. 83. Austro-Hungarian cavalry tree and cover, nineteenth century.

it in place. In addition, some riders cinched a surcingle of leather over the top of the whole rig.

The Hungarian *pusitas,* or cattle herders, usually dispensed with the cinch, using only the surcingle.

Medium-weight leather was used for covering these saddles. The seat was commonly padded and quilted. A pair of pouches were carried on the pommel, while another pouch for extra horseshoes, nails, and the like often occupied the left side back of the cantle. The cavalryman carried his rifle slung across his back, as did the Russians and French. The carrying of a saber was optional; some wore it on the hip while others slung it to the left cantle ring.

Breast collars were used to some extent in early times, but cruppers were seldom seen. Then the breast collars disappeared in most cases after 1860. Cavalry bridles had narrow headstalls with bits of a rather

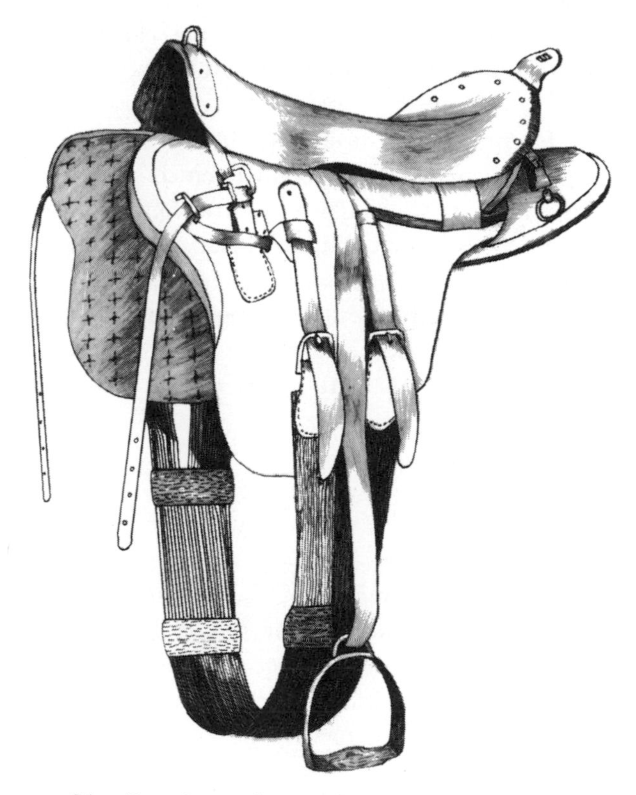

FIG. 84. French cavalry saddle, nineteenth century.

heavy, medium-high-port curb. See Fig. 86. Both curbs and snaffles on similar headstalls were in favor among the civilians.

The influence of the Hungarian saddle seems to have extended over into France. While employing a somewhat different principle, the heavy French tree with iron pommel and rather low cantle had a suspended seat with all the basic characteristics of its Eastern neighbor (Fig. 84). Skirts were fastened to the sidebars and stirrups hung the same as on the Hungarian rig. French skirts, however, were larger and bore quilted linings. The whole outfit was more finished in appearance than the Hungarian design. With the typical pommel pouches and back-of-cantle saddlebags, it weighed about twenty-eight pounds.

French cavalrymen favored breast collars and cruppers, and the straight-sidebar curb bits in Fig. 86. Stirrups were of the narrow iron variety with narrow treads. Carbines were carried on the men's backs, but sabers were slung on the left side of the cantles. The Dragoons carried lances held upright in stirrup buckets.

Very little different was the outfit used by the Belgian cavalry. Their saddle had the same arched-steel pommel, cinch rigging, stirrups, and saddlebags as the French. About the only variation was the seat construction. This was also a suspended seat; but instead of being merely a single piece of leather, it was made double. The upper layer was stretched into seat conformation while the lower length was allowed to sag down almost to the tree. The space in between was well stuffed with hair before sewing the two together. It made a very comfortable seat and weighed thirty-four pounds, six ounces.

Russia had the only cavalry saddle to be made on a double-rigged tree (Fig. 85). Former cavalry officer Colonel V. D. Krijanovsky says the old Russian Army had three kinds of saddles, namely, the officer's model, the regular issue for enlisted men, and the Cossack type.

The officer's model was quite similar to the English design, though built considerably heavier and bearing a higher pommel and cantle. It was double-rigged, having two leather cinches made to buckle. The cinch straps extended over the top of the tree and were laced to the sidebars. The sidebars were lined with felt pads which were held in place by pockets on their front ends and straps around the bars in the rear, similar to the French and German method. It had the suspension-type seat and was covered with light brown leather. Behind the cantle were two large saddlebags, while two smaller ones straddled the pommel. The rings on front and rear of the tree held straps to secure field equipment. Stirrup straps looped over and through the sidebars and carried plain iron stirrups.

Enlisted men's saddles were more like those of the American cavalry. Their pommels and cantles were higher and wider, both being the same height. They carried the big rear saddlebags only. Forage and equipment

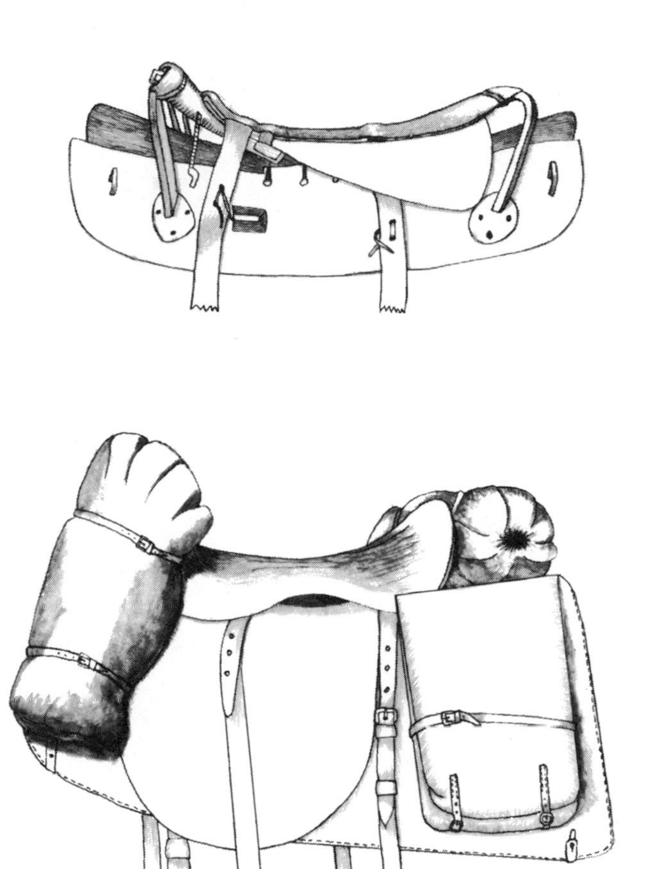

FIG. 85. Russian cavalry tree and complete saddle, 1890.

straps, stirrups, and skirts showed little variation from the officer's model. They were covered with dark brown leather.

The Cossack rigs were built much higher than either of the others. They had wooden cantles and pommels, which were uncovered, and

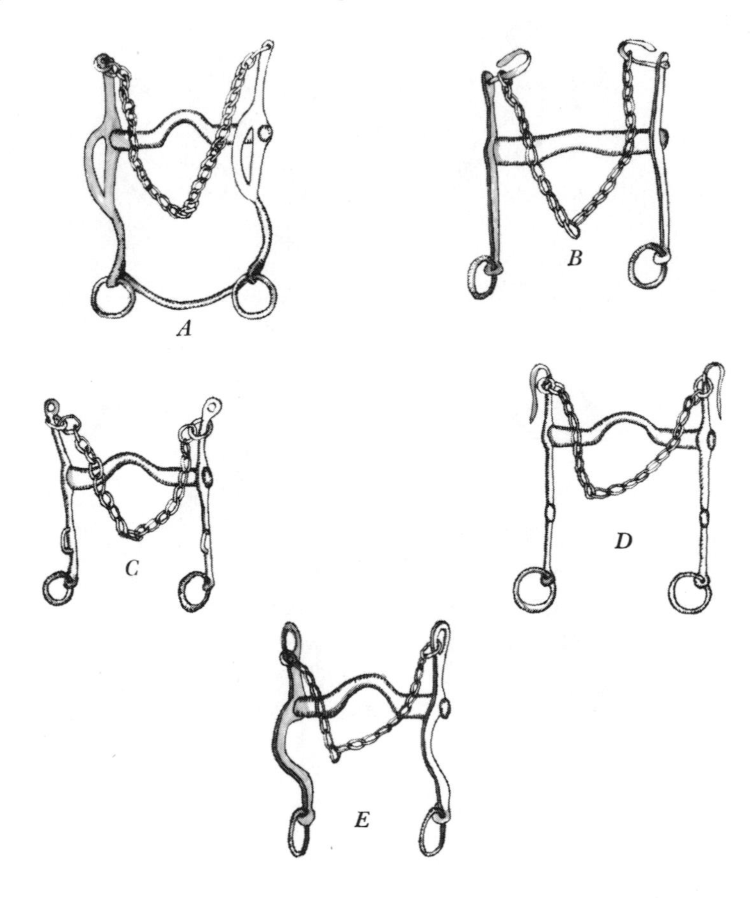

FIG. 86. European cavalry bits, nineteenth century: *A* English; *B* German; *C* French; *D* Russian; *E* Austrian.

horns similar to those on our cowboy saddles. The seat consisted of a pair of cushions placed over the tree, the whole being covered with black leather. Skirts were cut square and short. Stirrup straps were very short to permit the bent-knee style of riding which had been practiced by these people for centuries.

None of these saddles were equipped with stirrup covers, carbine boots, or saber straps. Open iron stirrups were standard, while carbines and sabers were always carried on the person. Curb bits, similar to the French type (Fig. 86) were used by the regular army. The Cossacks preferred, as they always had, the easier snaffles.

Special blankets, known as *voltraps,* were used on the mounts of the imperial guard for dress occasions. These had pipings to conform with the various regimental colors. Each had the czar's initials embroidered in its corner.

Civilian saddles followed the English pattern to a large extent until 1910. Shortly afterward, the Italian style of riding, which had developed in Italy's Pinerolo Cavalry School, was introduced into Russia. It stressed long stirrups and a saddle seat set slightly forward, allowing the rider to sit lower in the saddle and have better purchase with his legs. It became popular and gradually superseded the old Phillis School of the North, which had used short stirrups and elevated the body more above the horse. The Pinerolo ideas also brought an introduction to the Italian saddle. The southern rig had a single cinch and its skirts set more forward to bring the rider's weight nearer the center of gravity of the horse. It found general favor throughout Russia, practically replacing the English type in a short while.

As might be supposed, a certain amount of variation appeared among the riders of all nations. There can be no complete isolation among such a widespread fraternity as horsemen. European countries were small, and the man on horseback was never one to stay in his own little garden patch when unknown lands lay just over the hill. Centuries of intermittent warfare also left in their wake a scattering of customs and equipment from many regions. While national characteristics were more or less sharply defined at all times, each generation found the mounted man of various countries more and more a man of the world.

—15—

The Horse Returns to America

IN THE YEAR 1493, after unreckoned millenniums, the horse finally set foot again on his ancient homeland. The first to return to the Western Hemisphere arrived on the ships of Christopher Columbus. The old explorer had found himself a stock country on his original voyage the year before. Now he was back on Santo Domingo with twenty-four stallions and ten mares, plus a few head of cattle, as the nucleus of what he hoped would insure his old age against the eccentricities of crowned heads and unstable ships. Though his luck ran out before the plan fully materialized, the ranch he started on that part of the island now known as Haiti proved his vision was as good on land as on sea. The colony he established there grew to seventeen towns during the next twenty years, with most of the population's economy based on stock raising.

Others were quick to follow his example. The countless leagues of lush, unbroken lands were a paradise for grazing animals. And with a whole new continent to be explored and settled, horses to ride and beef to eat were of foremost consideration. Every ship from Spain was viewed as a possible transport for breeding stock. Each budding conquistador divided his mind between visions of gold and a well-stocked estate.

The Spanish crown established a royal farm on Santo Domingo in 1498, its purpose to breed first-class mounts for those engaged in further development of the New World. Esquivil's colony on Jamaica, Ponce de Leon's on Puerto Rico, and Velásquez' on Cuba were all established by about 1500. Ranching was the big attraction for most settlers of means. Similar ventures were in progress on all the main islands. Almost all of them were enjoying marketable increases by 1513.

Most of the later successes of Spanish conquest were due to the fecundity of domestic animals on these various islands. It is extremely doubtful if the Castilians could ever have made serious inroads on America had they been forced to depend on direct importations of livestock from Europe. Their ships were small and poorly equipped for carrying the feed and water necessary to transport large animals in quantity. Storms, calms, and contrary winds all added to basic difficulties of such voyages.

The horse latitudes first got their name because of the windless periods so often encountered in that section. Ships carrying horses were frequently becalmed there until water shortage forced them to jettison part of their stock in order to save the rest. At times, half or more of the horses had to be dumped overboard. With this hazard added to all the other perils of the long voyage, few and fortunate were the animals which survived to reach their distination. By the same token, imported stock was a prize which only the wealthy could enjoy. Horses on the islands were valued at around $1,000 each at the time Cortez was outfitting for his Mexican venture.

All early Spanish writers tell us that the horses first brought to the Western Hemisphere were of the famous Cordoba breed. These were the mounts which carried the conquistadors across North and South America to the Pacific and reshaped history from Canada to Patagonia.

Cordoban horses were famed for their excellence throughout Europe from the Middle Ages to the seventeenth century, while to ride like a Cordoban was a complimentary term denoting the epitome of horsemanship. These exceptional animals were a five-vertebrae Barb strain developed by the Moors during the 1200s. Cordoba was then the richest of the Moors' captive kingdoms in Spain and seat of their foremost horse-breeding activities. It is claimed that the Arab caliphate of that territory started the breed with four sires brought from either Yemen or the Hejaz, and a bunch of Spanish mares.

Cordobans were generally considered to be the best saddle horses in the world at the time America was discovered. Spanish adventurers, who saw a future in the New World for the man on horseback, quite understandably brought only the choicest horses they could obtain; these were Cordobans for the most part. Where shipping space was so limited and the hardships and dangers of the long voyage so great, there was no place for inferior animals. The ones which reached America might thus be considered the pick of the breed. It was fitting that so superior a contribution from the ancient horseman's world of the East should be the one to repropagate the horse's ancient home in the West.

And in America they moved into their heritage with surprising speed. By the second decade of the sixteenth century the imported horses throughout the islands had so increased that exploring expeditions and colonization attempts on the mainland could depend on home supply for their mounts. Throughout the years of the Spanish conquest, it was the island horses which carried the conquistadors toward new horizons and stocked their new ranches. Less than forty years after the first shod hoof stepped ashore on Santo Domingo, native stock was in use from the southern plains of North America to the Argentine pampas.

It was much the same with cattle, which generally abound in the horseman's world. Granted a few head of breeding stock, the equable climate of the Indies was almost sure to foster great increase. By the early 1500s herds were supplying beef necessary for home consumption, and they were also the source of seed stock taken to found new ranches in Florida, Mexico, and Central America.

In the main the cattle came from Andalusian stock. They were a wild, tough breed, chiefly black with needle-sharp horns. They ranged at will over the islands and became as salty an any untamed animals.

The six Andalusian heifers and one bull which Gregorio de Villalobos took from Santo Domingo to Vera Cruz in 1521 launched an epic of cattle raising which eventually encompassed the western half of North America.

Cortez established a ranch in the Oaxaca Valley of Mexico as soon as he finished bestowing Christianity on what natives had survived the introductory course. Many others followed the same procedure in Mexico and Central America during the next few years. Pedro de Mendoza staked himself out a spread in the Buenos Aires region in 1535, while Pedro Menendez de Avilés became Florida's first cowman in 1565.

Some twenty years after Villalobos first brought his cattle to Vera Cruz, there were going ranches strung the length of both the east and west coasts of Mexico. Coronado became the first American trail driver when he trailed five hundred head from Culiacán, Mexico, to Zuni, Arizona, in 1540. Luis de Carbajal set himself up in business at Cerralvo, just south of the Texas border in 1583, only fifteen years before Juan de Oñate founded Santa Fe as a ranching center.

All this is not to say that Spain was alone responsible for the introduction of livestock into America. True, the Spanish were the first:

Spanish horses and cattle were eating American grass from northern Mexico to the tip of South America almost a century before any other Europeans started bringing stock across the Atlantic. But the nations who sent colonists later made contributions of equal importance when they began colonizing the Atlantic seaboard.

Horses were landed in Arcadia in 1604 by the French settlers of that colony, though it was another fifty years before they were received there in any quantities. John Smith's company of adventurers brought six saddle mares and two stallions to Jamestown, Virginia, in 1609. Most of these were eaten during the "starving time" winter of 1609–1610, according to *A Trewe Relacyon* written by George Percy, a member of the company. Fresh importations, however, gave Virginians seventeen head in 1611. The Dutch in New Amsterdam imported Flemish and Belgian animals in 1623. Six years later Francis Higgins brought six Percheron mares and a stallion to Plymouth, Massachusetts. The Swedes brought some to their settlement the same year. Others arrived in increasing numbers at all the New England colonies soon afterward.

As the settlements grew and multiplied, the importation and breeding of horses assumed growing importance. Early America was strictly a horseman's country. Distances were great, horse racing and hunting were the chief sports, and business and pleasure travel were conducted over thoroughfares that were commonly mere trails totally unfit for wheeled vehicles.

Crude carts and wagons were the only vehicles the general public had to boast of during that period, and they were chiefly confined to small areas. Only the man on horseback was properly able to hold his position as an active citizen.

This was especially true in the southern colonies, where plantations quickly became the basis of the economy. There, plantation management, community gatherings, business affairs, pastoral duties, courtship, travel, and the advancement of civilization into new lands depended mainly on the feet of saddle horses. Horses, in fact, were the backbone of colonial life. It is small wonder that the late 1600s saw the South well on its way toward the fame that was to be hers as a region of fine saddle horses and superior horsemen.

This is not to say good mounts and riders were foreign to the North. The latter, too, moved swiftly and skillfully in increasing the motive power of a country designed for the man on horseback. Nevertheless, the North was more inclined toward industry and small farms than the

South. This fostered the development of heavier breeds and greater attention to draft animals. Also, as in all the world's history, where the populace turns most of its consideration toward working with its hands or following the plow there was a dearth of true horsemen. It was chiefly the cavalryman, the sporting gentleman, and the far-ranging adventurer who carried the banner of the mounted man north of the Potomac River. To those few must go the credit for promoting equestrian advancement in that area.

Thus it is that, while the English, French, Dutch, and Swedes all took part in the return of the horse to America, we must go back to the Spanish conquistadors for the most salient factors in putting the New World on horseback.

When Cortez put his little band ashore on the American mainland in 1519 there was probably no thought in his mind of founding a livestock economy and the horseman's dynasty that was to spring up in his wake. His primary quest was for gold. Horses were merely incidental adjuncts common to any explorer's venture. He had only sixteen head among the whole company. All were individually owned; some, due to the scarcity of mounts, were shared between partners.

An interesting record of these few horses has come down to us in an account written by Capitan Bernal Díaz del Castillo, a member of the company. He noted the various animals' descriptions and owners as follows:

Capitan General Cortez, a light chestnut stallion, which died in San Juan de Ulúa. Pedro de Alvarado and Hernando López de Avila, a very good chestnut mare. After our arrival in New Spain, Alvarado took this mare entirely to himself, either by purchase or by force. Alonzo Hernández Puertocarrero, a silver gray mare of good racing qualities. Juan Velásquez de León, another silver gray mare, very powerful, restless and a good racer, that we called La Rabona (the docked, or bob-tailed one). Christóbal de Oli, a dark chestnut stallion, very good. Francisco de Montejo and Alonso de Avila, a brownish sorrel stallion, unfit for war purposes. Francisco de Morla, a dark chestnut stallion, a great racer and restless. Juan de Escalante, a light chestnut stallion with three white feet; was no good. Diego de Ordás, a silver gray mare, barren, fair, but a poor racer. Gonzalo Dominguez, a dark chestnut stallion, very good and a great racer. Pedro Gonzalez de Trujillo, a good chestnut stallion, that ran very well. Moron de Vaimo (a native of Vaimo), a cream colored stallion, with marked forefeet and very restless. Vaeno de Trinidad (a native of Trinidad), a dun stallion with black points; does not go good. Lares, a very good stallion of a somewhat light chestnut color, and a good racer. Ortiz, the musician, and Bartolomé Garcia, a very good dark stallion that we called Muleteer, one of the best. Juan Sedeño, a native of Havana, a chestnut mare, which foaled on the ship. Two of these sixteen horses were killed in the first battle.

When the natives first saw the strange, unknown animals, they thought the horses were extended parts of the bearded, white-skinned gods who rode them. To oppose such wondrous creatures, who could produce thunder and lightning from sticks and race over the countryside with frightening speed, was surely the height of folly. No wonder they hauled out their richest treasures and fairest maidens as peace offerings. Without his little group of mounted men, Cortez might well have written the first chapter of a far different history. For, as more than one conquistador was wont to say, "After God, we owed the victory to our horses." We of today might not be amiss in echoing that statement when applauding the magical development of our western wilderness.

It was these animals, supplemented by later sporadic additions from the West Indies, which reinstated the horse in his ancient homeland to spawn the vast herds that roamed the western plains before the first Europeans crossed the Mississippi River. And it was these horses which carried the weight of the country on their backs throughout the hectic years of growth and expansion that led to world eminence among nations.

It was likewise the equipment of these visionary Castilians which set the fashion for most of what we of today consider typical western horsemen's gear. True, most of their accouterments were often overlarge and unwieldy—the heavy bit with its many jingling chains, and the 12½-inch spur in Fig. 87 are fair examples of the extravagant models used by the conquistadors. Most of them underwent alterations to accommodate them to later conditions; but the basic design is still seen among riders in the cattle country of America.

Much the same might be said for saddles. The early conquerors brought the old Spanish war saddles, already described, with them. These deep-seated rigs with their protective pommels, heavy leather cinches and elaborate iron or carved-wood stirrups were as suitable for warfare in America as they had been in Europe.

The carved and painted wooden stirrup (Fig. 90) was little changed from the Turkish-Moorish design of seven hundred years previously. This type continued in use in certain west coast sections of Mexico and South America until recent times. The conquistador stirrup in the same illustration was a product of the ironworker's art, large and heavy enough to knock down anything in its way. Stirrups of this kind were as good as battering rams to mow down poorly armed mobs of Indians. In their size and design we may see the germ which culminated in later-date tapaderas or leather stirrup hoods.

When the gentlemen from Spain finished enlightening the Indians and began turning their attention toward stock raising in Mexico, they found the cumbersome old war saddles poorly suited to ranch work and everyday riding. Many of them were remodeled for peacetime use, the pommels lowered, winglike thigh protectors cut down or eliminated and the chair-seat back reduced to conventional cantle shape. Also, there was some importation of the plainer *la jineta sillas* from Spain. The latter rigs, of the type shown in Fig. 74 came chiefly from Anda-

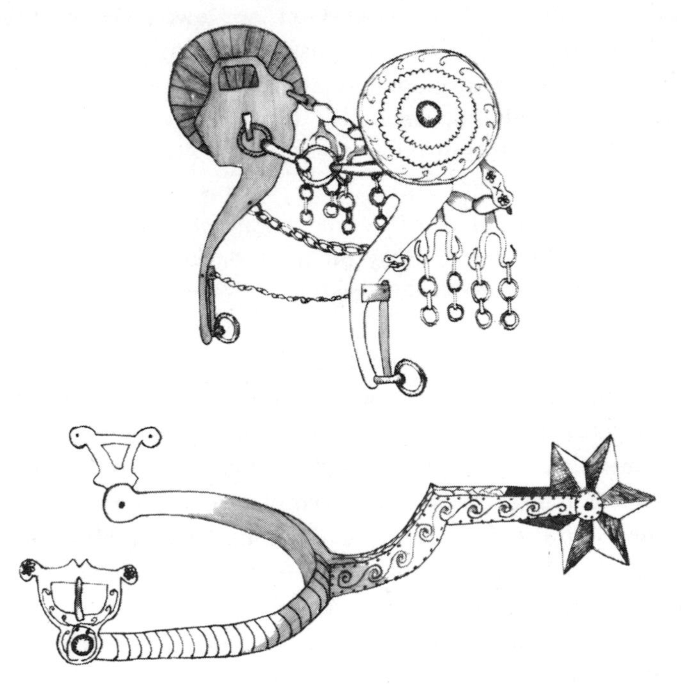

FIG. 87. Bit and spur, Spanish conquistador, sixteenth century.

lusia. Their similarity to the original Mexican-made charro saddles, which came along later, suggest a direct lineal descent.

Stong says the stockmen of Santo Domingo and Jamaica originated a Western saddle particularly adapted to their needs in the mid 1500s. He credits this as having considerable influence on the design of the original Mexican rigs. And it may well be so. Mexico was served for many years by these islands. If the islanders did create a saddle better suited for ranch work, it would naturally have migrated to the new territory, where ranching was the coming industry. And there, either with or without combining its form with that of the old *jineta* saddle, it would have served as a pattern on which Mexican craftsmen undoubtedly based their own creations.

Much obscurity clouds the transition period when Old World equipment was subject to various innovations and modifications designed to fit a new life in a new land. We can only be sure it was a long, drawn-out process, with much overlapping of styles drawn from many sources, until the true Mexican saddle emerged as a definite Western Hemisphere product in the seventeenth century.

—16—

South America on Horseback

WHILE THE MOUNTED MAN was coming into his own in the north, much the same thing was going on in the continent to the south. Early Spanish explorers penetrated the two Americas almost simultaneously, carrying into both lands the nucleus of a fabulous equine population and eight thousand years of horseman traditions.

Horses were taken from Spain and Santo Domingo to the northern ports of Colombia as early as 1509. Between 1514 and 1526 further importations reached the same section, as well as Panama. It was at Panama that Pizarro took aboard the horses for his mounted soldiers when his three ships embarked for the invasion of Peru in 1531. During his ten-year sojourn in the land of the Incas, further importations of Cordoban Barbs produced an increase that spread well into Bolivia and Ecuador and down into central Chile. Another forty years took them to the tip of Patagonia.

Over on the east coast, most of the horses were the famous Barbs from Spain and Portugal. Diego García's exploratory expeditions through Argentina from 1516 to 1526, with those of Diego de Rojas in 1542 and Domingo Martínez de Irala in 1548, took many animals into the interior. Pedro de Mendoza and Don Juan de Arjolas brought both horses and cattle to Buenos Aires in 1534. Álvar Cabeza de Vaca's records show that he reached Paraguay in 1540 with twenty-four of the forty horses with which he had sailed from Spain. The other sixteen had gone overboard during a water shortage while the ship was becalmed in the horse latitudes. Other shipments had reached Brazil in 1521 and the years following. The Dutch brought some to the northeast coast shortly after 1600.

From these early expeditions, horses lost, strayed, or stolen by the natives took up residence as naturalized citizens and went into production as quickly as circumstances permitted. Then, when ranching started on the heels of conquest, an increasing amount of stock found its way to freedom. By 1600, herds of wild horses roamed all the fertile grasslands of the southern continent.

All through the 1600s these wild bands ranged at will by uncounted thousands. In a book published in 1774, the English Jesuit Father Falkner, who spent forty years in Argentina, wrote:

> There is a prodigious number of wild horses, and likewise a great plenty of tame ones. The wild ones have no owners, but wander in great troops about the vast plains. They go from place to place, always moving with their heads against the current of the winds. . . . [They] were in such vast numbers that, during a fortnight, they continually surrounded me. Sometimes they passed me in thick troops, on full speed, for two or three hours together . . . greatest difficulty that I and my four Indians preserved ourselves from being run over and trampled to pieces by them.

In the beginning, these wild horses were invariably of solid colors, mostly bay, brown, and chestnut. The light colors and pintos which appeared early in North America were virtually unknown. In the later years the admixture of more imported stock led to the appearance of various colors not present in the original animals.

In Argentina wild horses were called *baguales*. The word came to mean the "wild ones." It was taken from the name of a freedom-loving Querendi Indian chief living near Buenos Aires, whose tribe never surrendered to the white man's restraints.

According to all contemporary accounts of that period, the South American wild horses, while as intolerant of restraint as the old chief whose name they bore, were excellent animals. Their immediate ancestors had all been of the best quality. Besides, on the great rolling pampas, winters were severe and summers were hot, with frequent extended droughts which necessitated traveling great distances for water. In such a land, survival depended on strength and durability. Infirm mares and weak colts fell by the wayside or became prey for lurking pumas, while inferior stallions were killed by stronger rivals or forced into solitary bachelorhood. The net result was a general upgrading all along the line. Surviving stock eventually became what we know as the South American Criollos, saddle horses with few equals.

As the descendants of the conqueror's horses grew and multiplied, developing finer qualities as they adapted themselves to their new home, the conqueror's riding gear took on new features peculiarly suitable to the great grazing lands of South America.

It was the old Spanish war saddle which first came to the southern continent, as to the north. It was soon discarded or modified to suit individual ideas and local working conditions. Bits, spurs, and other equipment went through a similar alteration and development.

In modifying the Spanish military saddle, the South Americans at first leaned heavily on civilian designs. Many of their original saddles were very similar to the treeless pad affairs so popular with the ordinary citizens of sixteenth century Spain. Especially in Argentina, there appeared a modified Moorish type built on a sidebar tree. Both employed the conquistador's single cinch, breast collar, and crupper. Unfortunately, neither style was very strongly made, and lack of horn made them poorly suited to roping.

The practice of roping from horseback was brought to America by the Spaniards, a heritage from the ancient horsemen of the East. It was, however, a mild thing compared to the new American art which soon developed. The wild herds which roamed the vast, unsettled regions of the new world evoked a skill with the rope such as no country on the globe had ever known. As ranching developed on the southern continent, the use of the lazo spread and flourished wherever men handled livestock on horseback.

Paraguay, in particular, claims some of the finest ropers in the world. Superbly trained through the centuries, the modern Gauchos of that country use braided rawhide ropes up to seventy-two feet in length. The men braid their own ropes, tapering them slightly so the noose end will be the heavier. The Paraguayans are reputed to make phenomenal catches in wooded country, throwing at fantastic distances through narrow openings among the trees. Unlike the North American *vaquero,* they never oil their ropes, preferring to retain the natural stiffness.

In contrast, the Argentine Gaucho has always shown a preference for the old Indian trick of catching animals by snaring their legs with bolas. This was perhaps because their early saddles were rather unsubstantial affairs which lacked any convenient holding points. The bolas needed no anchorage. They were merely sets of two or three fairly heavy balls fastened to the ends of connected thongs. Thrown with force, they would entangle and wrap around the legs of the creature to be caught, holding it securely.

When roping was done, it required the addition of an extra cinch over the saddle, both for securing the lightly-built rig and as a place to tie the rope. The rope was made fast to a ring set in the off side of the extra cinch to compensate for the lack of horn or other fork projection. This was obviously a rather awkward and inconvenient arrangement. It was only natural that the bolas eventually became a favorite instrument on the open grasslands of the pampas.

A somewhat similar method is practiced by the Goajira Indians along the north coast of Colombia. They use a long leather rope, called a *torahoa,* which is fitted with a heavy weight on one end. It is thrown so that the weighted end entangles the feet of the animal to be caught, in bola fashion. The long rope, however, allows the thrower to hold onto his victim. This is a decided advantage to the Goajiras, who do their roping on foot.

The various factors which helped put the South American on horseback were all more or less instrumental in designing the typical gaucho saddle of later years (Fig. 88). For its base, it had the old Moorish sidebar tree with heavy leather skirts. Onto this went a replica of the sixteenth century pad saddle, usually composed of sheepskin, with the wool side uppermost, and a seat cover of cloth or soft leather. The narrow, strap-like leather cinch ran through loops which held the pad to the tree. The whole rig was doubly secured to the horse by an extra cotton-cord cinch fastened to a wide leather strap that passed over the seat of the saddle. It needs little imagination to picture this extra cinch as a modern version of the old surcingle roping cinch. Stirrup straps were of the plain, fenderless variety common in Europe. Stirrups were usually of leather-covered iron or the toe-ring type.

The Gauchos rode with long stirrups and a firm seat in the saddle, like the North American cowboys. They also favored a similar style of long, open reins. For leg protection in brush country they used big leather flaps fastened to the saddle fork, much like the early Mexican leather shields which evolved into North American chaps. When they carried lariat ropes, they customarily tied them on the right side of the saddle behind the cantle, as do the Marajo Island cowboys of Brazil. (See Fig. 92.)

All but the very poorest of these horsemen expressed their love of ornamentation in fine displays of silver mountings on the various parts of the outfits. Such decorative features were especially evident on the big Spanish bits and spurs. The latter were commonly of the heavy variety with medium-long shanks and three- to six-inch spoke or buzz-saw rowels, styled similar to the Chilean design in Fig. 93.

A visitor to Paraguay in the middle 1700s wrote that ". . . for saddles in that country, they have a coarse and thick piece of stuff which is first put on the horse. A girth is fastened over this. Then a piece of leather the size of the saddle is added, which serves as a housing over the croup. Onto this goes the saddle, resembling a packsaddle. Over the saddle go some sheepskins, usually dyed in colors. The whole affair is secured by a second girth. Stirrups are small and narrow, as they never put the foot in beyond the toe. Their bridle bits are of solid iron with a half-circle iron curb." These must have been the old Arabian or Mameluke bits brought from Spain.

The writer went on to say the Paraguayan women rode as often and as well as the men. Later visitors to that country tell much the same story.

Toe-ring stirrups (Fig. 91) were a favorite style among the barefoot Gauchos and Indians throughout most of South America. In Chile, Argentina, Uruguay, and Paraguay the ring was commonly made to accommodate only the big toe. A slightly larger type for two or three toes predominated in the north. The latter kind is still in vogue in the Amazon Delta country. The idea behind such stirrups was chiefly to save weight. They were also convenient for men who habitually rode barefoot.

Down in Patagonia, the natives used toe-stirrups about two inches in diameter, designed for only the big toe. They were made by simply slitting both ends of a piece of leather, then doubling the strap over to receive the notched ends of a stick in the slits.

Straps for such stirrups were equally primitive, being merely raw-hide thongs looped through the stirrups and over the sidebars. The side-bars themselves were lashed to the wooden forks with rawhide. The Patagonian trees had a strong resemblance to the round bow trees of the

FIG. 88. South American Gaucho saddle.

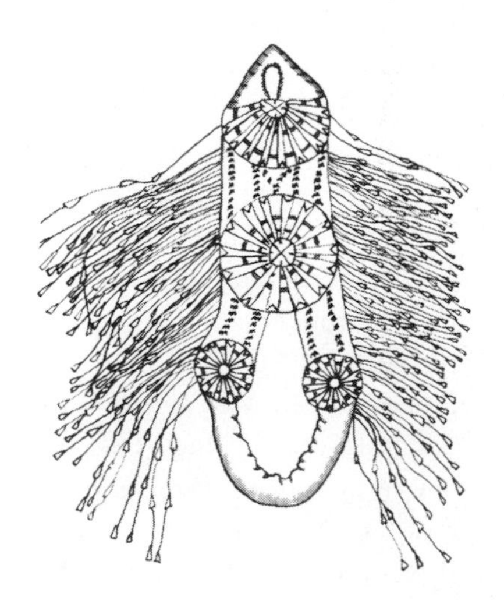

FIG. 89. Guatamalan horsehair cruppers.

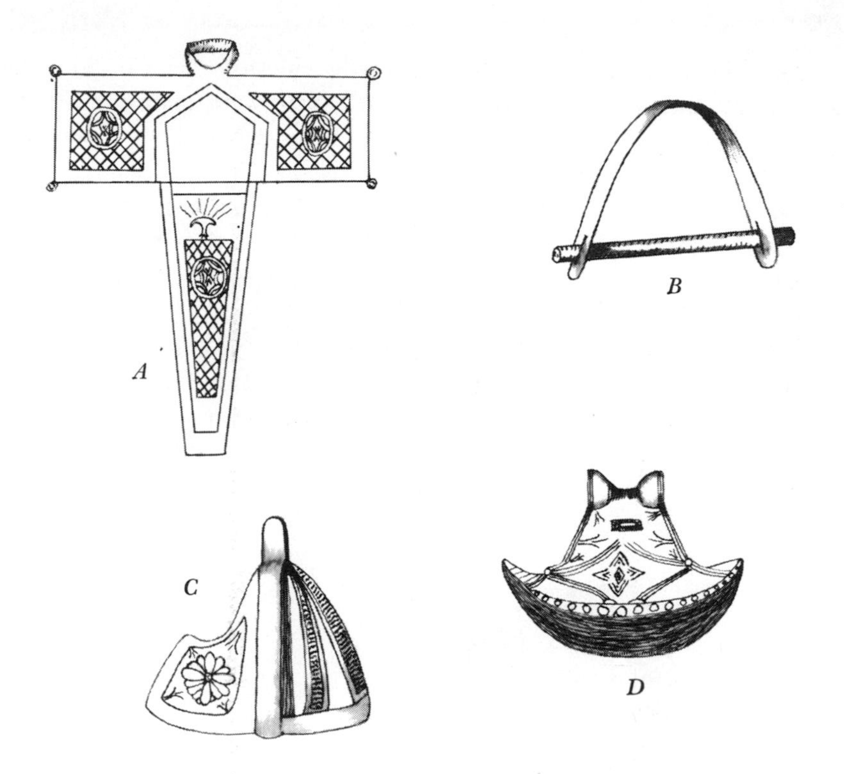

FIG. 90. Latin American stirrups: *A* Spanish conquistador; *B* Patagonian; *C* South American, carved wood; *D* Mexican, carved wood.

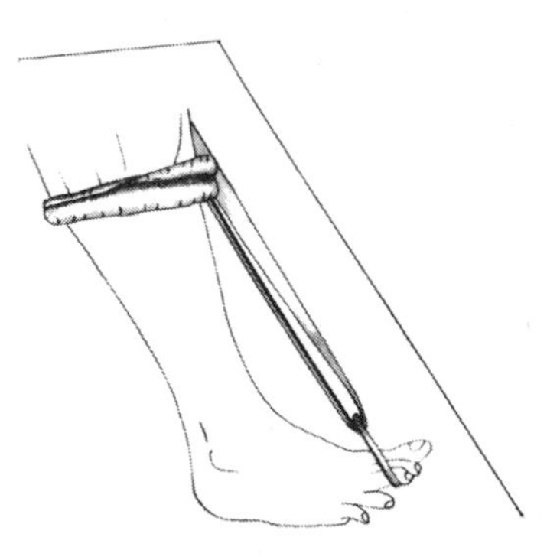

FIG. 91. Toe-ring stirrup.

Mandan and Crow Indian saddles in North America. See Fig. 96. Like those of the Indian saddles, the fork and cantle were almost alike. In some sections, especially among the Araucanians, a leather blanket over the thong-lashed tree served as a seat.

Spurs were very primitive, somewhat like the old goad spurs of medieval knights. Bridles were commonly of braided horsehide, often having a silver thread woven through them, and equipped with heavy Spanish bits.

The Spaniard's big bit, a heritage from Turkey and Morocco, was a favorite wherever obtainable throughout South America in the early years. Ring bits likewise enjoyed great popularity, even up into modern

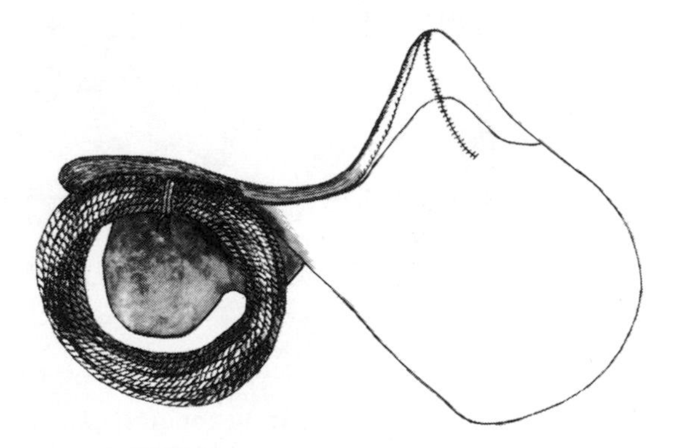

FIG. 92. Saddle and rope, Marajo Island.

times. The style shown in Fig. 93 saw widespread use in the Latin countries. But whatever the type, most of them were made up in rather elaborate designs with plenty of gold and silver inlays.

A bit frequently seen among the Gauchos of various sections had a mouthpiece of rawhide fitted with silver rings. This was a makeshift born of necessity in a land where manufactured goods were scarce. Better products soon superseded it as the country developed.

The early Chileans rode a saddle quite similar to that of the Patagonians. It was a bare tree over which was thrown a rug or blanket. Lieutenant Wise wrote that, in 1846, this covering was usually so bulky as to distend the rider's thighs in an unpleasant manner. In later years, however, a more comfortable rig built on the Mexican pattern prevailed among all except the poorer classes.

In Chile the toe-ring stirrups eventually gave way to the iron or leather-covered type to a large extent, following the style set by the pampas riders east of the Andes. Examples of the old Oriental carved and painted wooden stirrups (Fig. 90) appeared in scattered localities. Stirrups of this kind have shown up as far north as central Mexico.

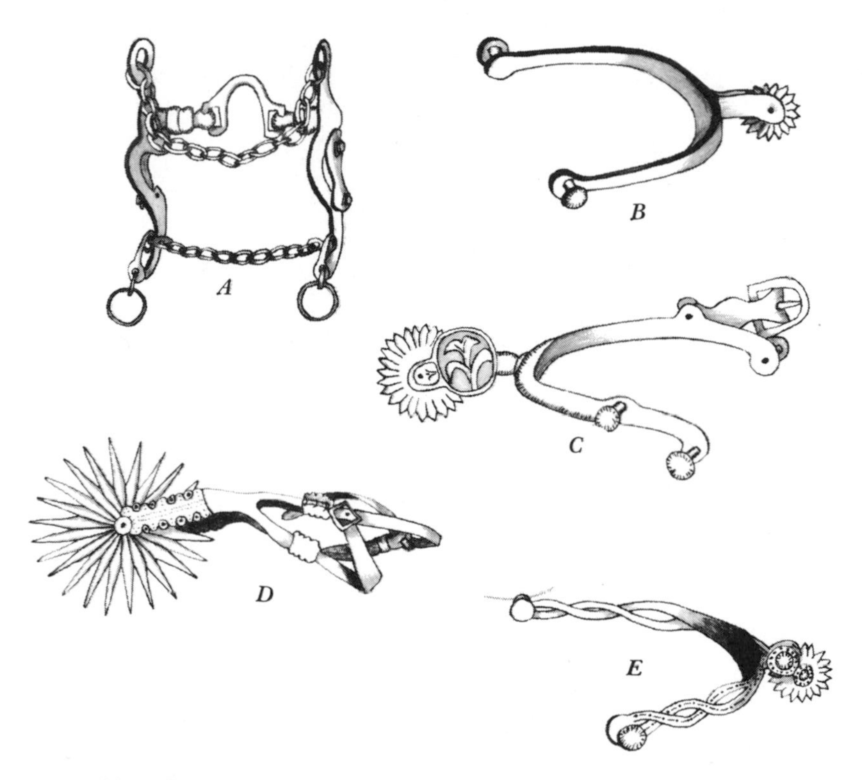

FIG. 93. Silver mountings: *A* South American bit; *B* and *C* Central American spurs; *D* and *E* spurs from Chile and Colombia.

Chilean bridles and bits were of the ornate Spanish variety common to the rest of South America. Spurs were the same, often carrying up to 6-inch rowels with twenty-four points (Fig. 93). Fancifully designed shanks and heel plates were ordinarily rich in silver and gold inlays. Narrow spur straps were preferred. They usually continued around under the instep to accommodate poorly shod and barefoot riders.

Shorter shanks and smaller rowels have won the favor of many Chilean *huasos* in various sections during later years, though the overlarge rowels with short shanks are generally preferred. Decorative features remain about the same. Fringed leather leggings that buckle around the leg just below the knee take the place of boots.

A better looking saddle appeared among the Colombian cowboys. It was full leather-covered, with full skirts and jockeys (Fig. 94). Its long seat, nublike horn and straight cantle were reminiscent of the old Arab-Moorish rig. The rope was carried on the right side, while a sheath knife

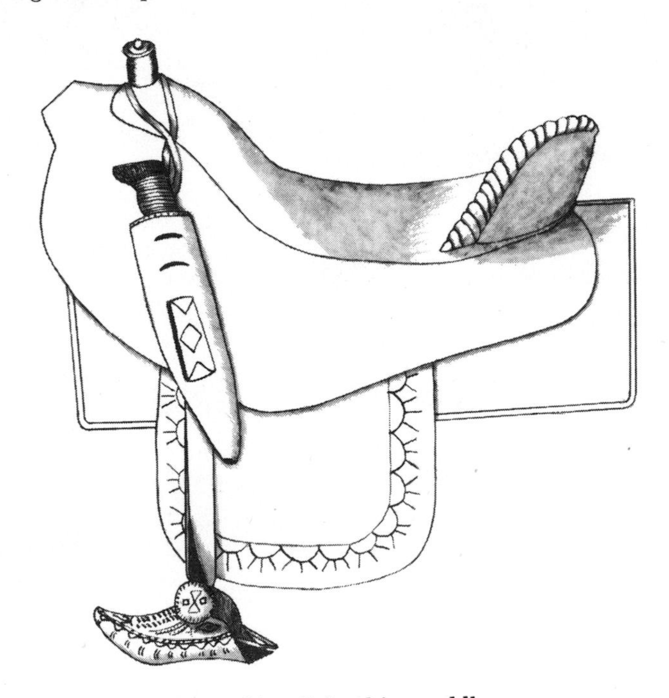

FIG. 94. Colombian saddle.

was commonly slung from the left side of the horn. The favorite stirrup was the enclosed shoe-shaped style of carved and decorated brass or copper in the Moorish design. Many of these were still in use in this century. A long, soft-leather carry-all pouch was frequently carried back of the cantle, like a blanket roll.

The Colombians clung to the big spurs of the Chilean type and the heavy Spanish bits. Both displayed the Latin love for rich embellishments. Colombian *zamorras* were very similar to Mexican chaps. With the customary bright Indian blanket under his saddle and an equally bright serape draped across his shoulder, this Southern horseman was as colorful as he was skillful in the practice of his chosen profession.

Another and quite different type of mounted man is found on Marajo Island in the delta of the Amazon River. The cowboys there do most of their riding on oxen. Marajo is a large, low-lying, often inundated island given over to cattle raising. The stock does much of its grazing in the floodlands. Working over the mud flats, flooded ground, and even out into the fairly deep water, the ranch hands have found the slow, splay-footed oxen more temperamentally suited to the task than horses. While the latter are employed to considerable extent, they are mostly held apart for use on the dry portions of the island.

Marajo saddles are of the hornless variety, light in weight, simply made and covered with plain leather (Fig. 92). The seat is frequently covered with red plush, while fenderless stirrup straps loop over the sidebars to swing free on top of the flaplike plain leather skirts. Stirrup straps are commonly of rawhide, as is the cinch rigging. Braided rawhide ropes are carried on the right side behind the rider's thigh. Because the outfit is unsubstantial, ropers usually tie the rope to the cinch or around their own bodies.

Very similar saddles and ropes are used by the Venezuelans. But there, instead of tying their ropes to the cinches, they tie them to the mount's tail. The same method was used in northern Mexico before good saddles made horn-tying practicable.

Moving from the open pampas grasslands into the mountainous jungle, we find the true horseman less in evidence. Men ride horseback through all these sections, especially the upper-class citizens. But aside from these, riding is more in the nature of European peasants jogging to market on work horses.

Their saddles are poor in quality and may be of any vintage or style. Cheapness and availability seem to be the chief governing factors. Old army saddles, English-type rigs and the cheaply constructed Morgan-tree muley saddles formerly made in the United States are much in evidence.

Farther north, in Central America, we meet the old Mexican-type saddles of the 1800s. Most of these are plain rawhide-covered trees with Mexican-style horns and cantles, minus skirts and fenders. They are single-rigged. Cruppers are fairly common and are usually trimmed with colored hair tassels. Those of Costa Rica are especially handsome.

A scattering of modern stock saddles from Mexico and the United

States are found along with these old rigs and assorted importations from Europe. Unfortunately, only a small part of the Central American population can afford such luxuries as good riding gear. The less privileged are forced to make do as their fathers did before them; they still habitually ride barefoot, a single spur adorning one naked heel.

Spurs are, as a rule, much lighter and less elaborate than those in either Mexico or South America (Fig. 93). Smallish sunset rowels and plain, narrow heel plates predominate. The kind which provides for a strap under the instep is usually favored by barefoot riders.

Hackamores and bitless bridles are used to a large extent. Bridles, with or without the heavy Spanish bits, are usually well decorated and trimmed with colored horsehair tassels.

Riding is not the popular diversion among women in Central America that it is in the land of the Gaucho. The few women who do ride are careful to observe the conventions which frown severely on any form of astride riding.

Similar conditions and practices prevail in most cases from Panama to Guatemala. Local customs in all sections have their peculiarities, but the overall picture holds few outstanding variations.

One rather interesting feature found in Guatemala is the large and elaborately decorated cruppers trimmed with black and white horsehair (Fig. 89). They are almost identical with those used by the North American Indians of the upper Missouri River country in early days. How two such widely separated peoples came to adopt the same type and design in one particular item makes an intriguing question.

—17—

The Indian Gets the Horse

When the horse first returned to its ancestral home in North America, it met that other original resident, the North American Indian. Still it was some time before the two came together on a companionable basis. Historians are in some disagreement as to exactly when this association first took place. Even the best of them can base their deductions only on probabilities. Moreover, the time varied considerably among scattered tribes.

As we know, the horse was a strange and forbidding animal to the Indians when the Spaniards made their initial landing in the New World. Dogs were the only domesticated animals the Indians had. When they became acquainted with the true nature of the horse, they discovered it was only another burden bearer and thought it was simply a large kind of dog. This idea was strengthened by the fact that some of Cortez's men used large dogs to run down and capture the Indians. These dogs performed much as did the man-and-horse combinations. To the savage mind, this may have signified that the two creatures were closely related.

In fact, Big Dog was the Snake Indians' original name for the horse. The Comanches called it the God Dog. Among the Sioux it was known as Shonka Wakon, or medicine dog. Ponoka Nita, or elklike dog, was the Blackfoot name. Various other tribes had similar doggish names for it.

At first, the Indians' one aim was to kill the fearsome creatures. It was not until they discovered the inherent value of horses to their own scheme of life that they began appropriating the animals as desirable possessions. When this turning point took place in various sections of the country is largely a matter of conjecture.

We know that Ponce de Leon took 50 horses to Florida on his expedition of 1521. Eighty-nine of the animals went with Ayllon's 500 settlers who attempted to found a colony near the mouth of the Pedee River in 1526. Two years later Narvaez landed 80 head at Tampa Bay. Then came de Soto's great pilgrimage of 1539–1543, marking a big crescent from Tampa to northwest Mississippi and down into Texas. The return to the Mississippi found the expedition with only 22 of the original 214 horses with which it had started.

The others fared even worse than de Soto, most of them losing all their mounts in the Florida wilderness. Chronicles of these expeditions speak of how the Indians treated the animals, killing them whenever possible. However, this is not to say that some were not captured alive by Indians awake to the potentialities of the new beasts.

The colony Luna founded at Pensacola in 1559 and Avila's settlement at St. Augustine seven years later both failed within a couple of years, but they were there long enough for the Indians to learn the truth about horses, and no doubt confiscate a few for experimental purposes.

Sketchy records all seem to agree that the southeastern tribes had a fair supply of horses early in the following century. Such animals must have been descendants of the early Spanish importations, as the Spaniards had directed little but minor coastal activities toward Florida after Mexico claimed their attention in the mid-1500s. The efforts of the English and French to consolidate their positions in the North kept them too busy for any southern ramblings. Travel difficulties and danger from Indians precluded much penetration of the South's interior by individuals until after 1650. We can only assume that, with no other visible source of seed stock, the southeastern nations developed their horse culture from animals lost or abandoned by the early explorers.

At any rate, the first adventurers to enter the southeast found a considerable number of horses. Berbner credits these animals to breeding stock obtained from de Soto. A number of old Indian legends also link their first horses with de Soto. Denhardt believes these Spanish descendants were ranging as far north as Tennessee and North Carolina by 1650. The La Salle expedition of 1682 found horses at the mouth of the Arkansas River, where they traded tomahawks for thirty-five head. Their chronicles also mention a report of similar stock on the lower Missouri River at that time.

West of the Mississippi, La Salle's ill-fated company, set afoot on the Texas coast, found horses among the Caddo Indians near the junction of the Brazos and Navasota rivers in 1687. A detachment of Spanish cavalry also saw some mounted Indians near the mouth of the Colorado River in 1690. Tonty, La Salle's companion, had a like experience the same year, while exploring the Red River near Texarkana, Arkansas.

As Benevides, del Bosque, and Mendoza, who separately covered most of central Texas to the Rio Grande between 1630 and 1683, found no horses throughout that region, it is evident that the animals seen nearer the Mississippi had not come from the West. Their origin could only have been stock brought to the southeast Gulf Coast at an early date. That they had risen from a limited source is evinced by their slow spread during the preceding century.

Things moved more swiftly in the West. A thousand horses went to Mexico the year after Cortez's conquest. More soon followed, as new ranchos came into being. Another twenty years saw both horses and mules ranging in quantities from Nicaragua to northern Mexico.

When Coronado organized his expedition to search for the seven golden cities of Cibola, he found it easy to outfit his entire company with home-grown stock. They pulled out of Culiacán on April 22, 1540, with 228 mounted horsemen, 559 saddle horses, and around 1,000 pack-horses and mules to carry the equipment for 336 white men, 3 women and 300 Indians. Also with the expedition went several bands of sheep, hogs, and a sizable herd of cattle. The latter gave Coronado the distinction of being the first trail driver across western America.

The sixteen hundred horses and mules Coronado took with him served as the western Indians' first introduction to mounted transport. It is fairly certain, however, that the Arizona natives had heard of, and perhaps seen, the new animals in the south earlier. Moreover, these native Americans were never backward in learning new ways and acquiring the things needed to carry them out.

At any rate, records of the Spaniards tell us that instead of falling in awe before the strange beasts, as the Aztecs had done, the northern tribes made continual attempts to capture horses for their own use. Castaneda, historian of the expedition, wrote that the natives stole some horses while the explorers were camped at Tiguex, near the present Bernalillo, New Mexico, the winter of 1540–1541.

The conquistadors knew that their power and supremacy rested largely on keeping their horses out of the hands of the Indians. Great care was taken to prevent any theft of the precious animals. Yet, on their long journey to the east and northeast in 1541, still following the trail of the golden mirage, some unavoidable losses definitely occurred. Castaneda wrote that several mounted soldiers disappeared, horses and all, while they were crossing the awesome Texas plains. Presumably they strayed off and got lost. It is equally probable that at least some of them fell prey to watchful Indians.

Other sixteenth century visionaries no doubt lost some of their horses the same way. Friars Rodriguez, Lopez, and Juan Santa Maria, with 9 soldiers; Espejo, with 15 soldiers; Bonilla and Humana, with a large company; and de Sosa, with 170 settlers bound for Taos, all traveled and explored through the New Mexico territory from Arizona to the Pecos River during the 1581–1593 period. All these parties were well supplied with riding stock. Though the Spaniards were chary about admitting successful thefts by their inferiors, it would have been odd if all of them had escaped the attentions of such crafty adversaries avid for the desirable animals.

The Comanches, Pueblos, Navajos, and Apaches throughout that region were the first western Indians to develop a horse culture. Our best authorities on the subject believe that these nations were, to a large extent, mounted soon after 1550.

The great spread of Indian horses, however, did not catch its stride until after Juan de Oñate founded his colony at Santa Fe in 1598. The breeding stock he brought north to supply his 530 soldiers and prospective ranchers might be called the actual fountainhead of the equine hordes which later covered the West.

Of course, like all early Spaniards, Oñate's colonists were opposed to the Indians' having horses. The newcomers recognized the fact that most of their strength lay in exclusive possession of the animals. Among the first resolutions passed for community welfare were stringent laws forbidding the natives even to ride the beasts.

The first hanging in North America took place at Santa Fe in 1598, when Oñate strung up a couple of Indians caught trying to steal a horse.

The very nature of the settlement's development, unfortunately, worked to defeat such rules. Farming and stockraising were the backbone of the colony. The myriad chores common to homemaking in new lands called for a great amount of labor. As the colonists were already overburdened with establishing themselves, the only source of extra laborers was the Indian neighbors.

In all such settlements a mission was one of the first things to be erected. The padres felt that nourishment for the soul, as meted out at the missions, was the primary objective in life. The missions also provided a place to teach the natives the beauty of swapping their carefree existence for a steady job in the cornfields. The training ran to small doses of religion mixed with a generous amount of ranch work. In a short while most of the farming and stock handling was being done by the natives.

As a way to get the unpleasant tasks done, it was a brilliant idea; but it wasn't the best scheme for keeping the horses out of alien hands. It didn't take the Indians, working about the herds, long to learn the value of horses and the main secrets of good horsemanship. They no doubt learned more than they cared to about the process of forced labor at the same time. With considerable enlightenment on both subjects under their scalps, it was natural for their next step to be in the direction of far distant and less exacting regions. Equally natural was their habit of taking a selection of the desirable animals with them in the interests of swift escape and future benefits.

In the course of the next fifty years, horse stealing became the highlight of Indian existence. It provided comfort for the foot-weary and more meat and hides for the hunter. As a game, it had no equal for demonstrating personal skill and bravery, rating even higher than war as a test of manhood. Horses provided a visible display of wealth and success for all who had the courage to acquire them. As a trade item, they ranked supreme.

One account, written in 1664, mentions the Plains Indians' bringing their captives and buffalo robes to trade for horses among the western tribes. By 1659, the Navajos northwest of Santa Fe had become a serious threat to the horse raisers of the settlement. Nor was it long until they, along with the Comanches and Apaches, were making raids deep into Mexico for the coveted animals.

With horses thus in Indian hands on all fronts, plus the phenomenal increase engendered by rich feed, temperate climate, and freedom from enemies, a wide dissemination of the animals was inevitable. This ran in three loosely defined streams from the Santa Fe region: one branch headed east, one northward across the High Plains east of the Rockies, and the third up the Rio Grande, Colorado, and Green River watershed toward the Northwest.

The eastbound branch made its way along the general line of the thirty-fifth parallel, gradually fanning out toward the Gulf Coast on the south and the Canadian and Red rivers on the north. It merged with the southeastern horses, slowly working westward toward the Plains, about 1700, thus establishing an unbroken horse population from the Colorado River of Arizona to the Atlantic seaboard.

Thus we find the Indians of various nations becoming mounted in the wake of each advance by the horses. The Comanches, farthest west, had possessed the animals almost from the advent of the Spaniards. By around 1680, they were famed as the leading horseback nation in the West. Another ten years found them rich in the possession of territory in northwest Texas and of multitudes of horses. Their neighbors on all sides followed the same pattern until, with the merging of the east and west movements, the whole southern Plains area emerged as a strictly horseback country.

The spread of horses toward the northwest followed a similar pattern during approximately the same period. As horses worked up through western Colorado, Utah, and southern Idaho, the Utes and their neighbors to the north, the Shoshoni-Snakes of the upper Snake River, were mounted around 1690.

Here, the movement forked off in two prongs leading toward the northeast and northwest. The latter prong brought horses to the Cayuses and Nez Percé tribes about 1700. Another thirty years found them in good supply all through the intermountain region as far north as the Okanogan and Kootenai valleys of British Columbia.

A host of Indian legends and accounts received from the older natives by early fur traders leaves little question about the progress of these northwestern horses. One venerable old Nez Percé confirmed much of it in a conversation with Meriwether Lewis in 1805. By that date, all the intermountain tribes were on horseback and assessing their wealth by the size of their herds.

The course of the northeastern migrants led up the Snake and Green rivers to western Montana and the Yellowstone. The Lemhi and Wind River Shoshonis, north of and related to the Snakes, were the first to become mounted. It is believed they were little behind the Snakes in getting their horses.

The Flatheads were next. Francis Haines dates the start of their horse culture at between 1700 and 1710. They were followed by the Crows and Blackfeet. Both of the latter nations obtained their first horses in the 1730s. All three appear to have received their original animals from the Shoshonis.

These dates coincide nicely with old tales told by the Keepers of History in all these tribes. They also reflect accounts written into the records by such early fur men as David Thompson, St. Pierre, and Anthony Hendry, who associated with these people in the 1700s.

All Crow legends, incidentally, agree that there were no horses south or east of their territory along the Yellowstone until some time after they got their original mounts from the west.

This supports other evidence that it was Plains horses which mounted all the tribes east of the Rockies. The migration there seems to have started about 1695. Most of it stemmed from the Comanche country in west Texas. At least, that is where the Pawnees told Claude du Tisne they had got the ones they had when he met some of them in central Kansas in 1719. Du Tisne judged the animals to have been a fairly recent acquisition, and apparently some of the first to arrive that far north.

Five years later, de Bourgmond discovered the advance guard had moved on to the extreme northwest corner of Kansas. That the animals were still in short supply and highly prized for their rarity is evinced by his statement that he managed to buy only seven head, "and they at a very costly figure."

De Bourgmond also wrote that the 1,100 Kaw foot-Indians he had brought from the Missouri River had never before seen horses. Neither had they found any of the creatures on their journey. All the eastern Kansas peoples were still traveling on foot and using dogs for packing.

Starting with the Pawnees shortly after 1700, it seems to have been the Comanche animal which put all the Plains tribes on horseback as far north as South Dakota by about 1740. Pierre de la Verendrye found them in the Black Hills three years later upon his return from explorations in Wyoming and Montana. His son took a couple of these horses, probably obtained from the Cheyennes, back to his Mandan friends in North Dakota as a gift. These were the Mandans' first horses, as none of the animals ranged east of the Missouri River at that time.

It was the summer of 1745 that Anthony Hendry reported the presence of horses among the Assiniboins along the Canadian border. He said they were recent arrivals. Later travelers found the Saskatchewan Assiniboins and Crees with only a few in the early 1800s. Maximilian wrote that the Crees had made little progress in the horse business by 1833. The fact that these people were predominantly canoe-Indians may have had something to do with the situation.

The Minnesota Sioux were also canoe-people. Horses, however, made a swift and radical change in their life. They knew nothing of the animals when Jonathan Carver visited them in 1767. Six years later, Peter Pond found them partly mounted on the few horses they had obtained. By 1796, horses had practically replaced canoes as a mode of travel, according to David Thompson's journals.

Meanwhile, this new horse consciousness had induced part of the tribe to move out on the South Dakota Plains east of the Missouri River. This was ideal horse country, made for such mounted Tartars as the Sioux were to become. They claim to have gotten their main start in the animals from the Cheyennes. Mari Sandoz places this notable event at the ancient trading site on Horse Creek, in southeastern Wyoming, where some quilled robes purchased the tribe's first "medicine dogs."

Contemporaneous with the spread of western horses was a minor introduction of eastern animals among the tribes east of the Mississippi. English and French stock from New England and Quebec began trickling out through Ohio and down from the Great Lakes shortly after 1700. Similar migrations from the eastern seaboard crossed the mountains into Kentucky and Tennessee. Together, they reached the Mississippi at such points as the mouths of the Minnesota, Des Moines, and Illinois rivers around 1750. By that time, all the tribes east of the Mississippi had become reasonably familiar with the beasts, as had the Iowas and Missouris farther west. Most of them used the animals to some extent, though none attained the stature of the Plains nations as horsemen.

Among the latter, bulwarked by unlimited breeding stock scattered from Mexico to Saskatchewan, the scene was set for the rapidly multiplying herds which were to amaze all western visitors after 1800.

Mules, too, were often present in these herds. Most Indians rated mules as particularly choice possessions, going to great lengths to obtain them. M. Menard, the French fur trader, wrote in 1792 that the Cheyennes, Kiowas, Arikaras, and Mandans had many Mexican mules in their herds. These all wore Spanish brands, as did many of their horses. As Menard had spent some fourteen years with the Mandans, he might be considered a knowledgeable reporter.

Though there is no record of any Indians' having bred mules at that time, all the various tribes owned and coveted them. Part of their value, in Indian eyes, hinged on the necessity of theft or uncertain trade to obtain them.

The journals of Lewis and Clark speak of mules in the Mandan and Hidatsa herds in 1805. The mules and many horses carried Spanish brands. Farther west, the explorers found the same thing among the Lemhi Shoshonis, whom they met above the Three Forks of the Missouri.

The one portion of the West where neither mules nor horses received particular attention was in the Pacific coastal valleys. The northern Indians of this section were mostly village-dwelling, canoe-people. Cut off from their horseback cousins by the Cascade Mountains, they had little contact with the new animals. It was not until the American mountain-men and Canadian fur traders began riding their sturdy mustangs through the high passes in search of new beaver streams during the early 1800s, that they became much acquainted with horses. Even then, they never actually adopted the animals nor developed any great fondness for riding.

Farther south, the California tribes were chiefly sedentary fishermen and agriculturists. Isolated from the southwestern nations by the high Sierras, they were comparatively ignorant of horses until Gaspar de Portolá brought some of the animals north with his expedition of 1769. Though others were soon to follow, they were forbidden to the natives for many years. Some were later appropriated by the Indian herdsmen impressed into service by the missions, but oppression and decimation by the Spaniards prevented any noticeable advance in horse culture.

In the over-all picture, none of the West Coast Indians appear as real horsemen. That was reserved for the hard-riding nomads of the Plains and Rocky Mountain region, where horses were such a vital part of life.

Foremost among the horse-Indians were the Comanches. They were among the first to have horses and the first to set the pattern for most Indian activities. Their horsemanship was equalled only by that of the Crows, to whom the Sioux ran a close second. General Crook called the Comanches the finest and most efficient light cavalry the world had ever known. Armed with their short, powerful bows and six-foot lances, they stood as the personifications of the ancient Huns who had conquered half the Old World thirteen centuries before.

One of their favorite pastimes was to ride alongside a fleeing buffalo, then leap from the horse to the shaggy brute's back and stab it to death with a knife while in full flight. As warriors, they were the dread of everyone who knew them. Experienced military men credited them with being foes more to be feared than any mounted troops known.

It was the horses of these people, supplemented by the wild bands of the Southwest, which developed the variety of colors later found among all western herds. The conquistadors had brought mostly solid-color animals to Mexico; but with uncontrolled breeding and the natural mating of settler stock that had escaped to the wilds, mixed and off-colors were bound to appear. Moreover, the Indian was a great lover of the colorful and flamboyant. He liked showy horses for ceremonial occasions, for his lady's use, for visiting excursions and, under certain conditions, for war. Aided by time, these factors eventually produced a generous sprinkling of off-colored mounts wherever the animals ranged.

The Cheyennes, by the way, won their names as the Painted Horse People through having owned the first pintos to appear on the central Plains.

It should be said, however, that pure love of color was not always the Indian's primary motive in breeding or trading for certain types of horses. There were invariably substantial reasons for most of his customs and practices, including the selection of coveted mounts for his *remuda*. He was one of our original camouflage experts, exercising his art at a time when the rest of the world tilted a supercilious nose at what it considered mere childish antics of untutored savages. But the red man was wise in the knowledge of his fathers. Often at war and usually averse to alarming the wild game on which his larder depended, he was a past master at moving in an unobtrusive manner that blended with his surroundings. That was probably why it took an overwhelming mob of European invaders three centuries to run him to earth.

As he painted his body to conform with particular backgrounds when on foot, so did the Indian achieve a measure of invisibility on horseback by riding an animal similarly disguised by color. In winter, when the ground was covered with snow, the Indian would choose a white horse from his multi-colored herd. Blacks, dark bays, or browns were best for night riding or in timbered country. Duns, roans, and creams held preferred positions in the sandy deserts or when the plains had become a bleached tawny sea of waving grass. Blues, roans, and grays offered the best security in sagebrush and juniper country. Pintos and light grays blended with certain seasonal backgrounds to perfection. They also lent themselves more readily to the skillful paint jobs which often added to the illusion.

But regardless of color, all horse-Indians found any of the animals to be an irresistible lure. From Canada to Mexico, the great international game of horse stealing was in constant operation.

All this thievery, however, must not be judged by the precept of the white man's Eighth Commandment. To the red man, it was more in the nature of a nice clean sport; the horse was a table stake in a most fascinating gamble. Success depended on skill, bravery, and physical prowess, being commonly rated a higher honor than killing an enemy. For the winner, the more difficult the theft or the stiffer the penalty for failure, the higher the honor. Consistently successful horse stealers walked in the highest social circle and brought much prestige to the tribe. To win such distinction, young men would train themselves in the craft from boyhood. That their neighbors might bring humiliation down upon their heads by retaliating in kind was all part of the game—something to guard against, but to accept with all possible grace as an example of one's medicine being overpowered by unknown forces. The old Omaha Indian saying went: "A horse you may possess, but never own."

Further dissemination of horses was aided by the widespread channels of Indian trade. This ancient barter system reached into every corner of the red man's homeland. From every direction, the many nations made yearly migrations to such centuries-old trading centers as the Three Forks of the Missouri in western Montana; the Chugwater Valley of southeastern Wyoming; The Dalles of the Columbia River; the Arkansas River near Pueblo, Colorado; and the Pueblo villages of the upper Pecos River. There, at the colorful conclaves, amidst gambling, dancing, feasting, horse racing and visiting, goods from myriad regions changed hands—dried meat and pemmican from the buffalo plains for the corn, beans, and dried fruits and fish of more sedentary tribes; buffalo robes and dressed skins for skillfully designed weapons and stone tools; choice furs and beadwork for sea shells from the Gulf Coast or copper ornaments from the North. And ever, when Indians got together, there was the inevitable bargaining for horses or their exchange as gifts.

Often retold by the Old Ones at such tribal gatherings, and still interesting sidelights for antiquarians, were such stories as the old Lacota-Sioux legend of the Thunder-horse. That was what they called it in the long, long-ago time, before the Sioux had ever heard of actual horses. It was a monstrous horselike animal which appeared occasionally out of the spirit world. According to the noted Sioux, American Horse, who personally related the legend to James H. Cook in the late 1800s, this great animal would sometimes come down to earth during thunderstorms and chase buffalo, often striking and killing them with his massive hoofs. On one notable occasion he saved the lives of a whole village of Sioux at a time when all game had mysteriously disappeared. When hope for salvation had all but vanished, the great spirit horse suddenly appeared out of a thunderstorm and drove a herd of buffalo into the midst of the camp. The confused animals, coming from no one knew where, fell easy prey to the hurriedly armed villagers, allowing much meat to be taken and all lives saved.

Equally intriguing is the story from the Southwest of Johano-ai. This is a Navajo legend which tells how the sun is carried through the sky on the back of a horse by the god, Johano-ai. The god is supposed to have five horses, all of different colors, which the rider uses in turn as he makes his daily trip from east to west. It is a very ancient legend in Navajo history, and strangely reminiscent of more ancient mythology in the distant East, when horses were still associated with the gods. At the same time, the specific colors designated for Johano-ai's horses, one each of white, black, dun, bay and chestnut, indicate later association with the Spanish Barbs. Or does it?

Man's life in America dates back into antiquity; horses existed here perhaps no longer than fifteen or twenty thousand years ago. Was the belief in spirit horses, present long before the European animals were ever known by the later Indians, some importation from ancient lands or a direct conception sprung from the country where horses first originated? Such legends make for interesting guesswork and invite a host of speculations.

—18—

Indian Saddle Makers

WITH THE POSSIBLE exception of a few isolated cases in the far Southwest, we might truthfully consider the Indian to be America's first saddle maker. While the French and English colonists along the Atlantic seaboard were importing their saddles from the old country, the native red men north of the Spanish settlements and west to the Pacific were building their own riding gear of native materials fifty to two hundred years before they were first induced to start swapping their own work for manufactured articles.

Unfortunately, practically nothing is known of the early craftsmen who first set the pattern for Indian saddlery. There are a few indications that some of the Indians were using saddles of their own making as early as 1630–1640. These accounts are so lacking in detail as to shed little light on exactly when, where, and how the rigs were made or to what extent used. According to Dr. John C. Ewers of the Smithsonian Institution, the oldest fully documented Indian saddle of native manufacture known to exist in any collection dates back only to the early 1830s. Any creations, changes, and developments that took place in the preceding centuries can only be a matter of conjecture. Nevertheless, considering the basic principles of saddle making, the limited range of materials available to the Indian, and man's inherent opposition to change, it seems logical to believe that native saddles varied little in style between their earliest conceptions and the designs commonly found in later years.

In the beginning, much of the new craft was influenced by captives from the Spanish settlements. There was considerable traffic in Mexican slaves during the seventeenth century. All the southern Plains people prized such captives very highly because of their knowledge of handling the new animals and constructing suitable saddlery, metal working, and the like. The crafts and skills thus displayed under duress were quickly adopted by the Indians.

Most of the native Americans possessed an inborn cleverness in contriving devices helpful to their mode of life. When the advent of the horse opened up a whole new world of progress to them, they had no trouble in selecting their needs from nature's storehouse. Just as they flaked stone arrowpoints into serviceable weapons and shaped buffalo hides into comfortable homes, so they selected crotched tree limbs and elk antlers for saddle forks and made stirrups from bent sticks. Thin slabs split from cedar or cottonwood served as sidebars, while sun-cured rawhide provided seat coverings and bound the several components together in a sturdy replica of the rigs used by the foreigners.

Indian saddles were made in three basic designs. One was the plain wood-frame packsaddle tree, very similar to the white man's old sawbuck variety, with curved pommel and cantle. While made for packing, it was often covered with a robe and used for riding by men who had nothing better at hand. The second was the treeless pad saddle, which will be discussed later in this chapter. The other was the sidebar tree model covered with rawhide and usually fitted with a suspended seat. The later bore a strong relationship to the packsaddle but had higher forks and a better appearance.

The most peculiar thing about all these sidebar saddles was their uniformity in size throughout the country. Though there was occasionally a variation in width when made to accommodate some particular horse, few saddle makers departed from, and none altered, the average length. In general, they gave the appearance of all having been cut from a single standard pattern. When we stop to consider that this held true throughout half a continent populated by a myriad unrelated primitive peoples who had no metallic tools, processed materials, printed diagrams, or even a common language, it would seem that civilization's bright minds might do well to ponder the native intellect of so-called savages.

Whether north, south, east or west, Indian saddles seldom fell outside of the common 17- to 21-inch length. That was only a 4-inch variation

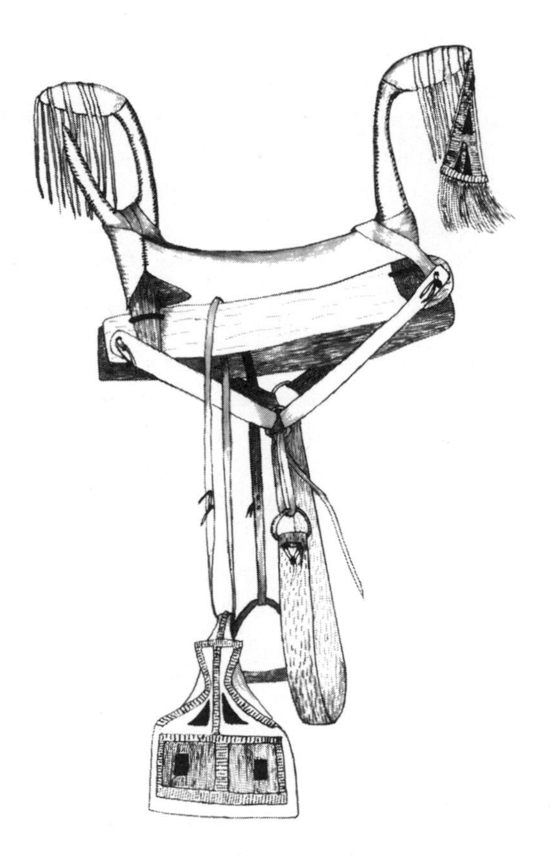

FIG. 95. Shoshoni Indian saddle.

for the whole country. Within individual tribes, the margin was usually less than half that. Those of the Utes stayed within a 17- to 18-inch limit. The Crows made theirs slightly longer, 19 to 20 inches. The Cheyennes had the widest variation, 16 to 19 inches. The 20- to 21-inch Shoshoni model was the longest of all. Other tribes held to similar ranges of length within the general limited scope.

In other dimensions, the sidebars held to the uniform three or four inches in width and one-half inch in thickness. Their profile shapes were usually fairly standard within each tribe, the slightly curved or sickle-shaped design being most common. Round, square, and tapered ends appeared as definite tribal patterns, as did the straight or deeply

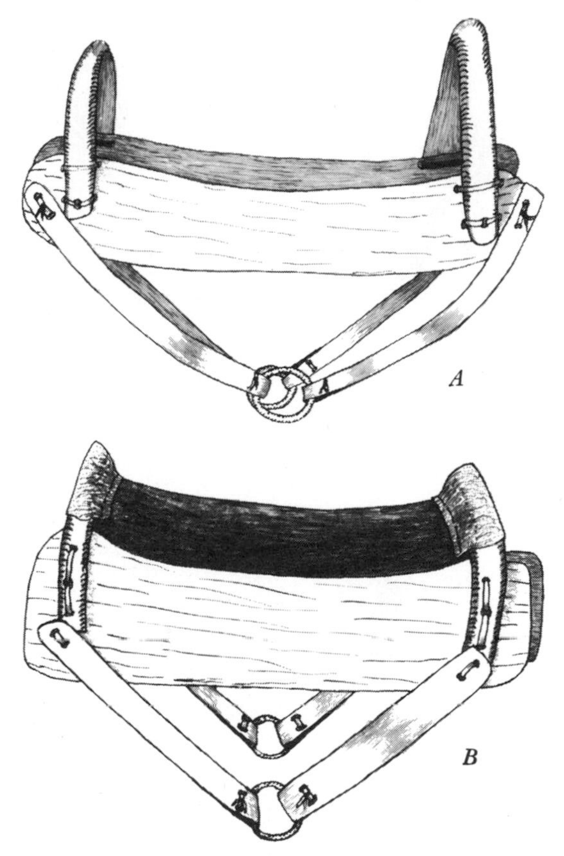

FIG. 96. Indian saddles: *A* Crow; *B* Mandan.

scalloped edges and the placement of holes for attaching the rigging. See Figs. 95–99.

The rigging was always about the same, two straps on either side, tied with thongs. All were made to accommodate a single cinch. The stirrup straps were simply looped over the sidebars and left free to slide forward or backward at will.

Forks were made from elk horns, bent wood, or natural tree forks. On the high-pommel model, the forks were shaped like an inverted Y.

Their angled ends were laced to opposite sidebars, allowing the shank part to extend upward and serve as a horn or cantle. There was usually little distinction between horn and cantle, both being about the same in size and shape.

Among the peoples of the northern Plains an upward protruding hook on the outside of the front fork was often present (Figs. 95, 97).

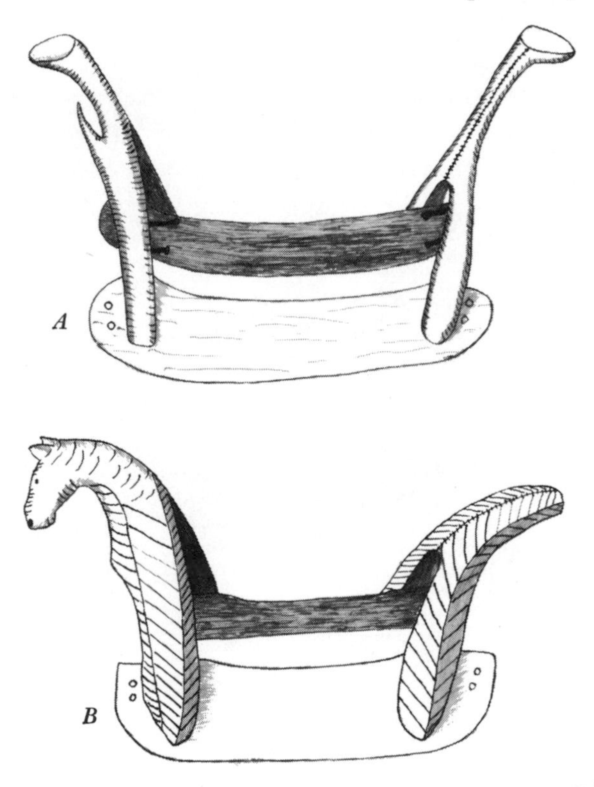

FIG. 97. Indian saddles: *A* Blackfoot; *B* Menomini.

The primary use of such hooks was to hold the front end of the suspended seat in place. It also provided a handy depository for quirt, arrow quiver, parfleche, or similar extras. As a place to swing a papoose carrier on moving day, it had few equals.

This was especially appreciated by women riders. And it was women riders who most commonly used these extremely high-forked saddles. Men usually showed a marked preference for the lower forks or treeless pad outfits. Early travelers in the West made frequent mention of the extravagant pommels and cantles seen on women's saddles. Francis Parkman wrote that they ran up to eighteen inches high among the Sioux of southeastern Wyoming. The Astor Fur Company men, Robert Stuart and Gabriel Franchère, reported similar extremes among the Walla Wallas and Nez Percé in 1812–1814. Clark Wissler says it was the general rule throughout the Plains country. Too, it was the saddles of the women which usually carried the most decoration.

Aside from ceremonial and parade outfits, men's sidebar saddles ran chiefly to bow forks (Fig. 96). The uncovered packsaddle style seems to have been in evidence to considerable extent in many sections. The Lewis and Clark journals speak of those seen among the Shoshonis of southwestern Montana as being much like the packsaddles used by the French and Spanish. Various observers mention similar rigs in other localities.

A design of the packsaddle variety was in use in early times east of the Mississippi River. James Adair left us a description of some of this type which he saw in the Chickasaw towns in 1775. He said they had the sawbuck end pieces notched together three inches below the ends, two pairs set fore and aft like a packsaddle and lashed to the sidebars with rawhide thongs. The sidebars were thin boards split out of oak. When assembled, the whole rig was covered with green buffalo hide, hair side out, and laced to the tree with rawhide strings. The whole was then dried to extreme hardness. "When thoroughly dried," he wrote, "it appears to have all the properties of a cuirass saddle." A trimmed bearskin was used for a saddle blanket.

He further commented at this time that among the southeastern Indians in general, "The shape of their saddles is very antiquated and mean, like those from the West Indies."

This would lead us to believe the original Spanish stock saddle, previously mentioned as a Santo Domingo development of the middle 1500s, might well have found its way to the southeastern mainland as it did to Mexico during the early period of Spanish expansion. Thus it could have fathered the original Indian saddles of the Southeast as its relative did those in the Southwest.

The majority of the Eastern nations, like those of the Deep South, seemed to favor the low sawbuck and bow-type forks. Fairly low Y forks were used to some extent among the Great Lakes tribes. These were often carved in artistic designs, especially among the Menomini. Fig. 97 shows a classic example of the latter type.

The fashioning of elk and deer antlers into saddle forks was practiced mainly in the West. East of the Mississippi, wood was the chief material. The bow forks were rounded strips of wood or horn bent in circular shape, while the Y style came from large elk horns or natural tree forks trimmed to a proper fit.

Edwin James describes an Indian saddle in the making. While returning with Major Long's Rocky Mountain expedition in 1820, James fell in with an Indian and his wife somewhere along the upper Arkansas River. The pair had suffered some recent misfortunes, and were reduced to one horse without a saddle. The explorers took pity on their plight and extended hospitality for the night at the camp.

That evening, the woman borrowed an axe from her hosts and chopped down a suitable cottonwood. She cut two forks out of the tree, hewing them to proper size and shape. Then she split a pair of thin, flat boards out of the tree body to serve as sidebars. These were smoothed down with the axe and trimmed to some twenty inches in length. Matching holes were bored through the forks and sidebars with a heated ramrod, and the parts lashed together with wet rawhide thongs. More wet rawhide was laced over the whole rig, after which it was set by the fire to dry and shrink itself tightly around the wood. The couple went on their way the following morning, the crude but serviceable saddle, padded with a robe, permitting them to ride one at a time in reasonable comfort.

Wood forks predominated among all the Plains tribes. Whether of the Y or bow type, wood was easily worked and, when covered with rawhide, as durable as the more brittle horn. Moreover, the tough forks found in most ash, elm, and cottonwood trees were nearly always available in good supply along the prairie streams. Wood was also better adapted to the making of fancy forms and extremely high forks.

In the fir and pine regions of the Pacific Northwest, the situation was reversed. Forks and heavy crotched limbs of suitable size and strength appear rarely in such straight-growing woods. Here, we find the native saddle makers turning more toward deer and elk antlers for material. Franchère, Ross, Wyeth, and many others mentioned the preponderance of horn forks among all the intermountain tribes between Great Salt Lake and British Columbia.

Among these people, cinches, latigos, and stirrup straps were of braided hair. Stirrups were of bent wood covered with rawhide. The horn was also usually covered with rawhide. This covering was more prevalent with the elaborately decorated high-forked women's saddles.

The high forks of horn and wood, similar to Figs. 95 and 97, were in considerable favor throughout the Rocky Mountain region. Garrard said high-forked saddles carrying much decoration were a particular characteristic of the Cheyennes. These often had bead- and quill-trimmed leather housings that covered the horse's back from withers to tail.

Bow forks, however, were not uncommon among all tribes. The use of bows tended to increase as one moved east from the Rocky Mountains. Most of them were made of horn. Individual saddles built with a Y fork and a bow cantle appeared indiscriminately in various sections but were by no means common.

The Crows, Mandans, Minitari, and Assiniboins rode mostly bow-type rigs (Fig. 96). They appear to have favored a somewhat higher style of bow than was used in the East. A few Y forks were also used.

In the Southwest, Indian saddles followed the old Spanish and Mexican styles more closely. The earlier ones, of course, employed the familiar Y- or bow-type forks and rawhide coverings, but even these showed the Latin influence. This was enhanced by the Spanish rigging and decorative materials which they somehow managed to acquire for most of their outfits.

As a general thing, such tribes as the Navajo, Hopi, and Pima showed a marked preference for the bow-type forks. With the Apaches, Comanches, and Caddoes, the inverted Y predominated. But this was not a hard and fast rule. According to early observers, both divisions used the opposite type to some extent, as in the North.

As foreign influence grew and expanded in the Southwest during the eighteenth century, the saddles of all these Indians steadily drew closer to the Spanish pattern, both through choice and availability of materials. Mexican trees were used whenever obtainable. In Fig. 98 we have a Navajo example from this transition period, showing the main characteristics of both Spanish and Indian parentage. Incidentally, nowhere else were Indian saddles ever known to carry double rigging.

Bear, buffalo, and cougar skins were used for saddle blankets throughout most of the Indian country. More often than not they were decorated around the edges with quill- and beadwork, colored hair tassels, and carved bone ornaments. In the Southwest, where cotton had been grown and woven into fabrics long before America was even known to Europeans, cloth blankets dyed in attractive colors appeared frequently.

As already noted, some saddles were simply crude rawhide-bound frames over which a buffalo-robe pad was thrown to ease the harsh jolts of rough angles. The majority, however, employed the suspended seat principle (Fig. 96, 97). This feature gives cause to wonder where the unread American Indian picked up an idea so plainly reminiscent of the ancient Hungarian aid to comfortable riding. We only know the earliest records of Indian saddles show this innovation already in operation.

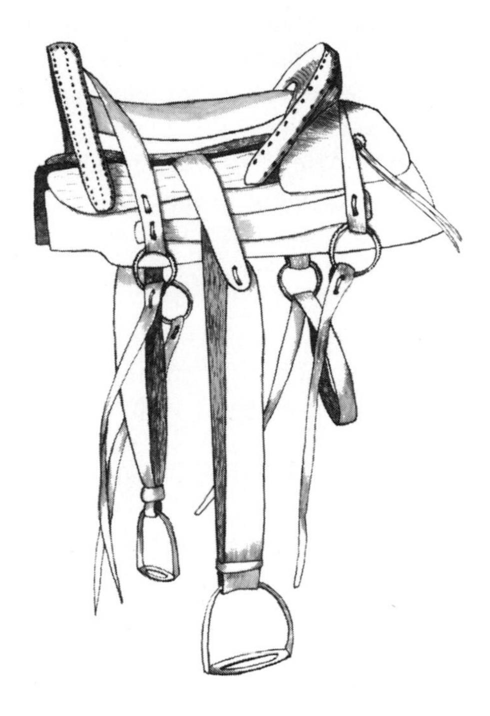

FIG. 98. Navajo saddle.

Along with the sidebar saddle came the treeless pad design. These ranged from rather crude rush-stuffed cushions used by the Pimas to the well-constructed and finely decorated creations of the North. Such saddles were light in weight and easy on both man and horse. Used almost exclusively by men, they were prime favorites among buffalo hunters, war parties, and for racing or long journeys. Wissler believes that they were used before the slower advancing frame saddles appeared.

Dr. Ewers follows this up by pointing to the sixteenth century pad saddle of Spain brought to Mexico in the middle 1700s. Such rigs likely made their initial appearance in America much earlier than that, as it was undoubtedly a first cousin to the Spanish pad on which the Argentine pioneers patterned their *Gaucho* saddles. They are described as four-cornered pads stuffed with hay and secured to the horse by a surcingle cinch.

When white men first penetrated the northern Plains and Rockies,

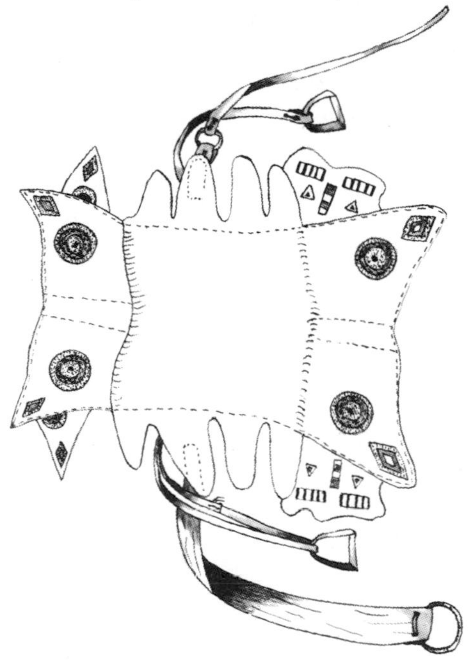

FIG. 99. Sioux pad saddle construction.

they found a similar pad of much improved design in general use among all the horseback nations of those regions. Hendry reported seeing them among the Blackfeet as far north as Calgary, Alberta, in 1754. Others noted their presence in various separate sections during the same period. As horses had reached those regions only some ten or fifteen years previously, there seems little doubt that the use of pads arrived with them, as Wissler's reasoning suggests.

A glance at the Sioux pad in Fig. 99 will show the ease of construction under primitive conditions, as well as the evident light weight, flexibility, and comfortable security under the press of war or buffalo chases. Two pieces of tanned skin, each about 24 by 30 inches, were cut to match in sort of an hourglass shape, with the greater width at the rear. These were placed one on top of the other with the edges even and then sewed down the center with two parallel rows of stitching spaced about two inches apart. Another line of stitching ran around the outside edge to hold the duplicate leather facings together after the interior was stuffed to the right thickness with deer hair.

Elk and deer hair, by the way, is hollow. Thus it remains fairly fluffy after extended use, instead of matting down like horsehair and most vegetable padding.

With the pad properly stuffed and sewn, a third piece of leather, 12 to 15 inches wide by twice that long, was placed crosswise in the center of the base pad and sewn in place to serve as a seat cover. This piece usually had scalloped or fringed ends. Onto its underside, near the edge, was sewn the 2- to 4-inch-wide strap used as a cinch. A latigo strap was attached to the opposite side. Stirrup straps were fastened to the seat cover or to the ends of a rawhide band which ran completely over the saddle. The latter method concealed the cinch attachments and also allowed a freer play to the stirrups. The completed rig seldom weighed over three pounds.

Such saddles were frequently embellished with bead- and quillwork. Four large rosettes of beadwork on the outer corners of the skirts were common decorations. Other fancywork on the edges and extra flaps usually ran to individual ideas. The outside seam was often concealed beneath a band of trimming.

Pad saddles were usually present in the ever-familiar picture of Indians riding around an enemy with their bodies slung on the off side of racing mounts. A warrior was reasonably secure in spread-eagling himself on the animal's side while he shot over or under its neck, if the pad was cinched tight enough to insure carrying his weight on one stirrup, his opposite heel hooked under a flap or ornamental knob on the back of the saddle and his head and one arm thrust through a rawhide loop suspended from the saddle or the horse's mane.

This style of fighting was practically the same method practiced by the old Cossack tribes of Europe a thousand years earlier. How it happened to spring up on opposite sides of the earth in such widely separated eras is something else for antiquarians to ponder over.

A variant of the pad saddle was the Cree war rig used in the middle 1800s. This was merely a broad band of rawhide cinched a trifle loosely about the horse. The rider took up the extra slack in the cinch by thrusting his feet under it as a substitute for stirrups.

A similar method was employed by the Comanche mustangers of Texas when chasing wild horses. They, too, depended on a single band of rawhide cinched around the horse. But as an added improvement, they attached small loops of braided rawhide to the bands for use as stirrups. The loops were made only large enough to receive the rider's big toes. Frank Collinson wrote of seeing this style used on the Staked Plains as late as 1882.

And here we have another one of those little riddles which persist in rearing their intriguing heads along the horseman's trail. How did plain surcingle rigs come to appear simultaneously among such widely separated peoples as the Texas mustangers and the Canadian Crees fifteen hundred miles to the north? And what, if any, is the relation of the Texas toe-loop stirrups to the toe rings of the South American Gauchos twice that far to the south? Pure coincidence, perhaps! Yet the mysterious long arm of common parentage remains to plague the imagination.

In the early days all Indian stirrups were of much the same general bent-wood pattern. Men of the Plains tribes west to the Rockies favored the simple triangular shape. Beyond the Shining Mountains and up into Canada the round-top style was the most popular. Round tops also predominated in the northern territories of the Mandans, Minitari, and Assiniboins. The large, square type with decorated sides was chiefly a woman's stirrup. It was native to the central and northern Plains and used most extensively east of the continental divide.

It was undoubtedly something of this sort that Maximilian referred to when he wrote of Assiniboin stirrups as being rawhide-covered affairs made in the shape of shoes. Occasional examples of this type had the footplates almost as long as the foot. The sides were also sometimes cut out in openwork patterns to suit individual artistic tastes.

The basic principle of all these stirrups, however, was the same. The cruder ones were simply willow withes bent into shape and tied together at the top. The better ones predominated, being well designed and carefully constructed. Cottonwood was a favorite material for this work; it was light, tough, and easily fashioned.

A scattering of Spanish iron stirrups, buckles, rings, bits, and other metal trappings began trickling into the northern regions in the early 1700s. Indians were avid gamblers, traders, and visitors. Their commerce was widespread throughout the continent. International warfare also added much to the dispersal of useful commodities. It is not surprising that items of Spanish manufacture antedated the arrival of white men into the West by many years.

A rope made from wild hemp was found to be much in use by the Nez Percé when Lewis and Clark arrived on the Clearwater Fork of Snake River in 1805. Clark wrote that it equalled any rope he had ever seen produced by white men.

Hair was used for strapwork to some extent by most of the Plains peoples, though they usually preferred buffalo hide. Hide bands made very durable cinches and were less inclined to chafe than those of hair. Bits were often made of twisted rawhide, especially by the Comanches. Thongs of the same material were excellent for latigos and stirrup straps. Braided rawhide or long strips of buffalo hide were used for ropes. The latter was favored for picketing horses because of its ability to give and stretch without weakening.

Rawhide from the heavier portions of buffalo skins was used by all the Plains tribes for shoeing horses. This was the same old method practiced by the ancient Tartars and brought west through Arabia, Spain, and Mexico.

Another thing that traveled from East to West without much alteration by passage of time was the rump housings and cruppers extending from the saddle cantle to the mount's tail. Some typical examples may be found in Fig. 100. A crupper design found among the Crows was strangely similar to one of far-off Guatemala. See Fig. 89.

With this single exception, and save for minor tribal peculiarities, such accouterments followed the same general pattern among all Indians. Made of well-dressed leather, often fringed or bordered, and heavy with elaborate designs worked in quills or beads, they added a handsome touch to spirited horses in holiday mood. As a rule, they were reserved for ceremonial occasions, visiting excursions, and capturing the eyes of admiring maidens. The patterns of colored beads overlaying alternating shades of leather had a way of rippling in the sunlight with the movements of the horse that would delight the eye of any beauty lover.

Fancy beaded and quilled breast collars were often used with such display outfits, though commonly dispensed with in everyday riding.

Watchful eyes might also catch a further bright, flashing message from a small mirror attached to the saddle. Indian riders often had a small trade mirror hung on their bodies or among the saddle ornaments.

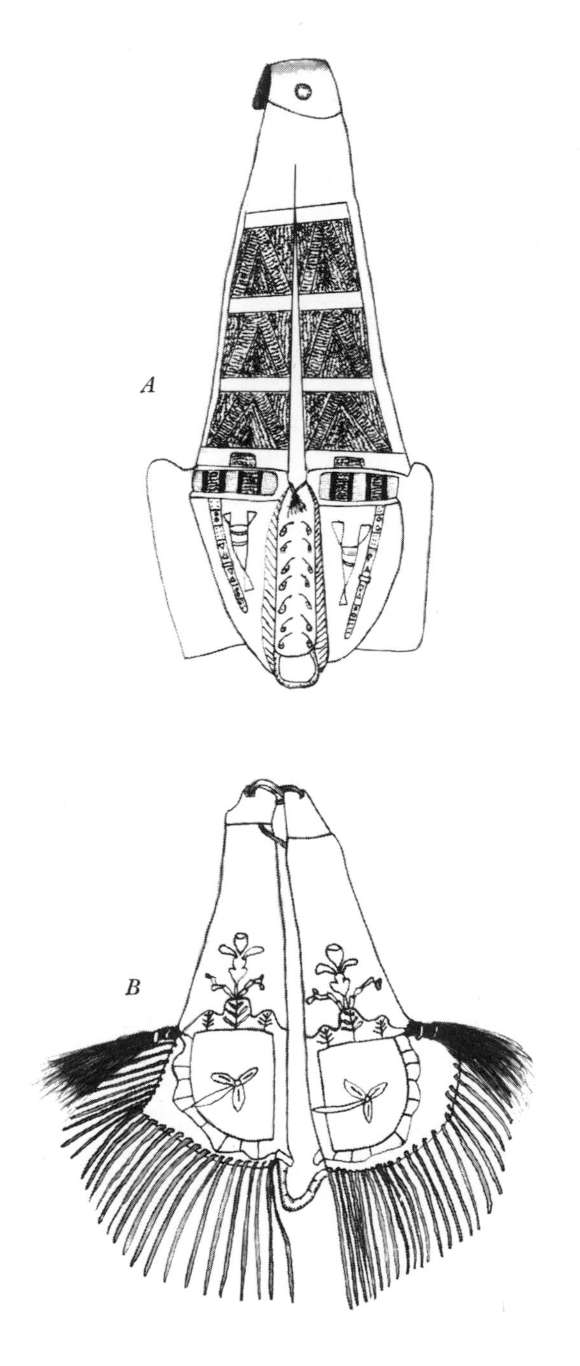

FIG. 100. Indian cruppers: *A* Shoshoni; *B* Blackfoot.

Many people harbor the erroneous idea that Indian warriors carried those little trade mirrors for the sole purpose of admiring themselves in unemployed moments. But that was not the most valuable function of the little glass, which was really the keystone to a country-wide communication system.

The Indian was probably America's first heliograph expert. With the shiny surface of the glass tilted toward the sun, he could communicate with his fellows across unmeasurable miles of wilderness.

The mirror was used to attract the innately curious antelope and draw them within range of concealed hunting companions. Horse-stealing parties found it a most valuable aid. With two or three mirror-armed lookouts posted miles away in either direction to observe any enemy movements and direct the escape route, it was comparatively easy for the main actors to steer the stolen herd clear of recapture or direct pursuit. Many kindred uses made the mirror the most sensible thing in the world.

Colonel Richard I. Dodge wrote that in drilling warriors for combat, a regular practice in most tribes, a chief would usually command the drill from an outside position, preferably the top of a knoll. His orders to the company would be communicated by signals in most cases, often with mirrors. Dodge felt that the Indians were far more proficient at such signaling than any of their white contemporaries.

While the Apaches were the only Indians to wear spurs, all the tribes considered quirts as standard equipment. These all followed the same general pattern, a bone or wooden handle with leather thong lashes affixed at one end. There was usually a wrist loop on the opposite end.

It was a common saying in the early West that you could tell a mounted Indian from a white man in two ways—the manner in which he kept his quirt going in time with every jump of his horse, and the way he sat his saddle.

As a matter of fact, no one familiar with the older Indian's style of riding would ever be in doubt about his identity. He habitually sat his mount in what appeared to be a constrained and rather awkward manner. On parade or at ease, his body was held stiffly erect; in motion, he rode bent slightly forward, his thighs nearly perpendicular and shanks bent back to bring his heels up against the horse's flanks. Likely his shoulders would be somewhat hunched and his arms anything but relaxed.

The one tribe departing from this general rule was the Apaches.

They rode more in the manner of their Mexican neighbors. Using the longest stirrup leathers of any tribe, their lower legs did not present the sharp angle commonly seen among other Indians.

But all this was merely superficial. Unorthodox as their style might have appeared, Indians knew few superiors as riding men. In war or on buffalo hunts or the trail they rode like centaurs and well deserved the title of Tartars of the Plains. Early writers agreed that they were among the world's most skillful horsemen. Colonel Dodge wrote of what he called their "incredible feats of horsemanship" on several occasions.

It should be noted in passing that the native red men all originally practiced man's natural habit of mounting from the off side of the horse, as have all primitive races. This was another source of disparaging remarks made about the Indian's peculiar riding methods by uniformed and intolerant white observers.

Indian women were often the recipients of even harsher criticism from form-conscious male outsiders. Judged by white standards current at that time, their style was undoubtedly a far cry from that decreed by Eastern fashion. Still, that doesn't alter the fact that they could ride where most white women couldn't even drag a halter. Habitually riding astride, as had their Sarmatian sisters of four thousand years before, they were somewhat inclined to show a lack of the feminine grace which white men deemed so important. But seated deeply in the high-forked saddle so admirably suited to a land that knew few refinements, they well deserved commemoration as horsewomen of the first order.

Perhaps it was their appreciation of good horsemanship that led them, as well as their men, to abandon the old homemade rigs for better equipment as soon as white traders began moving into the country. For good as they were and long as they had served a worthy purpose, the crude frame saddles were undeniably less comfortable to horse and rider than the better-designed rigs made by white craftsmen. The Indian recognized this as quickly as anybody. As soon as superior saddles began to show up, he rated them next to guns as desirable trade items.

Exactly when this branch of commerce saw birth is uncertain. In fact, it was more of an evolutionary process than a birth. We know Spanish equipment was coming out of Mexico and the Santa Fe country in the very early 1700s, some as the result of Indian raids. By the middle of the century a fair scattering of Indians were riding Mexican outfits. Spanish saddles and bridles were also present as individual specimens in practically every tribe throughout the North when the first white men arrived there.

In various portions of the Southwest, raiding, gambling, trading, and the passing back and forth of illicit French traders all helped to bring about a wide distribution of the Spanish gear. Wily traders working out of Natchitoches and Fort Chartres found a lucrative profit in bringing Mexican saddles from Santa Fe and Chihuahua. The bulk of them seem to have passed into the hands of western riders and traders bound for the Indian country. They apparently had little appeal among eastern horsemen. Few of them were in use east of the Mississippi.

The West's affinity for Spanish-type saddles stems to a large extent from their direct relationship to the old Indian-made rigs. Both apparently shared a common ancestor; then each departed in its own separate direction for over a century. During this separation, the cumbersome old Spanish saddle slowly evolved into something more suited to the *caballero's* taste and the *vaquero's* work, while the Indian was shaping his deep-seated, high-forked design toward the riding security demanded by wild horses, racing buffalo, war maneuvers, and hazardous mountain trails. When the creative developments of both factions met, it was to form a liaison which eventually produced the heir known as the western stock saddle.

Parkman's writings repeatedly mention Spanish saddles, bits, and spurs as those most commonly used among the mountain-men. Pommel holsters for pistols were often seen on such saddles.

It was this growing demand by both Indians and mountain-men that started the Spanish, or Santa Fe, saddles moving into the central and northern Plains in quantities shortly after 1820. The opening of the great Santa Fe trade which followed the Mexican Revolution of 1821 brought increased numbers of them to the Missouri River and added impetus to their distribution.

Along with all this was the profit factor, a not inconsiderable aid to any mercantile expansion. According to the diary of General George C. Sibley, there must have been an immense profit in transporting saddles to St. Louis. At Santa Fe, in 1826, the general itemized a list of equipment bought to outfit Captain Brannin for a trip to St. Louis. Included were "five Spanish saddles @ $4.70 each." As these rigs were then selling for twelve to fourteen dollars at the Missouri River, it is easy to see why traders were exerting themselves in bringing the finer things of life to the red men. A reflection of this rise in saddle business is found in the many new saddle shops that sprang up in St. Louis shortly after 1820.

The fact that the saddle trade in the Indian country was truly booming is pretty well documented by an account Thornton Grimsley had with the American Fur Company. This single account, one of many similar items from the old fur company records, brought to light by Barbara Kell of the Missouri Historical Society, covered the period of October, 1832, to October, 1833. During those twelve months this saddle maker sold the company approximately two hundred saddles. The Grimsley records through that period, and earlier, show numerous sales to the U.S. Indian agency.

Of course, not all of these saddles were of the Spanish model. Saddle makers then as now turned out whatever the customers wanted. There were always some who called for the more elite Eastern types, which were much cheaper, a factor which carried weight in the Indian trade as it did elsewhere. Of the two hundred Grimsley saddles sold to the American Fur Company in 1833, seventy were listed as "Spanish saddles." They sold at $12 or $14 and up. Thirty were "common saddles," at $8, apparently the hornless muley or English-style saddles popular in the convention-minded East. Pack saddles were $1.50 and "common bridles" $.75. Also listed were fifteen "Falbacke" or "Fullback" and thirty-six "Pigeon" or "Piegan" saddles.

There is some uncertainity about the spelling and consequent identity of the two latter models. Miss Kell found the writing, poorly penned and age dimmed, hard to decipher; some words were spelled differently in different places while others were almost illegible.

If we accept "Falbacke" as correct, we must consider the word to be merely the name of the maker or designer. "Fullback," on the other hand, would seem to denote a logical distinction between a full-cantled rig and the flat-seated English variety. The latter theory seems more plausible; a cheap saddle patterned after the Spanish type would carry a designation setting it apart from the common flat tree.

Concerning the other model in question: if "Piegan" is meant, we might consider it a saddle especially designed for the Indian trade on the upper Missouri River. The Piegans were an important division of the Blackfeet ranging along the east flank of the Montana Rockies. Attaching their name to an article intended for that general region would have been a most natural proceeding in commercial circles.

Dr. Ewers, however, presents an interesting alternative in describing a saddle used by some of the Plains tribes in the 1800s. It was made with a very low pommel and cantle. The Indians usually relegated it to the status of a packsaddle; but, like all Indian rigs, it was used for riding when need or inclination arose. In the Blackfoot country, where it saw considerable use, the Indians called it the "prairie chicken snare saddle." Knowing the early westerner's predilection for corrupting native names into words of his own choosing, it is easy to understand how such a name might quickly have become "pigeon" to Indian traders and saddle makers alike.

But whatever they were called and however made, the white man's saddles soon assumed an important position among all Indian horsemen. After about 1840, they were no novelty in most sections.

Maximilian said they were in noticeable numbers among the upper Missouri River tribes in 1833. He further noted that they soon lost much of their former identity after coming into Indian hands. One of the first things a native commonly did upon obtaining a manufactured saddle was to cut away everything that didn't appeal to him and then embellish it after his own fashion. Among the Mandans, Minitari and Assiniboins, this usually consisted of lining the inside with red or blue cloth and decorating its outer surface with colored cloth, beads, bone ornaments, hair tassels, buckskin fringes, and dyed quills. Silver and nickel trimmings were much sought after in later years.

The Blackfeet and Crows often covered their saddles with cougar skins. The hides were lined with a piece of red cloth large enough to form a broad border around the entire skin, head, tail, body, and legs. This was placed over the saddle with head and tail hanging down on opposite sides. Less important skins were used when the highly prized cougars were unavailable. Robes of this nature were rated very valuable, often commanding the price of a couple of good horses.

Similar practices held sway all over the West, varying only in minor details. Gregg, Farnham, and Garrard were among the many to mention the likeness of patterns among the various nations on the central and southern Plains. West of the Rockies, Mexican outfits from California began reaching the intermountain peoples after 1824. With this, the influence of the Hudson's Bay Company annual fur brigades, independent American and Mexican traders and wandering mountain-men fostered a distribution of white man's equipment in the Northwest that was equal to, if not ahead of, that on the Plains.

Along with their saddles, the Mexican ring bits were highly prized in the Indian country. The same might be said for the big heavily ornamented spade type. The *vaquero's* fancy leather headstalls, resplendent with silver and nickel trimmings, also held an irresistible appeal. Few Indians north or south could resist the elaborately designed metal stirrups, while reins of braided hair or contrasting colors of leather were universally popular.

Bridle decorations, especially among the Navajo, frequently included one of antiquity's oldest symbols in the form of a crescent-shaped amulet attached, points down, to the bridle browband. This was the same type of charm so popular with Roman, Arab, and Moorish horsemen in guarding their mounts against evil spirits.

There is a strangeness about such a unique charm and belief in its properties appearing halfway around the globe in almost identical form among unlettered red men. Its origin, a coincidental native creation of unknown times, or perhaps the bequest of some superstitious Spaniard? *Quien sabe?* All we can be sure of is that it found a reception that extended on to the twentieth century cowboy.

All this, however, is not to suggest that the old Indian-made gear vanished into the limbo of forgotten things overnight. Far from it! The transition period lasted, in most sections, for around three quarters of a century. As a matter of fact, there was still plenty of old-time native equipment in use when the Great White Father finally managed to set his wards afoot and relegate them to a round of maggoty agency bacon and tepee patrol.

In the meantime, the Indian rode whatever he could get, depending on luck, skill, or wealth. As there were few class distinctions in his democratic society, the available items of better grade simply took their place side by side with the less good. Up until the closing years of the last century, many an old Indian rode a manufactured outfit to chase the white man's cattle off his scanty reservation grass, while many a later-generation youth became a budding cowboy atop some old pad rig or rawhide-covered sidebar saddle.

—19—

Caballeros and Vaqueros

THE CONQUISTADORS WERE interested mainly in gold, glory, and conquest. Opportunists and soldiers of fortune for the most part, only a scattered few had eyes for future economic development. Orderly progress and the establishment of ranches and towns fell mostly to later colonizers, gentlemen with imagination to match their means, and men who saw possibilities in the limitless grazing lands of the New World. These latter bold spirits shared the same common heritage of independence, individuality, initiative, resourcefulness, and love of adventurous freedom which has ever placed the man on horseback in the forefront of pioneer expansion. From them, through the years, evolved the well-known figure of America's cattleman and cowboy. So also the riding gear of today's cowboy is a product of similar evolutionary developments dating far back.

The old cut-down *silla de montar,* or war saddle, a scattering of *la jineta* rigs from old Spain, and a limited number of the stock saddles developed in the West Indies outfitted the original Mexican stockmen for many years. But none of these saddles was completely satisfactory for the varied and exacting work required. It remained for the rangemen to figure out alterations and improvements best suited to their needs. Somewhere around 1600, saddle makers began combining the more desirable features of the older rigs into an all-Mexican creation.

It was a rather crude affair at first, simply a plain wood tree covered with thin rawhide. Some even lacked the rawhide covering, trees, and sidebars, being merely lashed together with thongs. Much depended on the materials available, as well as the skill of the craftsman. But generally speaking, the Mexican saddle had a low, fairly comfortable cantle that made mounting or dismounting easy even under adverse circumstances, and a horned pommel that made for riding security while being low enough to insure free movement for the rider.

The horn was not strong enough for very extensive roping. Most of the early *vaqueros* tied their ropes to the mount's tail when catching stock. Some tied to an extra surcingle cinch that encircled horse and saddle. The rope, when not in use, was carried on the right side, tied behind the cantle.

Complete details on these very early saddles are largely nonexistent. Some lacked any cinch rigging whatever, depending on the surcingle that passed over the saddle seat. Trees were often made from giant cactus wood. This light and unsubstantial material gave rise to the uncomplimentary term of "cactus trees," later applied indiscriminately to common Mexican saddles. Cottonwood and other soft, easily worked woods were also used for tree material.

It was to counteract the inherent weakness of such light, soft woods that Mexican saddle makers first developed the massive horns for their saddles. Once the big-horn custom was established, it remained to become a trademark of Mexican design up into modern times. However, bulky as they were, none of these early trees was overly strong. The poor quality leather produced in Mexico during that period did little to improve the situation.

But it was a start in the right direction. And each succeeding decade saw improvements in styling and construction. By the later 1600s, the basic form of the modern stock saddle had been achieved. The outsize horn had a top four to six inches in diameter surmounting a correspondingly thick neck. Heavier rawhide covering now enclosed the tree. The stirrup straps had been lengthened to allow a better knee-grip while riding the American-Barb wild mustangs, and also to bring the rider's weight below the center of gravity when braced in the stirrups. A more substantial style of single-cinch Spanish rigging had been installed. Saddle bags were appearing, often built onto the saddle. All-wood stirrups made by native craftsmen were quite generally adopted. Fig. 101 shows a saddle fairly typical of this period.

The early Mexican wood stirrups were strictly a New World creation designed to replace the hard-to-get European metal ones. Fig. 102 explains their make-up. The body of the stirrup was carved from oak, the hole being only large enough to admit the toe of the shoe. The tapadera-like covering was of leather made in a more or less fanciful design. Thonged to the stirrup, it presented a slightly curved face to accommodate the shoe tip. (Mexican riders of that period did not wear boots.) Such stirrups were in use from earliest times to the late 1800s.

Some of these stirrups did not have the hole cut entirely through the blocks. Instead, they were made of extra-thick material carved out from the back side. This left a layer of uncut wood over the face of the stirrup to take the place of the leather tapadera.

The Spanish padres of northern Mexico and California mounted their Indian neophytes around the missions on "mission saddles," which lacked any of the later refinements. They were simply rawhide-covered skeleton trees with open seats, usually lashed together with rawhide thongs. They had no skirts or other trappings. Though actual speci-

FIG. 101. Early Mexico-California saddle.

mens no longer exist, old records present them as being a more primitive version of the regular model (Fig. 103), but lacking cinch rigging and saddle bags. They were secured by a surcingle that ran over the seat of the saddle. Stirrups were of the wood-block variety, usually without tapadera coverings. A blanket, piece of leather or animal skin was commonly placed over the open-center tree to serve as a seat. Some of the better ones used by the overseers and early Mexican *vaqueros* appear to have had *mochila* coverings.

Mochilas were full leather covers made to fit over the entire saddle.

They had apertures cut in them through which horn and cantle were slipped to allow a smooth fit and hold them in place. They ordinarily extended well down over a horse's sides to serve as fenders and protect the rider's clothing. A later *mochila* model of similar design appears in Fig. 103.

Those old mission rigs were a pretty lean excuse for saddles, but they served their purpose. As the padres taught their Indian converts to rope

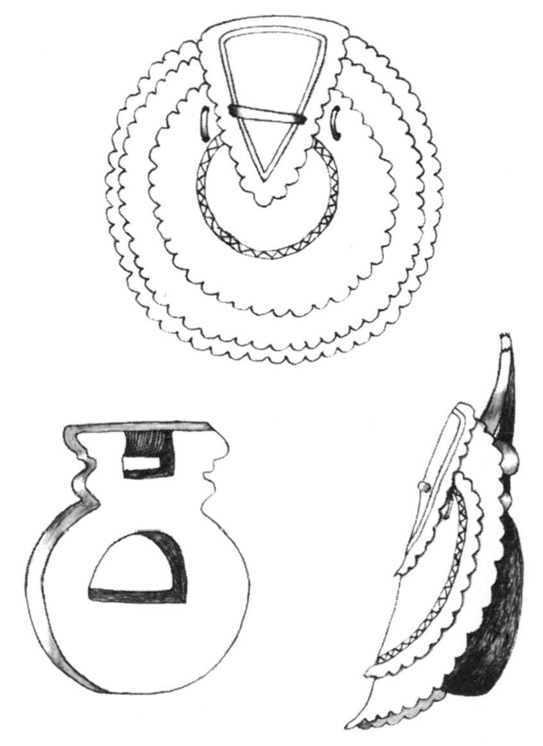

FIG. 102. California wood-block stirrup and flat tapadera.

and brand, ride herd and break horses, they did the best they could in fitting them out with passable equipment which at least carried a fair resemblance to that used by their superiors. Though the Indians were largely replaced by Mexican *vaqueros* riding a much-improved style of saddle in the later 1700s, the old mission outfits hung on as available rigs until well up into the late 1800s.

It might be proper to class the Spanish horseman's first two centuries in America, 1525–1725, as the transition, or coming-of-age, period. It was during this time that he shed his aging cocoon of European customs to emerge as a bright new creature indigenous to the Western world. Then it was that he discarded his old war saddle, *la jineta* rig, pad saddle and West Indies development in favor of a creation of his own devising. Likewise, he threw away his metal armor, swapped his age-old iron stirrups for those of wood, lengthened his stirrup straps and shortened his spur shanks. Shortly after 1730 he rode fully accoutered into the limelight of a definitely western stage.

Let us take a brief look at this New World, eighteenth century *caballero,* or gentleman on horseback. Raised in the saddle from infancy, he was one of the world's premier horsemen. The horse was his transportation, his workshop, his office, his daytime home. On its back he performed all necessary labors, sought his pleasures, and carried out his duties to society and government. Being on horseback meant to him the very essence of life.

By the same token, the attention lavished on his riding gear outrated most of his other interests. Money was usually only a means to an end; cattle would grow into beef and hides if given time; even the right *señorita* might walk into his life eventually if the saints were willing. But the best obtainable riding outfit was a must, here and now, if complete happiness was to be realized.

A later, but very typical, example of this regard for choice equipment appears in a story that came out of Pancho Villa's insurrection of 1914. When Villa began his triumphant march on Mexico City that fall, about all his rugged *discípules* could think of was the big store on the *Avenida Cinco de Mayo,* where reposed some of the finest saddles in the world. How their eyes brightened as they eased the weary miles with visions of themselves so soon to be in control of such a treasure. But alas! the rival forces under Emiliano Zapata were first to arrive on the avenue and clean out the coveted wealth. While Villa's *muchachos* knew that their opportunity to loot the national treasury, jewelry stores, and kindred establishments was an enviable one, well worth the long march and perhaps worth dying for, their hearts slowed to dispirited beats as they surveyed the great store so recently emptied of all its fine saddles.

Only lack of opportunity would have prevented his predecessor of a hundred years previously feeling the same way. The old *caballero* appreciated the comforting warmth of gold in his pocket, but after all, it was only gold. The carved leather and ornate metalwork that went on his horse was what signified the status of a heritage running back to Bellerophon.

In appearance, we find the *caballero* to be something of a dandy. His hair, which is never cut, is parted in the middle and brought back into a single braid behind. He shaves not very often, usually on Saturday, leaving long sideburns that run down almost to the jaw. His head is bound with a kerchief of black silk tied in the back. This is topped by the sombrero, low of crown and wide of brim, covered with black oilcloth and tied under the chin with a tinsel cord or silk ribbon. An inch-wide hatband of silver-studded buckskin, braided silver cord, or tinsel rope gives a finishing touch to the wool-felt hat. Less affluent *vaqueros* wore hats of leather, cheap felt, or woven palm fiber.

Next comes the *chaqueta,* or jacket, heavily embroidered and bright with braid trimmings and fancy metal buttons, worn over a loose white shirt. Trousers reaching to the knee are worn over drawers which are wrapped into knee-length leggings that resemble those worn by the Indians. The leggings, or *sotas,* are probably of embossed leather embroidered with tinsel thread in fetching designs. They are bound at the knee with handsomely tasseled garters.

A red silk sash or heavy leather belt encircles the waist—sometimes both are worn, the sash being uppermost. A brightly hued serape slung over one shoulder adds a final touch of color, helping to draw the eye away from the poorly made buckskin shoes fitted out with rawhide soles and flat heels.

If he happens to be a mounted soldier, he probably carries a sword horizontally under his left leg and a carbine in full-length scabbard slung vertically behind the right side of the cantle. Lacking a gun, he will likely be armed with a lance carried upright in a stirrup boot. A double-layer rawhide shield of round or slightly heart shape will complete his fighting outfit.

In any case, he will be a rather dashing fellow.

Around 1765–1775 he came out with a more pretentious saddle (Fig. 103). This had a large *mochila* covering which came down to about the knee. Fastened to the back of the cantle over the crupper strap was a leather housing that extended back to the horse's rump. Beneath this, and covering the rump to the root of the tail, went a gaily colored serape, its ends hanging down over the animal's thighs. The extensive covering provided protection for the rider's clothing and whatever extra gear he packed with him. It also made a nice place for the lady of his choice to ride. A jaguar skin or large piece of silk fabric often took the place of the regular housing. Saddle bags back of the cantle and square pockets with buttoned flaps on either side of the pommel were frequent additions. Made detachable, these were used to a great extent when traveling or enjoying the ever-present Spanish habit of going visiting.

Some of these rigs dispensed with the serape, having a complete skirt-

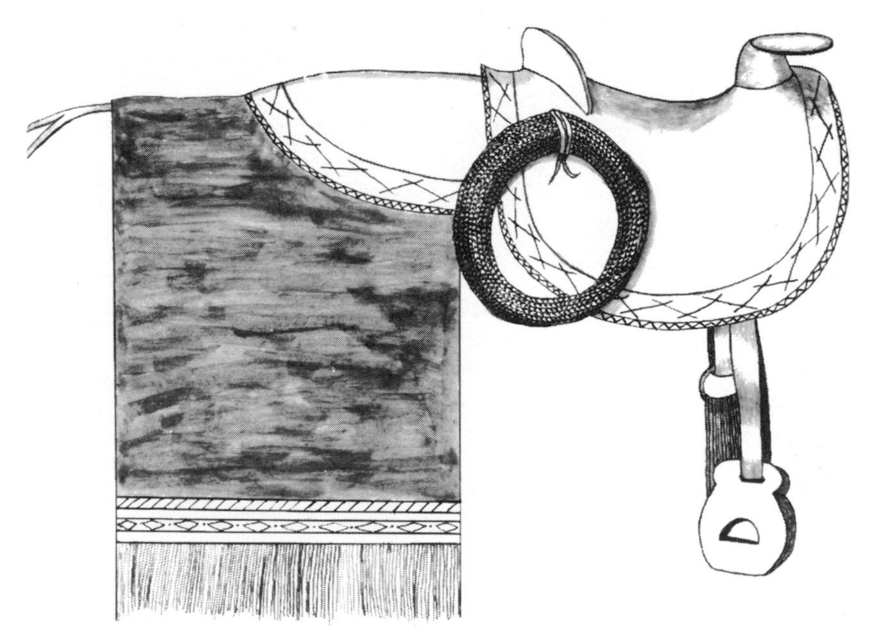

FIG. 103. California saddle, early 1800s.

like housing, or *colo de pato* (peacock's tail) that covered most of the horse's sides and extended back to the crupper. Up until about 1800, these were often fringed with jingling metal ornaments. Both the housing and *mochila* were usually well decorated in matching designs. Among the better class *caballeros,* this decoration invariably ran to elaborate representations of the leather carver's and silversmith's arts.

As we have seen, leather carving is one of civilization's oldest crafts. Supposedly originating among the ancient Nubians, it was carried westward by the Arabs, Moors, and Spaniards to reach California and the Southwest on the riding gear of Mexican horsemen. All along the way it rose step by step on the artistic skill of the various cultures through which it passed.

The same thing might be said for the worker in gold and silver. Like the leather carver, he came over the centuries-old road from the ancient East, bringing his craft to fulfillment in America. Both leather and metal work reached their zenith in beauty and design through a post-graduate course in the arts of the Incas and Aztecs. Their culmination in the American West was a triumph of creative handiwork rising step by step on their journey halfway around the globe.

But despite its handsomely worked covering, the eighteenth century Mexican saddle was still based on the crude old skeleton tree with front-fork rigging and no skirts. The *reata* or rope continued to be carried back of the cantle, while the bulky wood-block stirrups remained the best thing available.

It was not until about 1790 that a conventional type of wood stirrup appeared. These were big, boxlike affairs five or six inches in width, but a considerable improvement over the heavy wood-blocks formerly used. Some were of bent wood similar to our more modern style, while others were made up of squared pieces mortised together.

Somewhere in the 1780–1790 decade, the Mexican-California saddle maker began to rig his creations with fixed skirts. These were round, abbreviated affairs without jockeys, but quite an improvement over the old naked trees. He also developed a more substantial type of rigging about this time. Though it continued to be made in Spanish style—the cinch ring suspended in line with the front fork—it had a horizontal strap running to the back of the tree. This helped to equalize the pull of the cinch throughout the tree. Moreover, this saddle was evidently built much stronger in all respects. It was during this period that the Mexican *vaquero* began tying his *reata* to the saddle horn instead of his mount's tail.

Our earliest definite record of this change in roping methods comes from the log of Captain Vancouver, when he made his voyage to the West Coast in 1792. After visiting one of the ranchos near Santa Clara Mission during his stop at San Francisco Bay, he wrote: "I saw a rodeo there . . . they caught the cattle with hair or rawhide ropes . . . and having strong, high-peaked pommels to their saddles, they took a turn around it with the end of the line and by that means held the animal."

If this style of roping was a regular practice in 1792, it must have risen into considerable prominence during the preceding years and probably originated with the better built saddles. On the other hand, it might be more logical to conclude that the demands of the roping fraternity brought about the sturdier saddle.

There is no doubt that the voices of cattlemen carried weight in those times. The Mexican *vaquero* was a roper par excellence. His skill with the *reata* was a continuation of the art introduced by the ancient Persians. By the time it arrived in the hands of the *vaquero,* it was an indispensable craft in the horseman's world. And in his hands it reached the summit of artistic perfection. Considering his *reata* as his good right arm from childhood, he seldom let it out of reach of his nimble fingers. With it, he was equipped for almost any task that came along. Usually made of four to eight strands of braided rawhide oiled and softened to animated pliability, it did his work, served as a favorite plaything, armed him for offense or defense, and stood as a measure of his stature on all fronts. A growing awareness of his need for a more substantial anchorage when plying his craft would be answered by saddle improvement.

With the advent of better trees and fixed skirts, California saddle makers were turning out some handsome jobs by 1800. Of course, most of these top-quality rigs went into the hands of the affluent dons and upper-class *caballeros.* Fig. 104 shows a typical example of these plushier creations.

A completely fitted out saddle of this kind often weighed over a hundred pounds. The extremely large square skirts were carved in a variety of beautiful designs usually decorated with worked silver trim and rimmed with rosettes of the same material. The *pomo,* or horn, built higher and trimmer than on ordinary saddles, would be capped with silver; its neck might be covered with leather or completely encased in silver. On the *fuste,* or tree, would go a quilted cushion to serve as a seat. This would be covered with a *coraza,* or *mochila,* of embossed leather embroidered with silk and tinsel and studded with silver trimmings. Creamy white leather trimmed with black was a great favorite. Designed to match the *coraza* was the *colo de pato,* or peacock's tail, extending back over the horse's rump and hanging down over its sides. This might be either richly carved leather or heavy silk fabric finely embroidered and edged with silk fringe. The cantle would be covered with embossed leather, frequently so heavily decorated with silver as to display little of the leather. Carved leather tapaderas studded with silver concealed the wooden stirrups, or *estribos.*

Bridles were even more elaborate. The massive Spanish bits were often of solid silver exquisitely engraved in singular designs. The majority, however, were of iron. Most of the latter were artistically forged and inlaid with gold and silver. Spade or ring mouthpieces predominated, though the old Moorish-style Mameluke with solid iron curb was occasionally seen. Bit chains were invariably used, often being of burnished silver.

Headstalls commonly ran to carved leather almost completely cov-

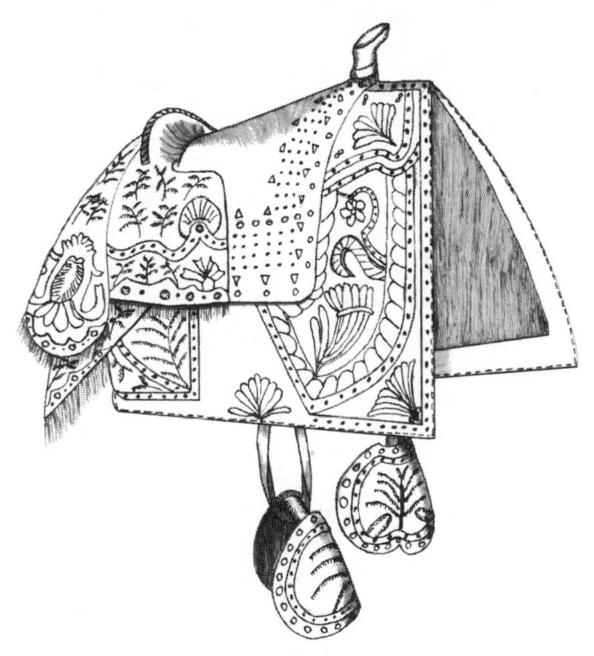

FIG. 104. Spanish-Mexican saddle, 1800.

ered with fluted and engraved silver. Crossed-chain browbands were highly favored. They consisted of two silver chains which crossed the brow diagonally under a six-pointed star. Braided leather reins with an attached *romal,* or single quirtlike end, were the preferred style. The whole bridle would often require as much as 250 silver dollars to decorate, and would weigh in the neighborhood of twelve pounds.

Solid silver spurs, too, would occasionally be found, though iron was more common. The latter were usually heavily inlaid and encrusted with gold and silver to match the saddle and bridle. Some of them were most imposing, being wrought in fanciful designs with shanks averaging around 5 inches long and rowels up to 6 inches in diameter. One well-documented pair measured slightly more than 10 inches in over-all length and carried 5¾-inch rowels. They weighed 2 pounds 11 ounces.

Most of the silverwork was made from Mexican silver dollars. Native artisans would forge them into rosettes, *conchos,* studs, and assorted ornaments. Some were cold-drawn into fine wire and then crocheted into sectional designs joined together with solid rings and links. Others were formed into flowers, wheat heads, ears of corn, delicate-stemmed plants, animal figures, and Aztec or Inca symbols that were already old when most Europeans were still painting themselves blue and beating each other over the head with stone clubs. Complete outfits fully adorned with such work were fabulously expensive.

About 1830, the *caballero* exchanged his knee pants for the long *calzoneras,* or trousers, commonly associated with the typical Mexican horseman. Those were made with side seams overlapping. Down the entire outside length of the leg ran a row of fancy buttons, often of engraved silver, arranged to fasten the seam together. Most riders left them unbuttoned below the knee, allowing the varicolored inner lining to display itself before admiring eyes. The customary red silk sash was used as a waistband support.

A matching garment was the short-waisted velvet jacket richly embroidered in fancy designs with contrasting colors of silk or tinsel thread. This was the forerunner of the short denim jacket so popular with latter-day cowboys. Worn over a loose white shirt and with a colorful serape draping one shoulder, such a jacket made the perfect foil for the dark-featured *caballero.*

His footgear was still soft buckskin shoes with rawhide soles and flat heels. A piece of heavy leather was fastened to the heels to hold up the big spurs.

Hats with 4- to 5-inch crowns began to replace the old, very low variety shortly before 1850. They were much the same style as the earlier ones—black flat-topped crowns with silk linings and chin straps. Most were made of yellow vicuna fur felt. Silk tassels or metal danglers were often suspended from the broad brim. The brim was bound with silk or a spiral gold cord. Twisted cords of silk, gold, silver, tinsel, or woven beads made up the hatbands.

The big, tapering, steeple-crowned hats did not appear until later in the century.

The ordinary *vaqueros* and poorer-class riders used outfits of a similar nature. Even the lowliest peon took pride in his clothing and horse-trappings, copying his don so far as he was able. But he had to content himself with things of poorer quality materials and workmanship.

One such lesser light was the *cibolero,* or buffalo hunter, in New Mexico. His dress was a flat-crowned straw hat, trousers and jacket of leather in a plain design, and soft buckskin shoes. Knee leggings of embossed leather or buckskin tied at the top with colored garters completed the ensemble.

A bow and arrow quiver hung from one shoulder, while his lance rode upright in a stirrup boot, its midshaft section fastened to the pommel by a strap. The point of the long lance swayed gently well above his head, a tassel of parti-colored stuff tied to its tip to flutter in the breeze. A scabbard on the opposite side of the saddle carried his old muzzle-loading fusil. To protect its load of loose powder from dampness and dirt, the muzzle of the gun would be lightly plugged with a gaily tasseled stopper.

The majority of working *vaqueros* carried on with the old *mochila*-covered skeleton tree through all those earlier years. It was usually the best they could afford, and it did serve the purpose. And to them must be given the credit for most of the pioneer ranch work throughout northern Mexico, southern California and the Southwest.

Cruppers, with or without rump housings, decorated or plain, were very popular with Mexican riders all through that period. Breast collars, on the other hand, were pretty well discarded along with the old war saddles. A few were used in later years with the more elaborate outfits, but the rank and file of Spanish Californians appear to have cared as little for them as did the later cowboys.

In the 1840 era a neater, better built saddle appeared. This style marked the transition from plain stirrup straps to regular fenders. It was still a *mochila* rig, but it had the big fixed skirts, a more comfortably rounded seat and better fitting cantle (Fig. 105). It was the opinion of Henry A. Wise, after riding one at Monterey in 1846, that these were the most comfortable saddles to be had at that time.

Mochilas for these later creations might be either rounded or square in shape. The rounded-corner type seems to have been preferred by more style-conscious riders. This might be called the parent design of the small, round skirts which arose as a uniquely California design a few decades later.

Among the gentry of California, saddles were often fitted with a plain

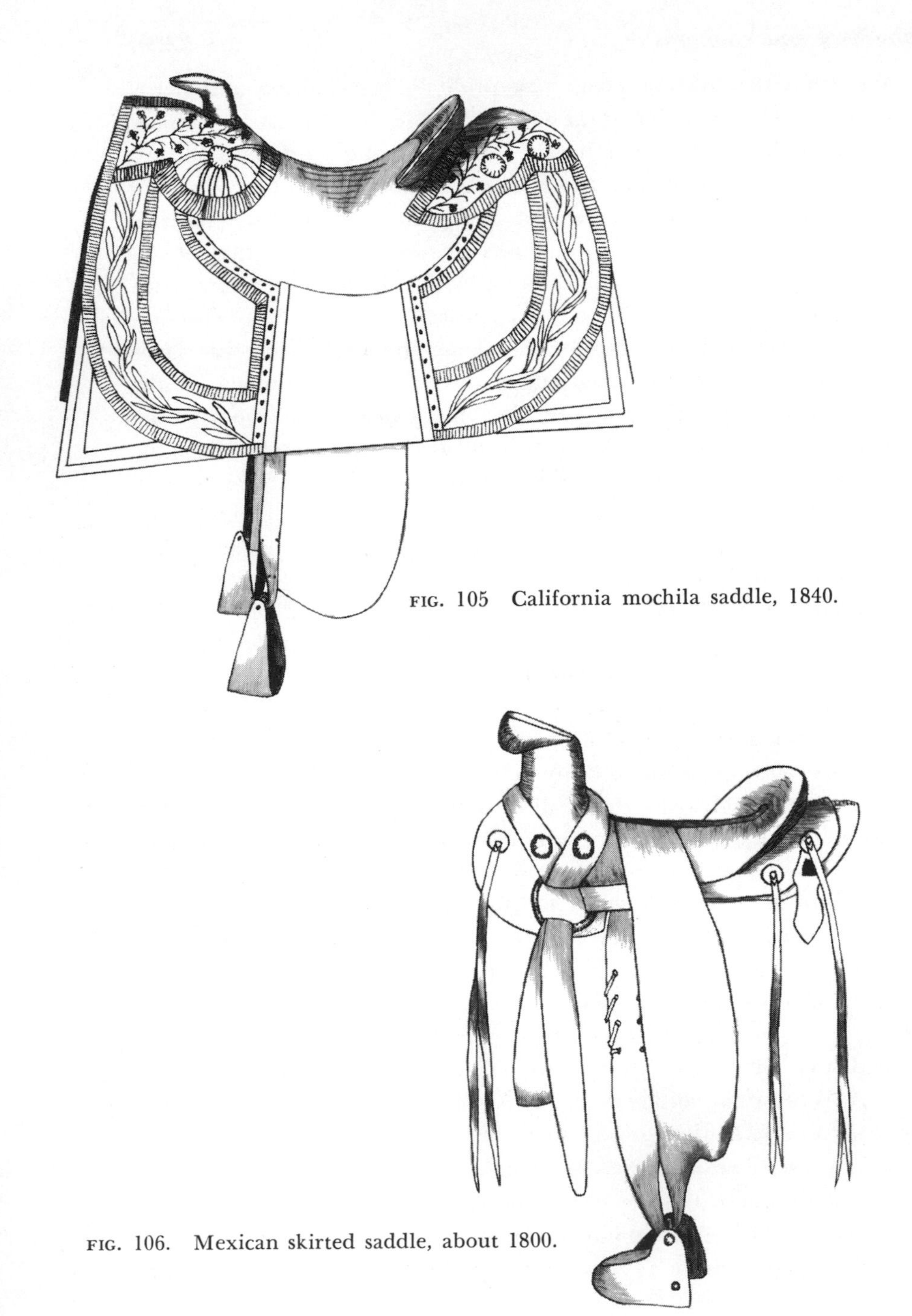

FIG. 105 California mochila saddle, 1840.

FIG. 106. Mexican skirted saddle, about 1800.

mochila for everyday use. When occasion demanded a more imposing appearance this would be covered with a second *mochila,* called a *coraza,* which carried the fancy carving and silver decorations so dear to Latin hearts. In case of a long journey or extended visiting excursion, a third cover, called a *corona,* might be added. This was also decorated and carried rectangular leather pockets with button-down flaps on either side of the pommel.

Meanwhile, around 1790, one branch of Mexican saddlery had turned off in a somewhat different direction. This offshoot was built on the old open-seat, rawhide-covered tree of earlier years. It had the same wide *aricones,* or stirrup straps, looped over the exposed sidebars, the flat seat, moderately low cantle and massive horn as its predecessor. There were still no fenders or jockeys. While the single-cinch, exposed Spanish rigging followed the old pattern, it was made heavier and had horizontal straps to transmit some of the pull to the back of the tree. The fixed *bastos,* or skirts, built onto the tree were an innovation, as were the boxlike stirrups of bent or mortised wood. These were usually covered with box-nose tapaderas. This was, and still is, the basic form of the Mexican *charro,* or common *vaquero* saddle. See Fig. 106 for one of these.

The favorite saddle blankets, called *tirutas,* were of heavy black and white wool, woven by the Indians of Sonora. Unfortunately, the ordinary *vaqueros* were forced to make out with less desirable items in most cases.

Horns on the *charro* saddles came in a variety of styles. They were created by individual makers who exercised their own imaginations or that of the customer in fashioning a chosen design. While they were all of plain wood built large for strength, they might be round, flat, squarish, crowned, tilted, clumsy, refined or any combination thereof. Many types were localized or popularized by certain groups of riders.

Sectional custom, too, had its effect on the whole saddle. As a matter of fact, the *charro* saddle soon divided itself into something resembling a pair of fraternal twins.

The original settlers in Mexico came in the most part from two different regions of Spain. Being rather provincial, each clan held to its own ideas. Each thus developed practices peculiar to itself in the new land. Those who settled on the West Coast were the ones who worked up into California. The eastern division spread out toward the Rio

Grande and Texas. Each sowed a heritage of regional peculiarities that is visible to this day.

The West Coast country contained a preponderance of affluent land owners and upper-echelon *caballeros.* They preferred less bulk and more style in their outfits. In consequence, the influence of the lighter-built *la jineta* rigs permeated the saddles of this section more than elsewhere. The same West Coast characteristics led to the original round, or round-cornered, saddle skirts and *mochilas,* as well as the refining of ill-shaped cantles and bulky horns.

The West Coast *vaquero* was a dally-man, one who takes a few turns of the rope around his saddle horn when catching stock, in contrast to the tie-down man who ties his rope hard and fast to the horn before making a catch. (The word "dally," by the way, is an English corruption of the Spanish *dale vuelta,* meaning to give or take a turn around something.)

The *vaquero* used a braided rawhide *reata,* which had a very satisfactory strength for all roping purposes if it were allowed to slip and give a trifle when the strain of stopping a catch came upon it. On the other hand, it was subject to breakage if used for hard and fast snubbing, or tying up close. Thus it was that the western riders quickly developed a preference for a taller horn with less top for swifter and surer action when taking a hurried dally. The thick neck, however, was retained as offering a larger and more secure surface for holding and allowing play of the rope when a caught animal was brought to a stop.

Farther east, where style was less important and economic conditions more harsh, we find a saddle more inclined to reflect relationship to the old *silla de montar* of the conquistador. The squatty, bull-necked horns with flat tops big enough to hold a three-card monte layout were especially designed for the tie-down ropers who predominated in that section. Plain rawhide-covered trees prevailed in most instances, while few refinements were worked on other features of the saddle.

We shall go into other differences between eastern and western cowboys in a later chapter.

—20—

East Is East

Oh, East is East, and West is West, and never the twain shall meet,
Till Earth and Sky stand presently at God's great Judgment Seat.

—Rudyard Kipling

HORSEMEN OF THE United States and Canada stand in a position somewhat similar to those in Mexico. Like the Latins, they are represented by two separate and distinctly individual schools of thought and action. While the two do meet at various places, even overlapping occasionally, each remains an entity unto itself. Aside from a scattering of western-minded pleasure riders and professional rodeo hands, the East's riding habits, stock, and equipment are basically as eastern today as they were three centuries ago. Beyond the Mississippi, the West is equally staunch in preserving its old-time heritage. Wherever either chances to intrude on the other's territory, it does so more with the air of a visitor than of one trying to promote hybrid developments.

It is not the fault of the people. Rather, it is due to the radically different influences that govern the life of horsemen in the two regions. Riding is not a way of life in the East as it is in the West. Basically, the East has never been a horseback country. With the exception of the southeastern plantation country, the mounted man never appeared as a dominant figure anywhere east of the Mississippi. Of course, horses have always been ridden throughout the whole region. They were the chief means of inland transportation during the years of early settlement. The military, sportsmen, circuit riders, race jockeys, mail carriers, dispatch bearers and travelers of all sorts had to be experienced horsemen. Yet the eastern pioneers, as a class, were mostly woodsmen, farmers, tradesmen, artisans, and the like, footmen by custom and inclination. Horses to them took on more the nature of something to work in harness or, in case of need, to ride temporarily on necessary errands. There was no riding as an everyday custom or as recreation and no regular working from horseback.

Certain sections of the East, however, did produce horsemen with all the skill and prideful heritage of their breed. Virginia has been famous for its riders and breeders from earliest times. The elite of the Old South spent most of its waking hours in the saddle. The Bluegrass region of Kentucky has ever been synonymous with horses and horsemen.

In the North, the sportive and wealthier citizens extended considerable attention toward their riding stables. Breeders working with imported stock developed American racing to a fine degree, while influencing a moderate spread of saddle animals into other walks of life. Countryside riding and horseback recreation enjoyed no great popularity until about 1890.

Even then, most localities offered it little recognition, deeming it merely a fad of the leisure class. These habitual footmen tended to follow the fashion of using buggies and carriages for pleasure outings, often scorning as eccentric foolishness the idea of mounting a horse for enjoyment. Horses kept exclusively for the saddle were not plentiful, and the whole horseback program worked as sort of a fragmentary adjunct to the more prosaic business of everyday life. Riding gear was likewise of a less progressive nature than that used elsewhere.

The style and equipment of most eastern horsemen were copied from designs brought across the sea by that much-touted old mentor of early American customs, the North European. They prevailed in our eastern region until they came up against the vastly different tack of the individualistic West.

Other factors which contributed in part to this state of affairs were the East's lack of need for a working horseman's outfit and the easterner's lack of interest in the life known to free-ranging knights of the saddle. From the Atlantic to the Mississippi, there was no roping from horseback, no hard riding; there were no bucking horses to conquer, no wild cattle to chase through forbidding territory, no endless trails to follow into desert, mountain, or plain. Plain pad saddles and nondescript bridles were light in weight, cheap in price and convenient to use in a country that made no excessive demands on a rider. Considered stylish by some and adequate by most, such rigs served to help the more earthbound and tidily conservative easterner preserve his identity as a species apart from the flamboyant, wild-riding barbarians his imagination pictured roaming the wilderness beyond the Mississippi.

The status of the eastern rider underwent little change in passing years. Few needs arose to encourage alterations or developments in his outfit. Considering the fact that he was, as a rule, basically more of a footman on horseback than a horseback man proper, we shall follow his trail only in its broader aspects as it applies to the general American scene.

When he first began to mount, around 1630, his riding gear was all imported from Europe, most of it from England or France. Styles and customs then prevalent in north Europe likewise took their place on this side of the Atlantic. All this, however, was almost negligible during the early period. Saddle horses were extremely scarce; only the few wealthier colonists could afford them. The settlers, as a whole, considered themselves lucky to own an ox or two or perhaps an all-purpose farm horse. It was not until up around 1700 that riding became anything like general among the populace, and then only as necessity demanded.

European saddles continued to dominate the scene all through this era. The styles shown in Figs. 80–81 were most in evidence. Bridles, bits, spurs, and other necessities corresponded with designs currently popular in the Old World.

Eastern horses were the offspring of English and French importations. English principles governed riding habits and customs. About the only deviation of note was the Virginia innovation of lengthening the stirrup straps to permit a better knee-grip on the mount's barrel. This came into general use around 1776, soon spreading throughout the South.

As a matter of fact, imported English gear and English styles were assiduously affected by some eastern Americans.

Even the wearisome custom of posting or bobbing up and down like an old-fashioned walking beam when riding, was simply a reproduction of English fashion. No other horseback nation practiced it. The only reason it came into use among the British was that they never had any easy-gaited mounts. Their horses were all so closely related to the old hard-trotting breed of Nordic animals that a person had to rise in his stirrups to avoid being pounded to death. Their imitators were merely slaves of fashion rather than intelligent horsemen.

North of the Potomac, the English style of short stirrups and bent knees prevailed over most of the country. Along with the aforementioned saddles, a couple of special-purpose designs from the 1750 period were quite popular (Fig. 107). Though developed for particular needs, these won much favor among horsemen with regular riding jobs. A man didn't have to be a postman to appreciate the smooth, leather-covered, sloping seat, moderately high cantle, and padded knee rolls copied from medieval saddles.

The postilion rig was used chiefly by men who drove the big four- and six-horse Conestoga wagons, military vehicles, fancy coaches, and heavy stages. They commonly rode the near, or left-hand, wheel horse, managing the team from there instead of from the vehicle seat. The saddle was designed primarily to provide a maximum of comfort for drivers who had nothing more strenuous in view than keeping their outfits in motion over long stretches of wilderness roads. The absence of cantle enabled the rider to relax in any direction when the way became tedious. The heavily quilted skirts were usually made long enough to extend down over the traces. The padded, half-roll pommel, like the one on the postman's saddle, was a revival from the days of knighthood. The built-in pouch was a measure of convenience for one in regular need of an extra horseshoe, nails, tools, harness repairs or a fresh plug of tobacco. Such saddles were in use until about 1834.

A later type of postilion saddle called the wagon saddle enjoyed considerable popularity during the 1800s. It was built more on the style of standard English saddles, but with big, outsize fenders (Fig. 108). Up until the close of the nineteenth century it was, with the inevitable variations, more or less standard equipment as far west as the Mississippi.

Most of the early western string-team skinners, who did their driving of the long ten- to twenty-horse teams, two abreast, from the back of the wheel horse, preferred the low-horned, long-seated Mexican design, but there was no stigma attached to one who outfitted himself with a wagon saddle. Drivers of four- and six-horse teams commonly drove from the vehicle seat. The army alone continued postilion driving for everything more than a two-horse span all through the 1800s. Army riders usually used the artillery saddle shown in Fig. 127.

In the East, the late 1700s found a more modern style of English saddle coming into vogue. These followed the pattern shown in Fig. 109. Pilches or pad saddles, which were described in Chapter 13, were also used to some extent, especially among the more genteel class.

Much the same conditions prevailed in eastern Canada. Canada and the United States might be considered similar in their entire riding history. Both nations continued to use a generous amount of European gear despite the progress of home manufacture. They still do. Eastern horsemen have always been inclined to string along with the English

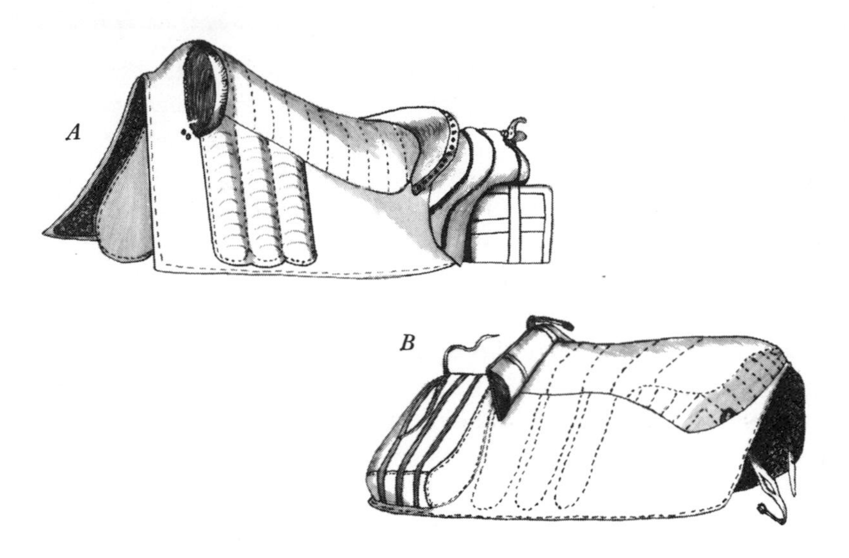

FIG. 107. *A* postman's saddle; *B* postilion saddle. Both English-American 1750–1775.

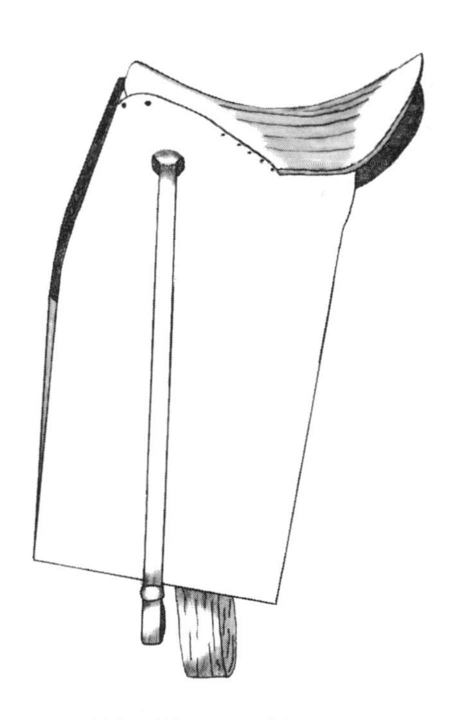

FIG. 108. Wagon saddle, 1800s.

tradition. The majority of their saddles hewed to the standard pattern of Britain's Somerset, Park, and Gentleman's models. The Somerset and its counterpart, the Shaftoe, were leading examples of this kind.

These saddles were built on 16-inch trees and covered with russet leather (Fig. 109). The 12- by 21-inch fenders might be either plain or padded with quilted calfskin. Padded knee and thigh rolls were often added, particularly in the early days. Quilted seats of soft glove leather were the rule, though the plain variety was not at all unusual. Customarily fitted with padded canvas inner skirts, some also came with small, square outside skirts back of the cantle. Equipped with single web cinches, they weighed around nine and a half pounds.

Stirrups on all these earlier saddles were of light-weight iron, mostly in plain designs, as shown in the accompanying illustrations. After America invented the bent-wood type in 1790, either kind might be used. The wooden variety with leather hoods (Figs. 110, 111) enjoyed considerable popularity after 1830, but the plain iron ones always predominated.

The plantation dwellers of the ante-bellum South were, as a class, the foremost horseback people east of the Mississippi. It naturally followed that their section of the country should show the widest variety of saddle developments. However, eastern saddles and saddle makers were by no means confined to definite boundaries, nor was saddle use governed by territorial lines. Many northerners found certain southern types more to their liking, and vice versa. Up until the disruption following the Civil War, neighborly interchange might be said to have placed all eastern saddlery under a common denominator.

Much the same applies to eastern horses. Both the North and South took a comparable interest in breeding saddle stock in line with their needs. The better-grade animals in both regions owed much of their parentage to English Thoroughbreds imported from time to time. Second-class stock was usually a mixture of British Isles ponies and light draft horses, also of European descent. In either case, most real horsemen worked wholeheartedly toward improvement as they went along. The result gave us such distinctive breeds as the Morgan, Quarter Horse, Tennessee Walking Horse, and American Saddle Horse, to name some of the most outstanding. Their excellence in conformity, speed, intelligence, spirit, tractability, gaits, beauty, and ease under the saddle is undebatable testimony to the skill of American horsemen in all regions.

Being in the main grain-fed and barn-lot raised, they naturally lacked something of the toughness and hardihood inherent in native western mustangs, but they raised the standard of American horse culture to a position that need bow to no nation.

Likewise, the eastern saddle maker forwarded his art to the zenith of superiority in variety, quantity, and workmanship. Encouraged by the demands of farmers, sportsmen, and cavalrymen, he developed assorted improvements on the old English saddle. This resulted in sort of a hybrid design, heavier in weight and of better riding qualities. Figs. 109–112 present a fair selection of the more popular American types in use during the 1800s. While varying to some degree in styles, they all had the typical hogskin or quilted calfskin seats and large leather fenders. Trees averaged around sixteen to seventeen inches, while single web cinches were universal. Many of these rigs in one style or another are still favorites with eastern riders.

Less pretentious in appearance than their contemporaries were styles like the Shackleford (Fig. 110). They were patterned more along the line of cavalry saddles. Though they had plain leather-covered trees with military-style split seats, they were built for a good fit and easy riding. Most dispensed entirely with fenders. Instead, the inner skirts were extended down almost to the stirrups underneath plain stirrup straps.

As representatives of the better designs, the Kilgore and Mosby stand as good examples (Fig. 111 and 112). These had the short 13- or 14-inch trees and full leather-covered seats. A glance at their construction will explain their popularity among discriminating riders. Saddles of this compact and comfortable style were chosen by a majority of hard-riding cavalrymen of the Civil War period.

Many former cavalrymen who had grown accustomed to the McClellan army saddles while in service wanted a similar rig for private use. In consequence, some were brought home by returning soldiers; others were purchased at army surplus sales.

Civilian riders, too, soon discovered their good qualities, creating a demand which, around 1870, brought about the manufacture of McClellan-type saddles for the general market. The more elaborate model was well furnished with short skirts, full leather seat, and jockeys. It also came with a quilted calfskin seat instead of the plain leather variety.

A racing or jockey saddle typical of the late 1800s had a rawhide-covered tree and plain leather skirts attached with brass screws. A later,

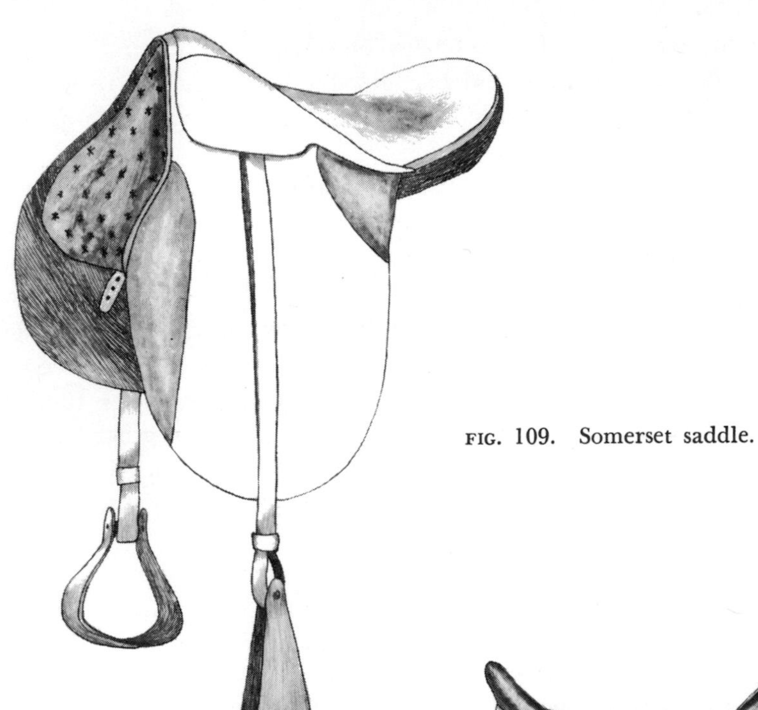

FIG. 109. Somerset saddle.

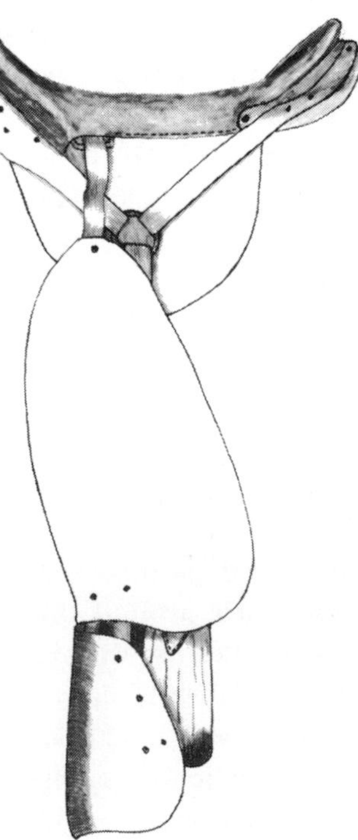

FIG. 110. Shackleford saddle.

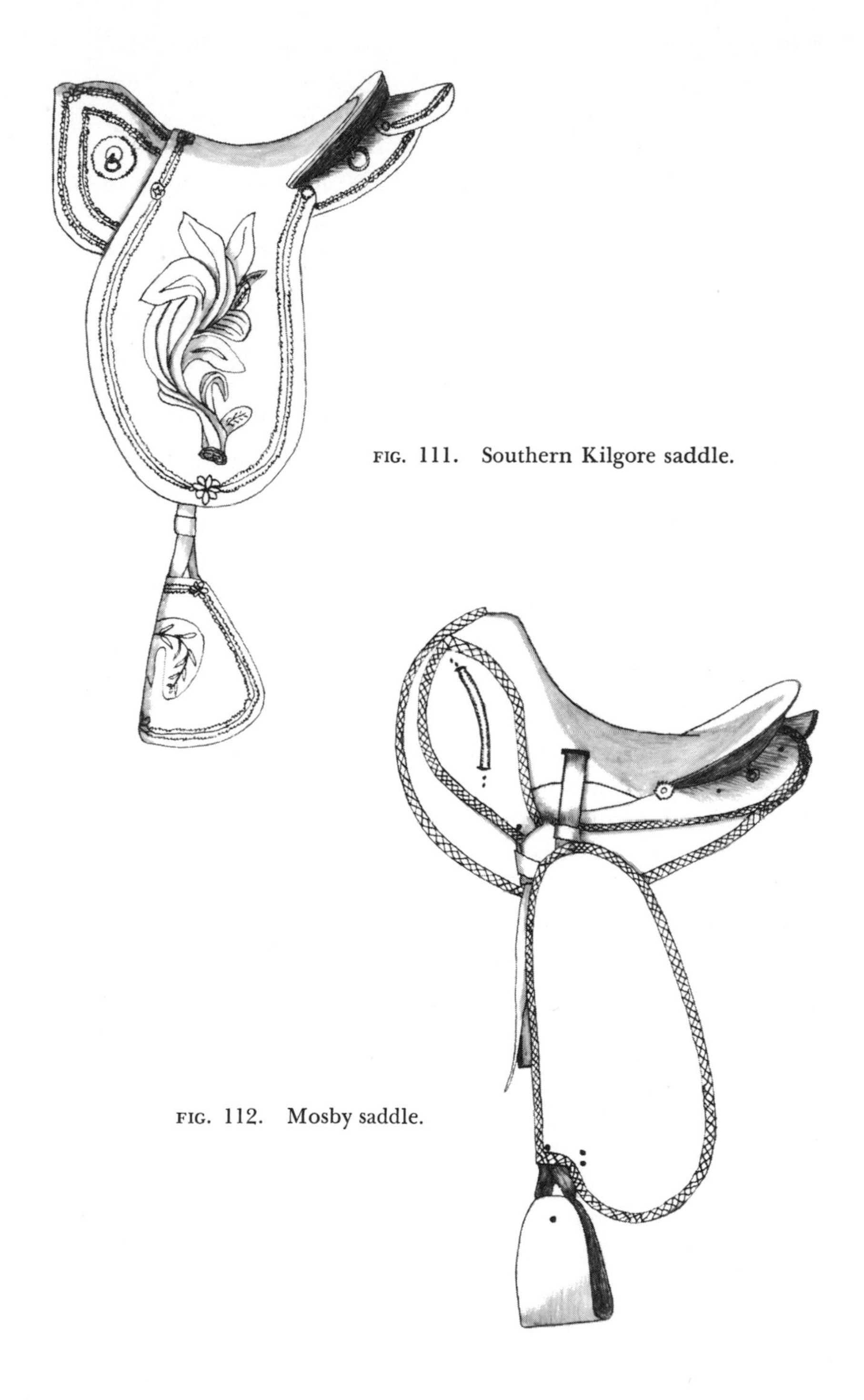

FIG. 111. Southern Kilgore saddle.

FIG. 112. Mosby saddle.

more modern design, lighter and less bulky, was built on a 6-ounce tree. This, with a few alterations, became the tiny, postage-stamp affair of today.

Eastern riders, like eastern footmen, have always swung to the genteel, conservative side in supplying their needs. Seldom did elaborate bridles with heavy ornamentation appear east of the Mississippi. The same applies to reins, which were usually of the closed type.

In bits (Fig. 113), jointed and solid-bar snaffles predominated. Among the gentlemen sports, bridoon and Pelham styles claimed a favorite position. The bridoon is simply a separate snaffle and curb bit used together. The snaffle is placed behind the curb. This requires a double headstall and a double set of reins, one for each bit.

The Pelham employs the bridoon's rein principle, but requires only a single headstall. It might be used with or without a curb strap, serving as either a snaffle or curb as the occasion demands. This is a very old style. It went under the name of "compass canon" some 250 years ago. One of these bits was dug up in Jamestown, Virginia, at the site of the first tavern, which was destroyed by fire in 1676.

Very similar was the American four-rein snaffle-curb. It differed from the Pelham only in having curved sidebars and solid rein rings.

The English bar-mouthpiece bit was made to accommodate either a two- or four-rein arrangement. It commonly used two reins and a curb strap, but was adaptable to any preferred style when an easy bit with good appearance was desired.

Another early English bit was the Chifney curb, invented in 1790. It saw considerable use on this side of the Atlantic, but was more or less superseded by the very similar Whitman model. In both of these, the main sidebars were solidly attached to the mouthpiece, their upper ends ringed to receive the curb strap and the lower ends of the reins. A short metal bar was made to swivel on the mouthpiece immediately inside the main sidebar and extend upward. The headstall was attached to this swiveled piece. This allowed extreme leverage on the curb without the customary interfering pull on the headstall.

Run-of-the-mill riders who wanted something more severe than plain snaffles ordinarily fell back on one of the common American port bits that followed the old Shoemaker pattern. These came with either high, medium, or low ports on the mouthpieces; the higher the port, the more severe the bit. Fitted with adjustable curb straps, they could be made to serve a wide variety of needs.

For those who preferred style over plain serviceable utility, there was a variety of port bits and snaffles fitted with fancy sidebars. The examples shown in Fig. 113 are typical of the styles in use during the 1800s. Usually lighter in construction than their unembellished contemporaries, they found their greatest use among women riders.

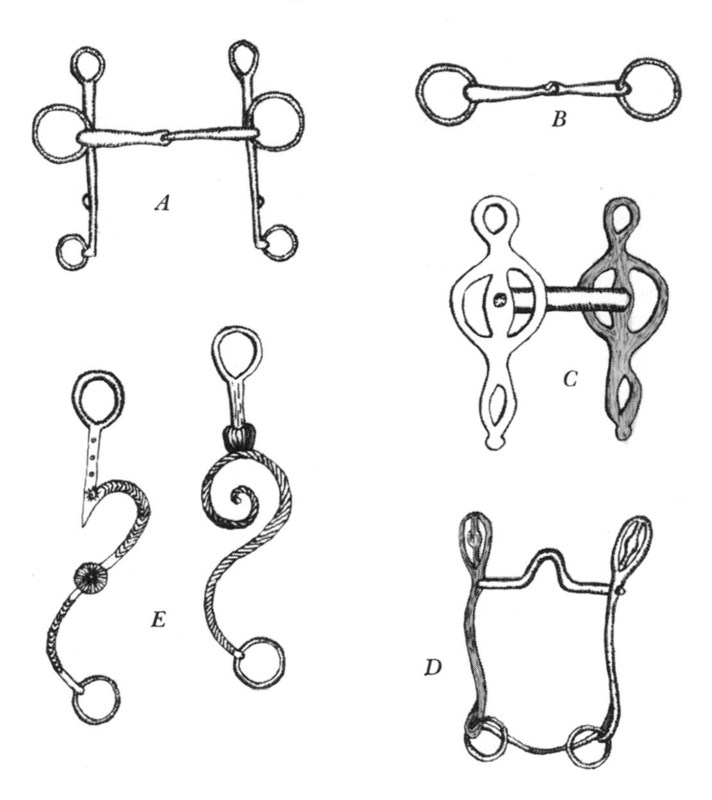

FIG. 113. Eastern bits: *A* pelham; *B* snaffle; *C* English pattern; *D* high port Shoemaker; *E* fancy sidebars, styled for ladies, 1875.

Women also seemed to favor martingales more than did men, although they were used to considerable extent by both sexes, particularly in the upper reaches of society. They were useful on horses with certain head-throwing habits and added a dressy touch for public appearances, but they never became as popular in America as in some of the old countries.

Breast collars, too, failed to win universal appeal on this side of the ocean. About the only places they saw much use were in some mountainous sections and on the saddles of army officers or mounted dignitaries. As better fitting saddles began to take over the American scene in the late 1800s, the need for breast collars to hold them in place diminished to where they are now seldom seen outside of fancy outfits designed for movie actors and dress parade.

Even more rare are cruppers. Aside from the early Spaniards, Indians, and occasional donkey or mule riders, America has never accepted this accouterment. Horsemen of this country seem to have the attitude of the philosophical old trail hand who said, "The kind of horses I ride ain't apt to let the saddle get ahead of 'em, even without it bein' anchored down by a stern line." Apparently the finely fitting saddles of this country make such bulky and bothersome appendages only an added nuisance.

Not so with spurs. All riding folk use that ancient badge of a horseman, men and women alike. Those of the East are usually of the lightweight English pattern, having narrow heel plates and short shanks that carry ½- to ⅝-inch rowels (Fig. 114). Many are of brass, designed for the gentleman or his lady.

The special trousers model was made to accommodate the bottoms of loose trousers when boots were not worn. The horizontal rowel was evidently for those who liked to do their spurring lengthwise of the goods. The wide-band Eureka, with its larger 1⅜-inch rowel, was a favorite with the farm-boot brethren.

The lady's guard spur in Fig. 115 is self-explanatory. The goad model had an inner spring which was of a strength to hold the goad in position for moderate spurring, but allowed it to withdraw into the shank when the rider's emotions went too far astray. Either type weighed four ounces.

The little 6-ounce Thompson model was devised as a handy aid to be screwed on or off the boot heel as desired. As a practical or popular item, however, it won few friends.

The whip spur was apparently a revival of the ancient Roman goad stuck in the butt of a *scorpio,* which had sprung up and died within a short period a millennium and a half before.

The old American phenomenon of anything being apt to appear at any time in any place holds as true with riding gear as with anything else. Eastern outfits have always shown up at odd times in various western spots. In return, western equipment is no great novelty in the East, where it has made strong inroads of late years. But despite all in-

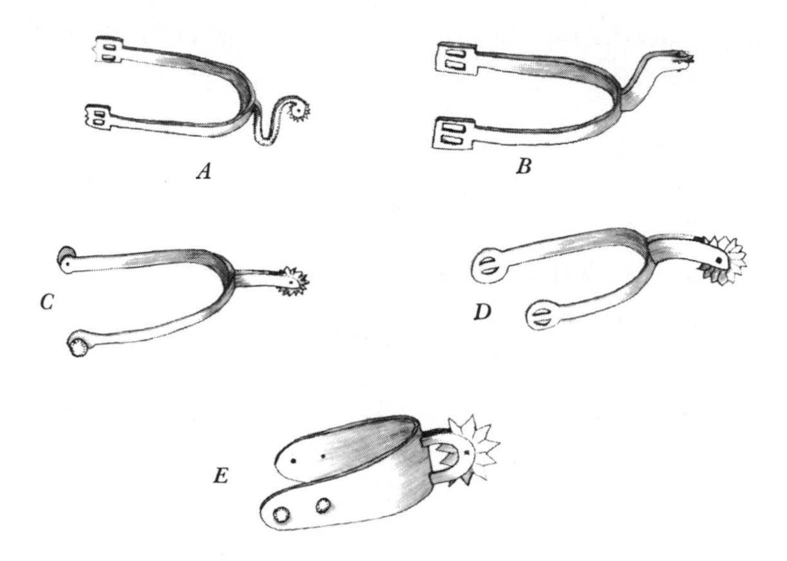

FIG. 114. Eastern spurs: *A* trousers; *B* horizontal; *C* jockey; D lady's or gentleman's; *E* eureka.

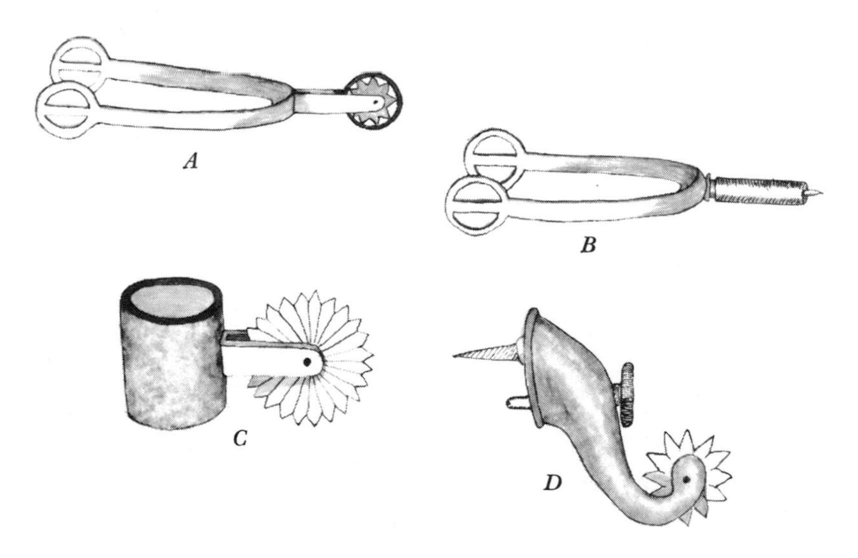

FIG. 115. Spur oddities: *A* lady's guard; *B* lady's goad; *C* whip; *D* Thompson's detachable.

terchange, there is still no real assimilation. East in West or West in East, each goes its own time-honored way.

—21—

The American Cavalry

AMERICA'S CAVALRYMAN was born along the eastern seaboard and went westward as he grew in stature. Most of his customs, traditions, and riding gear closely parallel that of the eastern horseman. Originating as he did in most cases from an eastern school, the first half century of his existence saw him drawing the bulk of his equipment from the ranks of his civilian contemporaries. Still, with all this, the average cavalryman had much in common with the westerner. His continuous hours in the saddle, his constant association with horses, his field of duty so often an untamed wilderness, all conformed to the western pattern. A love for adventure, hard riding, outdoor life, and unfettered freedom inherent in all true horseback men brought him, more than any other eastern American rider, into the fold of western thought and action. In art, literature, fable, and song we find him ranked side by side with the Indian, mountain-man, and cowboy.

His history dates back to the Revolutionary War. He started out under the name of Dragoon, graduating up through Mounted Ranger and Mounted Rifleman to his final status as a cavalryman.

During the pre-Revolutionary War era, European minds had been avoiding mounted warfare in favor of massed infantry battalions. Even George Washington would have nothing to do with cavalry during the early part of the war. It was not until 1777 that the old truth of a strong man on a high horse being superior to a weary man on the ground was borne in upon him enough to change his opinion about horses being only for officers.

Such faulty judgment by an otherwise excellent general was rather deplorable. The eminent historian, Charles Francis Adams, wrote that there were enough horses in the colonies at that time to have made a decisive striking force. In his book, *Washington and His Cavalry,* he reasons that the whole war would have been shortened by years, with a great saving in lives, had the general changed his thinking, based on conditions in Europe, for a more practical approach in the beginning.

It remained for the press of events to convince him that mounted troops were needed. Though Congress authorized the use of Dragoons late in 1777, it was only when Captain Allan McLane was placed in charge that winter that the new order took shape. Even then, the cavalrymen won small recognition until Thomas Sumter, Andrew Pickens, "Light Horse" Harry Lee and Francis Marion, the "Swamp Fox," demonstrated their real worth a year or so later.

These men were from the plantation lands of Virginia and the Carolinas, where horsemanship had reigned supreme for over a hundred years. To their standards flocked a kindred crew equally strong in the heritage of good horsemanship. That they had builded well was soon made clear. It was they who decimated Major Ferguson's command on King's Mountain in 1780. The mounted troops of Harry Lee and Daniel Morgan saved the day at Cowpens in 1781. Marion and Lee put Cornwallis on the run the same year. And it was their Dragoons which prevented Tarleton's men from overrunning the colonials and perhaps turning the whole course of American independence in an opposite direction.

The Dragoons were also a big factor in the War of 1812, as well as the Creek War of 1814. General Andrew Jackson attributed most of his success in the latter conflict to his mounted companies.

There was a dearth of standard equipment in the American army all through that period. Most of the Dragoons rode whatever they could get, mostly private gear brought from home similar to the current civilian saddlery discussed in a previous chapter. For arms, they carried Prussian-type sabers slung on the left side of the saddle, horse-pistols in pommel holsters, and flintlock carbines or musketoons on slings over the right shoulder, when they could get them. Flintlock rifles and muskets were often substituted when shorter guns were unobtainable.

The heavy-duty postilion saddle shown in Fig. 107 appears to have been quite a favorite with mounted troops. Drivers of artillery teams found them especially desirable. They were frequently equipped with horse-pistol pommel holsters like those shown in Fig. 123.

Although the mounted branch of the army almost disappeared after the War of 1812, it was revived in 1832 as the Mounted Rangers to provide a permanently effective cavalry. This was followed by the organization of two regiments of Dragoons the next year. A regiment of Mounted Riflemen was added in 1846. The First and Second Regiments of U.S. Cavalry came into being in 1855. All four divisions operated similarly and more or less simultaneously, until they were welded into a single unit under the head of cavalry in 1861.

About the only difference between the original Mounted Riflemen and the cavalry was the type of arms carried. The Riflemen were primarily designed as a swift mobile force of ground fighters. In consequence, they dispensed with the cumbersome sabers, using only percussion rifles and Colt army revolvers. The cavalry, having no intention of being on foot, clung to the heavy, down-striking sabers, short-barreled percussion carbines and Colt navy revolvers.

Civilian saddles of the English type, along with the South's Jenifer, Shackleford, Mosby, and Stonewall types, were used through most of this period. There is evidence of the army's efforts at standardization, but it was a slow and spotted proceeding. And as the Ordnance Department was not given charge of "horse equipment for the troops" until May, 1855, it is almost impossible to determine exact developments or precise dates for much of what went on.

Colonel Harry C. Larter says that during the early 1800s the heavy cavalry used a heavier full-covered saddle while the light cavalry preferred a less pretentious type built on the Hungarian design. Presumably, the heavier style copied those of north Europe.

Barbara Kell finds that records of the old Grimsley-Stark Company of St. Louis denotes Thornton Grimsley as the inventor of a patent Dragoon saddle, which was adopted by the army about January, 1848. This was somewhat like the Kilgore type (Fig. 111), though severely plain.

Dragoon saddles of this type, probably the Grimsley creation, were mentioned by General Henry C. Hodges as being in use at Fort Vancouver, Washington, in 1853. Henry Wise wrote of a Dragoon saddle he rode at Monterey, California, in 1847, apparently the same model. He preferred his own "easy and comfortable Spanish saddle." Theodore Winthrop felt that a saddle which he designated as an "Army Dragoon," seen at Fort Nisqually, Washington, in 1853, was far more uncomfortable than the Mexican and Indian rigs then in use around the fort. Probably the qualities found lacking in the Dragoon by these men caused its early discontinuance.

Apparently, the Jenifer appeared about this time. Styled like the Shackleford (Fig. 110), but with shorter, padded seats of 11- to 12-inch lengths, this remained the predominant model through the 1850–1860 period. The fairly high pommels and cantles were brass bound. Many were in use as artillery saddles until after the Civil War.

That there were changes, and perhaps duplications, during this time is borne out by Colonel Larter's statement that the Whitman model followed the Grimsley. The former was an open-seat tree covered with russet leather. It was later adopted by the New York City mounted police. Fig. 116 pictures this saddle.

Following the Grimsley, came the Campbell tree. Edgar W. Lancaster of the U.S. Ordnance Department says the Campbell was the standard design when the Ordnance Department assumed charge of the cavalry equipment in May, 1855.

This would give us, chronologically, the Grimsley, Jenifer, Whitman, and Campbell, between 1848 and 1855. Perhaps the cavalry was using them all more or less simultaneously as part of their general disordered condition at that time. This last would seem quite possible in the light of Mr. Lancaster's statement that most of these earlier saddles were furnished by contractors who showed a great lack of conformity in their measurements and dimensions. Their products, therefore, differed widely.

Unfortunately, we have little to go on regarding those old models. Records of details and descriptions are almost totally lacking prior to reorganization under the Ordnance Board. Very few examples have survived, while old prints are all too often so transposed through artistic license as to be unreliable.

One surviving specimen, used by Captain James Duncan during the Mexican War, and probably dating back to a much earlier period, is now preserved by the West Point Museum (Fig. 117). This saddle was a 22¾-inch seat padded with horsehair and covered with quilted leather. The seat leather is fastened to the tree with round-headed brass nails. Pommel and cantle are of wood, their edges being trimmed with brass. The stirrup straps, now missing, were looped through iron staples set in the tree beneath the seat jockeys. It bears the stamp of Company A, 2d U.S. Artillery, leaving no doubt about its authenticity as a military model. And it would no doubt stand as a fairly average representation of most better class cavalry saddles between 1815 and 1850.

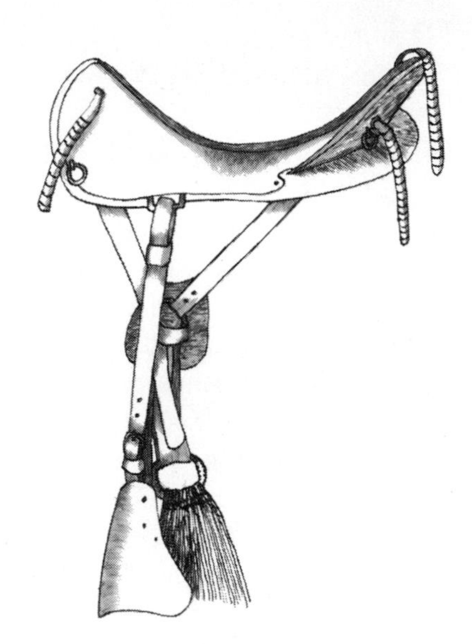

FIG. 116. Officer's Whitman saddle.

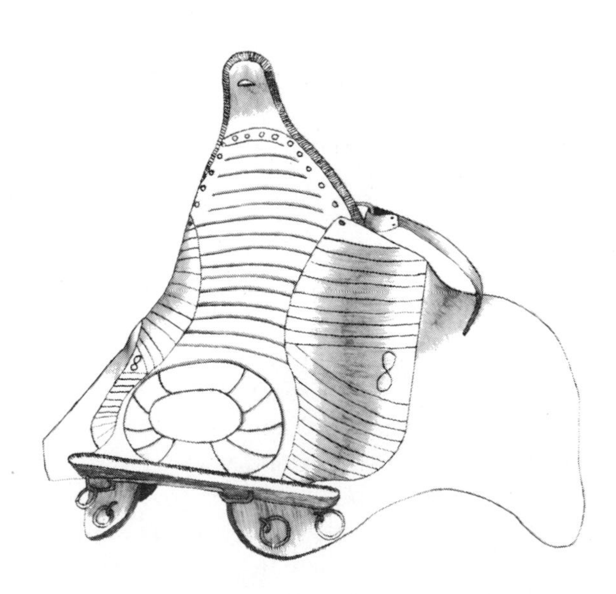

FIG. 117. Captain James Duncan saddle, 1846.

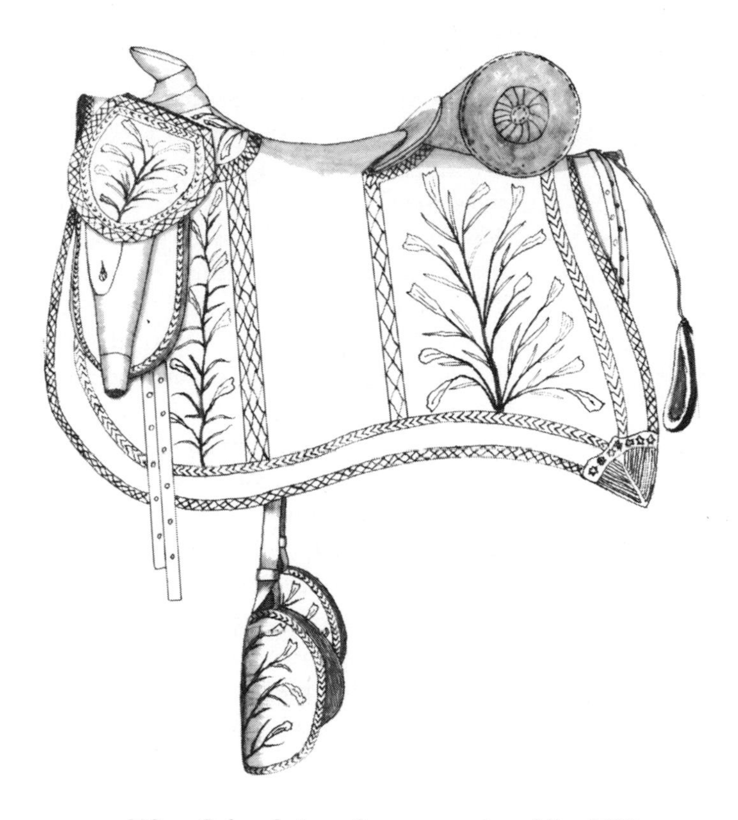

FIG. 118. Colonel Jesse Leavenworth saddle, 1862.

During that period the big, elaborate saddle blankets made their first appearance among American cavalrymen. They seem to have been absent prior to the Mexican War, flourished through the War Between the States, then disappeared for good. Their impressiveness apparently made a special appeal to officers and parade warriors.

Big-skirted saddle covers of finely carved leather were also very popular where appearance was a factor. A saddle ridden by Colonel Jesse Leavenworth in 1862, now in the Colorado State Museum at Denver, is a fine example of this type (Fig. 118). It appears to have been built on the old horned-model Whitman tree, or something similar.

Quite a few horned trees were in use during the Civil War. Many officers preferred them, but they were not common among the enlisted men. Evidently most were of civilian manufacture and personally purchased by individuals.

There is an account of one Confederate officer who had a broad, flat saddle horn designed as a miniature desk for use when writing command orders in the field.

All this variety, by the way, was not confined to saddles. Sporadic changes, alterations, individual purchases, and self-outfitted volunteers created a generous assortment of styles in all phases of cavalry equipment until after the end of the War Between the States.

Bridles invariably had narrow headstalls and closed reins. Most cavalrymen preferred single reins, though the double-rein type with bridoon or Pelham-style bits were not uncommon. Officers, in particular, seemed to have a special fondness for the Pelham. Enlisted men were usually found using single-rein bridles with snaffle or plain curb bits. The snaffle predominated among the earlier volunteer group. Curbs of various kinds appeared in regular army issues.

While it is doubtful that the army ever authorized any of the big, Mexican ring bits (Fig. 119), they were used to some extent by individuals. The regular 1850 port bits, with high, medium, or low ports and leather or chain curbs, were the standard issue until the Model 1863 appeared.

The latter came in four sizes, the ports being 2¼, 2, 1½, and ½ inches in height. The extra-high ones were equipped with ring curbs instead of the ordinary chain or strap, and were reserved for particularly mean horses. These bits were replaced in 1873 by the Shoemaker bit, which had only the three less severe heights of ports.

The Shoemaker was followed by a very similar model in 1892. Only open-bottom sidebars and the extremely high port differentiated it from the earlier style. It was accompanied by the officer's bit of the same period, made only with low ports, but rigged for either single or double reins.

Stirrups were likewise mostly a matter of choice until the late 1800s.

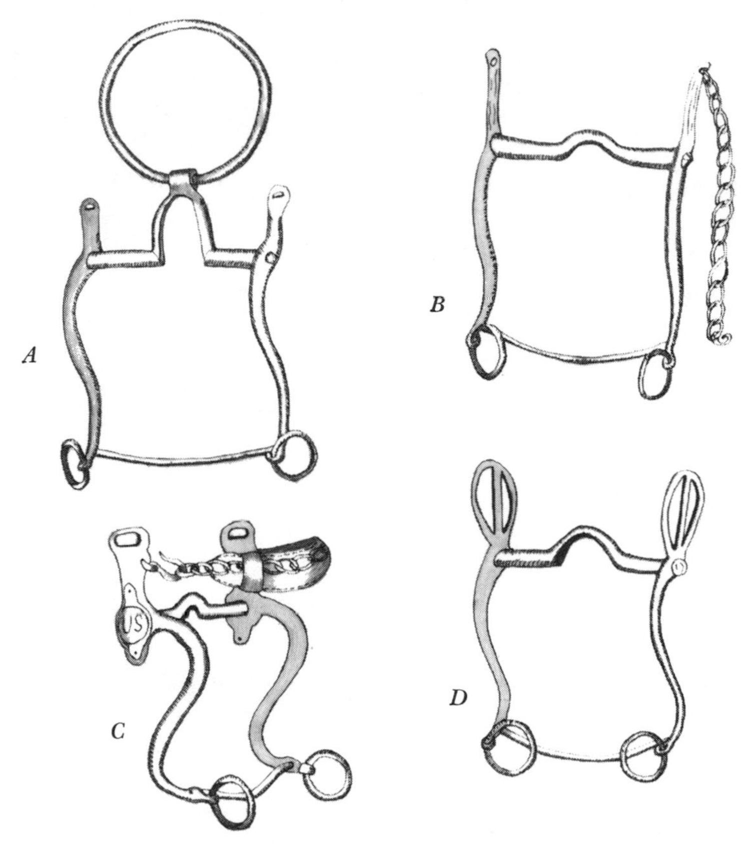

FIG. 119. U.S. Cavalry bits: *A* ring, early 1800s; *B* low port, 1850; *C* U.S.A. model, 1863; *D* Shoemaker model, 1873.

Though the bent-wood variety was available after 1790, and used extensively, the old open steel type that originated in Europe hung on until after the turn of the century, especially among officers. Those shown in Fig. 120 are quite representative of the whole. A grooved, solid-rubber tread appeared on the later ones. It will be noticed that the color-bearer's model carries a built-in socket to receive the butt of the guidon pole.

Though some wooden stirrups appeared in cavalry circles during the early 1800s, they were mostly confined to the North; southerners seldom used them. It was not until after the Civil War that they came into general use, relegating the open steel variety to fancy dress outfits and parade use. The wooden ones adopted were covered with short, close-fitting leather tapaderas that allowed only the ball of the foot to rest

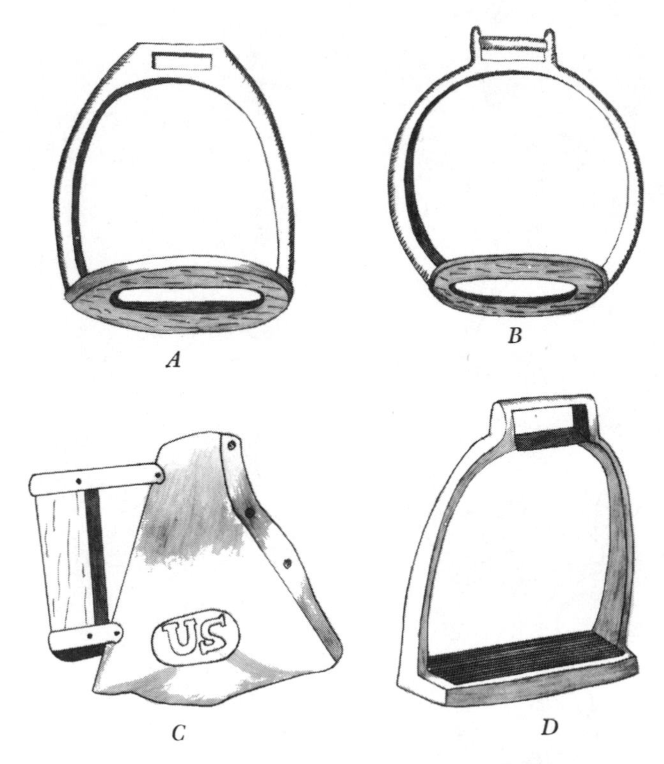

FIG. 120. U.S. Cavalry stirrups: *A* Union cavalry, 1864; *B* Confederate cavalry, 1864; *C* color bearer, 1900; *D* regular issue, 1900.

in the stirrup. They were well liked, even the officers preferring them for field work.

America, incidentally, was the only nation ever to rig its cavalry saddles with bent-wood stirrups.

In contrast, the American cavalry never got away from the European influence in its spurs. They started out by using, or copying, English and German models, apparently forming a habit that lasted as long as the cavalry. Of course, as with everything else, many troopers equipped themselves according to personal taste well into the middle 1800s. Army issue, too, was not always consistent. And the Mexican War indoctrinated some men into preference for the big Spanish spurs. There were individual examples of these all through the Civil War, but they never won much prominence among the better established English specimens.

The plain, simple spur of abbreviated size, fitted with single narrow straps (Fig. 121), graced cavalry boot heels for over a hundred years.

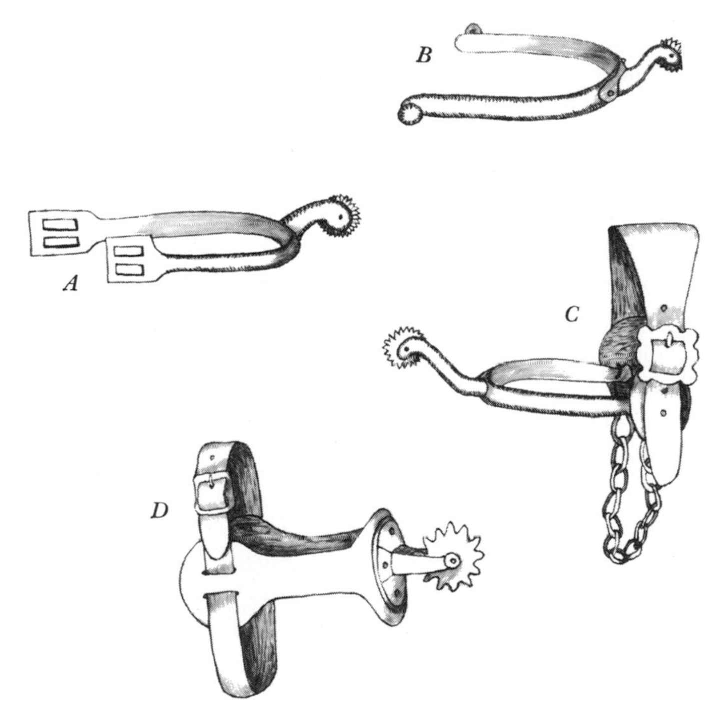

FIG. 121. U.S. Cavalry spurs: *A* standard brass; *B* cast brass; *C* standard steel; *D* Mills patent.

Unlike cowboy spurs, these small, goose-necked affairs were worn with the shanks turned up. There were certain minor variations, being made of brass, steel, or cast metal and having slight differences in strap attachments, heel plates, and shank lengths. All, however, had the ⅝- to ¾-inch rowels and followed the same general pattern until the nonrowel design was introduced out of deference to polished desk tops in later years.

The Mills Patent Model came out around 1900, practically the only odd ball in the lot. Its metal shank and rowel were riveted onto a heavy leather heel plate. It was used to a limited extent in some companies.

The boots that carried these spurs were mainly of the high-topped, jack-boot variety until Civil War times. This was the type so often worn by showmen, exhibitionists, and early army officers, the tops reaching to midway between knee and crotch. They survived as regular cavalry wear among officers until the middle 1800s. At that time the army cut them down to knee length.

The new design was of two styles: those for officers reached to just under the bend of the knee in the back and arched up over the kneecap in front. Ordinary troopers had to be satisfied with tops that were cut off square just below the knee. Both styles were larger in the leg than modern boots. All had low, flat heels and square toes.

The army apparently never included any martingales or breast collars in its early outfits. They were not used in the beginning of the Civil War except where certain individuals supplied their own. Few of the regulars cared to bother with them. Cruppers were also generally unpopular. Both, however, seem to have been issued for use in the latter part of the conflict.

Turning to saddle bags (Fig. 122), we find the earliest government issue was the smallish, 12- by 12-inch canvas affair (*A*). A later model was made of leather, having square flaps and two straps. A pair of these, owned by Colonel Ebenezer Gray of the Connecticut Militia, were of russet leather and measured 7 by 20 inches. (*B*) was a fairly early type. It measured 14 by 15 inches, one style being of canvas with a leather lining and the other entirely of leather.

All these seem to have been used more or less indiscriminately for the half dozen decades following the Revolutionary War. And with them were many of civilian design, ranging all the way from converted meal sacks to handsome creations of fine leather owned by those able to gratify expensive tastes. Old pictures show assorted kinds in both rectangular and half-round shape; of government, foreign, and civilian make—all overlapping in time periods until the middle 1800s.

The Ordnance Board established more uniform standards in 1855. The older styles disappeared soon after the black-leather 1865 Model (*C*) was adopted. This served until replaced by the square type (*D*) in the late 1890s.

The adoption of the bolt-action Krag carbine in 1894 also saw the first appearance of the full-length rifle scabbard. In the old muzzle-loading days, guns required special handling to protect the loose ammunition then in use and the rather intricate lock fixtures. With the big horse pistols, this was well taken care of by the covered holsters (Fig. 123, *A*). But the longer barreled rifles had to be carried across the saddle or by shoulder slings, with the muzzles up. It was not until

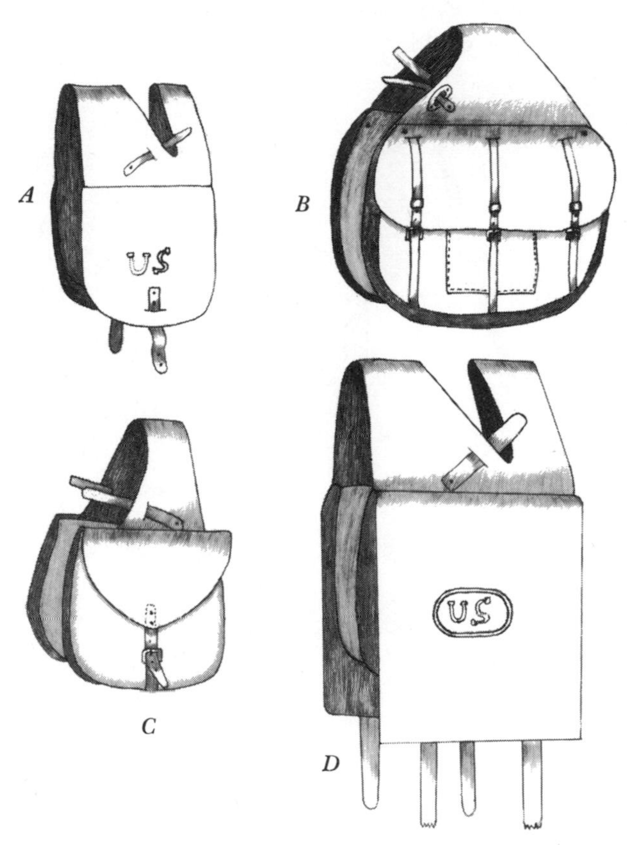

FIG. 122. U.S. Cavalry saddlebags: *A* 1750–1800; *B* 1775–1850; *C* 1865; *D* 1894.

breech-loading locks and metallic cartridges obviated the danger of breakage and rammed loads jarring loose by joltings of the horse that it became practical to carry a carbine muzzle down.

Swapping ends with the gun, however, brought little comfort to the rider's back. Carried by a sling over the left shoulder, with its muzzle pointing toward his right hip, it flopped around as aggravatingly as ever whenever the horse felt ambitious.

Thus a little black-leather socket was devised, 2⅛ inches long by 2¾ inches wide (Fig. 123, *B*) which could be straped to the off sidebar ring behind the cantle. The idea was to poke the muzzle tip of the loosely slung carbine into the socket as sort of a steadying measure for the weapon. In practice, the results were about what might be expected. It wasn't until four years later that progressive thinking finally discovered that the gun could be carried as easily by the horse as by the

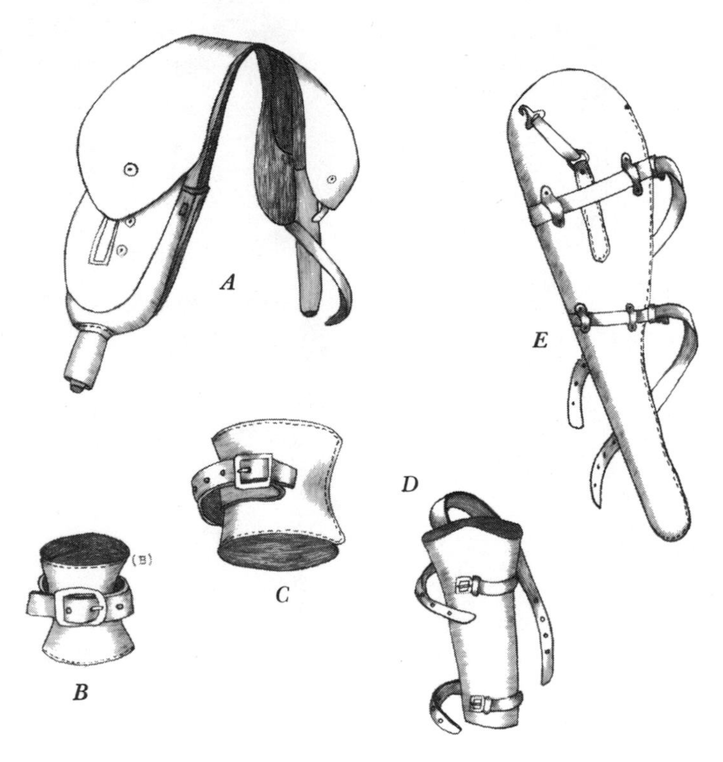

FIG. 123. U.S. Cavalry carbine boots: *A* horse pistol holsters; *B* 1861–1865; *C* 1865–1870; *D* 1870–1898; *E* 1898–.

man. Then a 14-inch boot (*C*) was adopted. It was made on the same principle as the short socket and was designed to receive the carbine bodily. It rode in the same position as its predecessor, taking its place in 1865.

Unfortunately, this too failed to provide the complete answer. It could be secured to the saddle at only the one central point. This allowed the carbine to do almost as much jerking about when the horse was in motion as it had before. Moreover, the fact that the boot could accommodate the carbine only to its midsection caused almost the entire length of the stock to stick up.

More thinking over the next five years eventually resolved itself around a revised model (*D*), which eliminated some of the others' worst failings. Slung by its upper strap to the right-hand rear sidebar ring, it was long enough to permit the lower end being secured to the off cinch ring. This not only tied the rig down, but also allowed the weapon to be carried lower and put it more out of the way. This served as the regulation boot until the full-length scabbard (*E*) arrived in 1894.

The latter was the first attempt to carry the cavalry carbine in a semi-horizontal position, butt foremost, under the right leg. The top and bottom sling straps were attached respectively to the fore and aft sidebar rings, holding the gun diagonally, its butt just above the horse's withers ahead of the saddle, the muzzle behind and slightly below the rider's knee.

When not worn on the person, the saber rode in a corresponding position on the left side of the saddle. Like the carbine, it was slung from the front sidebar ring, the lower end being fastened to the cinch ring so it could rest comfortably under the left knee.

Most of this diversity in equipment was on the way out after 1855. The newly authorized Ordnance Board was a believer in uniformity. One of the first objects of its attention was the cavalry saddle. The decision was for a single standard model that would eliminate the old miscellany and incorporate the best available qualities in riding comforts, serviceability, and ease for the horse. General George B. McClellan was assigned to select such a design.

The general's search for the necessary requirements resulted in his recommendation, the following year, for the adoption of a model copied from the ancestor of all military saddles, the ancient Hungarian laced tree (Fig. 84).

McClellan made his report to the Secretary of War, Jefferson Davis. The letter, now in the National Archives at Washington, D.C., was dated October 3, 1856, and reads in part: "Sir: I have shown to several officers passing through the city, the Prussian cavalry equipment. All agree that, with certain essential modifications, it would be a better equipment than any we have yet had in our service. The tree is what is known as the Hungarian. I would remove all the unnecessary iron with which the Prussians have encumbered it and reduce the height of the cantle."

After sundry recommendations from all concerned, McClellan was authorized to construct the modified saddle and other features at a cost not to exceed $75. This was approved and, on November 19, 1856, McClellan wrote to the Chief of Ordnance, accepting the offer.

Thanks to the general, whose name it now bears, 1858 found the McClellan rig formally introduced into the cavalry. The original appeared as in Fig. 124.

This came out with rawhide-covered, open seat on 11-, 11½-, and 12-inch trees. It had large, black-leather skirts fastened to the tree with brass nails. Both pommel and cantle were fitted with coat straps and exposed rigging. Leather-hooded wooden stirrups with 4-inch treads were used. The web cinch was of blue wool, leathered on the outside, with a latigo ring on the off side and a buckle on the opposite end. The blanket roll was usually carried across the pommel.

These were the standard saddles in use during the War Between the States. The South, which had been forced to depend mainly on civilian saddles in the early part of the conflict, acquired McClellans for most of their forces later on. It was said the troops exercised great care in keeping the saddles dry when not in use. Otherwise, repeated wetting and drying would often cause the rawhide covering to split and curl, giving the riders a foretaste of Sherman's definition of war.

No doubt that was the principle reason for the revised design which appeared soon after the war. The most important alterations that went into making the new model was the change to a smooth, leather-covered seat and removal of the big skirts (Fig. 125). From a copy of the Ordnance Board's specifications, supplied by Mr. Lancaster of that office, we find that other changes were of a minor nature.

This 17-pound 5-ounce model remained the regulation army saddle until the cavalry was abolished in 1942. About the only change made in subsequent years was the switch to a 7-inch hair-cord cinch around 1900, plus the substitution of russet color for the earlier black-leather covering to conform with the khaki uniforms adopted in 1898.

Many McClellan saddles, declared obsolete or surplus, eventually found their way into civilian trade channels and civic organizations. Canada acquired a quantity of them for outfitting her Northwest Mounted Police, when that force was organized in 1873. Others went to various police forces in the United States, to foreign republics, and to individual horsemen. Some are still in use.

The valise saddle dates back to before the Revolutionary War. It carried a built-in pillion contained behind the cantle, not unlike the mail pillion in Fig. 107. The pillion itself was made square, round, or oval at various times. It was a required item for those seeking to join cavalry units of the several state militias until about 1834. It continued in use until after the Mexican War.

The example in Fig. 126 was one of the later models which dispensed with the pillion. It had a rawhide-covered tree topped by a stitched and quilted black-leather seat. Pommel and cantle rim were bound with brass. Skirts and cinch were of black leather.

Quite similar was the saddle used by drivers of artillery teams. This was originated for the light cavalry units employed by Frederick II of Prussia. Napoleon copied it on an extensive scale as part of his grandiose scheme to conquer the world. From there, it migrated to Britain, and thence, in 1808, to America. It differed in some respects from the valise, but had the same black-leather covering, padded seat, and brass-bound pommel and cantle rims. The short front and back skirts gave it a neater appearance than the valise, while the longer fender-skirts were designed for maximum protection from the chain traces commonly used on artillery horses. Fig. 127 shows the Civil War model. It was equipped with the standard blue-wool cinch and the preferred stirrups of that period.

Following the Civil War, succeeding models gradually adopted more and more features of the regular cavalry saddle until there was little difference between the two. Then, after 1930, they turned in opposite directions to assume a marked distinction by the time the horse units were disbanded in 1942.

Of course, in the field or isolated outposts there was always a certain amount of interchanging and substitution. In studying old pictures we find civilian-type wagon saddles and cavalry models occasionally appearing on postilion mounts of supply vehicles, ambulance teams, and the like. Artillery and valise rigs also cropped up among regular troops. But it is safe to assume that such examples arose from temporary force of circumstances.

Much the same applies to cavalry horses. Mustangs, coach horses, and light work animals were ridden on occasion. But cavalry mounts were, as a regular thing, of eastern America saddle stock carrying a generous amount of Thoroughbred blood or strains of Arabian lineage. Pure Thoroughbreds were no novelty. The better ones were often privately owned, especially in the earlier years.

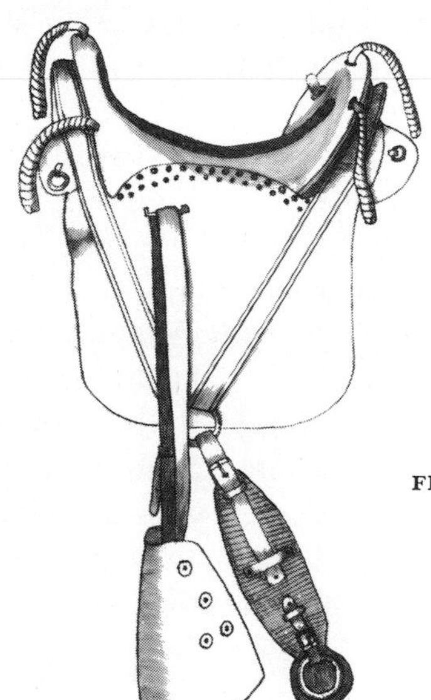

FIG. 124. McClellan saddle, 1868.

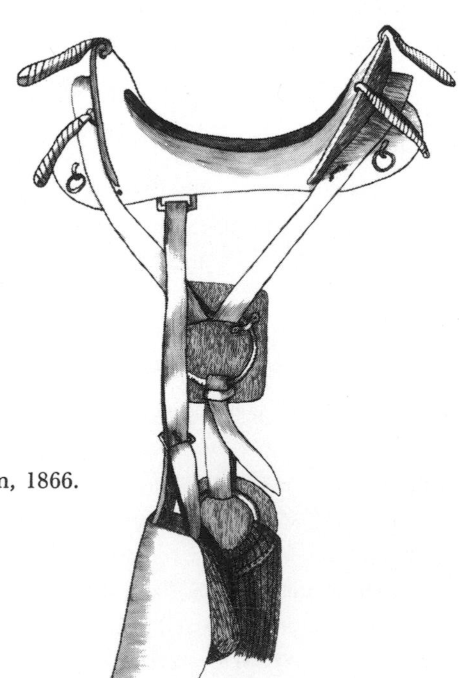

FIG. 125. Regulation McClellan, 1866.

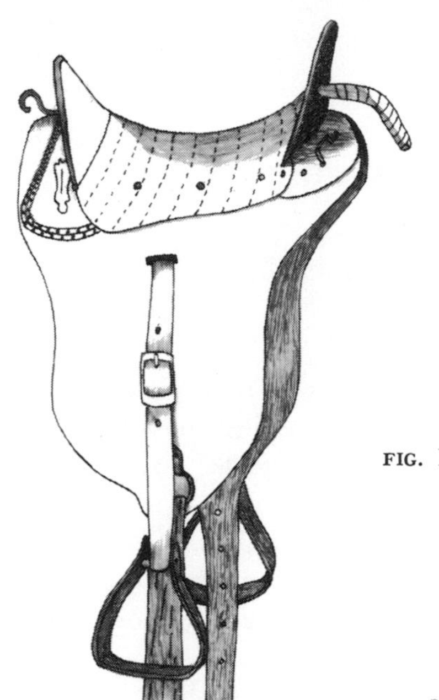

FIG. 126. Valise saddle.

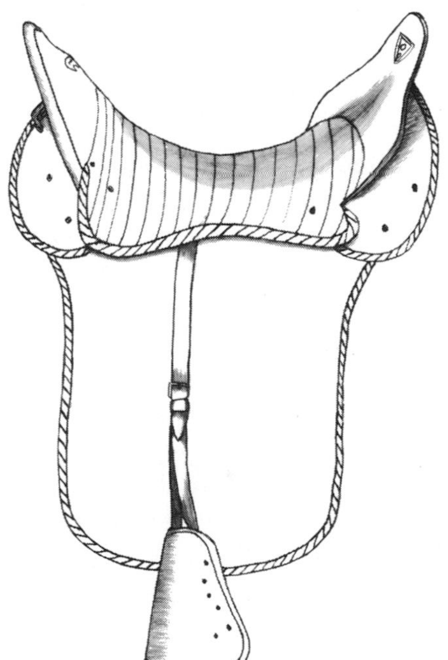

FIG. 127. Artillery saddle.

—22—

Sawdust and Spangles

RUNNING A RATHER close parallel to the cavalry horse is the horse of the circus. We find most good cavalry mounts very adept at answering bugle calls and going through intricate maneuvers with only a word, a body movement, or a prick of the spur to serve as a command. So, too, do the circus animals carry out their tasks with almost human response. Moreover, no other two branches of equine activities are so closely aligned in attracting attention or stirring the pulses of onlookers.

The circus animal, however, has always had the advantage of being allowed to perform on a prepared stage before assembled multitudes. He deserves that favor. Here is an animal whose beauty and intelligence have excited man's admiration from time immemorial. To watch him and his fellows waltz about the Big Top's sawdust ring, keeping perfect time to the music of the band, or going through a variety of formations with only the sound of the trainer's voice and popping whip to guide them, is to see perfection in the animal kingdom. And no less appealing than their skill in action is the pride of accomplishment each shows while performing.

Much of this pride, of course, is a reflection from the trainers and bespangled riders who put him through his paces. It is an arduous job to bring one of these four-footed actors to perfection in its work. Yet when the task is achieved the horse seems to take as much pride in a good performance as does the man who raised it to that level.

We have no way of knowing when horses of this type first began entertaining the human race. It was no doubt not long after man first adopted the animal as his best friend and was made aware of its intelligence and willingness to please. We know that the practice of training horses for exhibition purposes prevailed in ancient Greece during the times of Homer and Xenophon. Some of the methods used and acts taught by those people are still in use today; quite likely they were handed down to the Greeks by earlier Scythians, Parthians, and Persians. But however that may be, affairs which featured horse performances were popular attractions at most circuses around the dawn of the Christian Era.

Circus, by the way, is a Latin word used to denote the circuits around which chariots raced in the days of early Rome. At first, this was simply a circular course laid out in the open near the outskirts of the city. Later, the Romans put it inside an amphitheater, where the audience had the privilege of paying admission that they might be seated on the rising tiers of seats. One of the most famous of these structures was the Circus Maximus, built in Rome during the last century B.C. It was 115 rods long, built in a long oval 625 feet wide, and seated 260,000 spectators, the majority of whom found a special delight in watching the finely trained chariot teams race each other.

So great was the interest attending anything in which horses appeared that the sponsors incorporated various other equestrian features in their programs, even though it might mean postponing the regular attraction of watching Christians being devoured by lions.

After Rome collapsed under the weight of its own ego, Europe more or less slid back into a period of darkness that showed little heart for public entertainments. About the only thing in that line to survive was a primitive form of circus. Few definite details of this branch of history have come down to us. About all we know is that small troupes of performers wandered over western Europe during those unhappy ages. By the late 1300s, they were so plentiful that few public functions took place without such a company putting in its appearance. Closely related to the minstrel brotherhood, they roamed from the Mediterranean to the North Sea, performing their acts wherever there was a chance for some financial or gustatory reward.

From the earliest days, trained animals held a special appeal for audiences, and the adaptability of horses and dogs made them especially desirable for such purposes. So with a trained horse or two, a few dogs, and perhaps a tame bear, the embryonic circuses staged their exhibitions at fairs, on market days, in tavern and stagecoach courtyards and community gatherings throughout the Continent. Some of these grew to be quite extensive affairs, but large or small, they all used horses in some form as headline attractions for their shows.

The famous Hagenbeck Zoo of Hamburg, Germany, along with the Hagenbeck-Wallace Circus, was built on just such a foundation.

The highly trained performing circus horse, as we know him, did not come along until the 1770s. An Englishman by the name of Philip Astley was responsible for this development; and he might be termed the founder of the American circus.

Astley was a British sergeant-major in His Majesty's Royal Regiment of Light Dragoons. After his retirement from the army, he decided to gratify his love for horses and dislike of idleness by starting a regular performance of trained horse acts and trick riding. In a short while, he had his circus established in a vacant building near the Half-Penny Inn in London.

His venture was a success from the start, drawing attention from the Continent, as well as at home. He soon won so much acclaim for his circus that the Franconis of Italy and John Bill Ricketts of England were moved to come out with similar shows. Their new enterprises likewise proved so sucessful that horse circuses began springing up all over western Europe. Ricketts finally decided that the virgin field of America offered better opportunities than competitive Europe, so he shipped to America and set up his Equestrian Pantheon in Philadelphia about 1780.

This establishment was conducted as a riding academy, horse training school, and a circus featuring the best in trained horse acts. The place held a special appeal for George Washington, who often went there for relaxation during his Presidential years. It was Ricketts to whom the American circus owes much of its initial inspiration.

In America the circus came into being about 1820. It followed the old European pattern giving shows on the road and moving from town to town by horse-drawn wagons. The first of these circuses were chiefly horse and dog shows. By the time the circus came into full bloom, some sixty years later, horses were taking part in nearly all the acts except the high-wire acrobatics. From the gaily caparisoned teams pulling the parade wagons to the slow-cantering rosin-backs drifting around the ring, horses were ever the heart of the circus.

The annals of the circus are replete with equine performers of exceptional ability. The Schumann Circus of Copenhagen, Denmark, had a team of horses trained to play basketball. Others, here in America, were equally proficient in an amazing variety of acts. John Robinson, Adam Forepaugh, Ringling, Sells-Floto, Barnum and Bailey, Al G. Barnes were among the many who helped preserve the great tradition of filling the sawdust circle with the spectators' chief delight—well-trained horses. Whether jumping through blazing hoops of fire, as do Jimmy Murphy's pair of beautiful Palominos, or sneaking up on their knees to nip the seat of Toby the clown's baggy pants, all do their parts as only professionals can.

For the lovely girls in spangled costumes, who ride bareback, we have the broad-bodied, smooth-gaited Percherons called rosin-backs because their backs are sprinkled with powdered rosin to provide secure footing for performers who do standing rides and various acrobatics while in motion. The groups of dancing horses are second only to the liberty troupes, who go through their intricate drills and formations with neither riders nor controlling reins. Individual performers might be called the maestros of the profession, executing their solo acts with magnificent aplomb. All alike, however, show a marvelous sense of timing and precision.

Even the big draft horses, used to haul the parade wagons, are finished actors in their own field. Caparisoned in their circus finery and hitched in four- to eight-horse strings, their carefully timed movements when the calliope begins to play, and equally careful maneuvers in turning, circling, and cutting figure eights without getting tangled up, are as pridefully and precisely executed as the performance of any animal inside the Big Top. Most of them are so knowledgeable in their work that they could do fully as well without a driver.

The men and women who handle these various horses are no less adept in their profession. It commonly takes from two to four years to put the finishing touches on one of these animals. For best results most of the work has to be done by one master. Only true horsemen have the skill and patience to do such work successfully. And only true horsemen, experienced in their specialized craft, have any business on the backs of such performers. Anything less would not only spoil the act, but would probably ruin the horse as well.

As the circus horse exemplifies the ultimate in breeding and training for a most exacting art, so do the trainer and rider stand as the masters of a profession as old as human knowledge. Such notables as Will Rogers, Billie Burke, and Tom Mix were among the many who rose to fame from the ranks of outstanding circus riders.

The high intelligence and tractability of Arabians and Thoroughbred mixtures makes these animals specially favored for this type of work. Still, there are plenty of Hackneys, Palominos, Morgans, Appaloosas, Pintos, and other saddle-horse breeds, along with a generous sprinkling of mules, in the profession. Horses are much like people;

gifted minds turn up in all classes and many unexpected places. And, also like humans, most of them respond to kind teachers, hearty applause, and the music of the band.

To fully appreciate the height to which this response may lead, one has only to watch a performance of the famous Lipizzaner horses of Vienna. With a background of 223 years of continuous appearances before appreciative audiences on both sides of the Atlantic Ocean, they represent the epitome of training. These magnificent white animals, bearing the blood of Arabian, Andalusian, and the Vilanos horse of the Pyrenees, show a perfection of intelligence and performance which makes one wonder if the ancients were too far astray in their worship of the horse as one among the other gods. Though it requires some four years to train the Lipizzaners, starting when they are four years old, anyone who has seen them in action would surely vote the time well spent.

One horse that missed his calling by not being in the circus was King Philip. He was General Nathaniel B. Forrest's favorite mount during the Civil War. King Philip was rather easy-going and placid under ordinary circumstances. The fanfare of battle, however, brought out a different kind of animal. With the din of conflict in his ears, he was galvanized into immediate violent action. In the course of events, he even got to where he would take it upon himself to emulate the war horses of ancient knights, attacking the enemy with hoofs and teeth on sight. Anyone in blue uniform would raise his ire to fever pitch without any prompting from his rider.

Then, as though blessed with human understanding, he laid his savagery away with the coming of peace to become a quiet and inoffensive citizen again. As he grew old his continued docility and somewhat sluggish actions eventually won him a place between the shafts of an old lady's buggy. He was thus hauling his mistress up the street at his usual dispirited and sleepy jog when he suddenly spied a group of parading policemen dressed in blue uniforms.

That did it! An instant later, he was the young King Philip reincarnated. Up went his tail, back went his ears, and with bared teeth he drove headlong toward the hated bluecoats, the screaming lady bouncing behind him in the careening buggy like a hen caught in a whirlwind.

Fortunately, the fleeing minions of the law all made it to safety, if a trifle disheveled, through a series of convenient doorways and one shattered window. We are left to assume that the ruffled lady suffered damages to nothing but her dignity. With the disappearance of the blue uniforms King Philip himself returned immediately to his lack-luster plodding.

—23—

The Cowboy Arrives

THE NORTH AMERICAN cowboy is a unique breed. He represents a curious blend of California *caballero,* Mexican *vaquero,* and Rocky Mountain trapper, Dixie Land planter, Plains Indian, and eastern cavalryman. From each comes a different shade of his personality; each bequeathed characteristics blended *only* on western soil.

A large proportion of his basic qualities were inherited from the old-time western horsemen, the mountain men. Those hardy wilderness rovers represented the epitome of individualism, toughness, self-sufficiency, fierce independence, love of freedom, and daring. They were a colorful lot in words, looks, and deeds. Many of their traits combined the best qualities of Indian and white.

These original westerners represented a fusing of Indian customs, horsemanship, frontier knowledge, with Yankee ingenuity and the age-old indomitability of the man on horseback. The *vaquero* of Mexico and California added his characteristics to the mixture in most of the valleys of the southern Rockies and Sierras. The Latins brought with them the finer arts of roping practice, a more polished adroitness in the saddle, and an inborn sense of gracious living and hospitality, combined with a certain vanity.

Newcomers moving out of the southeastern states to the Texas Plains added a strong strain of southern gentleman and planter temperament. Springing mostly from the horseman's world, they brought cavalier courtliness, spirit, and pride. Infused with cooler, more direct qualities from the northern Rockies, plus a dash of the frontier cavalryman's traits, within a few years the corporate body brought forth that figure of world renown, the American cowboy.

The special skills and working tools of the cowboy, unlike his multi-sided personality, are mostly of a single origin. Though altered, refined and modified to fit American ideas and changing conditions, the basic design of whatever he does or uses in the line of work or sport is nearly always a heritage from the Mexican *vaquero*. This even extends to his language. Cowboys from Texas to Alberta commonly season their talk with words adopted from below the Mexican border. Various items of their equipment are still known only by their original Spanish names, Americanized by usage. Others carry translations so corrupted by the English tongue as to be almost beyond recognition, yet none the less rooted in the land of the *vaquero*.

Thus we find cinch to be from the Latin *cingo,* to surround, and Spanish *cincha*. The strap which connects it to the saddle is seldom referred to by any other term than the old Spanish name of *latigo*. Stirrup hoods are still *tapaderas*. Chaps are nothing more than a short version of *chaparreras*. *Sombrero* continues to mean a hat, in many sections. Our ranch needs only its original final *o* to again become the old *rancho* of the dons. We compounded the two words, *la reata,* the rope, to make lariat. Its companion term, lasso, derives from *lazo,* a snare or running knot. *Bozal,* a headstall for horses, is commonly applied to the nosepiece of a *jáquima,* or hackamore; the knotted theodore rope used to hold it in place gets its name from the Mexican *fiador,* meaning a fastener or security. The McCarty, or lead rope, for such rigs is simply the Yankee translation of *mecate*. In much the same category was the *mochila* saddle, which L. H. Hamley says was frequently referred to in the Northwest during the late 1800s as a "mercheer."

Out on the range we find a like situation. *Remuda,* which means a relay of mounts, became the name for any bunch of horses held for replacements by an outfit's riders. The similar designation, cavvy or cavvyard, comes from *caballada,* or simply a number of horses. A *manada* is a band of horses, usually a stud of mares, not held as a *remuda*. *Caverango,* a hostler, reaches us in the form of cavvy wrangler, or a plain old horse wrangler.

An unbroken horse starts out as a *potro,* to have its kinks shaken out by a *jinete,* or bronc buster. Then he is taken in hand by a *domador,* a tamer or horsebreaker, after which he becomes a *quebrantado,* or partly-broken animal. The *arrendador,* or teacher, finishes the job by training him in the ways of a good and useful *caballo de silla*.

The cook of an outfit often travels under the name of coosie, which derives from the Spanish name for that functionary, *cocinero*. This, however, should not be confused with coonie, which comes from *cuna,* or cradle. The latter is the name for the dry cowhide, also called a possum belly, that is slung under a chuck wagon for carrying the camp axe, shovel, dry wood for emergencies, and the like. If the cook has any dried beef on hand, it will probably be referred to as jerky. This term comes from its Spanish name of *charqui* because such meat was simply jerked off the carcass before being hung up to dry.

The Mexican's use of "gringo" and the American's "greaser" did not originate along the border as derogatory nicknames for each other, as many people suppose. "Gringo" comes from the Greek word *griego,* meaning foreigner or strange language. Mexican tongues twisted it into "gringo," from whence the pronunciation found its way up into our Southwest.

The origin of "greaser" took place a couple thousand miles northeast of Mexico and among a totally different class of people.

During the early days of the Canadian fur trade most of the men who worked for the big fur companies were French, known as *engagées,* to differentiate them from the individualistic free trappers. New replacements from abroad quite naturally found themselves relegated to the lowest tasks at the least pay. This augmented the usual homesickness and longing for things not available in the strange foreign land. One of their greatest plaints was the absence of pork from their diets. The well-seasoned *voyageurs,* cocky with frontier knowledge and experience, looked on the ineffectual greenhorns with amused contempt. The newcomers' lamentations for the old familiar sight of fat pork on the table, instead of the ever-present fresh meat, soon won them the ignoble title of *mangeurs de lard,* or lard eaters, from their comrades.

When American trappers spread north to mingle with the gay-spirited French-Canadians, they were not long in appropriating the name of lard eaters for their own misfits. At the same time, and with typical American pointedness, they shortened the term to "greasers." Also, with the peculiar single-mindedness of poorly educated men, some Americans came to use the name in blanket form for all dark-skinned foreigners with whom they came in contact. This included the few Mexicans and Spaniards who had drifted north to engage in the fur trade. By 1845, the term had become fairly common throughout the West.

It was those same French-Canadians who indirectly gave us the word "foofaraw" as a descriptive name for elaborate dress, gay trappings, and other fixings. The original word was the French *fanfaron,* meaning to display, brag, or boast. When the mountain-men got through with it, it was corrupted into the breezy foofaraw, and made to include almost anything of a gay or extravagant nature. They soon spread its use throughout the West, where it became an established term among the buckskinned fraternity. It was they who carried the word to California, where it met the very similar Spanish *fanfarron* without losing any of its American identity.

As to the cowboy himself, there will probably always be some controversy over the exact origin of his name. We know he was first a *vaquero,* the word deriving from the Spanish *vaca,* or cow. This term followed him all the way up the West Coast to central California and from south Mexico to north Texas. When the Californio moved on north into Oregon, Idaho, and Washington, the Yankee translation of *vaquero* turned him into a buckaroo. His trade thenceforth was to become known as buckarooing, while the first half of his name was commonly attached to the more unruly horses he often rode. The northwestern cowboy was for many years separated by distance, customs, and regional differences from his cousin east of the Rockies.

While the western *vaquero* was sowing the seeds of an undying culture in California, his counterpart was pounding out hoof-gouged trails across northeastern Mexico toward the Rio Grande. After crossing over into Texas, he was still the same old *vaquero.* And a *vaquero* he remained. His American likeness on this side of the border assumed the same name without regard to race or nationality throughout the Southwest. The late J. Frank Dobie tells us the word cowboy was seldom used in the Southwest prior to 1870.

Exactly where, when, and why ranch hands received the name of cowboy still continues to plague researchers. It apparently sprang up in the neighborhood of the Red River soon after the Civil War, gradually growing in popularity as it followed the spreading cattle industry.

We find the first record of the word cowboy in Ireland, around A.D. 1000. Though it crept into the English language, it apparently gained little prominence there as a general term. Whether it migrated from there to America, or Americans came up with it in their own right, is anybody's guess. We only know the name was sometimes applied to New England cattle drovers of the middle 1600s. It seemingly reflected no discredit at that time.

Later, during the Revolutionary War, the word gained an entirely different meaning. Many colonials of those troublesome days, as we know, lost heavily in possessions to both the Continental and British armies, depending on which side they were supposed to be supporting. Cattle were fairly easy to steal, and underpriced beef with no questions asked stirred the spirit of free enterprise in many commissary officers. The better element called the reversible British-American patriots who built up quite a business in cattle thievery "cowboys."

Some of the backwoods districts of the southern states are said to have continued using the word, but it received scant attention until it showed up in south Texas during the new republic's hassle with Mexico in 1836. It was still an uncomplimentary word, but it was then applied to army detachments sent out to find meat for the Texas soldiers, preferably on Mexican ranches.

In much the same vein the term was attached to the hard-riding, hard-fighting crew which made up the outfit of Colonel Ewen Cameron, the Scottish rancher of south Texas who set out to win a slice of the Mexican War on his own hook. His so-called cowboys seem to have passed out of the picture almost as quickly as the commotion he stirred up. The name still wasn't considered quite respectable. As a matter of fact, it was almost synonymous with that of rustler in south Texas for a good many years.

The most likely supposition is that the cowboy we know got off to a fresh start when somebody applied the name to some particular group of young fellows working together. Ranch boys went to work at an early age in those days. Kids of twelve or fourteen were no novelty out on the range. Many youngsters of eighteen or nineteen headed roundup crews and bossed trail drives. As all cattle were cows in range parlance, there would have been nothing unnatural in their handlers becoming known as cowmen and cowboys according to their positions in the different age groups. Moreover, when we consider that the spirit of the horseman is invariably young, it is easy to see how a predominant swing in the "boy" direction might have taken place as time went on. A further division appearing equally natural was that which set the cowmen pretty well apart as ranch owners or operators, leaving the men who worked for wages as the cowboys.

Some historians believe that the "boy" part, if not the whole word cowboy was implanted in the West by postwar settlers from the mountain country of the Southeast. Many of those people followed the custom of using "boy" as sort of a complimentary term when referring to favorite male acquaintances of any age. Transplanted to the south Plains by those who pioneered in the new land, the term won acceptance among their neighbors. It is a common figure of speech to this day in all that region between Oklahoma and Arizona.

"Roundup," as applied to the gathering of livestock, also probably comes from the Southeast. The term seems to have made its appearance on the Plains somewhere around 1865–1870. Previous to that, rangemen were known only as *vaqueros* or ranch hands, while a roundup was a cow-hunt, or gathering, and a roundup crew was a cow-crowd or bunch.

The later term cowpuncher did not appear until after the advent of steel rails and railroad cars. J. Frank Dobie gives us a most authoritative account of this word's origin in his *Vaquero of the Brush Country*. The story was told to him by one of the participants, a south Texas rancher named John Young. The place was Las Animas, Colorado; the year was 1879.

Young was helping load out a shipment of cattle for the Cimarron Cattle Company when some eastern boys, who had run away from home to see the storied West, got a ride east in return for helping with the stock. The boys were broke and anxious to get home; the cattle train bound for Kansas City would provide a quick escape from the coming Plains winter. Railroads then issued passes for a caretaker to accompany every car or two of stock, their duty being to help with the unloading and loading at feeding stations along the way and prod any animals to their feet at each stop. A full trainload would commonly permit more passes than there were men to use them.

The boys were a rollicking bunch; armed with their long prod poles, which they dubbed badges of office, they were soon calling themselves the cowpunchers. So apt a title caught the fancy of others forced to prod obstinate steers up loading chutes. In the course of time, it was expanded to include similar chores around the ranch, whence it spread to the outlying ranges and to cowboys in general.

"Cowpoke" was a colloquial variant of cowpuncher, often applied to older or less active hands. Its general use, however, was chiefly confined to self-appointed wits viewing the cowboy from out of a drugstore window or from between a pair of plow handles.

"Cowhand" was an old and very natural designation for anyone who worked with cattle, everywhere accepted as a fitting title, though it never attained the general popularity of the term cowpuncher. Rider almost replaced cowboy as an everyday name on the northern ranges during the first couple of decades after the turn of the century. Later years have happily seen a reverse trend toward cowboy.

The term rider is often misinterpreted in uninformed circles, being confused with bronc rider. While an ordinary rider may be, and often is, quite proficient at riding broncs, and a bronc rider often works as an ordinary rider between displays of his specialty, the two designations are distinctly different. In short, the rider is a working cowboy who may or may not turn his talents to bronc riding. Basically, he is a many-skilled workman plying his everyday craft on ranch and range without any attempt at showmanship. Only years of practice can win him recognition as a top-hand rider.

The bronc rider, on the other hand, is a specialist in the art of staying on top of an equine contortionist. He breaks out the rough string, tames the bad ones for less skillful riders, and competes at the rodeos. Given the proper physical qualities, he may be able to learn the trade in a matter of months. He might never be worth his salt as a cowboy or a passable ranch hand, yet all the while be a headliner in the bucking arena.

Bronc riders have worked under a variety of names. "Busters" is perhaps the oldest, coming up from the South with the trail herds. "Peeler" and "twister" were quite popular around the turn of the century. "Fighters" saw much use during the early 1900s, particularly in the North. "Stomper" is a fairly late addition, apparently an offspring of the rodeo circuit. "Rider" has had top billing in recent years. However, they are all one when it comes to topping off a "bucker."

"Bucker" and "bucking," by the way, are northern words. They derive from "buckaroo," the Northwest's version of *vaquero*. This word crossed the northern Rockies with Oregon trail drivers to meet its counterpart, "pitching," which came up from the Southwest. "Bucking" was seldom heard in the Texas-Arizona region until after 1890, while "pitching" never gained much of a hold north of Cheyenne. The central Plains area was about the only place where the two words were used more or less indiscriminately.

—24—

Tools of the Trade

THE BRANDING IRON, the rope, and the saddle! Symbolically, these items stand as the great central design in the cattleman's emblem; in reality, they are the foundation stones of his enterprise. No depiction of the range country could do without them; no rangeman could dispense with them.

The branding of livestock no doubt dates back to man's first domesticated herds. It stands in history as one of the earliest means of identifying possessions among both thieves and honest neighbors.

The practice, nearly a thousand years old in Britain, came to America with the first English settlers. History shows that one colonist recorded his brand at Plymouth, Massachusetts, in 1636. The other colonies were not far behind.

The New Haven, Connecticut, Code of 1643 stipulated how branding should be done to prevent trouble among "the rightful owners of horses running together in the woods." In 1751 the *Virginia Gayzette* carried a notice of strayed stock in which was defined certain brands and earmarks.

None of this eastern branding, however, assumed the proportions accorded it in the West. It was beyond the Mississippi that this vital part of stock raising came into its own. The Mexican *vaquero* brought it up the long trail as another of his gifts to American cattledom.

Cortez is credited with the introduction of brands into North America. He used them for branding his Indian captives on the cheek with a big G, which stood for *guerra*, or war. He sold many of these unfortunates to his friends as slaves. They, in turn, used the Indians to care for their cattle. Thus we find the first American cowboys wearing brands before they were used on animals.

But soon afterward brands were used for cattle. When the old conquistador established his ranch in Oaxaca Valley, in 1525, he started branding his Three Christian Crosses on the herd's flanks. This was the first herd brand in North America.

His neighbors were not long in following the example. With the cattle industry moving northward through Mexico and into the United States, the selection of an individual brand for each outfit became an established practice.

It was at branding time that another great tool of the *vaquero,* the lariat, came into its own. Born as a fraternal twin to the branding iron, on the ancient Mesopotamian Plains, it was an indispensable adjunct to all range work.

The *vaquero's* lariat was a long, snaky instrument made of braided rawhide. It commonly ran around 60 feet in length, though lengths of 85 feet were not unusual. Jo Mora mentions having seen them up to 100 feet long. And the men who used them were masters of a craft which demands the precise skill of a target shooter and a special sense of timing governed by the touch of sensitive fingers.

The *vaqueros* who came to California were dally-men, using free ropes that could be snubbed around the saddle horn after making a catch. Raised in the saddle with a rope in their hands, some of their practices bordered on the miraculous. It was not uncommon to manipulate an 80-foot rope in making catches at 60 or more feet. Assorted types of loops and methods of throwing were employed to meet the variety of circumstances under which a roper might find himself. Small loops would pass more easily between closely spaced trees or in brushy alleys. Vertical loops stood as open snares to capture animals running headlong. Loops that snaked out low to the ground would suddenly leap up to catch running feet. Each individual situation found its special answer in the skill of the roper.

All the ways of handling the lariat met a ready acceptance north of the border. Most of the horse-Indians learned the art at an early date, passing it along from the Spanish settlements to the northern tribes. Gabriel Franchère mentioned seeing Spanish style roping among the Nez Percé in 1814. Thomas James witnessed the Comanches' catching horses with ropes in 1823. George Catlin saw the same thing in Kansas ten years later. Maximilian wrote of similar roping among the upper Missouri River tribes in 1833. Such knowledge evidently traveled in company with the spreading horse population.

The mountain-men picked it up from both the Indians and the

Spaniards. As Indian saddles were not strong enough to hold roped animals, these early Americans followed the native practice of tying the rope to the cinch or around the mount's neck. This method was commonly used by both Comanches and white mustangers all through the middle 1800s. Early western stockmen simply adopted the lariat as the best aid to everyday work.

In southeast Texas, the overlong *vaquero* ropes were found to be at a disadvantage. In the crooked trails through trees or dense brush, long throws were usually impossible, and big loops were worse. The Texans, accordingly, cut their ropes down to 25 or 30 feet and learned to make their catches with small loops that would pass through openings scarcely wider than the steers' horns. Then, to be sure they stayed with any catch they made, they secured the rope to the saddle horn before throwing.

Later, Americans developed various innovations and modifications to fit the craft to conditions in different regions. Ropes held to the fairly standard length of 35 to 40 feet. Loops and throws suitable to the open plains came into more general use as ranching moved northward.

One of these was the throw introduced by John Blocker, one of the finest ropers early Texas produced. Though most modern cowboys are familiar with the overlarge Blocker loop, which is thrown over a critter's shoulders to catch both forelegs from the opposite side, the identity of its inventor is lost to many.

A deft twist of the hand which threw a half hitch around a post to check a running animal was in the repertory of the average cowboy. So was his ability to throw one or more half hitches around the feet of a critter upset by roping.

Various other distinctive ways of using a rope were, and are, common practice wherever cowboys ply their trade. Texas took her skills to the northern Plains; those of California drifted up the Pacific Coast, then east across the Rockies. Their combined forces fathered an institution that bows to no other nation on earth.

The Mexican saddle was the third heritage bequeathed us by the *vaquero*. Those that reached Texas came from northeastern Mexico, as did most of the practices that started the Plains cowboy on his way.

Many Texas pioneers were woodsmen and farmers from the East. Some were fine horsemen and stock raisers of experience. Others were the old, old breed of horseback men ever seeking wider freedoms. But one and all, they found the New World a land that called for more than plantation gear and farm experience. Cattle and horses were almost as dangerous and hard to control as wild beasts. They roamed a country as big as all outdoors, where they either hid in the brush at human approach or lay in wait for savage attack. The newcomer knew nothing of roping from horseback, nor was his flat, English-style saddle suitable for such purpose. It was no better for riding the country's explosive mustangs. Cactus and thornbrush tore his unprotected clothing to shreds and were almost as hard on feet fitted into narrow, uncovered iron stirrups.

But the budding Texan had come to stay. If cattle and grass constituted the only road to success, then cattle and grass it would be. He therefore got some of his *vaquero* neighbors to show him how, and went into business.

He learned quickly and well. The sturdy *vaquero* saddle was admirably suited to his needs. With a wiry little mustang between his knees, protective bullhide coverings over his trousers, and a rawhide rope in his hands, he was soon in pursuit of enough wild cattle to set himself up as a full-fledged cowman. Thus we find him in a few more years with a whole new mode of life established.

Here it was that the Plains cowboy was born. With the *vaquero* as a guide and his own pioneer initiative as a spur to achievement, he learned to break the wild mustangs to his bidding and lead the untamable longhorns over trails no white man had ever trod. When raiding Indian and outlaw rustlers threatened his progress, he joined with certain of his fellows to rid the land of the miscreants in a manner that is still a shining example to all law enforcement bodies.

This leading model of evil's nemesis was known as the Texas Rangers, mostly recruited from cowboy sources. The force was first organized in 1835 under the name of the Frontier Battalion. It consisted of three companies of twenty-five men each, combining outstanding horsemanship, fearlessness, and marksmanship. Though they received only $1.25 a day, they exemplified the spirit of the horseback man in all respects, regardless of opposition. It was claimed they would charge hell with a bucket of water.

Following the Mexican War, the Frontier Battalion was reorganized under Captain R. N. Coleman and expanded into a force of 1,200 men. Most of the men enlisted to fight with the Confederacy during the War Between the States. Home again after the war, they maintained a 300-man body until reorganized as the Texas Rangers in 1874. This latter outfit was composed of six companies of 75 men each under the command of Major John B. Jones. The oldest force of its kind in America, its effectiveness in maintaining law and order is still remembered as second to none in reputation and courage.

It is said that the famous Rebel yell of Civil War days sprang from the cowboy yell shouted as a battle cry by this famous troop.

With men of this caliber on his side, the cowman's progress could not be halted by Indians, rustlers, or frock-coated scalawags.

Returning from the war the Texan found his cattle had increased in fantastic numbers during his absence. There was an estimated six million head in the state in 1856. During the next two decades, he trailed these animals to all the farthest corners of the West. It was the greatest dissemination of livestock ever known. Some even started Chicago on its way to fame, in 1856.

The opening of the famous Chisholm Trail to Abilene, Kansas, in 1867, turned the world's spotlight on the Texas cowboy.

There is, incidentally, some disagreement over who brought the first trail herd to Abilene. W. P. Anderson, the railroad's agent at that place in the 1860s, wrote that Colonel J. J. Myers was first. A Mr. Hawkes, writing of the Abilene cattle trade, claims that Wheeler, Wilson, and Hicks took the lead with 2,400 head originally bound for California. The second herd, he says, was one started north by a Mr. Thompson and sold on the trail through the Indian Territory to Smith, McCord, and Chandler, who finished the drive. Brown and Schmitt reverse this order, stating the Thompson herd was first and the Wheeler drive second.

But regardless of who led the parade, the big movement was on. Some 35,000 head of cattle reached Abilene in 1867. The figure climbed to 600,000 by 1871. Other uncounted thousands went to Montana, California, and all points between.

And with them went the cowboy, the only man in America equipped by nature and training to build an empire on clacking hooves. He alone had the ability to turn half-broken mustangs into serviceable mounts and hold the great herds of longhorns on a prescribed course across an unmarked land. His course was often determined by pointing the tongue of the chuck wagon toward the North Star each night.

The ever-present chuck wagon, with drop board grub box on the rear end, was first designed by Colonel Charles Goodnight, of Texas. He had built the first model of *bois d'arc* (Osage orangewood) in 1866.

Pulled by ten yoke of oxen, it was heavy and cumbersome indeed. However, it stood the punishment of a roadless land and filled a long-felt want.

Roundup and trail crews had used pack animals for grub and equipment transportation all through the earlier years. It was not until 1857 that a shift had been made to wheeled vehicles. This started with a two-wheeled cart designed by a Texas trail boss named Thatcher for use while trailing a McCutcheon herd to Hannibal, Missouri. It was a crude affair, something like a Mexican *carreta,* pulled by four oxen. But it stood abuse well and could travel almost anywhere the herd went. It had no chuck box, the body serving as a catchall for everything that was taken along. By the time he rigged up a duplicate cart for a drive to New Orleans, in 1861, most of the Southwest had turned to similar outfits. These continued until Goodnight's chuck-box wagon was developed.

While all this was going on in the Southwest, similar activities had been carried on up the Pacific Slope into the Northwest. Armed with the *vaquero's* branding iron, rope and saddle, assorted individuals were establishing a cattle empire all the way to the Oregon Country. By 1875, they were trailing their surplus stock east to the north Plains and north to the Caribou. Thus it is that we might well accredit the conquering of half a continent to the mounted cattleman equipped with his trio of age-old tools.

—25—

Cowboys West

A GLANCE AT THE MAP will show how the Sierra Madres, the southern deserts, the gorge of the Colorado, and the backbone of the Rockies formed a roughly defined barrier between the territories of western and eastern cowboys. Although there was a moderate amount of casual association between the two divisions, each stood as an individual unit until the late 1800s. Basically, they were of the same school. Their differences, mostly minor, arose from regional conditions and local practices engendered during their apprenticeships.

Thus we find the open, rolling hills of southern California developing the dally-man. He found a high-forked saddle with tall, slender horn to be best suited for his needs. Likewise, the *vaquero's* single-cinch rig was adequate and more convenient for the type of work prevailing in that region.

Similar sectional needs and customs provided the evolutionary stimulus for other items of equipment in both East and West.

Most of the early Americans reaching California were traders, trappers, prospective ranchers, and horsemen in general. They commonly adopted the native *vaquero* gear, considering it best suited for the over-all needs of horseback work. The scattering of immigrants who came along later to settle under Mexican rule felt the same. This was in the 1825–1845 period, when foreigners and foreign goods were none too welcome in Spanish territory. Expediency prompted the average newcomer to copy the old adage of doing as the Romans did.

We have seen how Spanish saddles, bridles, bits, spurs, and the like were preferred trade goods as far east as the Mississippi River after 1820. Mountain-men, explorers, scouts, hunters, and mustangers all favored them. Visionary stockmen, following their dreams into the warm valleys of the Southwest, took over the *vaquero* outfits, hull, strap, and buckle.

At first, this was simply a matter of setting old things aside and going Californio. Saddles like those in Figs. 101 and 103 were most practical for everyday needs and readily at hand. For roping, breaking mustangs, riding mountain trails, or any of the other strenuous tasks that fell to the lot of the pioneer stockman, they met the day-to-day requirements as well as they had met the needs of the fur men. The roomy saddle bags, or *cantinas,* would accommodate a rider's necessities, pommel holsters carried his pistols, and the tapadera-covered wooden stirrups provided a most durable foot armor against thorns, cold rains, and falling horses. The bits, headstalls, and spurs that went with them were no less appropriate for the work required.

All this, however, is not to say there were no eastern saddles in early California. The records of Thomas O. Larkin, American consul and merchant at Monterey, contain an order for one hundred-odd saddles and bridle headstalls to be shipped from Boston in 1846. Probably other shipments were also made. Too, saddle makers at such jumping-off places as St. Louis and St. Joe, Missouri, and Omaha, Nebraska, were active in outfitting western travelers and eastern migrants bound for the Land of Promise. Many of these saddles reached California and Oregon to find long and useful service. Nevertheless, the majority of them wound up in the hands of townsmen, occasional riders, and farmers of agricultural sections. They attracted little notice in the range country, where only the *vaquero* style saddle met the needs of hard-riding buckaroos and ropers.

The newcomers had learned from the first that the *vaquero* knew what he was about when he created equipment for managing half-wild herds that knew only horseback men and unfenced ranges. This included his *chaparreras,* so well devised for providing comfort in seasons of cold storms and protection in the rugged business of horse breaking and cattle work.

Chaparreras, long since chaps, originated in the brush and cactus country of Old Mexico and Baja (Lower) California. They were designed as a protection for the rider's legs or, thrown forward, to shield the breast of his mount when forcing a way through dense thickets. The early Spaniards called them *armas,* their name for a leather protective armor. They first came into being about 1700 as merely the two sides of a dry cowhide hung, one on each side, over the pommel of the saddle. They were thus in a position to be pushed forward in front of the horse or pulled back, apron-fashion, over the rider's legs when needed. They first reached California in 1769 as items of equipment issued to Portola's cavalrymen. The soldiers used them extensively as leg and horse shields when fighting Indians.

This sort of leg covering is still used to some extent in Mexico and Baja California.

The *vaqueros* who moved north from Mexico with the expanding settlements naturally brought their *armas* with them. California, however, had fewer thorns and more agreeable surroundings, presenting little need for the hot and cumbersome cowhides. Besides, the crude, unwieldy *armas* did not appeal to the more refined tastes of gay *caballeros.* By the time the latter had taken over most of the cattle business from the missions, in the early 1800s, inventive minds had contrived a new leg covering better suited to that region. These were called *armitas,* or little armor.

Armitas were simply a couple of rectangular pieces of tanned buckskin or calfskin wide enough to cover two thirds of the leg and reaching down to below the knees. They were fastened to a belt at the top and had tie strings to hold the lower ends in place (Fig. 133). Perhaps a few silver conchos were laced onto the belt. Fringes decorated the outer edges and bottoms. They served as fairly standard wear in California and parts of Nevada until after the closed-leg shotgun style (Fig. 153) appeared.

The first of the closed-leg type was merely an improved version of the original *armitas*. The old apron-like facings had the bad habit of working around the leg out of position, while a broken tie string left them to flap like a wind-blown shirttail. Too, it was easy for a limb stub or sideswiping cow horn to slip under the loose edge to the detriment of the leg beneath.

By about 1870 the well-fitting standard design made of medium-weight leather had developed. The old *armitas,* however, hung on for a good many years in some sections, particularly in Nevada and southern California.

In the middle 1880s, the Californios came up with the idea of covering the fronts of their chaps with the skins of angora goats. The long, curly hair of naturally white or black animals gave a very pleasing appearance, adding a showy finishing touch to a well turned-out rider.

Cowboys farther north soon boomed the new "woolies" into popularity as the best protection against winter cold and storms; they continued through the years as a favored style. Some riders objected to their propensity for gaining weight when subjected to rain or snow. Others turned thumbs down on their use in heavy, hair-pulling brush. But for average range work they held their place in the field of individual choice. Wolf, dog, and bear skins often took the place of the more popular angoras. Dyed colors won considerable favor in later years.

It was the Yankee love of invention and development combined with the Spanish desire for better things that worked so many sweeping changes in California riding gear after 1850. Perhaps one of the first moves of this sort was to alter the rigging on the Mexican saddles.

All through the years they had carried the old Spanish rigging (Fig. 128). The heavy rump housings and cruppers used by the Californios served quite well as a balance for holding the back of the saddle in place, but the Americans disliked such trappings. Without them, the rigging set so far forward left the unanchored rear of the saddle with a tendency to creep and flip up. This was exceptionally objectionable when one had an uncooperative steer on the end of his rope. After a few unfortunate experiences with their adopted outfits, the new *ran-*

cheros began lengthening the front rigging so the cinch ring could be set farther back, then connecting the ring with another, newly devised, strap that extended back over the rear of the tree. By the late 1850s this innovation had converted most of California into center-fire rig country.

Incidentally, various historians claim it was fairly common for the mountain-men to restyle their early Spanish trade saddles into center-fire rigs in a similar manner. This seems reasonable. These men copied much from the Indians, and the Indians had been rigging their native saddles in that fashion from the start.

Another thing the newcomers didn't like was the crude wood-block

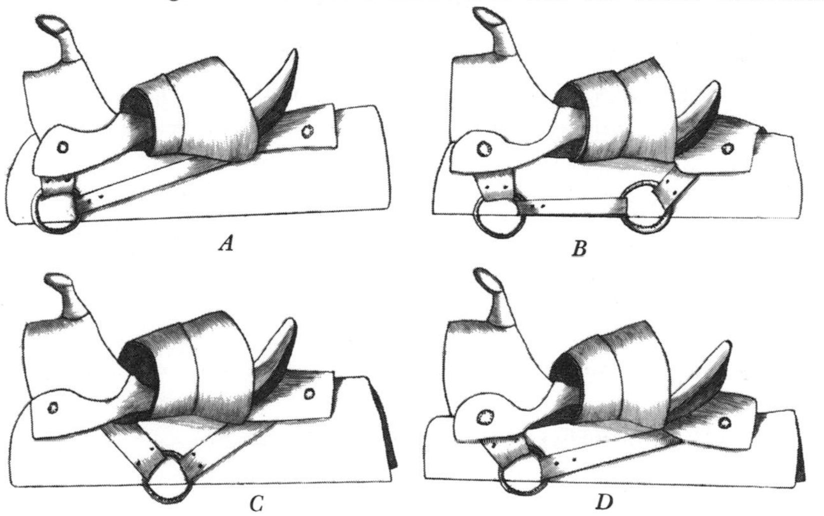

FIG. 128. Western rigging: *A* Spanish; *B* double; *C* center fire; *D* three-quarter.

stirrups and flat tapaderas present on the old Spanish saddles, as in Fig. 102. Nearly all western riders used this kind of stirrup for want of anything better at that time. Many were manufactured in Missouri for outfitting the Spanish-type saddles made at St. Louis. Occasional examples survived well into the latter part of the century. But the American cowboy never liked them, nor did he use them long after the initial experiment in western ranching.

Bent-wood stirrups had appeared in the East about 1790. They were familiar to many Americans who found their way into California forty years later. Not liking a heavy block of wood with a hole in it, it was natural for the Yankee to split some thin oak strips and bend them to shape. The result was rather crude by modern standards. They were almost square in shape, the tops equalling the 5- or 6-inch treads in width. But they were lighter, more comfortable and better appearing than the native style. Their size and conformity soon won them the name of doghouse stirrups (Fig. 147).

Later cowboys and discriminating *vaqueros* soon spread their popularity through all the western country. By 1865 they had pretty well superseded the old wood blocks among most working riders.

And with the vanishing of the more primitive stirrups went also the flat tapaderas. In their place appeared the short, rounded bullnose and shield type of 1830–1850. These were followed around 1870 by the long, trailing style so familiar in later years.

Shown in Fig. 129, the latter type ran around 14 inches wide at the stirrup. The eagle-bill design was 26 to 28 inches in length, while the pigeon-wing and monkey-nose types ranged between 18 and 24 inches. They weighed up to 14 pounds per pair. Their showiness as adjuncts to fine equipment was equalled by the practicality of their roominess and all-over foot protection. They were also almost as good as the old *armas* for throwing around in front of a mount's chest when forcing a way through heavy thornbush.

As the cowmen moved farther north, they found them fully as desirable for protection against rain, snow, cold, and bitter winds. They were often lined with sheepskin for additional warmth.

Reatas, too, went through a similar transition during this period. The increase of sailing ships and overland transportation to the West Coast after 1850 brought a growing supply of fiber rope into the country. The favorite among these was a particularly strong and durable rope made at Plymouth, Massachusetts, for the maritime trade. Brought in by visiting seamen, it won a great and lasting preference over the native rawhide lariats, especially among the Americans.

Ropes were likewise responsible for much of the change and development in saddles. The Yankee dally-man always had an eye out for convenience and speedier handling of his craft. Experience showed him that a higher, smaller horn was better adapted to receiving the quick turns of a rope. By the dawn of the 1860s his ingenuity was at work slenderizing the bulky Mexican horn and trimming down its saucer-sized top. Along with this, forks were heightened to bring the horns up into a handier position. This called for stronger trees and better rigging. The desire for added security and comfort resulted in the old 2½-inch

Mexican cantle going up to 5, 6, or even 7 inches in height, dished to conform with the human posterior and covered with an extension of the seat leather.

Cruppers and breast collars virtually disappeared; working cowboys considered them useless encumbrances. Martingales, too, were seldom used, and then only for special purposes on certain horses.

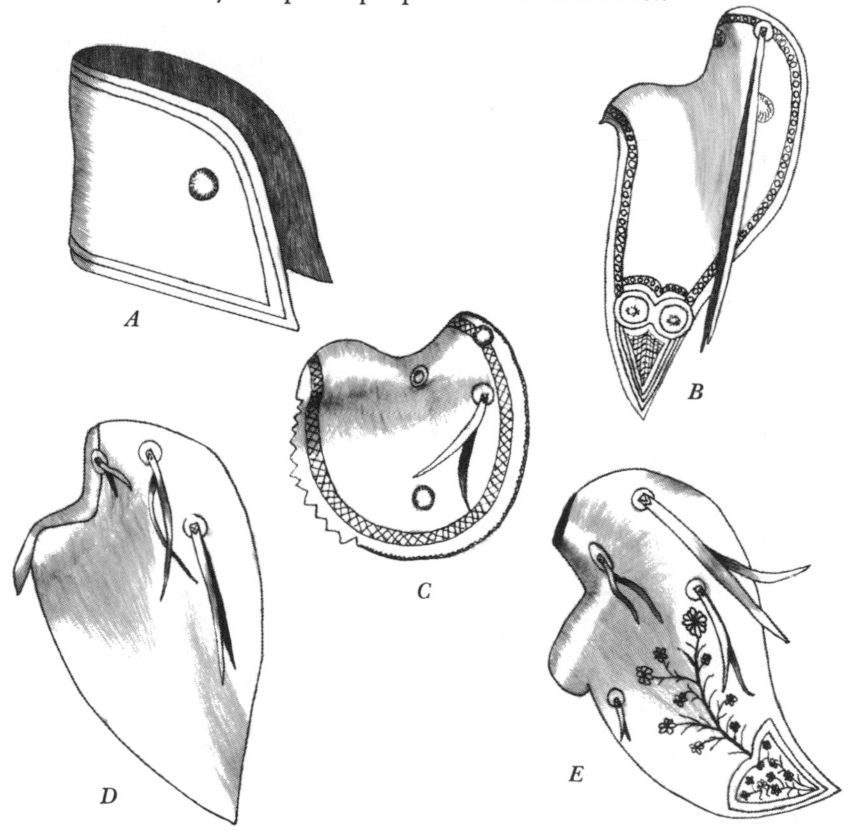

FIG. 129. California-Intermountain tapaderas: *A* shield; *B* eagle bill; *C* bullnose; *D* monkey nose; *E* pigeon wing.

Shortly before 1870 the old removable *mochila* gave way to a large, over-all covering made as an integral part of the saddle. This was known as the Mother Hubbard style. It differed from its predecessor only in having its cover built on as a permanent fixture (Fig. 141). Though well distributed throughout the West, this type was never so popular in the Pacific states as it was east of the Rockies.

The newer saddles, which began appearing shortly after 1880, however, were the predominant choice among most cowboys west of the mountains. These had full-covered seats, cantles, and pommels, regular jockeys, full skirts with sheepskin linings built in, and rigging concealed under the covering. Narrower stirrups of the Visalia type (Fig. 147) had replaced the earlier doghouse variety, some of which were full leather-covered. Forks were higher, with moderately slender, leather-covered horns, and 5- or 6-inch bound cantles were the rule. The big Mexican skirts had been made smaller and rounded off at the corners in most cases. Fig. 130 shows a typical round-skirted California saddle of this period.

Outside California, the square skirts continued in use through most of the intermountain territory. These, however, were of moderate size, seldom so large as those on the plains, except on occasional fancy turnouts where a broader base was needed for silver embellishments and the leather carver's art.

Steel tree forks made their initial appearance in western saddles during this time. An early catalogue put out by the Walsh Richardson Company of Sacramento, California, notes that they were one of the first saddle makers to use this innovation, starting in 1883.

Two- to four-fold wool blankets were commonly used under these saddles; nearly everyone west of the Rockies folded them small, with just the edges showing below the saddle skirts.

A few cowboys made their own blankets by quilting a pad of horsehair the proper size between two pieces of burlap. This would be soaked in water and then ridden while damp until the long horsehairs entwined themselves into a felted mass, after which the burlap could be removed to leave a very durable hair blanket.

The California saddle moved east into Nevada and north through Oregon, Idaho, and Washington. After 1890, forks grew even higher, with straight, narrow pommels running up to 10 or 12 inches in height. Straight cantles ran to 6 or 7 inches. Rather small, square skirts prevailed until Oregon began copying the round California style after 1900. Even then, the square ones gave way slowly to change, especially in Nevada and Utah. Narrow ox-bow stirrups became the general favorites after their appearance in the late 1890s. Horns were somewhat smaller and slimmer. They were full leather-covered in most cases during the earlier years. Later, many were covered with braided rawhide or plain leather and then wrapped around the neck with an extra length of wide

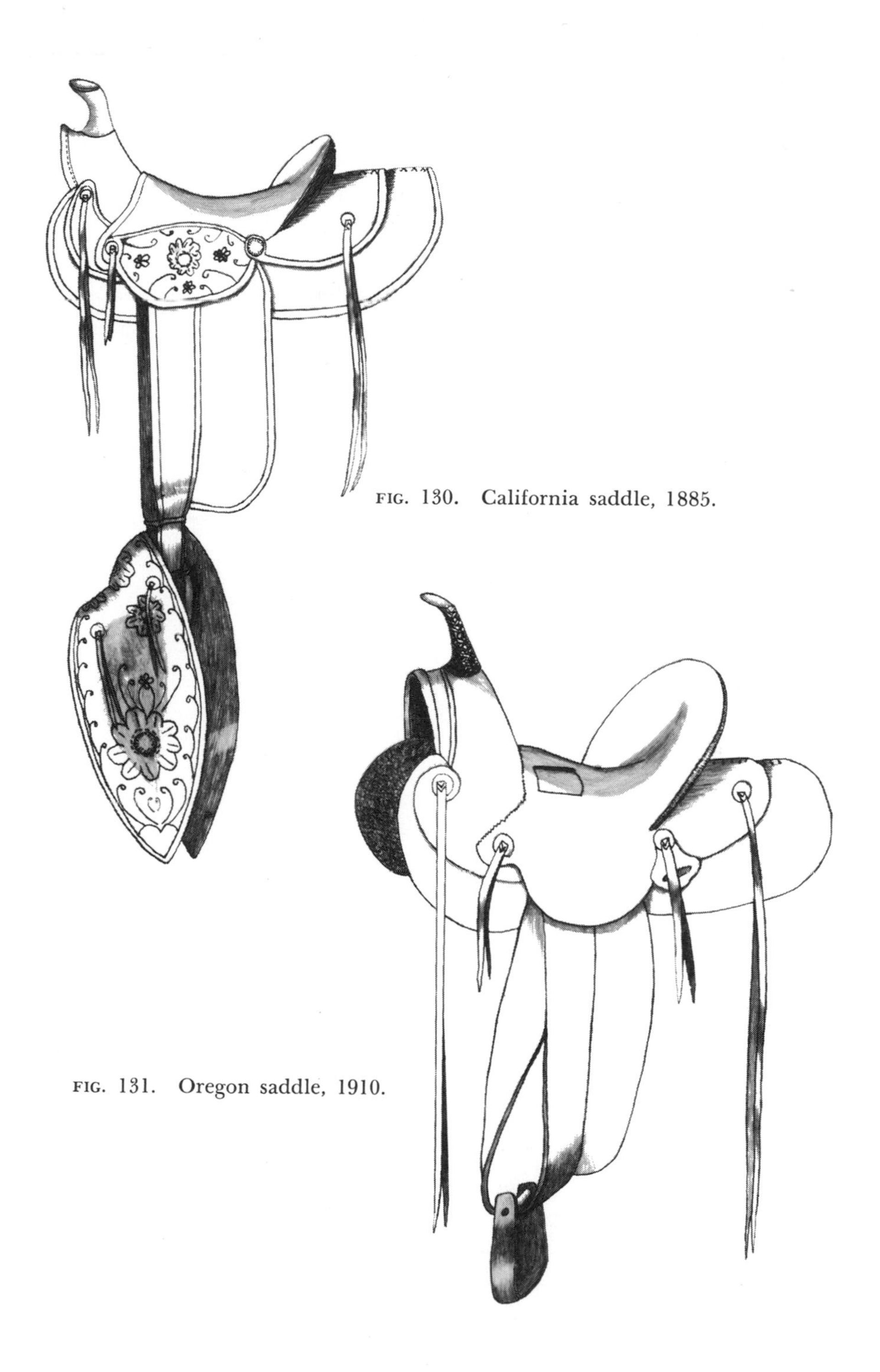

FIG. 130. California saddle, 1885.

FIG. 131. Oregon saddle, 1910.

lacing to take the wear of the rope. Typical examples appear in Figs. 131 and 132.

The smooth nickel-steel horn appeared in the Oregon country shortly after 1900, where it seemingly originated. It was neat and trimly shaped,

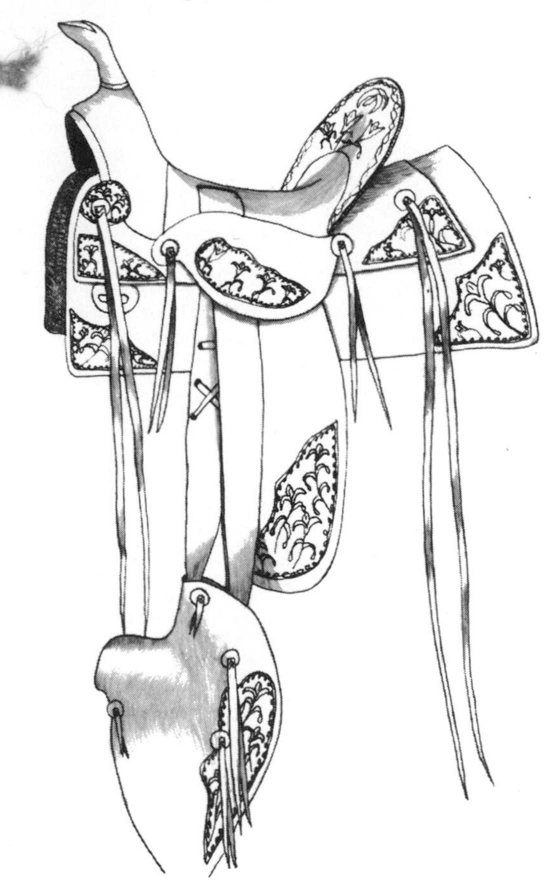

FIG. 132. Arizona-Nevada saddle, 1910.

very handsome in appearance and adding a bright finishing touch to a saddle.

Aside from certain localized superficialities, however, all these saddles followed the same basic pattern. Trees were improved and strengthened, while better materials and workmanship resulted in finer and sturdier outfits. Various minor developments improved some features from time to time.

Much the same might be said of all other equipment. The old dally-man continued to be a dally-man, and long ropes remained his favorites, averaging around 40 feet. California chaps, hair cinches, and the long tapaderas held their popularity all along the line. Even the regional method of breaking horses is much the same today as it was in the days of the Spaniards.

Far westerners have always preferred soft-mouthed horses. One of the surest ways to make a horse hard-mouthed is to use a harsh bit on him while he is fighting his way to understanding. This led to the use of hackamores in breaking young animals, as a guard against developing the unwanted characteristic. Bits were reserved for the educated horse, where bridle wisdom and neck reining kept even the most severe designs from being harsh.

This was diametrically opposite to the Great Plains, where horses were usually broken with bits, hackamores being used on experienced animals, if at all.

A hackamore consists of a braided leather noseband, or *bosal,* held in place by a light leather headstall and a braided cotton theodore rope (Fig. 133). The Plains people liked the *bosal* set low, down almost to the horse's nostrils; the western horseman lifted it well up on the nose to about the position of a regular bridle noseband, sometimes tipping forward and even higher. They believed the pressure of a low *bosal* on the horse's nostrils shut off its wind too severely, thus often causing the bad habit of head throwing.

A *mecate* rope, often doubled to serve as reins, is tied to the bottom loops of the theodore. The *bosal* can be made to exert strong pressure on the animal's nostrils, particularly when placed low, while the *mecate* rope may be knotted so that a sharp pull will force the knot up under the beast's chin in a compelling manner. In experienced hands, this outfit can be made to enforce a satisfactory amount of obedience without any harm to the horse.

Various styles of port bits with curbs were preferred by nearly all cowboys, as they command instant response in work that usually requires split-second timing. Moreover, they were the only type always ready for immediate and decisive severity when actual severity was needed, a most essential quality when riding all kinds and dispositions of more or less unpredictable range-bred mustangs. Yet they were seldom used harshly in the normal run of events, and then only to the degree necessity demanded. As a matter of fact, their usual application was less harmful to a horse's mouth than common snaffles in the hands of careless pull-and-haul, bit-guiding riders. The average cowboy valued the welfare of his mounts as much as he did his own, if not more so. He knew that a bridle-wise horse seldom needed a harsh hand on the reins, and acted accordingly. The horse, in turn, would respond to the light

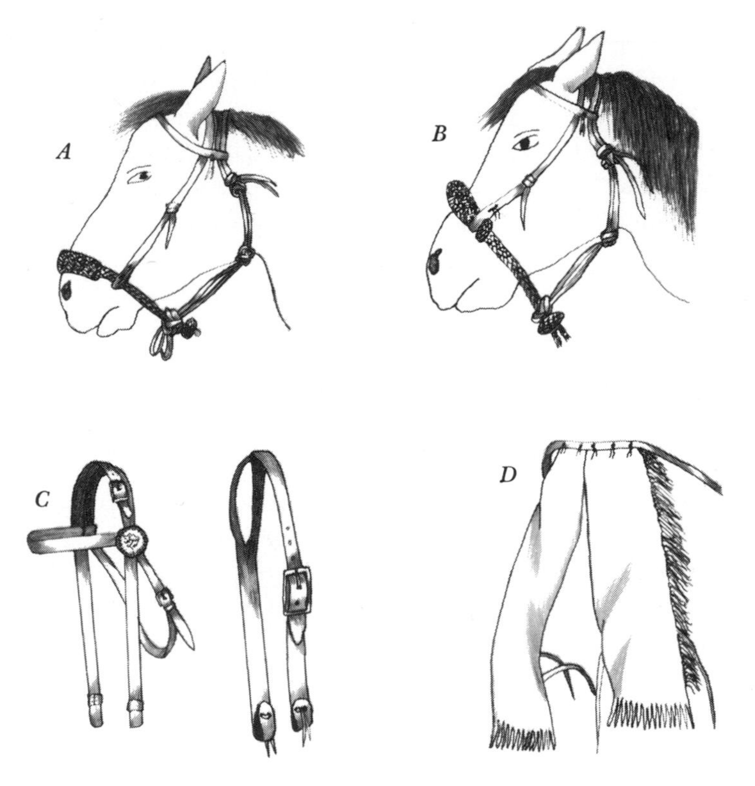

FIG. 133. *A* plains hackamore; *B* California hackamore; *C* California headstalls; *D* California armitas.

touch of a slack rein on its neck or rump-slide itself to a halt at the merest suggestion of a pull on the bit.

With this in mind, the Californio went ahead and chose a bit that suited his aesthetic taste, secure in the knowledge that its shape and construction would have no ill effects on the horse under his experienced hands. Always a lover of fine and showy equipment, he quite naturally followed the example of his ancestors in selecting the big Spanish bits. They were handsome in appearance, lending themselves well to engraving, gold and silver inlays, and ornate embellishments. And they were in tune with an atmosphere that has ever breathed the romance of *caballero* elegance.

Spade mouthpieces (Fig. 134) were perhaps the reigning favorite, with the half-breed running a close second. Ring bits were used quite extensively, especially in early California and Mexico. A jointed snaffle hinged onto the typical wide sidebars was a California invention attributed to Don Jose Ortega of Santa Barbara, in 1814. It went by the name of the Santa Barbara bit and was very popular during that period. However, it pretty well faded out of the picture later in the century.

Another rather unique bit came out of Mexico to find occasional, and usually obscure, use in the early days. Called the hairpin bit (Fig. 134), it seems to have been something of a rarity unknown to most modern horsemen. The Mexicans used it in cases where emergency demanded the immediate riding of a wild horse to a certain destination without the preliminaries of ordinary breaking. The hairpin fastened to the mouthbar was set so that it rested against the horse's teeth. There, it could be made to rattle against the teeth in a way that would distract the animal's thoughts from the strange burden on its back. It no doubt required someone familiar with its operation to get the desired results, but was said to have performed successfully in the right hands.

Bit chains, that ancient heritage of the bridle-cutting days of knighthood and Spanish grandees, were nearly always used on these western bits. Their musical tinkling, with the jingle of bright spurs, never fails to blend as a background for the cowboy symphony.

Odd as it may seem, California's love of embellishment and excessive styles was not shown in its bridles in later years. Rather plain, narrow headstalls were the rule after the mid-1800s (Fig. 133). Many were round, of braided leather or hair. Ear bridles in their simplest form appeared to some extent. Reins were usually of the round, braided variety or narrow, flat leather. Most *vaqueros* preferred closed reins with a *romal* end. The long *romal* had the appearance of a quirt, and served as such.

Real quirts were a Plains article that evolved out of the old wood- and bone-handled whips used by the Plains horse-Indians.

California horses were seldom led or tied by the reins as was common east of the Rockies. The *mecate* rope was usually employed instead. Also, there was little ground-tying as was so prevalent among the open-rein cowboys of the Plains. Thus the closed-rein style was eminently satisfactory for western riders.

A comparable difference between West and East marked the spurs worn on the Pacific slope, a situation still largely prevalent. The original spurs that came to the West Coast were those elaborate 10- and 12-inch creations brought by the conquistadors (Fig. 87). This was the type

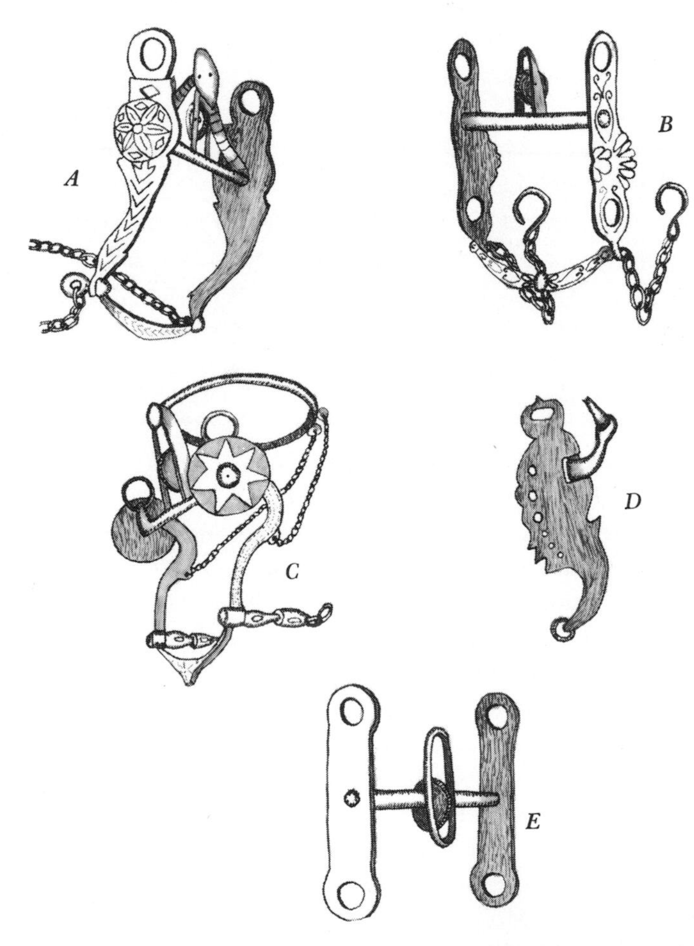

FIG. 134. California bits: *A* spade; *B* half-breed; *C* ring; *D* Santa Barbara hinged snaffle, 1814; *E* Mexico-California hairpin, 1830.

that traveled north with the first settlers into California, provided by the Spanish authorities in Mexico. The government-issue spurs were mostly made in Spain and patterned after those worn by the conquistadors. They had drooping shanks, straight heelbands, and solid buttons. Designed to ride low on the heel, they were held in place on the soft, homemade shoes by single or double chains that ran under the instep. The finer examples often carried beautiful engraving or gold and silver inlays that completely covered the outer heelbands and gracefully drooping shanks. Rich carving and silver conchos decorated the straps. Most of them, however, tended to be of plainer design and some-

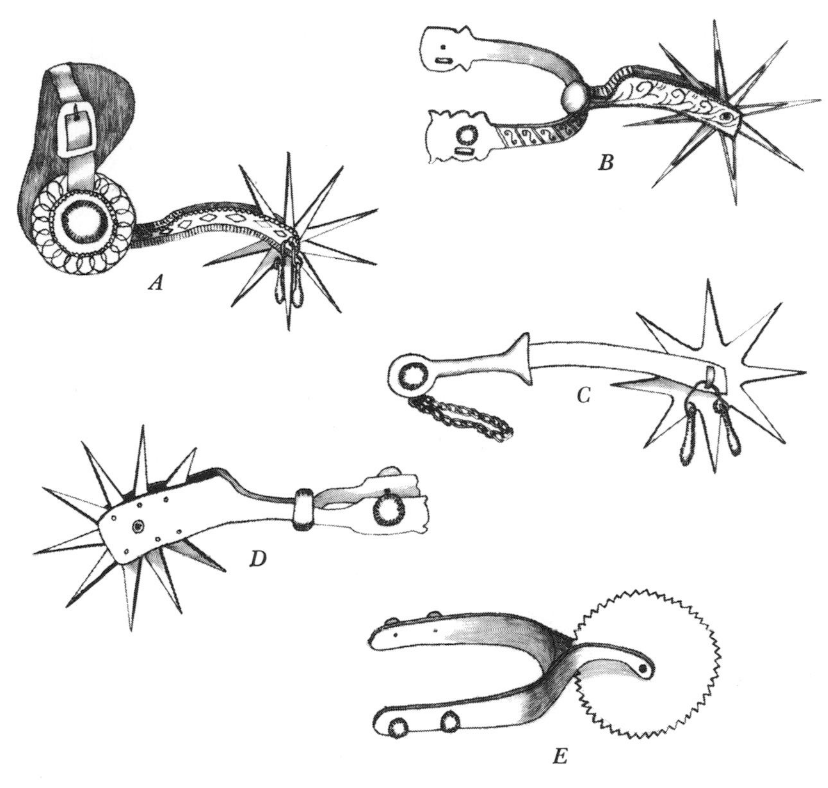

FIG. 135. Spurs: *A* Spanish-made for Mexico, 1760; *B* Mexico, 1785; *C* California, 1830; *D* California, 1840; *E* California, 1850.

what shorter than their predecessors, averaging 8 to 10 inches in length. Spoke rowels definitely predominated, running from 3 to 5 inches in diameter. A couple of pear-shaped steel danglers or tiny bells were ordinarily suspended from the head of the rowel rivet on the outside of each spur, to provide pleasing music for both horse and rider.

Fig. 135 shows some typical examples of early Mexican and California spurs, showing the gradual modification in size. Succeeding years and the spread of the American buckaroo worked a further decrease in rowel diameter and shank length, but they never shook off the influence of old Spain. From Monterey to Salt Lake, the elaborate shapes and ornate decorations continue to stamp West Coast spurs as a heritage of the dons.

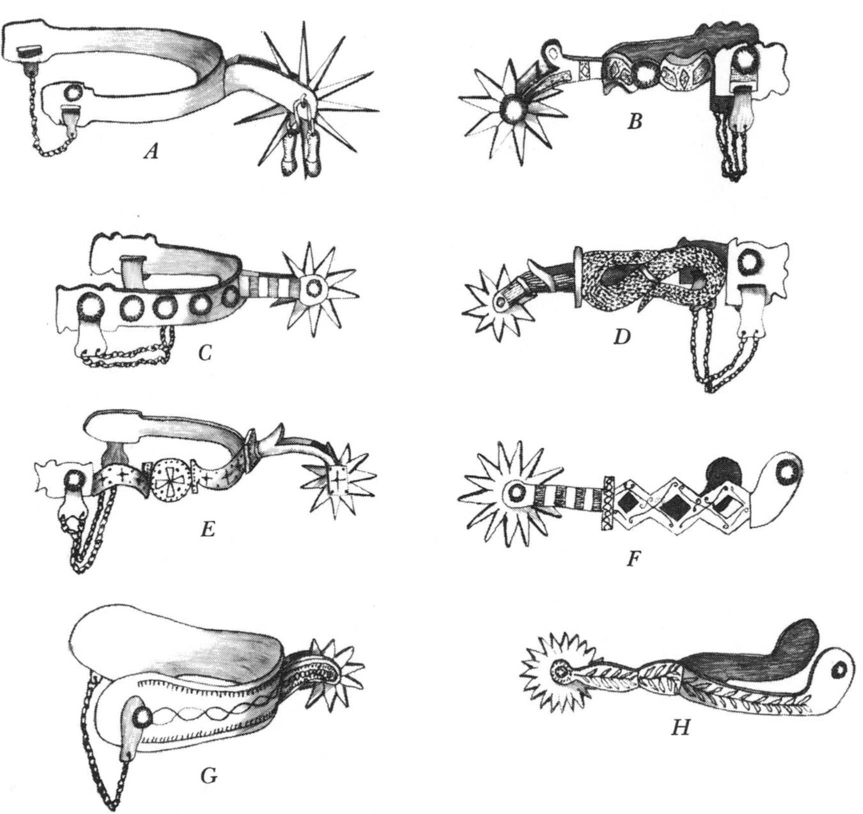

FIG. 136. California-Intermountain spurs: *A* California, 1860–1880; *B, C, D, E, G,* assorted California and Oregon, 1880–1910; *F* and *H* Oregon and Rocky Mountains, 1880–1920.

The spurs in Fig. 136 give a general idea of later developments. Shanks commonly run from 2 to 4 inches and carry 1⅜- to 2-inch rowels. The turned-up heelbands and swinging buttons are innovations adopted from east of the Rockies around the turn of the century; such styles never appeared on the original Californios.

The way spurs are worn is equally significant. Like other conflicting practices of buckaroo and cowboy, spur-wearing customs are sectional diversities bequeathed by the West-East *vaqueros*. Should a rider have the habit of taking them off when he dismounts from his horse, he is probably a native of the West slope.

The early-day Californios, like their Mexican mentors, had no stiff-countered boots. Their footgear was homemade shoes of buckskin or poorly tanned leather. Heels were flat and counters were unsubstantial or nonexistent. Some had an extra piece of stiff leather placed down next the heel for the spur to ride on. But in any case, it was necessary to wear the spur low enough to receive support from the heel.

The cumbersome spurs were fastened over the instep by a strap and secured underneath with chains, fairly secure when on horseback. But the heavy, 8- to 10-inch lowcurved shanks caused the 4- or 5-inch rowels to drag heavily, making it difficult to walk comfortably. In consequence, everyone took off his spurs when he dismounted, laying them aside until ready to ride again.

When the Americans started drifting in, they adopted the Californio's spurs along with the rest of his outfit and most of his customs. If they still had boots when they reached California, they were little better fitted for spurs than the native shoes. Thus it was easy to acquire the habit of removing the big dragging spurs when afoot. And though time brought good boots and shrank the size of the spurs, the old custom so well established continued to prevail over that region.

—26—

Cowboys East

THE TEXAS COWBOY set the pattern for most range life east of the continental divide. The pattern was copied and further refined by the growing ranks of cowboys spreading north with the longhorn herds to all parts of the Great Plains.

Quickly realizing the unsuitability of the various saddles brought to Texas from the East, the pioneer cattlemen turned to the northeastern Mexico model as far superior for all outdoor ranch work. This saddle

(Fig. 137) was built on a plain wooden tree, usually covered with rawhide, but sometimes left bare. The big inner skirts were fastened permanently to the underside of the tree, while attached saddle bags were common. The big doghouse stirrups, usually covered with boxnose tapaderas, like those in Fig. 106 were favorites. With its heavy rigging and tree-stump horn, the saddle made a rather substantial outfit for range work. Between 1830 and 1855 it held first place throughout the Southwest, appearing as far north as southern Colorado.

A lighter design (Fig. 138) saw considerable use in the Southwest around 1850. This was a rawhide-covered open tree with 1½-inch latigos, made to tie. Stirrup straps of the same width were looped over the sidebars and carried the current doghouse stirrups. There were very brief rear skirts, but none in front. A *mochila* was usually used. The handhold cut in the cantle was supposedly intended to facilitate handling, but old-timers tell us its popularity was greatest among riders who needed something more than skill to keep them aboard the Spanish mustangs.

Some of these saddles had matching holes cut in both sides of the cantle. They weren't popular. Except for isolated specimens, they soon passed out of the picture.

It was around 1850 that the Texan decided to do something about holding the rear of his saddle down. In the sharp battles to hold and handle the brush-popping longhorns, the single cinch set so far forward was hard on the horse and often punishing to the rider. He therefore took the rather ineffectual diagonal quarter-strap, which later Mexicans had used to anchor the back of the saddle to the cinch ring (Fig. 138), and installed it in a vertical position over the back of the tree. This hung straight down to accommodate a rear cinch, holding everything securely both fore and aft as in (Fig. 139). The net result was the double-rigged Plains saddle as opposed to California's center-fire rig developed about the same time.

The 1850 Texan also exchanged the Mexican's overlarge rigging rings for the smaller style and continued to use the narrow, tie-type latigos. A further change was made in the front rigging strap by wrapping it once around the horn as a means of strengthening that member. Then the horn was cut down to a slimmer and smaller size and fenders added to the stirrup straps. It was commonly used with a *mochila* covering, as pictured in Fig. 140.

Another saddle to come along at this time, and one of the first purely

FIG. 137.
Mexican charro saddle.

FIG. 138. Texas saddle, 1850.

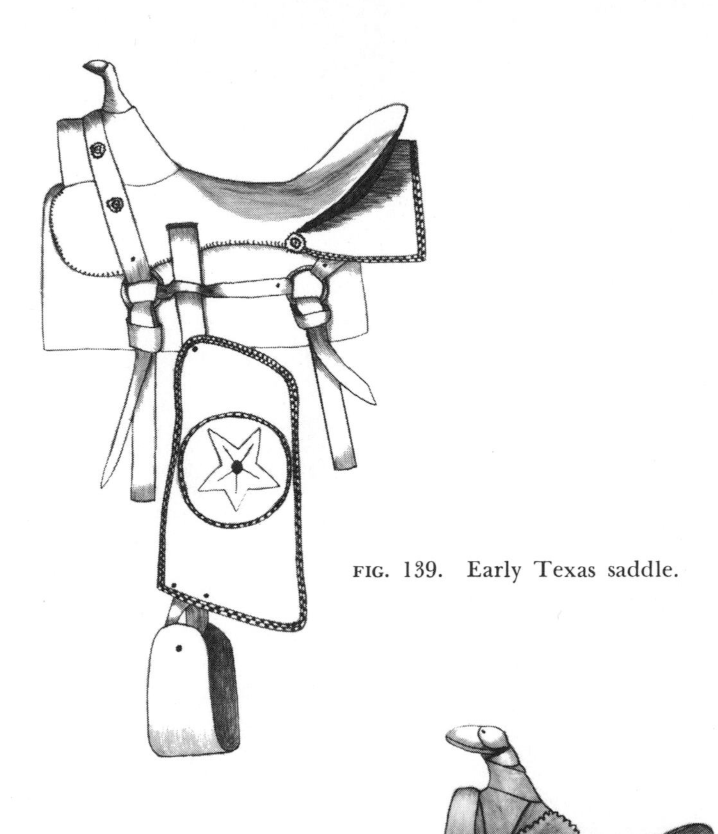

FIG. 139. Early Texas saddle.

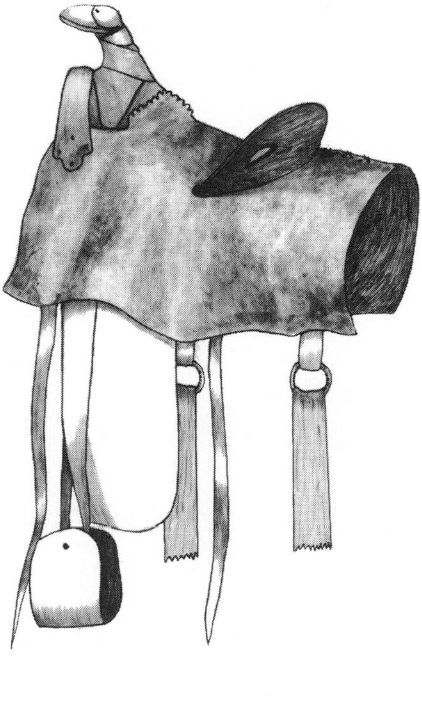

FIG. 140. Texas mochila saddle.

Texas creations, is that in Fig. 139. It had the sidebars lined with square leather inner skirts and carried short outer skirts back of the cantle. The full-covered seat was of rawhide stitched on, while leather often covered the fork. It had a better fitting cantle, regular fenders, and boxcar stirrups. However, it was built rather lightly, weighing only 12½ pounds, with the slender leather-covered wood horn being none too substantial. The majority of both *vaqueros* and Texans preferred the heavier Mexican tree with *mochila* covering.

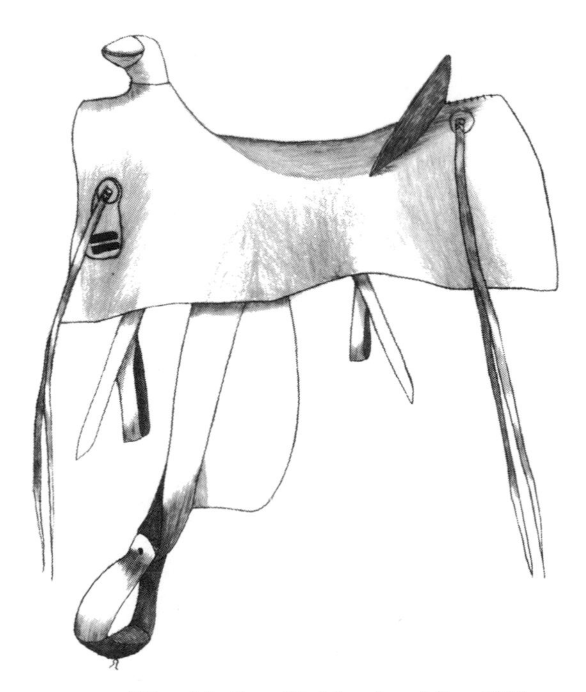

FIG. 141. Mother Hubbard saddle, 1868.

The *mochila* outfit was, as a rule, the most popular saddle on the south Plains until the Mother Hubbard appeared about 1868. The latter (Fig. 141) was nothing more than the old *mochila* rig made with the covering built on as an integral part of the saddle instead of being removable. It was, nevertheless, greeted as a great improvement and met countrywide approval.

During this early period of Texas saddle development tie strings first made their appearance. Both civilians and the military had always used straps or fixed rings on the saddle for carrying extra equipment, but the western frontiersman had ideas of his own. The old Indian and mountain-man practice of tying everything up with buckskin thongs made long enough to accommodate anything from a spare shirt to a bed-roll appealed to his practical nature. He accordingly discarded the conventional straps and fixed rings of his predecessors for the more convenient and adaptable tie strings of his own devising. Arranged to fasten the skirts and body of the saddle together, they quickly won a permanent position among all western riders.

Meanwhile, another version of the *vaquero* saddle had come out of Mexico to win friends among the pioneering Texans. This was a somewhat unique tree adapted from the old Spanish (not Mexican) saddle of early Mexico. Its pommel, seat and cantle, when viewed in profile, presented a semicircular effect. There was almost no flattening of the seat. When Texas saddle makers began copying it, they flattened the seat to a considerable degree in accordance with their ideas of comfort. They called it the Brazos tree.

Like all the western pioneering breed, the plainsmen had the habit of making needful items from materials at hand when the manufactured kind was unobtainable. A large majority rode homemade saddles during the budding years of development. These were usually covered with rawhide and carried rawhide rigging.

Rawhide also served for the making of latigos, tapaderas, chaps, *reatas,* bridles, quirts, and other strapwork. Most of the hackamores, stake ropes, cinches, and bridles were made of the equally plentiful horsehair. It was not until after the War Between the States that the products of professional leathermakers began to dominate the scene.

Rawhide or all-leather stirrups were common during this early period. They were patterned after the regular kind, but were made entirely of rawhide or leather built up in several layers, then soaked and sun-hardened to shape.

Sam D. Myers says the early Texans made the majority of their own saddletrees, using natural tree forks and hand-shaped sidebars. The top of the inverted Y-fork used on the front of the tree was carved into a large oval which was often called the "apple." This was similar to the way the Indians made saddles. Elm wood was most favored because of its strength and adaptability, giving rise to the old-time regional name, "elms," for saddles. This kind of fork was not very secure under the stress of heavy roping, and makers began bringing the front rigging strap up over the front to wrap around the horn. Mr. Myers said the old elms were in use until the iron horn was introduced around 1885.

When professional saddle makers began plying their craft in the new country, they followed along in the same old pattern. Most of them made their own trees of native woods. This led to a great individuality in material and construction. Regional customs and personal ideas among riders further flavored designs and occasionally founded new styles that became permanent.

L. H. Hamley quotes from an old tree maker who once told him the concern he worked for in Missouri around 1870 used only natural wood forks for trees. Cherry was preferred there, but oak and other hardwoods were used to some extent. Forks made from the hardwoods, however, were overly heavy and prone to split and warp. In the mid 1800s, most saddle makers turned to soft pine as tree material when they began to incorporate iron horns into the trees and use bullhide coverings.

A typical saddle of this period appears in Fig. 142. It came out about 1870, or shortly before, as one of the first to have full outside skirts and jockeys. The pommel cover served as part of the front rigging. The neatly covered cantle presented a far better appearance than the old style, whose rawhide seat cover was left only long enough to reach part way up the cantle face, leaving the rest bare.

By 1875, this had developed into the later Plains saddle shown in Fig. 143. It still had the half-seat and cantle covering in one piece, full skirts, and jockeys; but it was nicer shaped and better built all around. The skirts were full-lined with sheepskin, rigging was stronger, stirrups were narrower, and the cantle cover was carried on back to form a projecting cantle rim that became commonly known as the Cheyenne roll. The leather-covered wood horn was lower and sturdier, and, following the Texas scheme, was anchored down by the wrap-around outside rigging. The heavy buckle latigos and outsize double cinches insured its staying in place as long as any two parts of it hung together.

This was the saddle that followed the big trail herds north out of Texas, spreading the style up the Canadian, the Arkansas, and the Platte. L. H. Hamley says it was still a popular product of his father's shop at Ashton, South Dakota, in the 1880s. Many of the Plains cowboys were still riding them up into the 1900s.

This design used a rather long tree, with seats usually running from 15 to 17 inches in length. The makers reasoned that the extra leverage of long trees made them better for heavy roping. Unfortunately, this feature was also conducive to kidney sores on horses. The looseness of riding in overlong seats tended to induce chafing of human posteriors in an equally unpleasant manner.

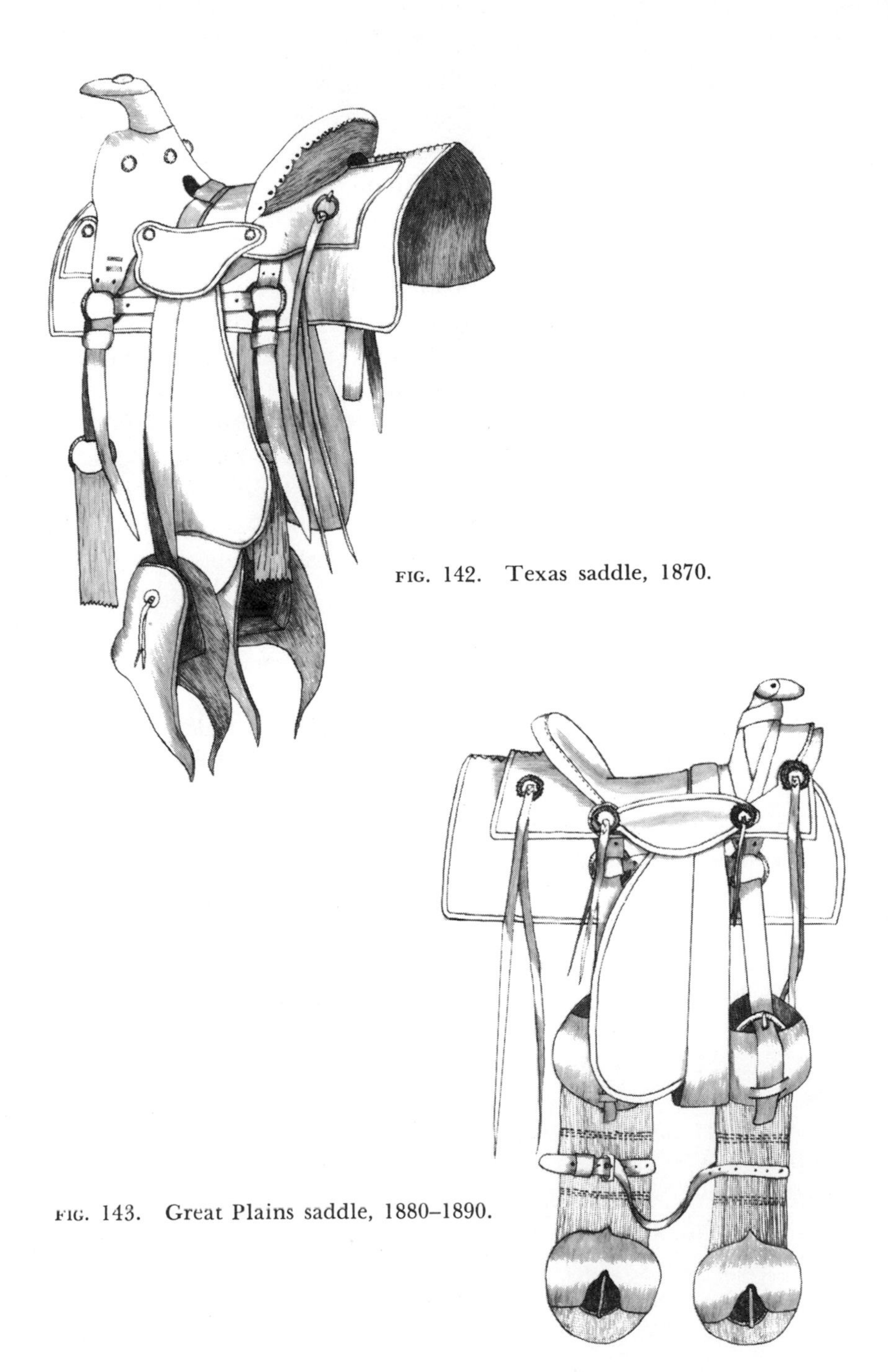

FIG. 142. Texas saddle, 1870.

FIG. 143. Great Plains saddle, 1880–1890.

A. E. (Teddy Blue) Abbott wrote that nearly all of these early saddles made in the 1860s and '70s had the bad habit of chewing up horses' backs and men's pistol pockets. Succeeding years, fortunately, saw a steady improvement in them. By 1883, he said, they were being made so they hardly ever hurt a horse.

Many of the improvements which raised this Plains saddle to its ultimate popularity may be attributed to the Collins brothers, John S. and Gilbert M. Though Collins saddles have long been rated highly throughout the Plains cow country, few people there today know how much the experimental developments done by these men were reflected in the splendid saddles of later years.

Old Eli Collins, a pioneer midwestern saddle maker, operated a shop at Galena, Illinois, during the early 1800s. There his two sons learned the trade under their father's direction. In 1864, the brothers answered the call of the West by opening a shop at Omaha, Nebraska. Their chief aim was to make the best saddles for any needful purpose. When President Grant, an old friend of the Collins family, appointed John as post trader at Fort Laramie, Wyoming, in December, 1872, the brothers saw opportunity in the offing.

At that time, there was in the North a dearth of saddles that were fit for stock work. True, many of the old Spanish rigs from Santa Fe were still in evidencc, but most of the upper Missouri River country's new residents had to depend on eastern equipment. Such hornless, flat-seated rigs were useless for roping, riding wild mustangs, and similar rangeland chores.

By the mid-1860s, it had been well demonstrated that domestic stock could thrive the year round on the rich grasses covering the north Plains. Cattle-conscious men of vision from everywhere were casting their eyes on this new empire. The Collins brothers saw it as a burgeoning field for the kind of saddles hard-riding rangemen would be needing.

Fortunately, John's Fort Laramie appointment arrived at this most opportune time. The brothers promptly decided that, backed by the lucrative position as post trader, they would have the means to develop the best saddle anyone could want.

But it was to be a long and often difficult task. There were years of disappointments and frustrations. Basing their work on the old homemade Mexican and Texas saddles, they needed imagination and experimentation to produce results. Natural hardwood forks were inclined to warp the trees out of shape. New and better ways had to be found for fastening horns to the forks and the forks to the sidebars to insure durability under severe punishment. Overlong trees produced kidney sores; skimpy ones caused sore backs. Seats made too long led to sloppy sitting, and made too short led to cramped muscles. Only trial and error could determine the height for pommels and cantles that would give a maximum of security without being awkward or dangerous. Rigging had to withstand the contortions of untamed mustangs and the savage jerk of a thousand-pound steer hitting the end of a rope and at the same time possess an alignment that prevented crawling and saddle sores.

Numerous saddles were loaned or given to rangemen, the only requirement being that they use them in the roughest way and report any shortcomings or failures that appeared, and make whatever suggestions for improvement practical field experience might have discovered. Then the damaged, wrecked, or unfit saddles were torn down in order that necessary corrections might be made in future productions.

It was a costly process. Only heavy financing could have accomplished it. Hours of painstaking work and valuable material went into saddles destined for the junk pile. But it eventually paid off in success for the makers and satisfaction for the users. The year 1882 found the cowboy assured of finishing any horseback job he undertook without worrying about his saddle, when mounted on one of the new Collins models.

This great saddle of the Plains, typified in Fig. 143, marked a new milestone in development. Though often built with variations to suit individual requirements, it usually came with about a 15-inch tree, 5- or 6-inch Cheyenne roll cantle, and large, square sheepskin lined skirts. The stirrup straps were looped over the bars immediately forward of the half-covered seat. The jockeys were separate, being fastened to the sidebars over the seat cover. The pommel was 5 or 6 inches high, built on a narrow, straight, or "slick" fork, with a leather-covered wooden horn. The front rigging strap came up over the fork to wrap around the horn in the old familiar way. Made of the choicest material throughout, it was a saddle for long wear and the hardest of service. By the time John Collins gave up his position as fort trader to join his brother in setting up a string of new shops at Cheyenne, Billings, and Great Falls, the Collins trademark had taken its place as an emblem of superiority wherever the north Plains cowboy rode.

The Collins brothers' leadership in these developments, thus dealt with so extensively, is not intended to imply that they were alone in producing good saddles. Quite comparable was the lone German leatherworker named Hermann H. Heiser, whose tiny shop, opened in 1858 at Denver, Colorado, flourished among the top-flight saddle-making establishments to become one of the oldest firms still in continuous operation in the West.

Many others were busily incorporating all the advanced improvements into saddles. Some even went ahead to create original designs of note.

One of these appeared over in the southern Rockies in the 1880s. It was known as the Pueblo saddle, in honor of its birthplace at Pueblo, Colorado. It was designed by either R. T. Frazier or G. C. Gallup of that city. Perhaps they shared in its creation; both firms were putting it out to meet a very heavy demand throughout the Rocky Mountain region well into the 1900s.

This saddle (Fig. 144) was easily distinguishable in having its full-covered seat leather cut through to expose the stirrup straps. It carried a bound 6-inch cantle with a 2-inch form-fitting dish. As opposed to the straight, tapering fork and outside front rigging of the Plains saddle, this one had a somewhat wider fork rounded out in the suggestion of a bulge on either side. All rigging was concealed under the cover. Pommels ran to 10 or 12 inches in height. Skirts were of the large, square type so popular throughout the Plains. Coming along in the dawn of the metal-horn era, it was fitted with a rather long, small-necked, leather-covered iron horn.

While all this progress was going on in the cow country, another type of saddle rose into considerable prominence in the agricultural regions of the South and Middle West. This was the well-known Morgan tree style. It got its name from the cheap, light-weight tree which was designed for the farm trade and knockabout use among footmen who rode horseback occasionally. It was built in a wide variety of models. In later years, various saddle makers made a bid for the cowboy trade by patterning it after the current stock saddles, but without much success. It had neither the strength nor quality for rough and tumble ranch work nor desirable comfort for man and beast in hard riding. With few exceptions, the only ones to find use on the range were scattered examples brought West by tenderfeet and nesters. Old-timers agree they were rarities on the Plains or in the Rockies, while saddle makers of the Northwest never heard of any being made in that region.

Unfortunately, first-class stock saddles called for a heavy cash outlay that was beyond the means of a large portion of the West's new inhabitants. Various models of the Morgan were rigged up to appeal to inexperienced eyes as satisfactory imitations of real cowboy saddles. Their cost was much more in line with the average settler's finances, and they served reasonably well for knockabout use or casual riding. The result led to their widespread distribution through the central and southern states for several decades.

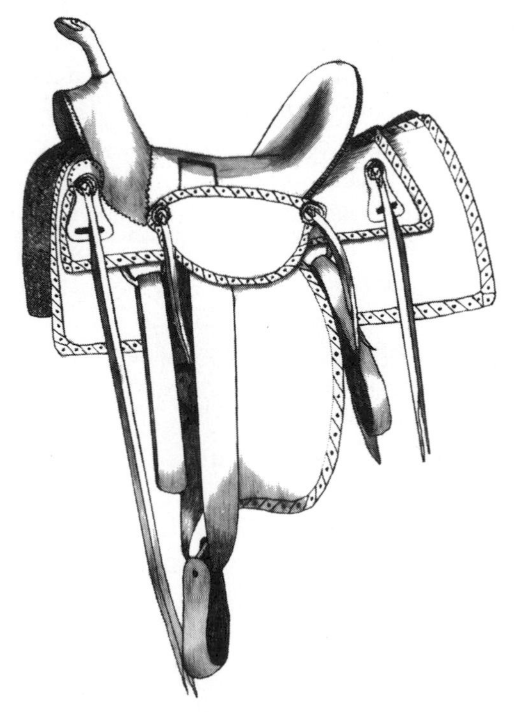

FIG. 144. Pueblo saddle.

The Morgan tree was originally designed about 1870, or shortly before. It was an unlined, 15-inch, straight-bar tree covered with canvas or goatskin in the cheaper models, or light rawhide in the better grades. The holes through the sidebars were made to receive the 1¼-inch stirrup straps. A few of the later and heavier ones dispensed with holes in the bars, looping the straps over their tops in the Texas fashion.

The original makers of these trees seem to have been the inmates of the Missouri State Penitentiary at Jefferson City, Missouri. Independent makers later carried the work to other parts of the country.

The individual saddle makers finished the trees according to local demands. The completed saddles thus appeared in a wide range of styles. Half-covered seats predominated, though full covers were often seen. The seat covers were simply nailed to the sidebars and upper part of the cantles. Rigging also avoided expensive construction by being nailed onto the outside of the tree, though some covered rigging appeared among the better examples. The 1¼-inch latigos made to tie were fairly standard throughout. Single web cinches on Spanish-style rigging were used on all but the heavier double-rigged models built to resemble genuine cowboy saddles. Many had no skirts or sidebar linings whatever; others were finished off with the briefest of token skirts for appearance. Rawhide-covered wooden horns were the rule; some had an extra leather cover in later years. Fenders ran from 6 by 11½ inches to 8½ by 15 inches, riveted to the narrow stirrup straps. Stirrups were of the prevailing boxcar variety in 4- to 6-inch widths. Many were hooded with the plain box or Dragoon-type tapaderas (Fig. 124). The completed saddles weighed from 7 to 14 pounds. They sold for $5 to $15 each. An occasional very elaborate model ran up to 25 pounds and was priced at a corresponding number of dollars. Fig. 145 shows typical examples of these.

Even men of gentler pursuits, who recognized the value of a properly fitting saddle built to last, began turning to the better types around 1890. By 1900, the old Morgan horned rigs had pretty well disappeared from the market, except in a few backward farming districts and as a cheap grade of skimpily rigged boy's saddle. Another five years found these remnants a closed chapter in the saddle-making trade.

There was a hornless model, however, which lasted well up into recent years in some localities. This was the muley design (Fig. 146), built on the rawhide-covered Morgan tree and weighing 10 to 12 pounds. It was similar in style to the old Mosby and Stonewall, with smooth, rounded pommel and full-covered seat. Made with or without jockeys and a semblance of skirts, it was favored by many individuals in the East.

It was no doubt their rarity in the West which moved Mari Sandoz to make particular mention in her *Buffalo Hunters* of a muley used by an early resident of Dodge City, Kansas. Other observers in the Plains area noted a similar scarcity, when not attesting to their absence altogether.

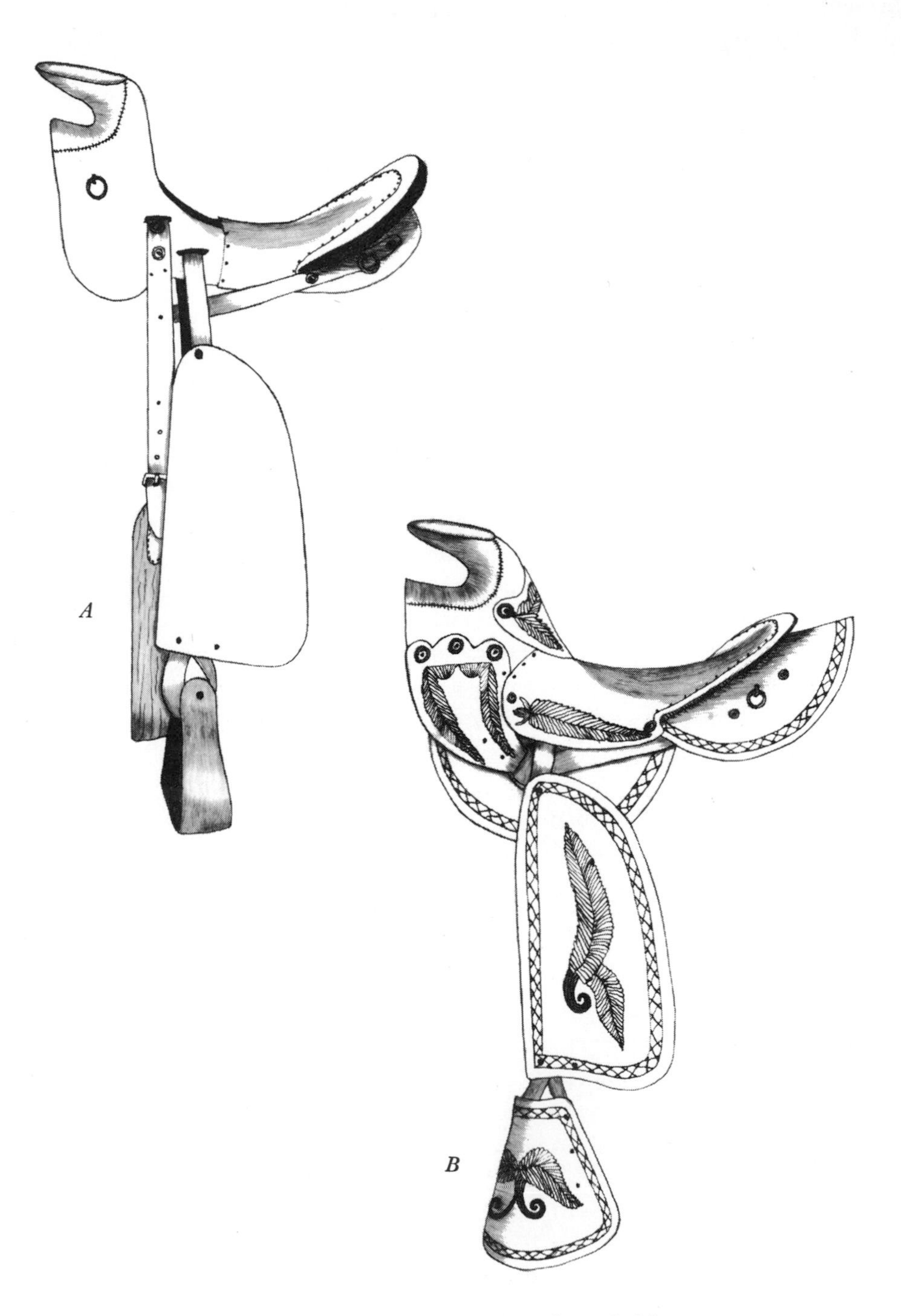

FIG. 145. *A* boy's Morgan; *B* cattleman's Morgan.

The muley was virtually unknown on the north Plains, in the Rockies and west to the Cascade Mountains. No real rangeman would be caught dead riding one. A few, however, were made on the Pacific Coast for residents of neighboring agricultural valleys, presumably homesick easterners.

Charles E. Bohlman says that while the George H. Lawrence Company of Portland, Oregon, listed a muley in their catalogue as late as 1894,

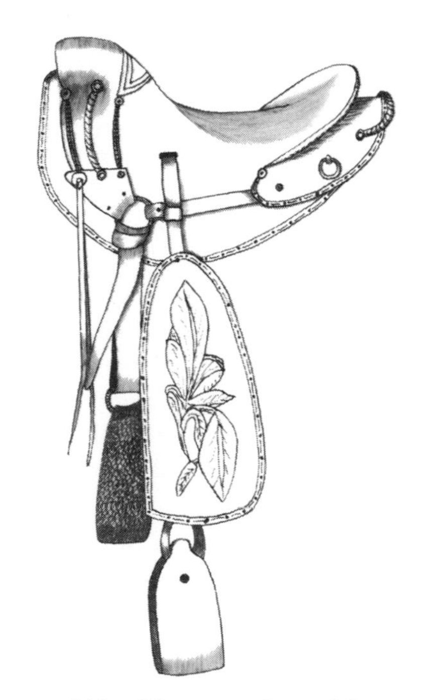

FIG. 146. Morgan muley saddle.

his half century of association with the company saw only a limited number made on order. These were chiefly boy's or children's saddles, usually fitted with the more or less typical hand loops on pommel and behind the cantle as a security measure for inexperienced riders. Mr. Bohlman adds that these were not genuine muleys; instead, they were built on regular trees with the horns removed. There wasn't enough demand for this style in the Northwest to warrant the stocking of special trees. It is his opinion that the same situation prevailed among the other saddle makers of that region.

L. H. Hamley, whose company has led in serving the Northwest since 1890, has no recollection of the regular muley saddles ever having been made in the intermountain region. The nearest thing to it was a special hornless job they turned out in the early 1900s. Only a few of these were made on order for customers who disliked the ordinary stockman's saddle. They were built on McClellan-type trees and had big, skirtlike jockeys similar to those on Eastern Park saddles. They were called East-West saddles, no attempt being made to class them with the standard muleys.

In California, however, the genuine muley again appeared. But its sale was not focused on local trade to any extent. Some were sold as lady's astride saddles at the time sidesaddles were going out of style, but they found little favor among horsewomen in general. Their manufacture was aimed primarily at the South and Central American trade. Considerable quantities of them went to the neighboring republics until heavy import duties after 1918 crippled this outlet to such an extent that California saddle makers quit making them entirely after 1921.

In the Kansas City region, a moderate demand continued until about 1917, when most saddle makers dropped the muley from their lists.

Some sections of the South, however, continued to use them in limited numbers. Victor Alexander says they are still the choice among a certain class of customers in various southern localities served by the Bona Allen Company.

But to get back to the cowboy: he rode through this era, slowly creating and developing new designs to fit his needs as he went along. As the old wood-block stirrups brought from Mexico or turned out by a German factory in Missouri were crude and bunglesome, he turned to the lighter bent-wood design in the middle 1800s. These he whittled down to a more convenient size during the following years, finally graduating to the neat ox-bows in the late 1890s. Then he leathered the treads of most of them for protection of the wood and comfort of the foot.

Fig. 147 shows a variety of stirrups common to the Plains. The iron models came in about 1900. Some of these were full-leather covered. Stirrups which were nothing more than plain iron rings enjoyed some regional popularity in the 1909–1916 period, especially in the central Rockies. Many riders objected to their coldness in winter, as well as having chunks of iron flopping around on the ends of their stirrup straps. Too, they were rather heavy and noisy. Most cowboys shied away from them, as they did from such freakish innovations as the offset stockman model and the light-weight aluminum creations of recent years.

Similar efforts to impress the cowboy have had poor success in weaning him away from whale-line and Plymouth ropes or the yellow Fish

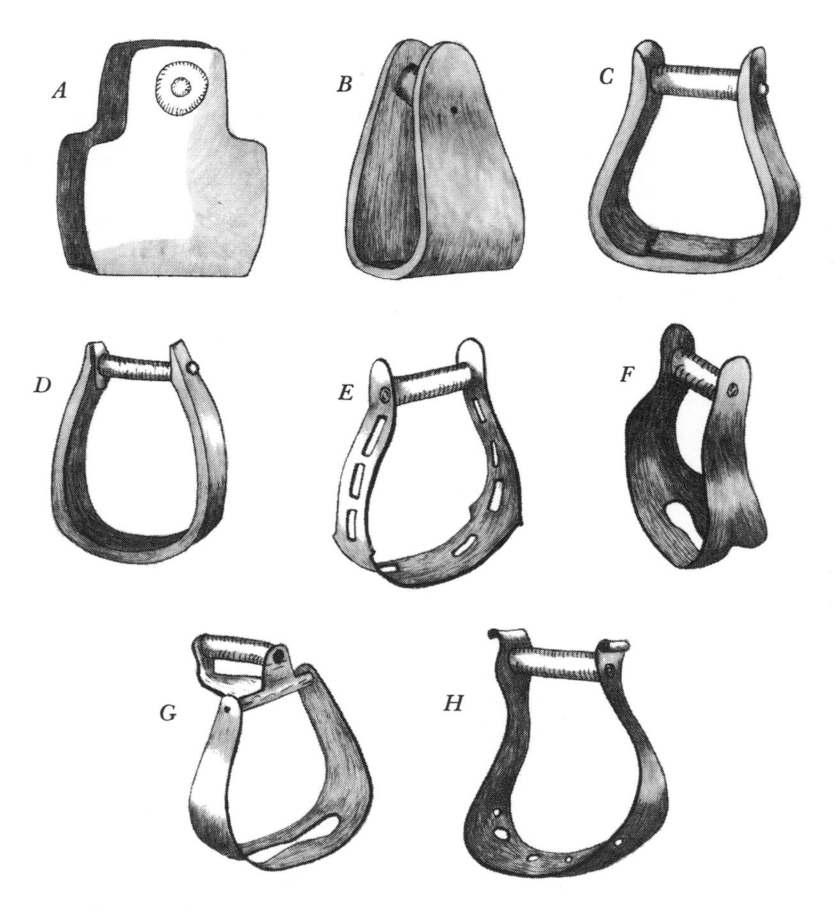

FIG. 147. Rocky Mountains–Plains stirrups; *A* doghouse; *B* boxcar; *C* Visalia; *D* oxbow; *E* Turner; *F* Wilson; *G* Stockman; *H* Goodman.

Brand slickers from Gloucester, Massachusetts. The old maguey grass ropes have never lost their moderate measure of popularity, while braided rawhide examples still appear occasionally.

As a means of carrying their ropes, the early Texans naturally adopted the *vaquero* custom of tying them onto the right side of the saddle fork with a thong. Then someone decided to slit one end of a thong made fast to the saddle fork. The slitted end could then be given a couple wraps around the rope and slipped over the horn. When the rope was in use, the tie strap would simply hang down out of the way. It was a convenient arrangement, serving until the regular buckled rope strap became a standard fixture in the 1890s. Some cowboys even yet prefer the old horn-string.

The Plains country likewise continued to favor the old-style two- or four-fold woollen blankets. Colored blankets with bright borders are still favored, folded large enough to expose a generous edge beyond the saddle skirts. Ever since the brightly patterned Navajo blankets became easily available, cowboys throughout the country have shown a great fondness for them.

Saddlebags never held much appeal for cowboys east of the Rockies. There, the average rider preferred to roll things up in the ever-present slicker tied behind the cantle. Travelers, messengers, stock buyers, and the like, however, made considerable use of saddlebags. Such as were used on the Plains commonly ran to the plain leather variety, though some angora and carved-leather specimens appeared occasionally. Fig. 148 presents some typical styles.

The use of tapaderas marked a similar difference between East and West. Those of the Plains ran smaller and plainer, when they were not dispensed with as useless encumbrances. Texas used the old Mexican box-nose type (Fig. 106) in the early days. The 10- or 12-inch style with drooping tips appeared around 1865 (Fig. 142), as did the similar shield (Fig. 129). These were liked all up through the central Plains area. Northern and Rocky Mountain cowboys, however, if they used any, favored a modification of the California-Oregon eagle bill (Fig. 129) after 1880.

Most working cowboys viewed breast collars as somewhat comparable to a harness left on the old plow mare ridden by a nester's boy. It was a rarity to see one on the Plains except for the purpose of added ornamentation in parades or rodeos.

Martingales and cruppers were even more scarce. Cruppers were used only on packsaddles.

As opposed to California's predilection for light bridles and heavy bits, Plains cowboys were almost unanimous in their choice of heavy bridles, open reins, and light bits that carried no chains. The headstalls in Fig. 149 are typical. The simpler ear bridles made up something like 20 to 30 per cent of the whole. Flat reins 1¼-inch wide and 6 or 7 feet long were left separate. In the absence of bit chains, reins were looped directly into the bits.

On the open, treeless Plains, usually devoid of anything to which a horse could be tied, it was a general practice to ground-tie mounts —simply dropping the reins to the ground, whereby the trained animals would stand as though securely fastened. Open reins were more con-

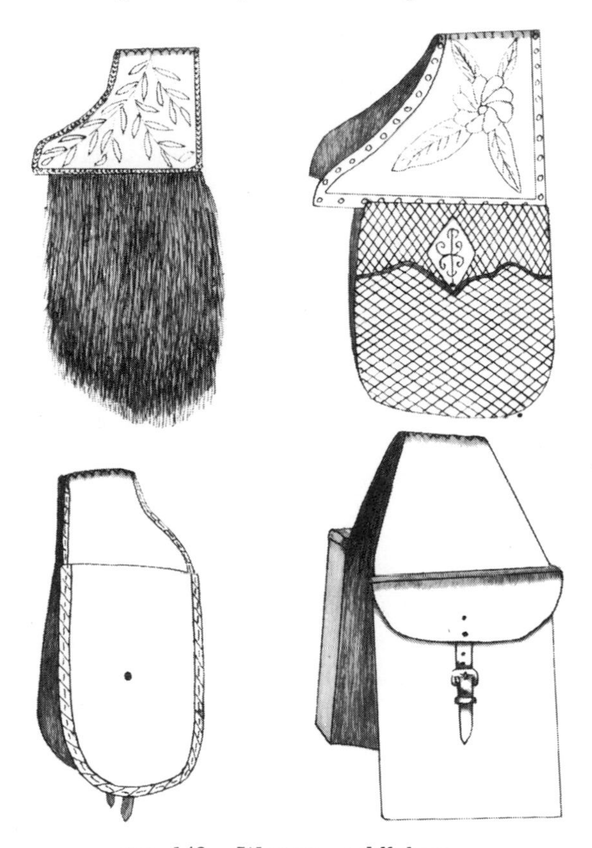

FIG. 148. Western saddlebags.

venient for this, besides offering less entanglement for the horse's feet.

In the North and the Rocky Mountain area, the California-Oregon bit chains frequently appeared with the Plainsman's open reins. Riders there and in Texas practiced the old Spanish art of neck reining in common with the Californios.

Bits of the Plains were usually either the lightweight, medium-high open port—a variation of the Shoemaker—or one of the high ports with a roller (Fig. 150). Leather curb straps were used with both. Snaffles appeared to a minor degree. The half-breed (Fig. 151) was used extensively, especially in the North after its introduction by Oregon buckaroos. It was not popular farther south. The roping bit is a modern creation designed to avoid entanglements with the lariat when contesting. Ring bits were seldom seen east of the Rockies.

Eastern cowboys were content with either bits or hackamores used separately as needs might demand. Most working cowboys, fated to do their daily tasks without frills on the miscellany of horses found in the average *remuda,* feel much the same way.

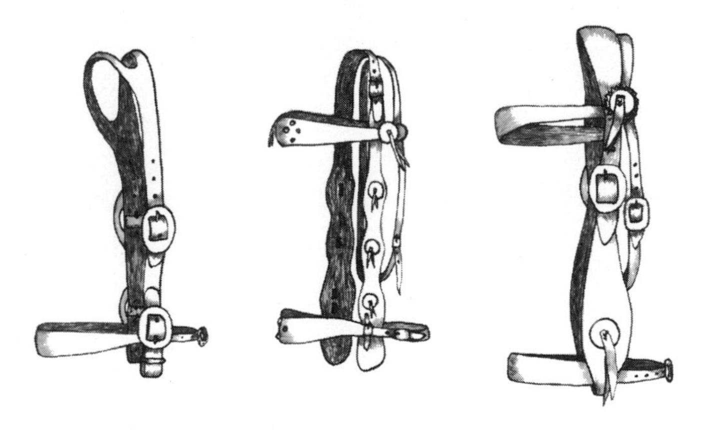

FIG. 149. Rocky Mountains–Plains bridles.

The eastern Mexican spur that came up into Texas was, like its owner, from a different section of Spain from that of the West Coast *vaquero.* The eastern spur had shorter shanks with less curve than the conquistador style. This allowed it to ride the heel higher and in a straighter line with the foot. Rowels, as a rule, ran to smaller sizes; only their tips came in contact with the ground when a rider was on foot. This made them quite convenient to wear when walking. They appealed to the Americans, who were accustomed to wearing boots that would hold the spurs in position under most circumstances.

Middle and west Texas was largely settled by scions of the more dashing cavalier type lately removed from southern plantations and cavalry service. Their spurs had long been the mark of a gentleman. They habitually wore them ahorse or afoot. When they met the Mexican from across the Rio Grande, they discovered a spur much more suitable for rough range work than the lighter sort they had known in the East. They immediately changed to the new style, made a few modifications and alterations, and set the future of cowboy life to the tempo of softly jingling rowels.

Spur shanks are of four basic designs (Fig. 152*A*), regardless of length. Many are entirely plain; others have upturned chap guards set behind the heelbands. Shape, curve, length, and other variation within any certain design depend on individual preference rather than locality.

The original eastern Mexico spurs were similar to the style *B* in Fig. 152. They had 2- to 4-inch rowels, moderately short shanks, and either plain or ornate heelbands.

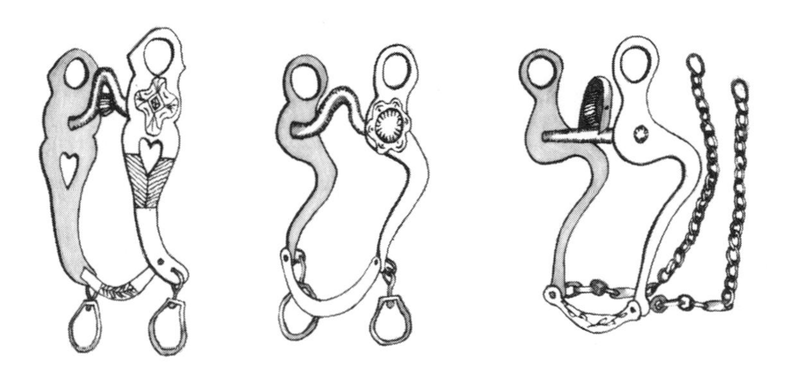

FIG. 150. Rocky Mountains–Plains bits.

Texas made little change in them until after the War Between the States. Then they only reduced the width of the heelbands, shortened the shanks a trifle, and substituted smaller rowels. The example shown in Fig. 152*B* carried 2-inch rowels and was the predominant type in the Southwest and Plains territory for a good many years. Spoke rowels were the favorites all through the early days, and still hold a major position among working cowboys. The sunset *C* and *D* and star *H* rowels were later developments. The cloverleaf *J* did not show up until after 1900, then being used mainly for parades and rodeos guarded by humane societies.

While the Americans in general liked the Mexican spurs, many of them objected to having chains under the instep. They dragged on the

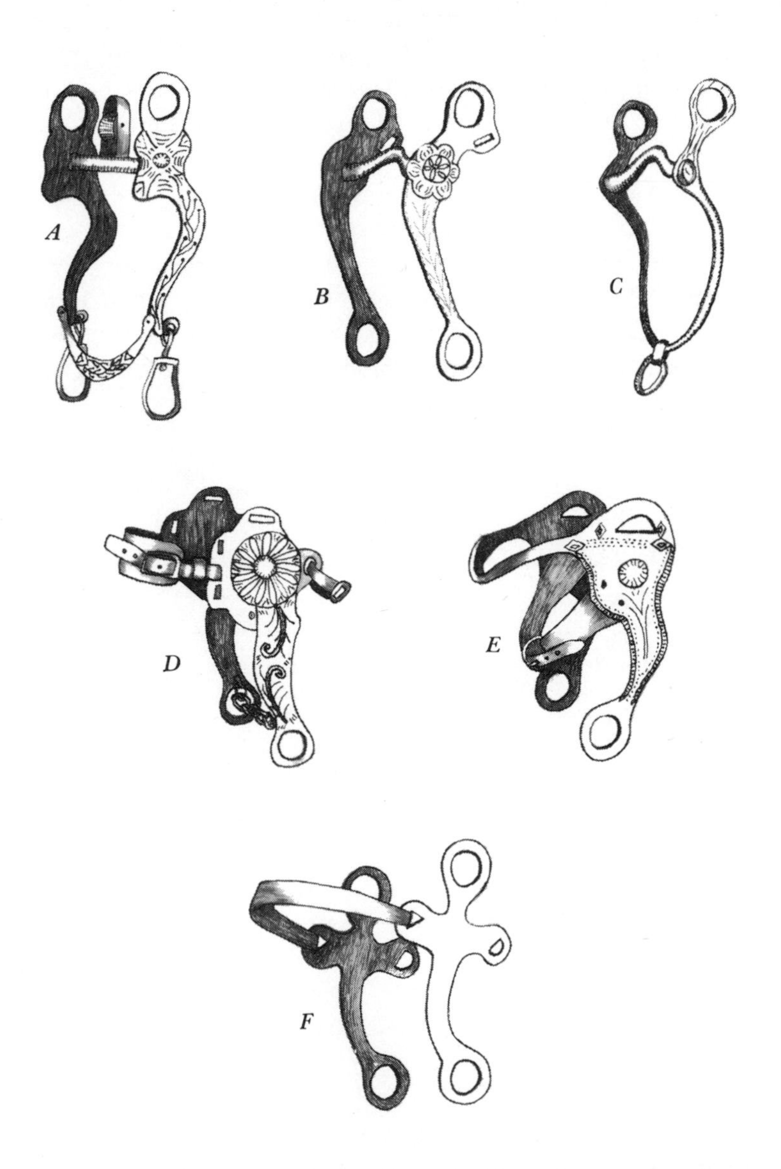

FIG. 151. Rocky Mountains–Plains bits: *A* half-breed; *B* grazing; *C* roper; *D*, *E* and *F* hackamore bits.

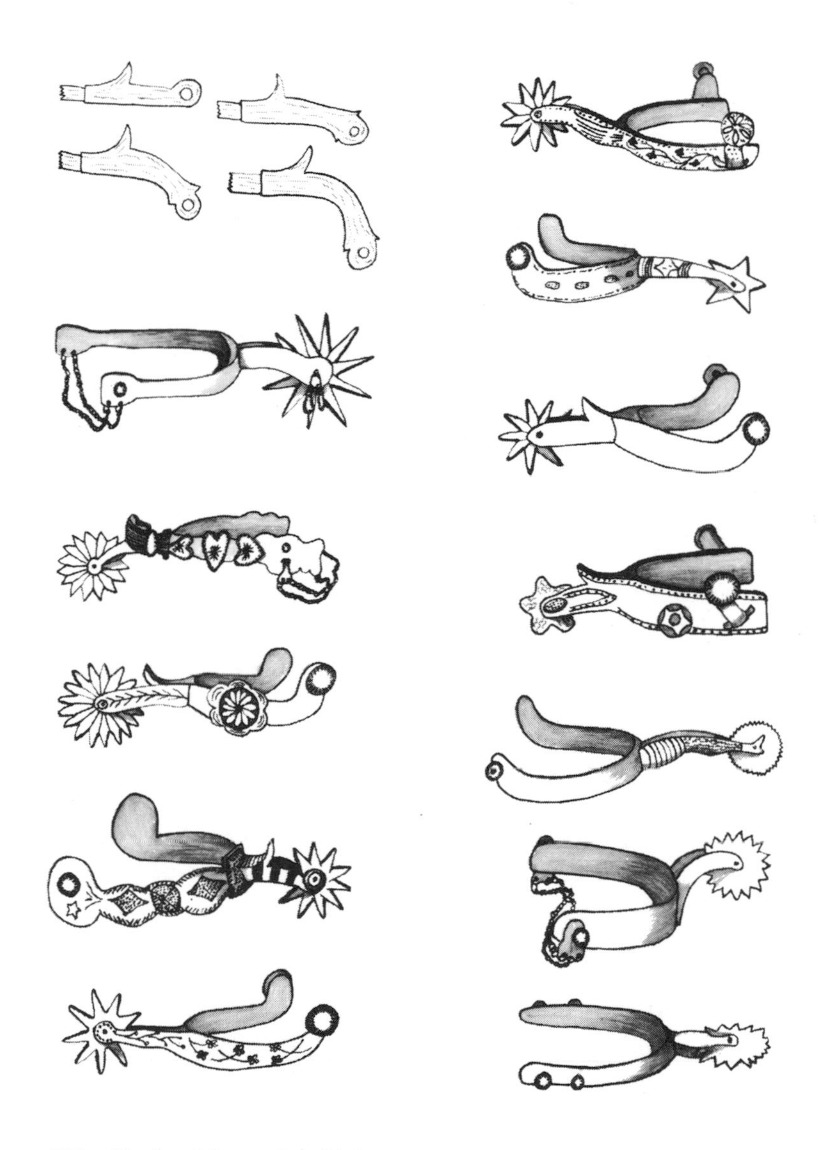

FIG. 152. Rocky Mountains–Plains spurs: upper left, four examples of spur shanks: straight, quarter-curve, half-curve, full curve; other style variations.

ground and were prone to snag on underfoot objects when one walked. They also offered the chance of becoming hung on a stirrup when one rode a mean horse. Along in the 1880s, someone developed an upturned end on the heelband which placed the strap button above the level of the spur body (*D, E, F, H, I, K*). These were strictly boot spurs, unsuited to any other footwear; but as few western horsemen ever rode without boots, this was no detriment. The swinging strap buttons (*G, J*) extending above a straight heelband served the same purpose. They came along about the turn of the century, but never achieved the general popularity of the upturned band.

Some of the early straight heelbands with instep chains hung on until recent years among the farmer group and country-lane joggers, who needed something to fit low-heeled shoes. The OK model (*L*) made with an extremely wide heelband and either straight or curved shank, was popular in this class.

The horizontal spur (*M*) was simply an off-trail creation. As an oddity to hang on the wall, it may have had some value.

Chaps followed much the same course as did other items of equipment. The northeastern Mexicans used the old apronlike *armas,* already described, well into the days of American occupation. The kind of thorn growth in south Texas had discouraged any attempt to introduce the lightweight buckskin *armitas* developed among the Californios. It remained for the Texan, growing progressively more displeased with the cumbersome *armas,* to find a substitute. Early in the 1860s, he began lacing together the edges of pieces of rawhide or medium-weight leather to form wearable leggings. These were fastened to a belt so they stayed with a rider wherever he might be. The extra edge of leather outside the lacing was cut into fringe, copying the old Indian and mountain-man pattern.

This gave the stiff, protruding edges more pliability, added a decorative touch, and furnished a handy supply of tie strings for repair work and other purposes. The result met a ready acceptance among *vaqueros,* white and brown, on both sides of the border. It answered all the purposes of the old *armas,* besides affording more complete leg protection against the everyday hazards of range work.

Although many *vaqueros* used the old rawhide chaps until the turn of the century, the year 1870 and the opening of the drive trails saw the birth of the familiar shotgun pattern (Fig. 153). Made of medium-weight tanned steerhide, these came with either smooth laced legs or fringed seams, the latter predominating. A belt in two pieces ran straight across the front of the legs, and the halves were laced securely together in the center. The buckle was at the back.

The idea of tying the belt together with a string, so it would break with a quick jerk if hung on the saddle horn at a critical moment, did not materialize until about 1900. The drop-front belt, a further precaution in that direction, appeared about 1915.

The shotgun style, with a few variations, was practically the only kind

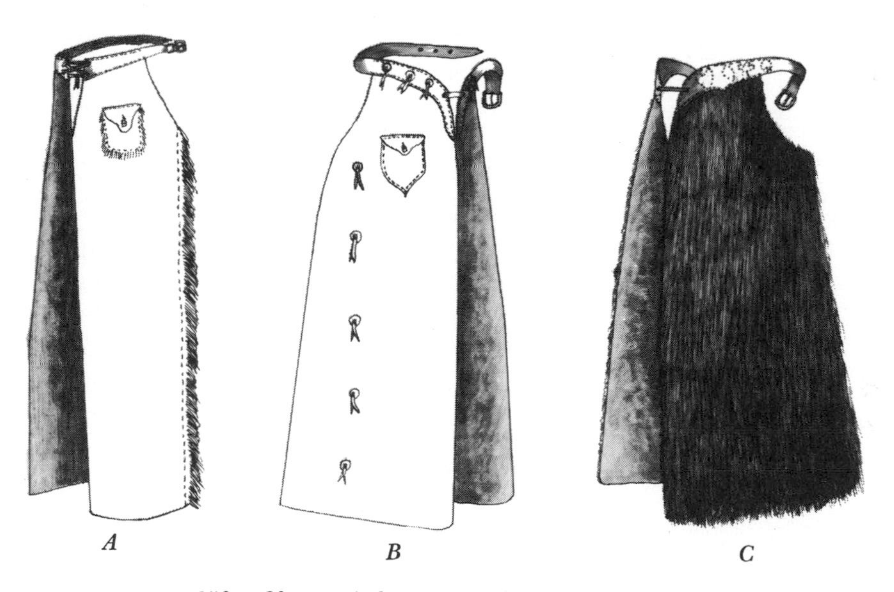

FIG. 153. Chaps: *A* shotguns; *B* batwings; *C* woollies.

found on the Plains prior to 1900. The ensuing decade saw a gradual change to the batwing design, though the old straight leg was used in diminishing quantities up into the present days.

The batwing, however, was the favorite after the beginning of the century. It apparently originated along the eastern foot of the Colorado Rockies. Fitted with five snaps and rings on the outer edge of the leg beneath the wing, it was much easier to unfasten it for removal than to try to drag a spurred boot through it. Such chaps also looked nice and added a little extra weight and balance in bronc riding, and the wings provided a generous field for decoration. They were often attractively trimmed with conchos and brass or nickel spots. Initials, brands, and fancy designs in contrasting colors of leather were often seen, especially among rodeo contestants and on display outfits.

Angora chaps came across the divide to Montana from Oregon in the late 1880s, spreading south in later years. The inner part of the leg was made of soft calfskin, much lighter in weight than anything used for the sturdier Plains variety. The light canvas lining underneath the thick angora covering made them very pliable and much warmer in cold weather than the others. Cowboys of the north Plains and Rockies used them quite extensively, especially in winter. They seldom showed up in the South, and never in the brush country.

The only other major change in chaps began about 1920. A big upswing in rodeo contests followed World War I. Many professional bronc riders had found that by leaving the bottoms of the chap legs unfastened they got better and freer leg action in spurring their mounts toward winning performances. As the unfastened leg left a sizable loose corner, often bothersome about doubling back on itself when catching a stirrup, they took to cutting the corner entirely away. Soon they were ordering their chaps made with one or two less snaps and the bottom corners trimmed circular. The style became known as the Cheyenne leg, since it originated among the champion riders who vied for honors at the Cheyenne Frontier Days. Other riders followed the example until Cheyenne legs became commonplace everywhere.

—27—

From Hat to Boots

HATS ALSO RAN the gamut of fashion's decrees in ensuing generations of cowboys (Fig. 154). The Mexican and the Californio initiated the use of a low-crowned, flat-brimmed, black-felt creation with a wide decorative band and tie strings under the chin (*A*). With the advent of Americans, this was changed in California for a soft felt hat of moderate crown and brim (*B*). In Texas, both the cavalryman's hat and the wide-brimmed planter's style (*C*) were favorites, when they could be had. The cavalry type predominated, claiming considerable popularity up into the late 1800s.

In early Texas, however, a man's hat was often anything he could get, including homemade specimens of rawhide shrunk to shape around a chunk of wood, the brim staked out on the ground to give it its horizontal form. Americanization of the territory and expanding cattle wealth eventually allowed him to discard both makeshift and Mexican headpieces for regular hats of eastern manufacture. But this wasn't the full answer. Eastern hats were made for eastern men, mostly foot-men gravitating between home and office or farm. The cowboy, faced by the year-round capricious Plains weather and a life spent almost entirely in the open, needed something quite different. He didn't know just what it should be, and he had no way of getting it if he did, but he was a prospective customer waiting at the door.

The door was opened by a Philadelphia hatmaker's son. A tuberculosis-wracked body was all the thirty-year-old John Batterson Stetson had left after business reverses destroyed his father's fortune. With empty pockets and mere shreds of hope, he decided to seek out the magical curative powers reportedly existing in the West. The West responded by putting him back on his feet during a year's sojourn in St. Louis, Missouri. The Colorado gold strike in 1861 induced him to pursue both health and wealth in broader fields.

During his trip across the Plains, he became disgusted with the inadequate little hat he had brought from Philadelphia. He called up his hatmaking experience and felted some rabbit hair, from which he fashioned a hat more to his liking. The result was not overly handsome, but it represented his idea of a Plainsman's hat. The high crown provided air space above his head, while the wide brim shielded his face from sun, rain, and blowing sand. A particularly observant miner eventually traded him a five-dollar gold piece for it.

Back in Philadelphia, with restored health and $100 got in the gold fields, his thoughts of the bartered hat stirred his imagination. With $10 worth of fur and the big idea, he made up some hats patterned after the Colorado experiment, naming them "The Boss of the Plains." The samples he distributed to retail dealers received an overwhelming welcome throughout the West. Almost overnight, this man, denied any education except the reading and writing taught him by his mother, found himself a living legend wherever fine hats were known.

The original Boss of the Plains had a moderately high crown and 5- or 6-inch brim. It stood as a symbol of that era in the eyes of the nation. Fig. 154 (*D*) shows this style. Age and weather often made it necessary to stiffen the brim by lacing a string around its edge.

By 1880, cowboys were unanimous in voicing an old saddle veteran's

FIG. 154. A century of hats: *A* Mexican, 1840–1850; *B* California; *C* southeastern planter; *D* plainsman; *E* Stetson, 1885; *F* Central Plains; *G* southwestern; *H* Big Four; *I* cavalry; *J, K, L* Western, 1940, 1960.

declaration that "Ya can beat a John B. plumb to death, but danged if ya can make 'er unravel!" These hats came to be so permanently associated with cattlemen that all large western hats of the type pass loosely under the name of Stetsons. In fact, the Oxford English Dictionary frankly lists "Stetson" as a synonym for "hat."

In the mid-eighties, Stetson corrected the brim's flapping tendencies by cutting it down to 3 or 4 inches and making a curled edge that prevented its losing shape (*E*). This style soon became popular from the Rio Grande to Canada, a great favorite all through the 1890s. The higher 6- to 6½-inch crown was worn uncreased or dented in various manners, such as Montana's sloping front crease (*H*), four dents of the Southwest (*G*), or the horizontal center crease of the Central Plains. Before 1918, one usually had a fair chance of guessing a stranger's home range by the way he wore his hat.

After 1900, cowboy hats took another spurt of growing. That great favorite, the "Big Four," came out with its 7-inch crown and 4-inch curled edge brim to win a foremost position wherever cowboys rode (see *H*).

This was the original "ten-gallon hat." We called it a "four-quart" hat in those days, which went with its Big Four name and its approximate capacity. It remained for movie-goers and sidewalk cowboys to boost the measure. This started with four gallons about 1917, jumping to five gallons shortly afterward. The late 1920s lifted it to the full ten gallons. Some governmental-arithmetic minds have lately been bestowing the twenty-gallon misnomer on it.

Or perhaps the term "gallon" came from the Mexican word *gallones,* which means decorations. The *vaquero* enjoyed putting *gallones* on his sombrero in the form of fancy braid, silver trimmings, silk tassels, and the like. American linguistics being what they are, the whole hat could have become a gallon affair in a short while; or, in its meeting with the Big Four, lost its identity under the four-quart designation.

The great popularity of the Big Four, and its fraternal twin, the "Carlsbad," led to the host of similar styles in various weights and dimensions. Most ran from 3 to 4½ inches of brim and 5- to 7-inch crowns. Some went the other way, increasing in size to 7- or 8-inch crowns and up to 5½-inch brims, after about 1914. These extreme sizes were widely popular with working cowboys for over thirty years. Many still prefer them, though the trend has been toward smaller styles in recent years.

The modern generation of horsemen has been turning the hat clock back to the 1860s. Low crowns folded in on themselves and stiffly molded brims have been used by the growing army of western movie actors, dude-ranch vacationists, sheriff posses, and twentieth century cowboys down the back trail since World War II.

Even some working cowboys have gone along with the backward trend in a very human manner. But whether crowned with the vintage of 1860 or 1960, the cowboy's hat will in all probability continue to stand as it always has, second only to his boots as a major item of attire. Given a first-class hat and boots, he will feel well dressed, even though the rest of his clothes wouldn't do to wad a shotgun.

His boots, fortunately, have not been subjected to so much change as his hat. Ever since the familiar cowboy style came into being, only minor variations have marked its course.

In the beginning, of course, he wore whatever he could get. Moccasins, shoes, farmer boots, cavalry boots, and boots of the eastern gentleman type—all did yeoman service in keeping the cowboy shod. Cavalry and southern planter styles were in the majority until an open-minded bootmaker and a cowboy got their heads together to create a design with features unique in horseback history.

This event took place at Spanish Fort, Texas, in 1878. The cowboy's name seems to be buried under the debris of time, but the bootmaker was a young fellow by the name of H. J. Justin. Justin had shown up in Spanish Fort that year, newly arrived from Indiana. He had two bits in his pocket and a roll of boot leather under his arm. He was looking for an opportunity.

Fortunately, one of the first customers to enter the tiny shed room where he had set up shop was the cowboy who had some revolutionary ideas about boots suitable to his occupation. He, too, was looking for an opportunity to get what he wanted. Their conference opened the door to a new era in cowboy footwear.

The product thus born of kindred minds took its departure from old standards by having a slender toe which would not hang in the stirrup, a steel-shank arch for riding comfort, and a uniquely shaped heel built for utmost foot security when braced against a rope, while eliminating most of the old danger of a foot going through the stirrup when mounted.

Those who saw the new creation were quick to recognize the features so ideally devised for range work. As a body, they approved, making Justin's style the leader it still is.

This turn of affairs naturally cracked the shell of bootmakers all over the West. By shortly after 1880, the new style was fairly standard wherever men rode. Most of the fraternity considered it a development exceeded only by the invention of the saddle.

These first boots still retained their plain square tops and straight legs reaching almost to the bend of the knee. They were commonly worn outside the pantsleg.

It was not until the late 1890s that the custom of wearing them inside the pantsleg appeared. By 1900, fancier designs were in demand. This brought out the rounded tops, V-notched in front and back; big mule-ear pulls to replace the old webbing straps; elaborate stitching to pattern the sides. Basically, however, it was the same boot. Leg length remained about the same, around 16 inches.

The short boot did not attract much notice until after 1920. Its height ran around 12 inches. Inlaid designs in contrasting colors appeared about the same time. Both features appealed to those who required less in the way of boots built for hard service and good leg protection. Recent years have seen the advent of flat, farmer-style heels and still shorter tops for a growing horde of occasionally mounted foot-men basking in the reflection of yesterday's West. Still, regardless of styles, it is ever the ancient spirit of the cavalier that expresses itself in neatly turned riding boots.

The close-fitting pants worn by cowboys reflect the style which once insured a smooth undergarment for armor-clad knights. The disappearance of armor found most horsemen still prone to avoid the unpleasant chafing caused by loosely wrinkled clothing. Fashionable eastern horsemen turned to the Englishman's jodhpurs, a full-cut garment developed by colonizers in India. Many southerners adopted the neatly tailored trousers similar to those used for dress wear. Fashionable breeches of the nineteenth century were favored in various sections. But all these fell far short of the requirements needed by the hard-riding workmen of the West. The cowboy wanted a durable and uncumbersome garment suitable to the myriad demands of rough rangework.

The answer to his problem was already on the way. It had started in 1850, when twenty-year-old Levi Strauss landed in San Francisco with an assortment of merchandise intended for sale in the California gold fields. Included in his cargo was a supply of canvas which he hoped to sell for wagon covers. But the California gold hunters were not interested in going elsewhere just then. They bought the rest of his goods directly off the boat but had no use for the canvas.

It was then that he met a miner who told him he should have substituted pants for the canvas part of his shipment. Gold mining was hard on pants; the local supply was limited and of poor quality for such work. This information sparked an idea in Strauss's head. He forthwith took some of his canvas to a local tailor and had it made up into a couple of pair of pants for himself and the miner. The goods was too heavy for ordinary thread, so he had the tailor sew them with harness thread.

Within twenty-four hours, the miner was bragging all over town about those "wonderful pants of Levi's." The walking advertisement soon brought a growing demand for more of them. Levi obliged by having the rest of his unsalable canvas made up into the new pants.

Meanwhile, Strauss arranged for regular shipments of canvas, took his brothers in as partners, and opened another store in Sacramento. Those "pants of Levi's" were beginning to be the tail that wagged the dog. They were in demand by outdoor workers all over the country, who soon shortened the name to plain Levi's. In 1860 Strauss moved his burgeoning business to Battery Street in San Francisco, where it still continues to flourish.

At this time he switched from canvas to a heavyweight blue denim material for these garments. (The name "denim," incidentally, comes from Nimes, France, a place famous for the weaving of a cloth called *serge de Nimes.*) The pants were styled with tapered legs, low-cut waist and snug-fitting hips. This is the same design that appears in the present-day Levi's, the only garment in America to go through a century of progress without need of style change. Practically the only addition ever made to the original design was the distinctive yellow thread used in sewing and the copper rivets at the pocket corners. This occurred in the late 1860s.

With the use of copper rivets to avoid rust stains, this notable contribution to Western culture had come of age. Outdoor workers the world around found it the answer to their everyday needs. When the cowboy began trailing his herds to ranges far and near, he promptly adopted Levi's as standard wear for the ultimate in saddle comfort, durability, and strength. He also used them to stuff cracks in bunkhouse walls, tie up calves, mop floors, blindfold mean horses, tow stranded vehicles, or any of the hundred and one other things that called for a soft, strong, and pliable material.

As with Colt's revolver and Stetson's hat, users the country over have made the name of Strauss's Levi's synonymous with cowboy pants. In like manner have western writers and illustrators clothed their characters in Levi's for the best part of a century. And for the phenomenal popularity which raised the item to the status of an American institution, we can only point to the man on horseback. Without the latter's bold figure drawing envious eyes toward the unfenced trails of romance, the durable Levi's would no doubt still be regarded as only the badge of hard labor, while coeds and vacation enthusiasts searched in vain for suitable clothing.

The cotton bandana, or large silk muffler, was equally versatile. Tied loosely around the neck, it was always available for emergency use, without being an encumbrance. Primarily, it was intended to shield the neck from the sun or be pulled up over the face, like a mask, as protection against blizzards, burning wind, or choking dust. Secondly, it was a handy substitute for everything from a hand towel to a pigging string; from a bandage to a broken headstall. It was handy for signaling, men have been hanged with it, and it has covered the face of many a dead cowboy buried on the unsettled prairie. J. Frank Dobie voices the sentiments of many old-timers when he says, "The bandana deserves to be called the flag of the cowcountry."

The short jackets, vests, and gloves so closely associated with the cowboy date back to medieval times. During the days of knighthood, a sleeveless leather jacket, or jerkin, was usually worn as padding under the suits of heavy mail. Among the unarmored serfs and ordinary horsemen, the jerkin alone was worn for protection. Its brief and fitted styling made it very suitable to the man on horseback, as did its sturdiness, warmth, and serviceability. Succeeding generations found it no less ideal for general wear.

It eventually found its way to the New World on the backs of hostlers, grooms, and those bringing up the rear of explorers' expeditions. The following century found it being reborn in the Spanish territories of the West as the *caballero's* short velvet jacket. When the practical-minded Americans, who cared more for utility than for style, came along, they exchanged the velvet for heavy denim or duck, put sleeves in it, and made a snug, all-purpose garment that combined the brevity and serviceability of the jerkin with the warmth and comfort of a burdensome coat. So satisfactorily did it fill the cowboy's needs that its use fanned out all over the West and crossed the mountains into Montana. From there, it drifted south until, by 1900, its association with the cowboy was accepted everywhere.

That other version of the jerkin, the vest, followed a parallel course. When peacetime pursuits allowed the knight to shed his armor and release his trusty squire to the village spit-and-whittle club, the latter simply put a decorative front on what was left of the old jerkin and wore a coat over the rest of it. By the time he reached America, he was making the whole thing of the more comfortable cloth.

The Texan appreciated the suitability of the short, sleeveless horseman's jacket that came up through Mexico, but he had a strong antipathy toward anything the Mexican wore. In consequence, he turned to the European's vest as a comparable garment. It would not hamper his movements, afforded a measure of extra warmth, kept the trail dust off his shirt, made a handy repository for cigarette makin's, herd tallies, and an occasional unanswered letter, and furnished a touch of refinement when he hit town. He spread its virtues northward across the Plains until it met the western jacket on the Montana ranges. Then it and the jacket traveled side by side into every corner of the cow country.

The cowboy had all the old cavalier's regard for his hands. His work demanded supple fingers while his pride called for good looks. Usually carefully gloved against the harshness of his surroundings, we find him invariably portrayed with the big gauntlets that had followed the man on horseback all the way down from medieval Europe. These were traditional items of ensemble among cavalrymen, conquistadors, and gentleman cavaliers alike. The cowboy borrowed from the Indian to add a row of decorative fringe down the cuff and from his native Texas to emblazon a lone star or a steer's head on the back of it. The cuff itself remained large and sturdy as a protective shield against brush, thorns, rope burns, hot branding irons, cantankerous animals, and the elements of nature. Throughout the West gauntlets served as effectively and carried as much prestige as they ever had in knighthood's greatest heyday.

It was not until the early part of this century that these big, fringed gloves began to give way to lighter, wrist-length styles. The change followed the demise of the western cavalryman and the rise of the rodeo influence. Rodeo contestants working against time objected to any dangling fringe or other extra appendages that might get in the way and slow their movements. Changing times and modified requirements of later generations further shifted the weight of fashion to where the great glove of nobility's horseman has almost sunk into the oblivion which engulfs so many of his other traditions.

—28—

The Pony Express

WHILE THE COWBOYS across the country were building their heritage toward a permanent place in the sun, a singular event in American history shaped an institution that still beckons to the spirit of western horsemen. This was the famed pony express, whose relay stations linked the Missouri River with the Pacific Ocean like beads on a string.

The idea of the pony express was not new; it dates back to Abd-al-Malik's Arabian courier service of A.D. 700, and probably much earlier to Persia at the time of Darius and the earlier Hittites and Assyrians. Mounted riders carried mail to a limited extent in America's colonial era, as well as among the gold camps of California. But it remained for William H. Russell, of the noted Russell, Majors, and Waddell freighting and stagecoaching firm, to conceive the scheme of linking the two halves of the nation together with a system of mounted postmen strung out over 1,980 miles of desert, mountain, and plain.

Russell may have been something of an impractical romanticist, as many claim, but his plan was quite in keeping with the breadth of vision peculiar to the West. And though it failed to make money for its supporters, it did establish the fact that men on horseback could deliver the mail from Missouri to California in ten to twelve days, regardless of roadless terrain, unpredictable weather, and hostile red men. This time was cut down by little more than half even in a half century of steel roadbed and mechanical progress. Moreover, the pony express lost only one mail during its seventy-nine weeks of operation, a record that any mail service might well envy.

The complicated details of Russell's project were presented to the company at Salt Lake City the winter of 1859. With only months to go, the idea was accepted and plans made for inauguration the following spring. One hundred ninety relay stations, located ten to twelve miles apart, were built along the route that winter. Two hundred station tenders and eighty riders were engaged.

The riders selected were the cream of western horsemen, over 21 years old and under 130 pounds in weight. These limits, however, were somewhat elastic for otherwise suitable individuals. Each rider was scheduled to make a 75- to 100-mile run each day, traveling at top speed between stations. Following a rest at the division point, he would return over the same route with mail headed in the opposite direction. Thus the loaded pouches were in motion night and day, through storm and fair weather, pausing at the relay stations only long enough to change horses.

Most of the horses for the western division were California mustangs. A. B. Miller, one of the company's executives, bought 200 head of Utah stock to be distributed over the eastern division. These were further augmented by additions obtained from Iowa and Missouri, plus a few bought from the army. The number of animals for the entire route totaled over 500.

In selection of riding gear, lightness and uniformity were the main objectives. Riders were to dress as lightly as possible in keeping with the weather. Arms were confined to a single Colt revolver with an extra loaded cylinder carried in reserve. Spurs, bits, and bridles ran to the current western designs in light weights. Saddles alone stood as original creations developed for this special work.

These saddles were constructed under the direction of William A. Cates, one of the line's supervisors. They were built on a stock saddle type of California tree made shorter and lighter than the ordinary rig. Although extra strength was built into the trees, the complete job weighed only one third that of regular stock saddles. It was the open-seat style covered with rawhide, had no skirts, and was fitted with outside rigging for a single center-fire cinch. The cantle was low and sloping; the horn short-necked with a flat top. Lightweight stirrups were used, either with or without tapaderas, according to the weather. The whole thing was covered with a *mochila* carrying four built-in mail pouches. In appearance, it closely resembled the Mexican saddle of early California, though made much lighter. The complete outfit, including bridle, weighed only 13 pounds.

Fig. 155 shows one of the pony express saddles and its separate *mochila*. The *mochila,* by the way, was the only part of the outfit to be transferred at relay stations. The weary horse was turned over to the station tender immediately upon arrival in exchange for another already saddled. The rider merely slipped the pouched covering with its load of mail from the saddle as he alighted, quickly tossed its slitted apertures over horn and cantle of the fresh mount's saddle, then swung aboard with part of the same motion before disappearing in another cloud of dust.

The mail pouches were fitted with padlocks which could be opened only at the stations where keys were kept. They would accommodate twenty pounds of mail. At the standard rate of $5 per half ounce for letters, full pouches represented a tidy bit of revenue. Unfortunately, they seldom carried a full load.

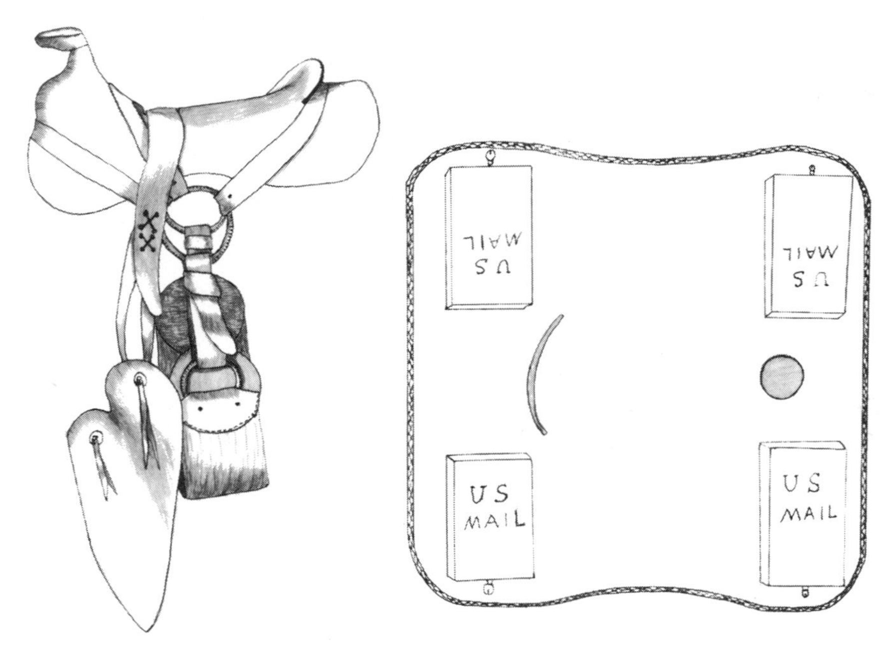

FIG. 155. Pony express saddle and mochila.

Dependable utility and convenience in the constant interchange of saddles and *mochilas* among mounts and riders demanded a complete uniformity in equipment. To assure this, Mr. Cates confined his purchases to only a few of the more reliable saddlery firms in the West. These were given exclusive contracts for manufacturing the required saddles.

Both Lee M. Rice and A. R. Mortensen cite San Francisco as the place where those for the western division (Salt Lake City–Sacramento) were made. Mr. Rice's research shows that Main and Winchester, of San Francisco, held the contract for supplying this section. These same authorities also believe that a few were made at Sacramento, by either Goldberg and Bowen or the Van Voorhies Company. The best supposition is that Main and Winchester sublet a portion of their contract to one of the latter firms.

Outfitting of the eastern end of the line was awarded to Israel Landis of St. Joseph, Missouri, although the Hermann H. Heiser Company of Denver, Colorado, is known to have made some of these saddles. It is not known to what extent the latter firm participated and whether they received an individual contract or sublet from Landis. Walter D. King, now president of the Heiser Company, says that definite records of the transaction have been lost or destroyed, but that there is no question that their company had a hand in equipping the pony express.

The bulk of the saddles used east of Salt Lake City, however, came from the Landis shop in St. Joe. Landis was one of the best known saddle makers in the Plains area during that period. His shop, established in 1844 as the Sign of the Big Saddle, was known to all travelers of the western trails.

An early believer in the power of advertising, Landis maintained a large wooden frame in front of his shop, where he would post each day a catchy poem recommending his product. Called "Big Saddle Poetry," the verses would usually wind up with some pithy comment on local affairs in which he, a civic-minded man, had taken part. His down-to-earth poetry and witticisms were repeated around campfires and stage stations as far west as San Francisco. Such tactics won for his saddlery a general recognition far beyond the bounds of the pony express.

It is uncertain whether or not Landis and his western contemporaries also made the *mochilas* for the pony express saddles. One would naturally expect such outfits to be turned out as complete units. But the press of time at that juncture was rather critical; and it was no job of a moment to construct properly fitting *mochilas* equipped with the special mail pouches.

Information gathered by Irene Simpson indicates that the Wyeth Company of St. Joe made many, if not all, of the *mochilas*. The pony express saddle in the Wells-Fargo History Room at San Francisco carries a *mochila* copied from a design supposedly used by Wyeths in outfitting the original pony express in 1860. Wyeth probably either had a special contract for that part of the outfit or worked as a subsidiary under Israel Landis.

In any case, the afternoon of April 3, 1860, found the pony express fully equipped and ready to roll. The first rider left St. Joe that evening, carrying forty-nine letters, five telegrams, and a few newspapers. According to the *St. Joseph Weekly Post* for April 7, 1860, the rider was Billy Richardson, "wearing high-topped boots, blue pants, red shirt, Plainsman hat, and riding a bay mare. The start was made from Patee Park, across the street from the Pony Express stable, at 7:15 P.M., April 3."

Frank A. Root, writing 41 years later, gives credit for this first westbond ride to Johnny Frey, a companion rider of great repute, mounted on a black horse. The sifting of contributory evidence, however, seems to favor Billy Richardson. The best supposition is that Mr. Root confused Richardson's starting ride with Frey's 120-mile run in 8½ hours to bring the first eastbound mail into St. Joe. The latter took place on April 13, at 3:55 P.M., 9 days, 13 hours and 55 minutes out of Sacramento.

The pony express actually ran only to Sacramento, the mail being carried on to San Francisco by boat. But the inauguration of such a momentous enterprise stirred the people of the latter city to throw a celebration in its honor. The idea of a ten-day mail service to the Missouri River was something to stir the imagination and call forth the best efforts of all good and true citizens. The promoters of the affair accordingly arranged to highlight the occasion by having the first mail for the east carried by a pony rider from the office of the Alta Telegraph Company, on Montgomery Street, to the waiting river boat bound for Sacramento.

Harry Roff may have been the man who galloped down the street through admiring throngs, as various writers have claimed. But the San Francisco *Alta Californian,* which carried an account of the affair the following day, stated that "the rider was James Randall, mounted on a nankeen-colored pony."

In any event, there seems to be no dispute over who was first to start the mail eastward on its regular land route when the boat reached Sacramento. It was 2 A.M., April 4, when Billy Hamilton tossed the pouched *mochila,* containing 85 letters, onto his saddled white mustang and started its hoofs flying up the American River toward Sportsman Hall and the Missouri River. It is noted that he covered the first 20 miles in 59 minutes.

The list of dauntless riders who kept this enterprise in continuous operation against all odds until its demise on October 26, 1861, numbers many who became legendary figures in the horseback West. Among them we find such indomitable individuals as Bob Haslam, Jack Keetly, Bill Cody, Alex Carlisle, Don Rising, Ras Egan, Wash Perkins, Nick Wilson, and George Towne. But all who took part in this accomplishment, which only bred-in-the-bone horseback men could have achieved, deserve equal honors.

Though this unique mail system was forced out of business by the advancing transcontinental telegraph and falling revenues, several other pony express lines operated over shorter outlying routes in later years. Wells, Fargo & Company had one between Queen's River, California, and the Owyhee River in Oregon in 1862. Ike Mossman operated a line from Walla Walla, Washington, to the Idaho gold camps in 1862 or '63. There was one between Reno and Virginia City, Nevada, in 1868. Dick Seymour and Charley Utter ran one from Fort Laramie, Wyoming, to Deadwood, South Dakota, the summer of 1876. Various others served isolated districts of the West until superseded by stagecoaches and railroads. Mail carrying on horseback was, in fact, no novelty in many back-country sections well up into the early 1900s.

These mail carriers all stood as equals in their disregard for temperamental weather, unimproved wilderness trails, animal perversity, or the machinations of lawless humans. It was truly a task that only men who rode tall in the saddle could have accomplished. That they did such an exemplary job of it was no surprise to them—nor to those familiar with the heritage of the horseback man.

—29—

The Blending of the Cowboy

THE DEVELOPMENT OF the cow country had a certain resemblance to a pair of pinchers in action. Rising out of the handlelike base of Old Mexico, it swept north in a pair of long arms on either side of the continental divide, the upper ends curving back together a couple of hundred miles north of the Canadian Border. When the jaws snapped shut, they locked within their grasp that vast and unique territory which was never to relinquish its identity as a region apart.

The force behind the movement of this great pincher's western jaw was supplied by the Oregon buckaroo. Rich in his heritage from the California *vaquero,* and supplied with multitudinous descendants of Spanish cattle brought north in the 1840–1860 period, he trailed his surplus herds east with the same efficient skill displayed by his Texan contemporary of the Great Plains. Starting in the late 1870s, the two met on the new northern ranges east of the Rockies. There, they began fusing the union of West and East which was to develop the American cowboy into a single entity.

The first and most important item to stem from this affiliation was the Montana saddle. This was the single-cinch design built on a three-quarter rig. It carried the high, straight fork and straight, bound cantle of the western saddle and the square skirts of the Plains model. Like the Plains model it lacked excessive carving and ornamentation, while it copied the western covered rigging and trimness of design. Narrow ox-bow stirrups with leathered treads predominated. The brass-bound Visalia type appeared quite frequently, along with a scattering of leather-covered iron ones. Iron stirrups, however, were never very popular in cold climates.

But to give this saddle its true perspective we must turn back to an earlier era. The Texans, as we know, brought their double-rigged Plains saddle, built for heavy roping, with them when they came north. It was a fine saddle that had established itself the breadth of the Plains.

At that time, the North had just emerged from the fur trade and buffalo days. Many of its inhabitants still reflected the influence of the old mountain-men, Indian associates, and hide hunters. They, as a class, had never cared very much for double-rigged outfits. They either used Spanish rigs or devised makeshift affairs that would accommodate a single cinch, something on the order of the early Indian saddles. Though they had more or less come to accept the Plains saddle by the time northern ranching was established around 1877, they still objected to the extra cinch. There was far less need for a heavy roping rig in their region; northern horses were not habitually conditioned to flank cinches, and men recently turned from game trails and cavalry life were prone to view them as needless encumbrances. Many riders simply threw away the rear cinch, using the saddle as though Spanish-rigged. Others lengthened out the front and back latigos to permit both being attached to the cinch ring in a manner that would set the front cinch back of its original position. Of course, such alterations were in the minority; the Plainsman and his outfit held a commanding position in all ranching pictures during the formative years. It was not until the late 1800s that the coming of the buckaroo tipped the balance toward new designs.

John K. Rollinson quotes an old Wyoming cowboy friend as saying he never saw a regular single-rigged saddle in the Wyoming-Montana country until he met an Oregon man using one in 1885. Another writer mentioned that little else but double rigs were to be found between Texas and Canada until after 1888. What few single rigs there were had been brought in from the Northwest.

Obviously, there was a moderate scattering of these over the North after Oregon trail driving began in 1879. Settlers and sheepmen were crowding in on the northwestern ranges by 1880, turning the cattlemen's faces toward the open prairies east of the Rockies. They, like their buckaroos, naturally preferred a continued use of the gear they were accustomed to when they shifted bases of operation. Conversely many Plains cowboys, sent west to drive their employers' cattle purchases home, found the buckaroo's center-fire saddle with smaller-sized square skirts more to their liking than those previously used. The result could only have given the North a generous sprinkling of the western style at a fairly early date.

Incidentally, in speaking of the northern cowboys it is meant here, as elsewhere in this book, to include all those who ranged up through Canada as far north as cattle grazed.

As additional single rigs came into the country, they grew steadily more popular. They were more convenient, served well for the somewhat limited roping needs of that region, and were eminently satisfactory for teaching orey-eyed broncs the sober facts of life. By the time the northern cowboy had come into his own estate as an individual, around 1890, influences past and present had pretty well converted him to the western design.

Still, the California-Oregon creation was not exactly what he wanted. The center-fire cinch had the bad habit of allowing the saddle to creep forward on horses with low withers. They were prone to cause ring sores under extensive roping, and often fitted poorly on potbellied mounts. The Montanan harkened back to the old mountain-man's ideas of a modified rig, somewhere between the Spanish and center-fire, and set about developing a style of his own. This resulted in the great favorite of most later cowboys, the three-quarter rig (Fig. 128). It had the cinch ring set three quarters of the way forward, or midway between the Spanish and center-fire position.

It is not known who actually put up the first regular three-quarter rig. Or precisely when. It seems to have been more of a cumulative effort among several Montana saddle makers at Miles City to satisfy the demands of neighboring cowboys. E. C. Abbott says Cogshall of Miles City claimed to have been one of the first in that field. He was one of the first saddle makers to set up shop in that city, starting about 1881. Under the name of Miles City Saddlery Company, the business he founded held a foremost place in western saddle making for over three quarters of a century.

Courtenay Terrett thinks a share of the credit should go to E. Gottlich, who opened a shop at Miles City in 1880 or '81, and Robbins and Lenoir, who founded a business there in 1884. Perhaps others were working along the same lines in neighboring towns. Time has erased definite records. We can only point to a small area around Miles City as the birthplace of the celebrated Montana three-quarter rig (Fig. 156).

Pin-pointing the date of this saddle's origin is equally difficult. A sifting of contemporary references made during that period, all brief and indefinite, would draw the line roughly around 1889–1891. It was fairly well established in the North by 1900.

From there, it spread progressively to the east, south, and west. Another ten years took it out through the Dakotas, down into Oklahoma and southern Colorado, and west to the Cascade Mountains. Many cowboys who still preferred the older types of saddles had their favorites fitted with three-quarter rigging.

The Southwest was the last to follow the new trend. Observations of Lee M. Rice denote few, if any, three-quarter rigs appearing in that section until after 1910.

Meanwhile, another modification in rigging had been developed in the Miles City region around 1900. This was the five-eighths rig, which carried the cinch halfway between center-fire and three-quarter rig. It has advantages and disadvantages readily pointed out by conflicting opinions. Many prefer it for certain types of horses or particular work. And it has stood the test of time. Yet it never attained the over-all popularity of the three-quarter rig.

It was during these early years that the short, round skirts, which California and Oregon had developed in the 1880s, began to attract attention on the north Plains. They were convenient to handle, lighter in weight, and had less inclination to warp or curl. They soon won a wide assortment of friends east of the Rockies. Oregon's nickel horn followed a similar course, though to a lesser degree.

In return, the Northwest gave the Montana saddle a warm reception

FIG. 156. Montana three-quarter rig, 1890–1910.

almost from the start, merging it into their center-fire world as a welcome improvement. It worked its way down into California in the early years of the century, often as sort of an Oregon round-skirted hybrid. The Walsh Richardson Company of Sacramento listed a "three-quarter," or "Montana rig," in its 1910 catalogue.

It is quite understandable how the Montana saddle's similarity to the California-Oregon type should have taken it down the West Coast at a swifter rate than east of the Rockies. On the Plains it ran head-on into the radically different Texas saddle, where it required more time for adjustment in the melting pot of the central states. It was around 1914 before the Plains yielded superiority to the northern rig.

Even then, the big, square skirts made a strong bid for survival. Double rigs and Cheyenne roll cantles, too, hung on in the South and along the eastern fringe of the Plains until later years. Single rigs, round skirts, and bound cantles did not become standard equipment throughout the West until about 1920.

Oregon is responsible for the most significant contribution to stock saddles developed in this century—the swell fork. Why no one ever resurrected the old European war saddle's front-fork bulges as an aid to security and protection during the earlier two centuries of steady riding is hard to understand. Everyone knew something of the sort was needed. All through the years that riders had been moving north from Mexico, cowboys had been improvising bucking rolls in one form or another to help anchor themselves in the saddle and protect tenderer parts of the anatomy from injury.

The first, and simplest, of such affairs was a coat or blanket rolled up and tied across the pommel behind the horn. The upper part made a good cushion for the body while the jockey strings held the ends in first-rate position for knee grips (Fig. 157 A). Altogether, it furnished the rider a snug, comfortable fit in the long seats prevalent in early days. Some of the boys improved on this by making up a tube of canvas or buckskin and stuffing it with hair.

These improvisions led to the invention of the regular bucking rolls brought out by the John Clark Saddlery Company of Portland, Oregon. Clark saw in the blanket rolls the suggestion for a padded leather roll that could be used as an integral part of the saddle. Development of the idea resulted in a pair of soft-leather rolls built onto a heavy-leather base and stuffed with hair. The rolls were spaced the proper distance apart on a strap which could be fastened to the front tie strings or buckled around the fork. In position, the rolls held down and back against the upper part of the thighs much as did the later swell fork. Clark patented the new creation under the name of Clark's Bucking Roll about 1900. It met a ready acceptance among both men and women riders, as a handy arrangement, easily removable if desired, and well suited to its purpose. Rolls of various shapes and sizes were later made to suit the usual variety of tastes. Many of these detachable rigs continued in use, particularly on the older saddles, until after World War I. Occasional specimens show up even to this day.

Such bucking rolls might be called the direct parents of the swell fork. The latter did not appear in its present form until 1904, according to the best available evidence. Of course, it is possible there were a few

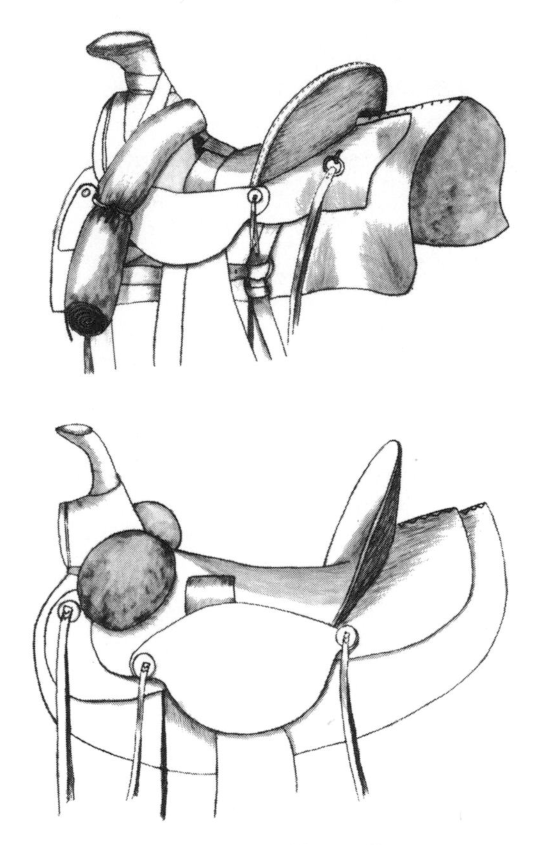

FIG. 157. Bucking rolls.

homemade improvisations of this sort in earlier years. Charles B. Roth says that a friend of his, Will Thomas, claimed to have originated the idea by sawing a croquet ball in two, screwing each half to opposite sides of the saddle fork and covering the whole thing with leather. Perhaps the claim is valid. Not a few outmoded saddles have been revamped in this way through the years.

Still, such isolated examples of home remodeling probably did little to promote the style. That remained, so far as we have been able to determine, for the Victor Marden Saddlery Company of The Dalles, Oregon. Mr. Marden is quite positive in his statement that he brought out the first swell fork saddle in 1904, having developed it as an improvement on detachable rolls. It was advertised as "The new fork to take the place of bucking rolls." Several of these saddles were made for the 1912 Calgary Stampede.

Swell fork trees used by Marden, as well as those used by other saddle makers of that period, were manufactured by the Ringhoffer Brothers of Walla Walla, Washington. The Ringhoffers, incidentally, were descendants of an old tree-making family of early-day St. Louis, Missouri. Leisure and Van Bebber of Portland, Oregon, and the Petaluma Saddle Tree Company of Petaluma, California, soon followed the Ringhoffers in making these trees.

We find in a 1916 catalogue of the Al Frustnow Saddlery Company of Miles City, Montana, the statement that they originated the design. As Frustnow took over the old Robbins and Lenoir firm early enough to have had the time element in his favor, it is possible that his model preceded Marden's, or was at least a contemporary. The weight of evidence, however, is in Mr. Marden's favor, as the date of his creation is authenticated.

The new Marden swell fork won almost immediate approval throughout the Northwest. E. G. Noble of Heppner, Oregon, adopted the pattern in 1905 or 1906. The Hamley Company of Pendleton started making them in 1907, though slick forks retained a reasonable popularity among their customers until around 1910. W. R. Thompson of Rifle, Colorado, had turned almost entirely to swell forks before 1910. Other saddle makers followed in the same direction.

Cowboy response to the new form was like a chain reaction. Increasing demands brought the swell fork into every saddle shop on the Pacific slope. Its singular appeal created one of the greatest turnovers in saddle history. By 1911 or 1912, it had crossed the continental divide and was spreading like a prairie fire across the Plains. Another three or four years saw very few of the old slick forks being made west of Omaha and Kansas City.

As with most great inventions in their early years, everyone had his own idea of how to design the swell for most satisfactory results. Some were built straight out at the sides, parallel with the fork; others, called back swells, slanted backward to hold the most vulnerable part of the rider away from the saddle horn; many carried their curve down to the short skirts, while some were more of a projection out over the leg. There were further variations in height, thickness, width, and taper. They came in a host of designs under such names as Ladesma, Taylor, Montana, Meanea, Porter, Scheck, Ellensburg, Portland, Cheyenne, and Mueller.

Originally, the swells were merely rounded bulges on the sides of the fork, describing semi-circular curves from the base of the horn to a point just above the end of the seat jockeys. Outside width measurement seldom exceeded 10 inches. But following the old adage that if something is good, more should be better, customer demand soon brought a great increase in size. By 1914, saddles with 18-, 20-, and 22-inch swells were no novelty. The great majority, however, fell within the 14- to 17-inch range decreed by experienced riders as the most practical size.

Thus it was that the first decade of the twentieth century saw the final blending of the Plains cowboy, the western buckaroo, the northern puncher, and the southwestern *vaquero*. Out of the melting pot came the only American to preserve his identity almost intact through two centuries of economic and social conflict. Though in the North he may show a marked preference for elaborate Mexican spurs and bits, he also uses the open reins and leather chaps of the Plains, California's long rope, and a brightly patterned saddle blanket from Navajoland. And close beside him rides a liquid-voiced individual from down along the Border, happy in possession of spoke-roweled Texas spurs, Kansas boots, California *romal* bridle, straight-legged angora chaps from Oregon, and a fine wool blanket recently purchased at a Hudson's Bay store in Alberta. Both will undoubtedly be mounted on Montana-style, three-quarter rigged saddles fitted with Oregon round skirts, Colorado dished cantles, and the moderately wide swells that symbolize the cow country wherever seen.

By 1912, the basic principles of this saddle governed most of the outfits in both East and West. Naturally, there were some minor differences of a superficial nature. East of the Rockies and in the Southwest pommels and cantles tended to run higher. Square skirts also lasted longer there, holding a fair majority until after 1920. Elaborately carved leather, silver trimming, and nickel steel horns claimed more attention in the West; while eastward, plainer styles predominated from Canada to Texas.

Indian riders, particularly in the Northwest, preferred saddles with exceptionally high forks, high cantles, and long-necked horns. Nickel-steel horns were very popular in this quarter, as was a generous display of nickel and silver trimming.

Examples of typical saddles most common in the Northwest and north Plains during the 1912–1920 period appear respectively in Figs. 158 and 159. They differ mainly in horns, stirrups, skirts, and pommel and cantle variations. These were occasionally interspersed with the old double-rigged Texas style in confirmed tie-down regions.

Another notable feature developed during this period was the undercut swell fork. There were certain disadvantages in swells that had to be built overwide in order to extend out over the legs. They made extra weight and often interfered with comfortable seating. In 1914, the Hamley Company employed a whole new concept in designing a narrower swell that gave increased security. Its lower edge was cut away to accommodate the thigh, allowing a tighter and more effective knee grip with a very comfortable seat. Patented under the name of Hamley's Form Fitter, its ease in ordinary riding and holding qualities on the "bad ones" won it a prominent place in the cowboy world from the start. Fig. 160 exemplifies this saddle.

Other saddle makers developed similar models in succeeding years. All were good rigs, although the original Form Fitter has perhaps more features to recommend it for general use. They were excellent for bronc riding, appearing frequently among rodeo contestants until the Association Saddle was adopted as standard equipment for that event.

It was during this 1919–1920 period that saddles built on a skeleton tree with the leather covering turned rough side out found considerable favor among bronc riders. The tree used was usually the one the Hamley Company developed for Yakima Canutt, the World Champion Rider at Pendleton in 1919.

Unfortunately, there was a bad side to such diversity in contest saddles. Serious supporters of rodeo, concerned for its future welfare, had long been advocating a standard set of rules under which riders should operate throughout the nation. These men took a dim view of allowing unrestricted innovations by individual contestants. Some of the professional riders had been going all out at making their saddles more ridable by shifting the rigging, building up the bars underneath, altering the shape of the swells, and devising various schemes which tended to work disadvantages against the horse and competing riders. As a move toward establishing better order in this direction, the managements of some of the principal rodeos decided that a uniform saddle

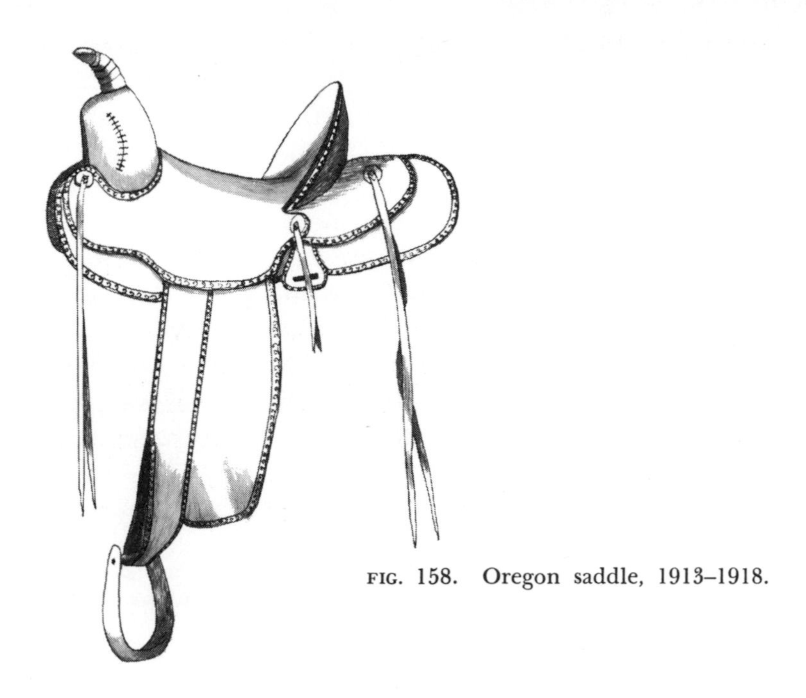

FIG. 158. Oregon saddle, 1913–1918.

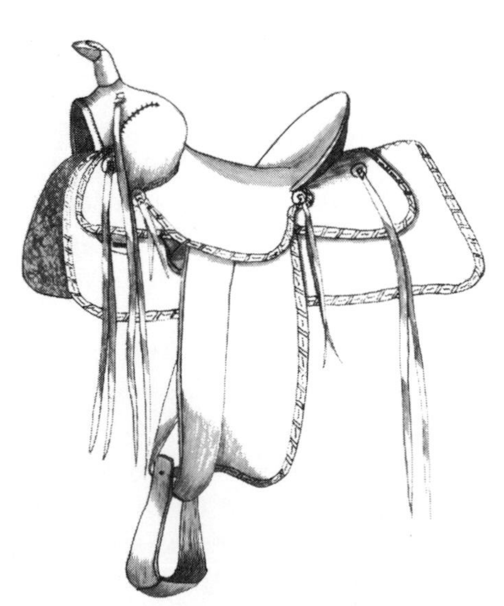

FIG. 159. Montana-Wyoming saddle, 1912–1916.

should be made obligatory for all participants in rodeo bronc riding. These several organizations thereupon appointed representatives to decide on a design for such a saddle.

The committee held a meeting at Pendleton, Oregon, on the Sunday following the 1919 Pendleton Roundup. Those attending were George Drumheller of the Walla Walla Frontier Days, S. R. "Sam" Thompson of the Pendleton Roundup, a member of the Cheyenne Frontier Days Association and one from the Boise Rodeo, the last two names not recorded.

These four met with L. H. Hamley, president of the Hamley Company, whose suggestions for a saddle built on a modification of the Ellensburg tree were followed. The approved saddle was to have a 13½- to 14½-inch tree with plain 14-inch swells slightly less undercut than the Ellensburg, 5-inch dished cantle, rather low, leather-covered horn, round skirts, and single three-quarter rigging. It also carried a flank rigging set somewhat farther back than the rear rigging on ordinary double-rigged saddles. These gentlemen named it the Committee Saddle and passed a resolution that it should be the only type of saddle permitted in the bucking contests at the rodeos which they represented, beginning with the 1920 season.

The Committee Saddle and the reasons for its adoption so impressed the rodeo fraternity as a whole that 1920 and 1921 saw most of the managements incorporating it into their bucking contests. When the Rodeo Association of America was formed in 1928, this rig was ruled to be the regulation saddle for use within the organization. Along about this time, popular phraseology changed its name from Committee to Association Saddle.

In speaking of rodeo saddles, we cannot overlook the elaborately decorated specimens that have appeared along with the development of the sport. The horseman's innate pride and love of colorful gear have always called out his best efforts at making a striking and pleasing appearance, especially for regional celebrations, parades, and rodeos. Any advance in position or wealth is usually reflected in the outfit he rides. Many notable public figures express their love of beauty or recognition through fine saddlery, exhibiting the old ostentation of the cavalier.

Among the many such superior saddles to claim public attention was the $10,000 creation made for Joe C. Miller of the famous 101 Ranch in Oklahoma. Designed and manufactured by that premier saddle maker, Sam D. Myers, of El Paso, Texas, in 1914, its cost today would be many times that figure.

Less elaborate and costly, but still in the royalty class, was the $1,500 saddle that Victor Marden of The Dalles, Oregon, made for Jess Willard, in 1910. Al Frustnow of Miles City turned out a $5,000 beauty for motion picture cowboy Tim McCoy. Tom Mix also flashed through the stratosphere aboard a $1,500 Frustnow saddle.

It was the contemporary Miles City Saddlery Company who made the $2,500 outfit for the Crown Prince and Princess of Norway, in 1938. The chewing gum magnate, P. K. Wrigley, invested $5,250 in a still more fanciful carved and silver-mounted job.

One of today's finest is the $50,000 masterpiece mounted with gold, silver, and Czechoslovakian rubies, and owned by the motion picture star Roy Rogers.

Other saddles of this type, not so elaborate but still outstanding in beauty and cost, have appeared from time to time all along the line. Inadequate finances has probably been the only thing that prevented more of them being seen.

Rodeo is also chiefly responsible for the invention of that rather unique creation, the trick rider's saddle (Fig. 161). It is a rather late addition to the horseman's world. L. H. Hamley believes it originated about 1912, or shortly before, and developed to full stature within a couple of seasons.

Another development that owes much of its being to rodeo is the low roper saddle (Fig. 162). Roping contestants were not much interested in saddles built for hard riding or security of seat; they wanted something that would hold their catches and be easy to get out of in a hurry. Consequently, they bid for a low, sturdy fork; a short, stubby horn of the Mexican duck-bill variety; and a 2-inch cantle flattened out to present no hinderance in throwing oneself off in an instantaneous attack on a roped animal. They also reinstated the rear cinch as a further aid to their special work.

Bulldoggers also found this style ideally suited to their needs. This led to the appearance of a considerable number of the low saddles among rodeo outfits after 1930. Many professional ropers and bulldoggers, who had actual need of them in daily contests, used them as general purpose rigs instead of bothering with an extra saddle. Others simply took them along for the tasks required. Altogether, a lot of cowboys made use of them.

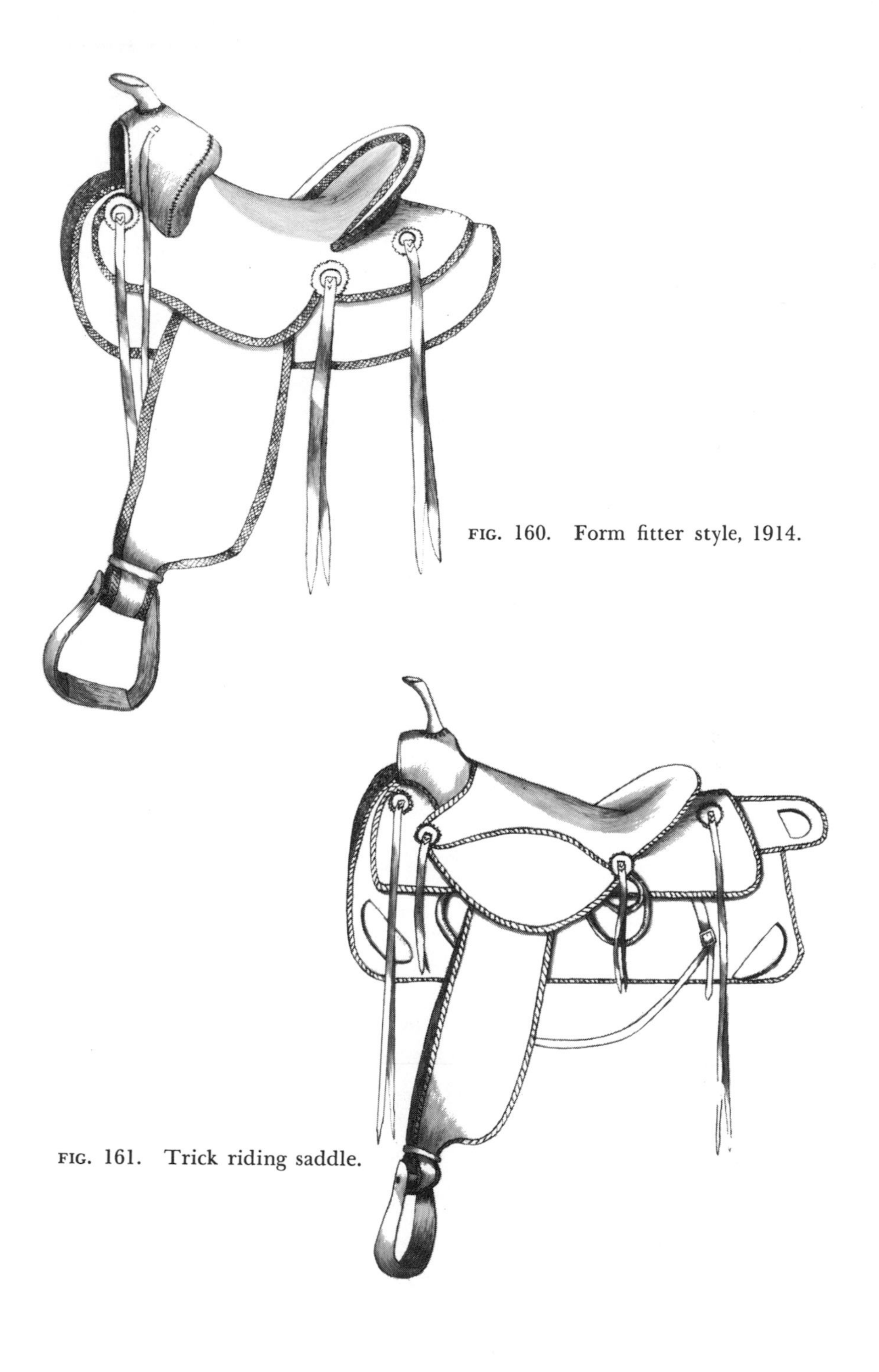

FIG. 160. Form fitter style, 1914.

FIG. 161. Trick riding saddle.

The example they set, without anybody thinking to explain their special reasons, quickly caught the eyes of movie actors, pleasure riders, and vacationing dudes, whose posteriors had never been conditioned to the deep, close-fitting cowboy saddles. They saw in these new flat-seated creations an overflowing comfort never before experienced. Saddle makers heightened the lure by putting Cheyenne rolls on the simulated cantles and padding the long seats with everything from quilted calf-

FIG. 162. Quarter-horse roper.

skin to sponge rubber, thus assuring solid comfort anywhere the rider happened to land. Then came the great urge for a mounted sheriff's posse on every Main Street. Most of their recruits found the flat, padded cantles with extra rolled rims a soothing place for creaky desk muscles, adding fresh impetus to the trend. The recent nationwide interest in horseback riding brought with it a host of new and inexperienced novitiates who based most of their choice on equipment seen in the movies and street parades.

Although it is the old-time cowboy saddle which still meets the demands of actual rangework, a great majority of riding gear is now being presented in styles popularized by the new crop of riders. And who is to say that many of these innovations are not good? Surely they are no more a sign of eccentricity than the rattlesnake skins plastered on a saddle by a decoration minded cowboy, or the heavily feathered loon breasts glued to saddle seats by upper British Columbia riders in search of added warmth. In any event, they are the stimulus which lifts the earth-bound mortal up onto the back of a horse and turns his face toward the far horizons of physical well-being and mental clarity.

—30—

Always the Horsewomen

WOMEN HAVE UNDOUBTEDLY been riding ever since some daring soul first mounted her mate's riderless horse to go back and see where the drunken lout had fallen off this time. We know that women of all primitive peoples in historical times have been as horse-conscious as their lords and masters. There is no reason to think they were any different before history got around to keeping score.

Thus we see the horsewoman riding out of the mists of antiquity and up through the ages into the Christian Era mounted astride in the natural way. Records are extremely vague as to when affected modesty impelled her to keep both feet on one side of the horse.

Nicetas, the Byzantine historian (1118–1205), tells us that in his day "Persian women do not ride as they used to do, sitting on a sidesaddle, but mount their horses with their legs indecently astride," thus indicating that sidesaddles had been in rather common use in that country during an era far antedating their appearance in the West.

A further suggestion in this direction is found in Shakespeare's *Comedy of Errors,* where he has those fabled Greeks, Antipholus of Syracuse and Dromio of Ephesus speak of buying a crupper for the saddle of a mistress.

Basing assumptions on statements of this sort, we can only conclude that the sidesaddle, or some variation thereof, originated in the East at a very early date. From there it traveled westward, reaching Europe in the middle 1100s, possibly brought by returning crusaders, after changing fashions had abolished it in the East.

The East apparently never restored the earlier uncomfortable style of riding. Della Valle wrote, while visiting Persia in 1617, that his wife rode astride while there, "as is the custom of the country." This type of riding no doubt impressed Della Valle in particular, because sidesaddles were then the proper thing for ladies in his native Italy.

Other writers of that and earlier periods spoke of astride riding being usual among the women of Eastern countries. The same fashion still prevails among the majority of these peoples from Mongolia to the Mediterranean.

But not so in western Europe. There the advent of the sidesaddle led to its acceptance as a permanent and steadily growing custom. Its popularity seems to have risen first in the south, moving northward through Spain and France. Ladies of the Italian, Spanish, and French nobility had adapted the new saddles quite extensively prior to 1200. At least, they had become the proper thing for polite occasions. An old French manuscript of that period pictures a lady of fashion riding sidewise. Various writers of that era also mention the custom. These women, however, were still riding astride when hunting or hawking.

Farther north things were moving more slowly. Though Stowe and Thomas Hearn, among others, tell us that sidesaddles appeared in England during the reign of Richard II and Anne, they apparently attracted little attention among the general populace.

One Latin historian of that period, circa 1150, wrote "—noble ladies then used high heads and corsets, and robes with long trains, and seats or sidesaddles on their horses, by example of their respectable Queen Anne, daughter of the king of Bohemia, who first introduced the custom into the kingdom; for before that, women of every rank rode as men do, with their legs astraddle of the backs of their horses."

Chaucer, in the fourteenth century, makes mention of one of the lady pilgrims to Canterbury wearing a "pair of spurrs sharpe." Obviously, the woman would not have been wearing a *pair* of spurs in riding sidesaddle.

In commenting on the modern trend toward astride riding in the early part of this century, the *London Illustrated News* said, "Now we look upon riding astride as novel. Some parents regard it with holy terror.

Possibly they have overlooked the historical fact that all women rode astride before 1380."

Bannerman's historical notes say English women rode astride until the late 1300s; an unidentified collector of odd facts says 1380. Jack Bishop's research reveals only a limited use of sidesaddles in England prior to the reign of Queen Elizabeth I. Various writers and artists of that period present most of the ladies as riding astride.

All agree, however, it was Elizabeth's use of the sidesaddle that brought it into general favor in Britain. Whether or not she turned to sidesaddles through a desire to hide her crooked legs, as some historians claim, does not concern us here. We can only say she chose the style of riding which, following her accession to the throne in 1558, blazed a trail that the majority of Western women followed for over three centuries.

History has neglected to tell us just what the first sidesaddle was like or who devised it. We are fairly safe in believing it was nothing more than an enlarged pillion, a treeless, hornless pad, equipped with its own cinch, crupper, and breast collar. Perhaps it carried a stirrup, though it may have used a footboard similar to those of later dates.

There is little doubt but what this pillion-style rig was the reputed sidesaddle of the time of Queen Anne, Richard's wife, as there is little to indicate a regular sidesaddle until several hundred years later. It is equally probable that even then the pillion and sidesaddle traveled side by side for a long time, the former often masquerading as a sidesaddle.

As few but the nobility ever had saddles of any kind in those days, most commoners were forced to continue riding bareback or on blanket pads. They naturally rode astride since this was the only practical method. At any rate, the sidesaddle does not appear as a distinctive, separate form until the Elizabethan period.

And here we come upon a rather odd proposition: All civilized peoples had mounted from the left side of the horse since the days of early Rome. This would naturally leave the legs of a sidewise rider on that side of the animal. And so they were generally pictured in drawings of all European horsewomen. But there must have been a contrary custom in some parts of France, Germany and perhaps elsewhere.

In a thirteenth-century manuscript, the *Livre du Roi Modus,* as well as in another contemporary manuscript, we find French ladies depicted as riding sidesaddle on the right side of their horses. This might be attributed to artistic license on the part of the illustrator. Art is ever wont to take liberties with realism in obtaining certain effects.

Yet, the same thing appears two hundred years later in still another French manuscript of the fifteenth century. This one also shows a group of ladies mounted on the right side.

Along with this, Hans Schäufelein (1490–1540) has left us the drawing of a German woman riding sidesaddle in company with a companion mounted on a pillion. Both sit on the right side of their horses. This, the drawing claimed, was the regular style of riding at that time by all well-bred people. Whether this statement referred to the right-side position or sidewise riding in general is an unanswered question.

So much evidence of this style would suggest that it existed in certain sections of France, Germany, and perhaps Spain as sort of localized fashions. It is also possible that the formless sidesaddles of that day allowed a woman to mount indiscriminately from either side, remaining in whatever position her efforts landed her.

Though some of the early sidesaddles might have been built on side-bar trees after the idea caught on, most were of the pad variety. They lacked either horns or cantles, the riders being seated completely sidewise, their feet resting on a shelflike platform.

Fig. 163 shows a somewhat later date saddle equipped with such a wooden footboard. These boards were five or six inches wide by about a foot long. Their use was extended to pillions and continued up through the colonial days in America.

Spain evidently made use of the footboard idea on sidesaddles. It appears to have been a rig of this sort that Pattie saw some of the Santa Fe Latins using in 1824. He said it looked like an English saddle with an armchair fastened to it in which the rider sat sidewise. No other known saddle so well fits his brief description. And the shelflike footrest would give a rider the appearance of being enthroned in a chair.

Pattie went on to say that the rider faced the right side of the horse when mounted in this saddle. This would seem to be a direct throwback to those old French manuscripts of the thirteenth century, showing riders similarly mounted. Had such a custom actually prevailed among a certain group of people for over five hundred years? Or was it an oddity, perhaps crossbred with the Indian custom of mounting from the off side? Lacking any contributory evidence in the records at Santa Fe, we can only put it down as another undefinable track left along the trail of history's horseback man.

But that Pattie knew what he was talking about is strengthened by the existence, in the Los Angeles County Museum at Los Angeles, California, of an old, single-horned, deep-seated, footboard sidesaddle which might well have looked like an armchair to one unfamiliar with such styles. Though this specimen is designed for nigh-side riding, it suggests that similar examples might have come to the New World with Spaniards of other riding habits.

The Los Angeles saddle (Fig. 164), of Spanish make, was brought from

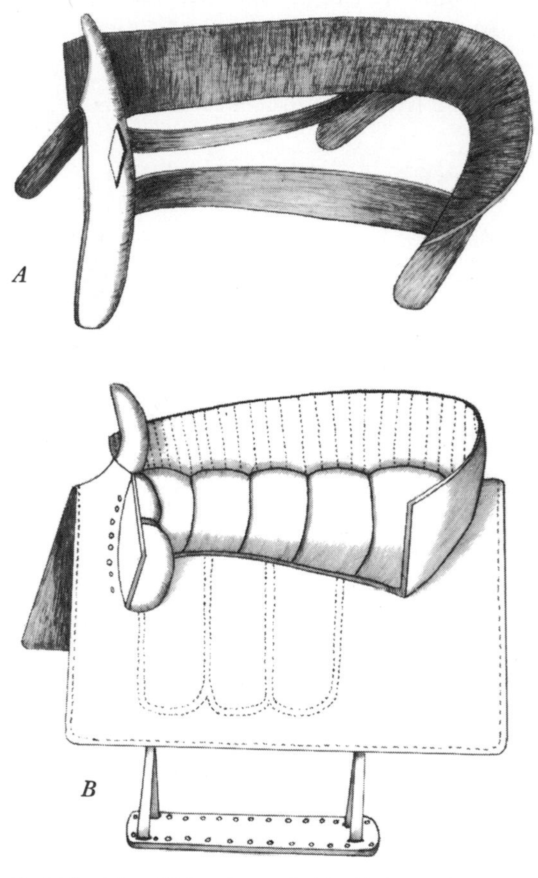

FIG. 163. French sidesaddle, about 1700; *A* tree; *B* complete saddle.

Monterrey, Mexico, to the Santa Anna Mission of California by the Jesus Angelo Larades family in 1704. Used by four generations of that family, it descended to Señora Doña Josefa Ybarra, a great granddaughter of the original owner, in 1854. She donated it to the museum in 1918. It is 23 inches long, with a fabric-covered seat and leather skirts decorated with corded embroidery. The 7- by 11-inch footboard is suspended 25 inches below the top of the pommel.

Having this saddle definitely dated as being in use in 1704, we must assume that it came from Spain somewhat earlier, being representative of styles used by Europeans in the late 1600s.

Sidesaddles as we know them did not arrive in Europe until 1650. It is unlikely that they saw much improvement during the first few decades of their existence. Thus we might conclude that the Los Angeles specimen, which is little more than a lightweight astride saddle rigged for sidewise riding, was very much in the nature of the original design which first supplanted the old hybrid pillion of earlier times.

FIG. 164. Spanish-made saddle, sent to California, 1704.

The saddle in Fig. 163, which was in use around 1700, is obviously a later development. It still carried the old wooden footrest, but the cantle had been replaced with an encircling cradleback, perhaps inspired by the lusty figures of that day. The seat had been flattened and lengthened and more heavily padded in deference to the same end. A padded pommel bulge added further comfort and security. The raw tree shown in the same plate was probably one of the first types made expressly for sidesaddles.

Sometime during the next twenty-five years the eighteenth century lady finally got tired of being jerked sidewise by every motion of the horse instead of being allowed to sway forward and back in a natural manner. It was then that she tossed the old footboard out the barn window and hitched on a regular stirrup for the left foot. She then hooked her right knee around the horn, sat up straight in the saddle, and proceeded to enjoy life in a straightforward manner. When she found a certain discomfort in clenching the knee tightly around the slender horn, she had the boys rig a comfortable knee-rest extending out

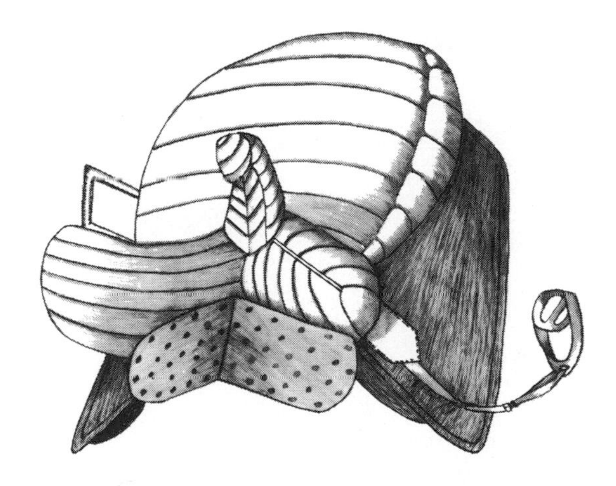

FIG. 165. French sidesaddle, 1735.

to the right of the horn base and enlarge the fork bulge to give a more secure bracing for the left thigh. Then, finding herself so well anchored forward, she jettisoned the old cradleback guard rail as excess baggage and went on her way. The net achievement took place around 1735 or 1740 in the form seen in Fig. 165.

Unfortunately, the slender-necked horn with its rimlike top was none too comfortable on the inside of the leg during long rides. It also had the bad habit of snagging on the voluminous riding skirts when mounting or dismounting and it always reminded her of a harpoon aimed at her midriff. About 1750, she had a lower, smooth-edged knee support installed in its place. She also revived an abbreviated version of the cantle to eliminate some of the end sway inevitable with backless seats. These added developments gave her the design shown in Fig. 166.

It was, for the most part, sidesaddles of this type which came to America with the colonists. Of course, it must be remembered that there were plenty of obsolete models from many countries, old styles and new, in contemporary use all through this nation's formative years. Thus there is no set rule as to time and design until after America was able to stand on its own feet and be independent of the Old World.

The same principle applies to the pillions used in America. They were the same as styles currently popular in Europe. Examples now preserved at Colonial Williamsburg, Virginia, are described by Assistant Curator Eleanor L. Duncan as being merely pads attached by straps to rings affixed to the saddle cantle. The seats are made square in shape, with rounded corners. They are around 12 inches in diameter, though some

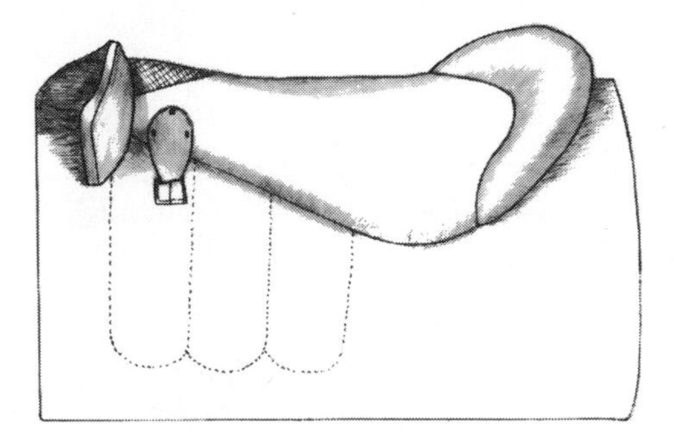

FIG. 166. French sidesaddle, 1753.

run slightly larger. Pigskin or linsey-woolsey was used for coverings, being stuffed with feathers, hair, wool, or quilted padding. Cruppers were standard equipment. Individual cinches appeared occasionally. The greater part of them were fitted with wooden footboards, as noted on the early European rigs.

Alice M. Earle gives a very similar description of those in use through the Revolutionary War period, including the footboards.

Pillions were the predominating riding gear for women in America's northern colonies. They sufficed for the Sunday-morning jog to church or a call on a nearby neighbor. They also fitted in better with Puritanism and straight-laced New England consciences. Even those trail blazers who accompanied their menfolk across the mountains to the new frontiers of Kentucky and Ohio, in the late 1700s, depended on pillions for the most part when horseback riding was necessary. It was not until the broader visioned planter class began to rise in the South that sidesaddles received more than cursory attention.

Pillions continued in use over most of the East until up into the 1800s, gradually tapering off until they were something of a rarity in most places by the time of the Civil War. The West never saw them except in a few sections of eastern Missouri and Arkansas, and there only in early days. Nor did they appear to any extent in the Deep South, where women ran more to the horseback breed.

Southern women were predominantly horsewomen. As such, they were strongly inclined toward spirited individualism. They enjoyed riding and hunting with their men, but objected to playing second fiddle on the rear end of someone else's horse while doing it. In consequence, sidesaddles were in common use throughout the plantation region from very early times.

But North or South, American horsewomen rode as a body into the new era around 1800. Flat, leather-covered horns curved to fit the leg had replaced the wooden knee-rests. Quilted seats had given way to the regular leather style. Trees were better shaped and stronger made. Various refinements in style and design came along from time to time as added improvements.

The belief is often voiced that there were many different kinds of sidesaddles during the nineteenth century. On the contrary, there were but two basic forms. One used wide sidebars which formed the fork and carried a rather low pommel. The rather narrow sidebars of the other were ironed to a tall A-fork carrying a high pommel. Otherwise, the differences were mainly variations designed to meet the regional demands of certain localities or social circles.

Practically the only innovation of importance to appear in these later years was the downcurving third, or leaping, horn (Fig. 167). It originated in 1830. This was an English invention growing out of the British love for jumping horses. This special horn gave the sidesaddle rider an extra purchase by furnishing a bearing for the left knee, thus forming a three-cornered brace between saddle seat, stirrup, and horn.

All the trees were made of wood, light in weight and well ironed. Those used in the better saddles were covered with rawhide, while canvas covering went onto the cheaper models. All the better trees were lined with leather or padded canvas. In the lower brackets was found plain canvas or nothing at all.

Seats were built on the same kind of foundations previously described for men's English-style saddles. They were covered with plush, velvet, Brussels carpeting, heavy cloth, enameled leather or pigskin. Choice of covering material usually conformed with the quality of the saddle. The standard length was 17 to 19 inches. In shape, they ranged from the perfectly flat English type without any cantle whatever to high-cantled, deep-seated rigs that lacked only off-side skirts and stirrups to make them fairly representative of men's saddles. Those made in America invariably had some sort of a cantle, ranging from 3 to 6 inches in height and with straight, bound edges. A few revived the old cradleback guard rail (Fig. 163), by attaching a felt-padded, leather-covered steel band to cantle and pommel in semicircular fashion. The taller cantles were commonly found with the higher pommels. Most of the deep-seated type appeared in the heavier and stronger models designed for serious riding. These ranged in weight from 18 to 25 pounds, as opposed to the 10 to 16 pounds for the ordinary variety. The former were especially favored in the West, where women often rode the unpredictable Spanish mustangs, helped with range work, and rode the dangerous mountain trails. They went under the name of mountain saddles in some sections.

Some of the cheaper specimens were built without skirts, having only small 10- by 12-inch flaps under the stirrup leathers. Most, however, carried big, square, leather skirts with rounded corners, often lined with canvas. Average-size skirts were around 14 by 20 inches, though the big mountain styles ran up to 16 or 18 by 28 inches. The larger ones were usually made to lace together behind the cantle and in front of the pommel, being nailed to the tree around the edge of the seat. Conchoed tie strings in front and back often helped secure them in place. A pocket for gloves or knickknacks occasionally adorned the rear end of the off skirt. These were patch pockets about 3½ by 4½ inches in size, made with gussets in the sides and closed with a button-down flap.

As with the trees, there were only two basic types of horns, though assorted variations were wont to appear. The single-horn style (Fig. 168) had a curved, fairly broad knee-rest extending out and up from the right side of the horn base for the disposition of the leg. These were usually seen on the lower pommeled trees. A higher, squarish pommel was commonly found with the two horns spaced to receive the knee between them. The leaping horn (Fig. 167), being sort of a special addition, might or might not be incorporated into saddles of any design. A few of these horns were entirely separate items, made to be screwed onto the outside of any finished saddle. They were approximately 8 inches in length by 2 inches wide. The upright horns ranged from 3½

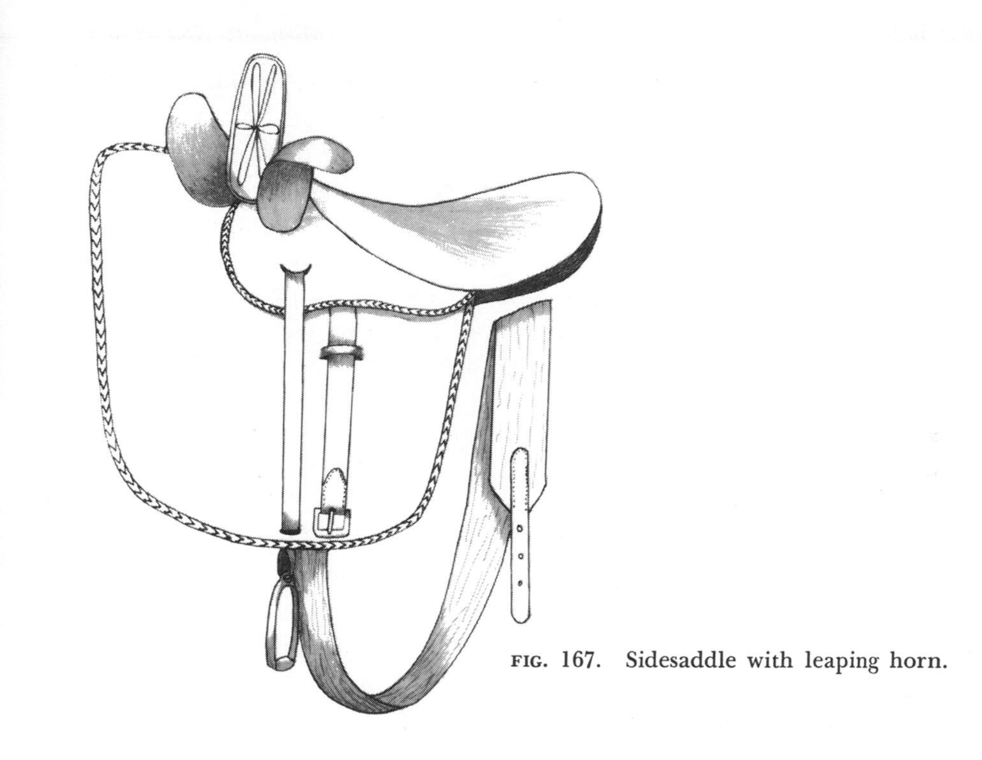

FIG. 167. Sidesaddle with leaping horn.

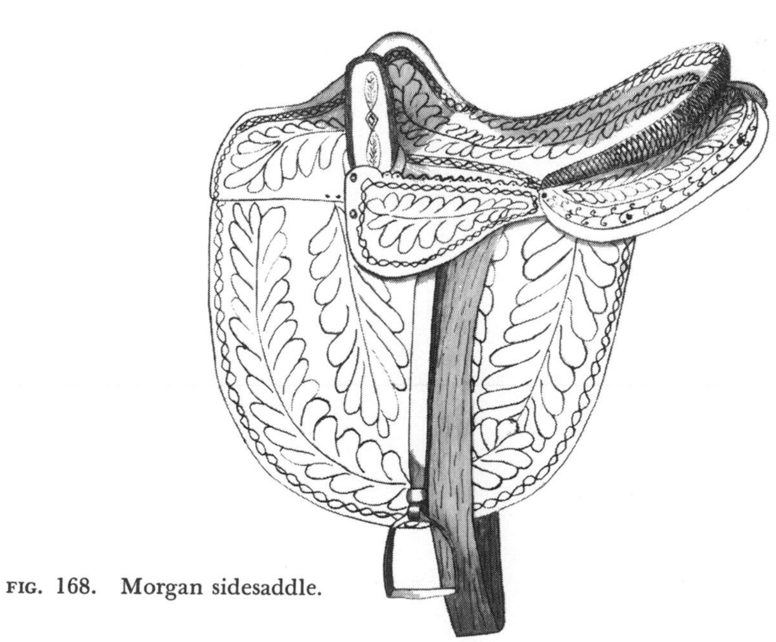

FIG. 168. Morgan sidesaddle.

to 6 inches high and 2 to 3 inches wide at the base. All were felt padded and covered with leather.

The stirrup straps and single center-fire cinch came down over the outside of the skirt in most cases. An extra webbing surcingle, running over the top of the tree beneath the seat covering, was often used in addition to the regular cinch. It passed through loops on the inside of the skirt, binding the whole rig into one unit. Occasionally specimens, usually English, employed an extra quarter strap on the off side, running from the rear of the tree to the cinch ring, as an aid to anchoring the back end of the saddle down more securely.

Sidesaddle stirrups were predominantly of the open-style iron variety, common to Park and Gentleman's saddles. A smaller, lightweight wooden stirrup of the boxcar type, with short, box-type tapaderas riveted on, was occasionally used but never very popular. The slipper style, which has appeared in some form ever since the days of the ancient Moors, enjoyed much favor as long as sidesaddles were used.

Then there was a wide variety of freaks and patented contraptions designed to impress the ladies who had visions of being thrown and dragged to death in some unsightly manner. Some were good, while others were better in theory than in practice. Fig. 169 carries a few of the more widely used creations of this sort. They employed a variety of swivel treads, spring releases, and patent catches that flipped over, jerked loose, or flew apart under the stress of any undue strain from the wrong direction.

Fig. 170 shows a sidesaddle that met a very favorable reception in the West. It was designed in 1890 or 1891 by Colonel Charles Goodnight, of Texas, for his wife. The ordinary commercial sidesaddles did not appeal to Goodnight as the ultimate in security and comfort for a lady often alone and always subject to the vicissitudes of hard riding in an uncivilized region. He therefore planned one which would fit his own ideas of what was needed. He then turned his design over to S. C. Gallup, a leading saddle maker at Pueblo, Colorado. The result was so satisfactory in the eyes of other western women that the Southwest was soon calling on Gallup for more of the Goodnight saddles. It was a demand that was to last as long as the West rode sidesaddles.

But this style of riding was already entering into its twilight years. Its knell was sounded in America shortly after 1900. It lasted somewhat longer in most of Europe, but eventually fell under the same general worldwide movement.

The *London Illustrated News,* around 1910 or 1912, said, in mentioning certain princesses seen riding astride: "There is nothing immodest in the situation at the present time, but twenty years ago a girl or woman astride was looked upon with grave apprehension by all who

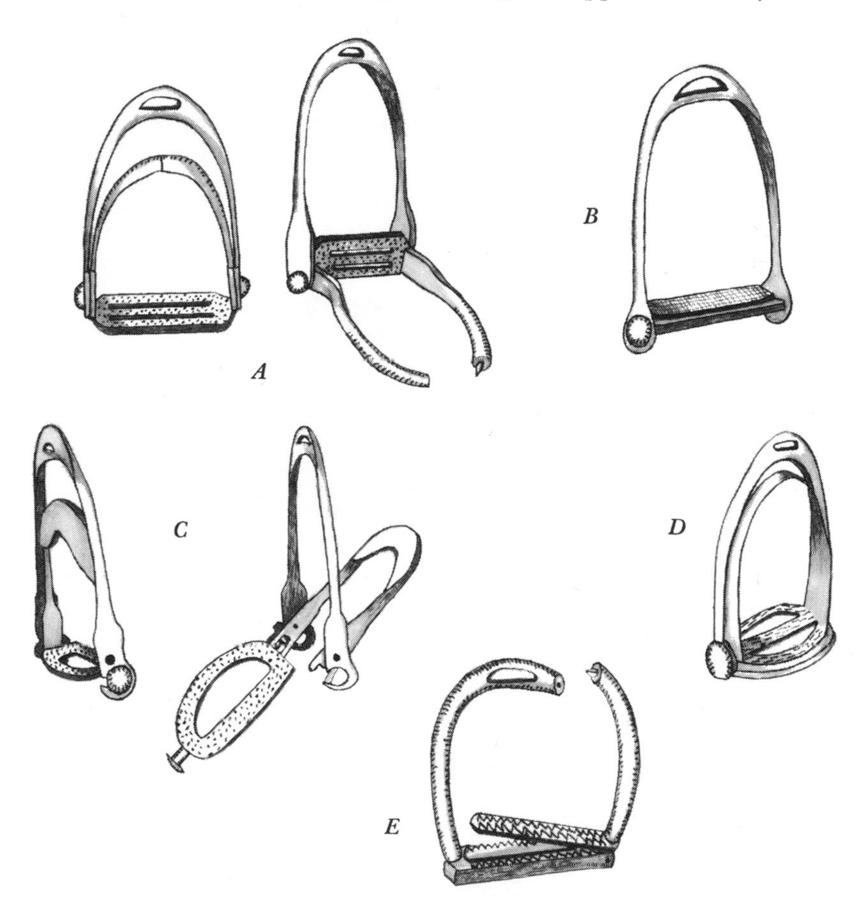

FIG. 169. Women's safety stirrups: *A* Scott's Safety, closed and open; *B* Turnfoot; *C* Cope's Safety, closed and open; *D* swivel tread; *E* Springside.

had her welfare at heart. She was classed among the tomboys and wicked rascals who climbed trees and stoned cats."

This was some three or four years after astride riding first started there. Colonel Downing says it began in 1907. The style was evidently practiced in a limited way, however, by a few very select individuals safely ensconced in assured positions during those earlier years. It was another decade before it became general enough that the largely insecure majority dared flout public opinion.

The change moved at much the same pace in France and other more forward countries. It was slower in the central regions of Europe. Colonel Krijanovsky says sidesaddles were used exclusively by all Russian ladies of any pretense previous to his departure from Russia in 1920. Other central European nations were quite comparable.

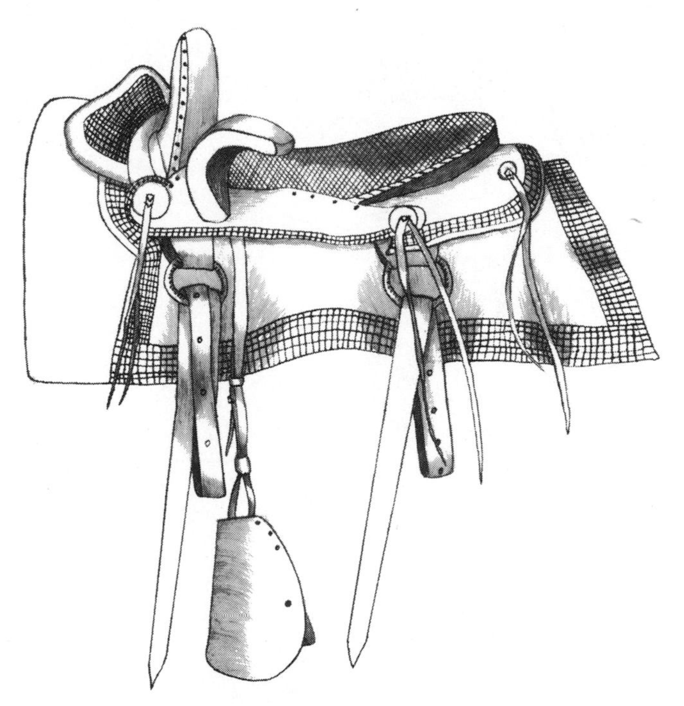

FIG. 170. Goodnight sidesaddle, 1890.

The sidewise riding of asses in a few sections around the east end of the Mediterranean continued up into modern times. Even the old pillion with its wooden footrest hung on in Sardinia.

Among the American Indians, of course, astride riding by women had been practiced since the dawn of their horse culture. They were a practical people, not to be swayed by inferior imported fashions.

Californios were similarly inclined. Caughey, Garrison, and Wise all say these ladies, especially the younger ones, rode and hunted to considerable extent, using *vaquero* saddles ridden astride. They had no saddles made expressly for women. Neither were there any pillions in evidence.

On festive occasions the older señoritas commonly rode double with their escorts. The lady was seated sidewise in the saddle, her satin slippers thrust through a loop of gold or silver braid, while the man mounted himself on the big rump housing behind the cantle. Less frequently, the señorita would ride behind, seated sidewise on a bright serape thrown over the rump housing. The señoras and older women habitually chose a more decorous position in the accompanying ox-drawn *carretas*.

Considerable research by Lee M. Rice and Ruth Mahood has failed to uncover any record of women's saddles having been made by the Californios in early days. Miss Mahood, however, has some evidence that a few sidesaddles of the type represented by the Larades saddle in the Los Angeles County Museum may have been brought from Spain or Mexico to California; but if such was the case, they were so few and isolated as to be practically negligible in the general picture.

American women, however, clung to their sidesaddles, as a general rule. And despite the shortcomings of this style, they did a good job of riding throughout the West.

Trail driving history has its quota of ladies who accompanied their men north on the big drives. Mrs. Amanda Burks is usually credited with being the first to brave such a venture. She made the trip with her husband, W. F. Burks, trailing a herd from Bandera, Texas, to the Smoky Hill River in Kansas in the summer of 1871. The heroine in Emerson Hough's novel, *North of 36,* is supposed to have been modeled on Mrs. Burks.

She was perhaps preceded by Sally Redus, who is said to have gone with a Redus herd from Hondo, Texas, to Kansas about 1870. It was the summer of 1879 that John Chapman and his new bride spent their honeymoon trailing a big Oregon herd across the divide to their new range in northern Wyoming. Even in the final chapter of trail driving days we find Mrs. W. B. Slaughter present on her husband's drive from Fort Sumner, New Mexico, to Liberal, Kansas, in 1896.

Sally Skull rode all over Texas in the 1870s, trailing horses and ramrodding her own trail drives with a crew of Mexican *vaqueros.*

Up in northern Wyoming, Frannie Morris ran her own outfit for years, riding with the best of them.

One of the first pioneers to bring cattle into southeastern Oregon and establish a ranch on Sucker Creek was a rather salty character who went by the name of McCoy. Years later, an unfortunate demise revealed McCoy to be a woman.

Countless others, most of whose stories will never be told, brightened the roster of valiant ladies who will ever ride the unfenced trails of that great Valhalla dedicated to true horsemanship.

Most of these women rode sidesaddle until after the turn of the century. Then, curious as it may seem, it was the eastern women who first broached the defenses of astride taboos in anything like an open-faced manner. These pioneers were mostly fashion leaders whose social positions enabled them to express themselves without catering to shop-worn customs.

In 1901 horrified Boston agitatedly popped its window curtains at sight of a lady riding astride—only they didn't call her a lady.

The following year, Mrs. Adolph Ladenburg threw heaving bosoms and clacking tongues into a turmoil by riding astride through the streets of Saratoga, New York, in broad daylight. One shocked newspaper reported that "There was no attempt on her part to conceal the fact that she was riding cross-saddle, wearing skin-tight riding breeches!" Another account of the affair stated that she wore the breeches under a divided skirt. Either way, it was quite a scandal.

Incidentally, they called it riding cross-saddle at that time, astride being considered a rather indelicate, if not frankly bawdy, word in better circles. The rougher element farther down the street, openly referred to such riders as clothespins, straddle-bugs, strumpets, and other terms reminiscent of the old livery barn and barbershop.

By December of 1906, the *Ladies Home Journal* threw in the sponge and stated, "Many young girls are now taught to ride cross-saddle, as the old style of sidesaddle riding is thought to make a girl become slightly crooked."

Another five years and Kate Field, writing in the *Chicago Times Herald,* said, "Mankind naturally rides astride, because in no other way can he attain perfect balance and complete control without artificial aid. Primitive women copied her mate even after bareback riding gave way to saddles. It remained for civilized convention to devise the sidesaddle and skirt of dangerous length with death in every inch. All because in the days of Queen Elizabeth a noble dame was too deformed to ride astride as women had always ridden up to that time. To cover the physical defects of one woman, a whole sex has been punished for centuries."

But it was a last war cry. The opposition had already picked up its marbles and gone home.

There were naturally some die-hards. Sidesaddles hung on for a long time in some sections of the East. Particularly among some of the mountain people of the Southeast, World War I found them still in much demand. Saddle makers were stocking them in the Kansas City region as late as 1917. In the South and Southeast, they were in evidence until after 1920. In fact, one or two manufacturers in the Southeast were still turning them out for a limited regional market up around 1950.

The West showed its usual impetuosity by making the switch in a shorter time. Its more extensive riding over rough, broken country probably had something to do with it. Too, horses were less gentle as a rule, while rangework by women was fairly common rather than an exception.

Charles E. Bohlman says the last sidesaddle he saw made on the Pacific Coast was in 1902 or 1903. L. H. Hamley says their company made very few sales after 1905. They were becoming a scarcity throughout the Rocky Mountain and Plains region by 1907. Only a few farming centers near the Missouri and Mississippi rivers had any use for them after 1909, and then only as scattered hangovers.

But the smothering tentacles of entrenched convention made a last desperate struggle to salvage female purity from the insidious lure of masculine customs. If the gals wouldn't ride sidesaddles, they should at least have saddles of a distinct type made expressly for their use, something, anything that would help preserve precious femininity by holding it apart from articles designed for male crudities.

The answer was women's astride saddles. It is thought this new creation first appeared in California around 1903 or 1904, probably designed by the D. E. Walker Company of Visalia, or Main and Winchester of San Francisco. They came into their greatest popularity in the 1906–1912 period. After about 1914, they tapered off sharply until they practically passed out of the picture by 1919. They lingered on in a few sections of the South and East for a few more years, but even there they soon disappeared.

The astride saddle was a hybrid design, recalling the old seventeenth century horned sidesaddle rigged for astride riding. The first ones were simply a modification of the old California-Spanish horned tree fitted with English-type skirts. As a matter of fact, they went by the name of Spanish saddles in most places. These rigs developed a little later into a roll-cantle, nickel-horned design, with quilted glove-leather seats, knee-rolls, and back skirts, built on the popular Canby tree. The English skirts with exposed stirrup straps were retained.

The greatest trouble with these original styles was that very few, outside of the painfully feminine element, liked them. Women who used saddles for serious riding, which included the majority of the western class, wanted something patterned more on the order of practical all-purpose stock saddles. Their demands brought forth an assortment of styles similar to the one in Fig. 171. The majority were basically little more than lightweight versions of the men's rigs. Weighing from 17 to 25 pounds, they were built for the supposedly more trivial needs of western women.

But all this was only a transitional phase designed by outside minds to bridge the chasm of change for weaker souls. Real horsewomen in general never received these cross-bred saddles with much enthusiasm. In the West, the majority turned directly to stock saddles upon acceptance of astride riding. Their counterparts in the East moved in a similar fashion toward the standard men's rigs in current use.

Along with the rebirth of astride riding came a similar reversal in the horsewoman's clothing. Her dress in all ages had been subject to the usual vagaries common to current whims of fashion. In general, though, with the exception of the voluminous skirts prevalent during the sidesaddle era, it closely followed the clothing worn by men. In ancient and medieval times, and always in the Oriental-Asian countries, women chose man-type trousers and short jackets as the only suitable style for their habitual astride riding. In Europe and colonial America, the ordinary long-skirted dresses were all that was required for sitting on pillions. These gave way to the extravagant and impractical riding skirts deemed so necessary as adjuncts to sidesaddles when the latter became popular.

When women quit their sidesaddles for those that had to be straddled, it was quite obvious that they could no longer use the old-style riding skirts, which were large enough to cover both them and their mounts. Still, if they weren't important enough or inconsequential enough to flout convention, they certainly couldn't be expected to appear before the forest of thumbs already turned down without wearing something voluminous enough to leave no doubt about their respectability. The genius who gave them the divided skirt furnished the solution in both volume and modesty.

History records this notable event as occurring around 1903 or 1904. It presented a design which was simply a pair of skirts, one for each leg, attached to a belt. The front was prefaced with a double-breasted panel which could be unbuttoned down one side to permit astride riding,

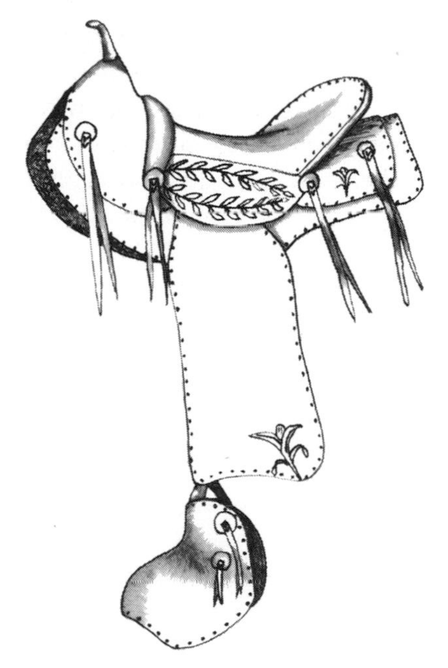

FIG. 171. Canby Western saddle.

or closed to give the appearance of an ordinary full skirt as soon as one dismounted. They were commonly made of heavyweight khaki or corduroy in ankle length, providing the most practical riding costume for women since Europe crawled out of the Dark Ages.

Around 1909, popular favor turned to a less bulky and somewhat shorter style just covering the tops of the boots. A good many westerners, especially in the practicing cowgirl group, developed a fondness for a model made of buckskin or soft glove leather fringed around the bottom and on the sides. These were more in keeping with the western tradition, wore longer and clung to the saddle leather better than khaki.

Like the advent of astride riding, riding breeches first appeared in the East. It was the upper-echelon horsewomen, fox hunters, steeplechase riders, and the like, who were first to adopt men's-style breeches, much as they had previously turned to astride saddles. Riding breeches at that time were of the jodhpur variety, made full in the hips and fitting tight below the knees. They were far more convenient and practical for strenuous horseback work than any kind of skirts. It wasn't long before they became the regular costume for most of the women of this class.

When dude-ranch vacations began to attract the attention of people of means, it was only natural that horse-conscious sportswomen should be the first to turn in that direction. The West was a land of horses, and the main allure of its ranches was horseback riding. It consequently followed that women bent on such a vacation should bring with them clothes to which they had become accustomed and found suitable for such pastimes.

Beginning about 1914, the home girls began looking with more and more envy at the freedom and practicality inherent in this type of wear. As the majority of ordinary ranch women could ill afford expensively tailored breeches, besides having an aversion to aping the dudes, they turned to the men's regular denim Levi's. Checked shirts soon followed in place of tailored blouses.

With the change in style, the younger women came into their own. The late 1930s saw the metamorphosis complete. Like the blending of East and West cowboys, American horsewomen on both fronts had become an indivisible sorority.

—31—

The Dudes Came Riding

THERE IS A PRIMAL urge in all red-blooded men and women which responds to the call of the wilderness and wide, free horizons. This is particularly true of the horseback fraternity. In their veins still runs the spirit of bold venture and derring-do that rode up over the rim of the world in the dawn of antiquity. Though often lulled into passivity by civilization's refinements, the ancient cry of the wild gods seldom fails to waken a response.

Such was the voice that has come out of the West ever since the first venturer filled his lungs with air sifting down out of the high Rockies. In pioneer days it was discovered only by those not economically and personally bound to the East, hardy souls who dared to make the land their own. Later years and swifter means of communication found increasing numbers of the more circumscribed individuals turning westward in search of the freedoms that are man's natural birthright. This eventually resulted in the creation of the dude-ranch industry, perhaps the most significant development to engulf the West since the cowboy chased the last Indian over the hill and replaced his tepee with a pine-board shack.

Men who might come under the present classification of dudes began visiting the West in the early days of the fur trade. These were mostly wealthy sportsmen from Europe, interested in unlimited slaughter of big game, plus a few scientific naturalists investigating the secrets of the New World. They set the pattern of hiring local guides, camp attendants, and horses while adopting a temporary facsimile of western life as their own.

Later on, after the spread of ranching and budding settlement crowded the remaining wild life back into the mountain areas, big-game hunting continued to hold a strong appeal for all sportsmen of means. It was still a big country, rugged and forbidding to the uninitiated and accessible only to men on horseback. The only practical course for visiting nimrods was to engage guides, horses, and equipment at conveniently located ranches for such back-country expeditions. As the bulk of the regular ranch work was out of the way by hunting season, and habitually lean purses welcomed a bit of extra revenue, various cattlemen began the practice of accommodating nonresident hunting parties during this off season. It was a profitable business for the rancher and assured the hunter a profitable trip. It also gave the man from the East a chance to slough off his ultracivilized veneer for a time and, without undue discomfort, feel himself a part of the romantic and free-spirited West. The idea grew and spread until various individuals, more interested in the West itself than in mere hunting, spent the season experiencing everyday ranch life as a new kind of vacation. The hunting just gave it an added fillip.

Sometime in the late 1880s, a couple of English-born Wyoming ranchers by the name of Greeley and Robbins came up with the belief that some of their countrymen would pay for the privilege of participating in Western ranch life. Wyoming was known to the rest of the world at that time as the heart of the real Wild West. Stories of its cowboys, Indians, and great open ranges had captured the interest of all peoples in all lands. The old, old urge for boys to play raiding Tartar, plumed knight, or dashing cowboy lay more or less dormant in every man. Greeley and Robbins knew the disposition of wealthy noblemen able to gratify suppressed desires in search for the unusual. They reasoned that there were plenty of such persons who would shell out $500 to spend a year at their ranch on the Laramie plains, enjoying the status of a guest while being free to partake of the region's activities at will.

The decision proved well founded. Their first customer was a titled Britisher by the name of Clement Bengough. A scholar and a sportsman, he soon succumbed to the haunting charm of the country and the easy familiarity which made him known simply as Ben to his associates. Foregoing the right to return to his $300,000 castle in England, he held hands with his adopted land until his death at Moran, Wyoming, in 1934.

Meanwhile, the Greeley-Robbins experiment had caught the attention of a few keen minds. Wealthy foreigners and eastern city dwellers alike seemed to find great delight in western visits, invariably living to the full the ordinary ranch life of the natives while there. Why shouldn't similar fare appeal to other classes as a special type of vacation? The West had a wealth of attractions, while people everywhere displayed an inordinate interest in all its many facets.

Howard Eaton was evidently the first to put such a plan into operation. Eaton was running a horse ranch in western South Dakota in the 1880s. He followed the customary western practice of keeping open house for all visitors. Unfortunately for him, he had a host of outdoor-minded city friends who viewed his hospitality and horses as an ideal vacation proposition. Each year found the summer deluge of guests increasing until he was hard put to make the ranch pay the expenses of entertainment. It was hard on his horses, too. He decided some drastic change had to be made if he was to stay in the kind of work he loved.

He knew from painful experience how simulated range life appealed to the imaginations of average individuals from other regions, especially city dwellers. And he had the Greeley-Robbins venture as an encouraging precedent. Why not, he reasoned, put the thing on a broad-scale, regular-vacation basis within reach of the moderate-income group? People other than noblemen and financial tycoons indulged in vacations, and there were many more of them. A guest ranch available to the general public, arranged for the convenience of visitors from May to November, should meet a favorable reception. He accordingly moved his outfit across the line into Wyoming, establishing himself at Wolf, about 1890. The growing response to his faith in western vacations put him back in business as a stockman and established the Eaton ranch as a permanent paying-guest enterprise. It likewise inaugurated a development that was to eventually blanket the entire West.

Here were born those distinctive terms "dudes," "dude wranglers," and "dude ranches," though it was some twenty years before the names lost the uncomplimentary implications formerly associated with derby-hatted easterners in store clothes appearing on the early western scene.

Eaton's success caused the lifting of many a grizzled eyebrow, but the march of events was against such scoffers. Feed shortages and falling beef prices were seen to have no crippling effect on a ranch which netted a good dude crop. Lonesome cowboys found a goodly measure of solace in the high percentage of unattached and nicely appreciative female dudes placed in their care. The work was easier and more agreeable, too. And what was most important, closer association revealed the fact that most of the dudes shared the ancient heritage of the man on horseback.

Various ranchers opened their doors to paying guests in succeeding years. William Wells followed the Eaton example at his ranch in Sublette County, Wyoming, in 1897, continuing the operation until his death in 1914. Struthers Burt launched his B Bar J spread in Jackson Hole as a dude enterprise around 1908. All along the east slope of the Rockies, necessity or hope of easy profits was drawing more and more outfits into the business, either as working ranches willing to accept a few guests as a side line, or planned establishments designed especially for the growing trade.

American vacationists had discovered a fascinating new field. And they loved it. Here, the old frontier existed to a fair degree of reality; here, they could feel themselves actual participants for a time in the storied romance that had stirred red-blooded minds for generations. Among those in whom the spirit of the mounted man either flared actively or struggled to raise its long-dormant head, the call of the wild trails, unpeopled distances, and the free, adventurous life of western rangeland offered an irresistible appeal. Lovers of magnificent scenery and those who simply wanted temporary relief from the madly whirling squirrel cage of conventional society followed in hopeful uncertainty and remained to worship at the altar of the horseback kingdom.

In the earlier years of this development most of such visitors stood somewhat as a race apart, quite comparable to Maine's Summer People. They brought their own clothes, manners, and customs with them. It was with something less than admiration that the West viewed tailored riding breeches, puttees, flat-heeled boots, derby hats and long-tailed coats. And it had even less regard for the custom of eastern women going about in clothing similar to that worn by the men. Western women were still properly distinguishable by their divided skirts and feminine jackets and blouses. Such a radical departure from local convention as was affected by the lady-dudes moved the average native to a variety of disparaging remarks. Perhaps the kindest expression current at that time was that of calling them "dudeens."

The word dudeen was coined the summer of 1916 by Bill Miller, a newspaperman of Cody, Wyoming. It caught the public fancy and spread to some extent at the time, but soon disappeared from the dude-ranch lexicon. Thereafter, "dude" was used indiscriminately for all paying guests of both sexes.

The idea of calling western visitors dudes was another little idiosyncrasy peculiar to the cowboy. Cowboys retained the old Indian practice of setting aside the real names of outsiders who came among them, preferring to bestow nicknames of their own choosing, usually more or less descriptive, on such persons. The early-day sportsmen who occasionally appeared on the western scene were commonly men of wealth and position who dressed the part. They looked like the popular conception of dudes to the westerner, so dudes they remained so far as he was concerned. Later-day paying guests, togged out in everything "the well-dressed vacationist should wear," and awkward in their strange surroundings, appeared to him as much the same breed as the English duke in hard hat and spats expecting a butler to materialize out of the nearest fir thicket. They went into the same category forthwith. As the cowboy is seldom one to change his ways in deference to foreign customs, he gave his paying guests the choice of accepting his outlook or else. The guests soon came to view the term as a sort of honorary degree awarded members admitted to the western fraternity.

All this helped people outgrow provincialism in both West and East. Eastern women had discovered the superior advantages of cowboy garb and gear for western use; western women, in turn, began copying their eastern sisters in turning toward man-style clothing for horseback work. Outmoded, hampering conventions thus swept aside, both factions settled on the happy medium of Levi's and close-fitting riding pants styled in the manner of regular cowboy garments. The year 1920 and the full emancipation of women saw the new order in full swing.

And with the common meeting ground of outward appearance established, easterners and westerners found each other to be much the same inside. Joining hands in that old, old Brotherhood of the Mounted Man, they forgot minor differences of birth, ambition, and culture as they picked their way along the horseback trails of mutual respect.

—32—

Out of the Chutes

ONE OF THE MOST significant things the West has given the world is the rodeo. This unique sport, as American as apple pie, baseball, and Huckleberry Finn, was, is and continues to be a distinct product of western horseback man. It has no exact counterpart in world history. It is the one group-sport where the individual must rely solely on his own efforts; where a large percentage of his winnings come out of his own pockets; where he must provide his own transportation and living expenses, accident and medical costs, equipment and clothing, and depend on luck in a lottery drawing for every chance to win an animal worthy of his talents in any given contest. It is the cowboy's playground. Its activities embody the more dramatic phases of his everyday life. And in it appears all the glamor and pageantry which has always symbolized the calling that is his.

Where did it start? And when? There are as many answers, none complete. You might say it just growed, like Topsy. Or perhaps it would be better to describe it as something that was spawned on the open range of the early West and nourished to maturity by an earth-bound multitude ever captivated by the lure of the man on horseback.

The word itself is of Spanish origin, meaning a roundup or gathering of livestock for sorting, marking, counting, and marketing. It was pronounced ro-day'-o, and was so passed on to American cowboys by the old-time *vaqueros*. Among these men, it remained the accepted term throughout the Southwest and Pacific states. East of the Rockies, where Anglo tongues prevailed, such work came under the head of "roundup." Time and the blending of the cowboy tended to bracket the two words as interchangeable, although regional preference continued to separate their use to considerable extent. It was not until the dawn of the twentieth century that "roundup" began to emerge as a definite phase of ranch work, leaving "rodeo" to designate the cowboy playtime.

Vaqueros and cowboys were ever a gay-hearted lot. Their rare opportunities for fun and frolic were met with joyous abandon. Roundup or rodeo time always meant the congregation of numbers and a brief recess from duty. Then it was that pleasure-starved spirits, lacking outside entertainment, gave themselves over to whatever festivities or carefree enjoyments were available. As with any craftsmen, it was only natural that thir sports should reflect the skills and objects of their trade.

Nobody knows when this sort of pastime started. It is no doubt an offspring of antiquity's horse racing and the jousting of medieval knights. We can be sure it is as old as cattle ranching in America. Some of the earliest visitors to California mention rodeos being held at the old Spanish ranchos.

Captain Vancouver wrote of seeing one at Santa Clara Mission during his stop at San Francisco in 1792. It was sort of a neighborhood fiesta, with roping and horse racing among the men and great rounds of dancing and dining by everyone.

Josiah Gregg wrote of a similar fiesta seen at Santa Fe in 1832. Captain Mayne Reid apparently enjoyed the one he attended at the same place during his visit to New Mexico in 1847. Under date of June 10 of that year he wrote: "This rodeo is a great thing for the cowhands, a Donnybrook Fair it is indeed. They contest with each other for the best roping and throwing, and there are horse races and whiskeys and wines; at night in the moonlight there is much dancing in the streets."

What was perhaps the first event of this kind to attract special attention took place at Deer Trail, Colorado, in 1869. It was primarily a bronc-riding contest which grew out of rivalry between the neighboring Campstool, Hashknife, and Milliron outfits. The only rewards, aside from certain lucky bets, was the impromptu title of Champion Bronco Buster of the Plains. It was won by a fellow with the highly decorative name of Emilnie Gardenshire.

All through these years there were the inevitable riding, roping, and similar contests when prideful outfits got together or met for mutual enjoyment at community celebrations. Cowboys out for a good time were never bashful about topping off some outfit's prize bucker or showing how quick a cagy old moss-horn steer could be tied down. Most were spontaneous affairs of the moment, similar to pick-up ball games and foot races common to other regions.

It was merely for a little fun and excitement that the boys got together and rigged up a steer-riding contest for the Fourth of July celebration at Cheyenne, Wyoming, in 1872. It was the same impulse which caused them to expand the affair to include bronc riding and some roping when beef roundup and shipping time assembled them again in Cheyenne that fall. Nobody then visualized the fame that was to make the name of Cheyenne synonymous with a national sport, a sport that is now exceeded only by baseball in paid spectator attendance.

However, it was not until 1882 that rodeo began to fall into its stride. That was the year Colonel George Miller, of the famous 101 Ranch, staged his first Wild West Show as an impromptu cowboy contest at Winfield, Kansas.

Austin, Texas, put on a steer-roping contest as an added attraction at the state fair in December of that year. Ten entrants competed for the $300 silver-mounted saddle, which was won by a time of 1 minute 45 seconds.

Another notable contest thought to have occurred in 1882, though the exact date is open to some question, took place at Canadian, Texas. It arose from a challenge between the men of the Laurel Leaf and Jaybuckle outfits. Both ranches had exceptional ropers for which their backers claimed supremacy. The arguments led to a countrywide interest and an agreement for a public contest to decide the issue.

About that time, the town merchants caught the faint scent of profit in such a drawing card. They promptly proffered a free barbecue with all the trimmings if the cowmen would hold the match there on the Fourth of July. Satisfactory arrangements led to plans for a gala day with horse races and other customary sports. The event evidently met all expectations: the saloons did a big business; considerable money found a new home; and a fine time was had by all.

The much disputed roping championship went to the Jaybuckle outfit's entrant J. Ellison Carroll. He tied his steer in 1 minute and 2 seconds from a 100-foot start.

Carroll subsequently set a record on December 31, 1907, that was to stand for over thirty years. This took place at San Antonio, Texas, in a 10-steer match with Clay McGonigal. Carroll's time on one steer was 16 seconds, the animal being given a 60-foot start. It was a feat seldom equaled by the best of today's arena professionals.

On another occasion he roped and tied a whole carload of steers as a demonstration of his consistent skill. His average time for the 22 head was 22½ seconds each.

This grand old craftsman remained a threat to younger competitors all through the early days of contest roping. Nor was he one to be taken lightly in his declining years. At the ripe old age of seventy-two he was able to give a good account of himself by taking part in the roping at the Texas Cowboy Reunion, held at Stamford, Texas, on July 4, 1935.

In 1882 William F. (Buffalo Bill) Cody had rounded up some of the boys for an exhibition of riding, roping, and other western features in conjunction with the Fourth of July celebration at North Platte, Nebraska. This was the prelude to Cody's Wild West Rocky Mountain and Prairie Exhibition which he took east to the delight of New York audiences the following year.

The year 1883 saw what is usually regarded as the first rodeo to have been planned along modern lines. This was another Fourth of July celebration. The place was Pecos, Texas. It was held on an open flat adjoining the courthouse. The courthouse yard was used as a corral for holding the stock, while the street became the roping arena. Morgan Livingstone, of the NA ranch, won the roping contest.

The Pecos affair, like all early rodeos, and many later ones, was of the old free-for-all, get-together pattern aimed solely at enlivening the holiday for that region. It was also good for business and helped instill a measure of community pride in the old home town. The idea for similar functions soon spread all over the West.

Albuquerque, New Mexico, put one on in 1887 with gratifying results. Denver, Colorado, presented its first efforts to a large and enthusiastic audience the same year.

The first regular rodeo to be organized on a paid admission basis appeared at Prescott, Arizona, in 1888. It was designed as a feature attraction for the Frontier Days celebration on July 4. This event also marked the first special rodeo trophy to be awarded a contestant. It was in the form of a commemorative plaque donated by the town's leading citizens. Juan Levias won it by placing first in both bronc riding and roping.

John Merrill took the crown at Agua Fría, Arizona, the following year by tying a steer in a fraction over 30 seconds. Other men who were to ride, rope, or race their way to fame were appearing all over the West.

Miles City, Montana, staged its first cowboy contest at a meeting of the Stock Growers' Association in 1891. Denver had continued its 1887 performance until 1895, when it laid off until 1901–1904. The year 1895 also saw a rodeo inaugurated at Billings, Montana, where Ben (Packsaddle) Greenough, father of the later-day champion Turk Greenough, won the bucking contest. Wilbaux, Montana, came along with a full-scale production in 1896. The annual Frontier Days event was established at Cheyenne, Wyoming, in 1897. Oklahoma City, Oklahoma, joined the parade about 1902. The Pendleton, Oregon, Roundup was born in 1910.

Up in Alberta, Calgary's *Weekly Herald* reported that city's first rodeo in 1893 as being held in conjunction with the Midsummer Fair on June 20–23. It consisted of a roping contest and a stake race. Bronc riding and Indian races were added in 1894. Public interest then allowed the affair to lapse until 1901, when the Duke of York's visit caused the local cowmen to put on a full-scale rodeo in his honor. This was followed by another recess until 1912–1913, after which it was set aside during the more serious business attending World War I. The year 1919 saw it permanently reestablished as the Calgary Stampede, one of the leading greats in rodeoland.

Meanwhile, towns large and small throughout the cow country had incorporated rodeo events into most of their holiday celebrations to some degree. By the early 1920s, the rodeo circuit was maintaining a year-round performance throughout the West, with branches in nearly every state in the Union.

This far-reaching interest was given its first shove by the old-time, commercial Wild West shows. It started with Colonel Cody's venture in 1883. E. Farlow put together a show, called the Frontier Days, at Lander, Wyoming, in 1893. Major Gordon W. (Pawnee Bill) Lillie, Tex Austin, Colonel Zack Mulhall, Tom and Lucille Burnett, the Miller Brothers, Colonel James Eskew, and Joe Bartles were foremost among the many who took to the road with cowboy troupes during the early 1900s.

Most of them were good shows, presenting stay-at-home audiences with a realistic introduction to the West. Few were to survive after 1914. Their personnel gravitated toward the open arena.

All through the early years rodeo had been sort of an unorganized proposition. Officials were anybody who happened to be handy; arenas were vacant lots, local fairgrounds or out in the open; rules were usually what any individual group chose to make them. There were no precisely clocked eight-second rides, contestants commonly being required to ride their horses out until they quit bucking or the judges were satisfied. A simple corral usually sufficed for holding the stock. Mounts were roped out and dragged into the open, there to be eared down or snubbed to a saddle horn while being saddled. There were no chutes or split-second starting gates. Everyone helped wherever he could, and conflicting efforts often resulted in anything but smooth execution.

However, it was colorful. Earing down raw broncs and saddling them in the open often provided unpredictable thrills unknown to the more methodical chute method. Steer roping in the open may have lacked much of the precise professionalism found in the up-to-date catching of calves automatically released from a spring gate, but it proved the mettle of man and horse, besides holding the suspense and the element of unscheduled excitement seen nowhere but on the range.

As for the cowboys themselves, that was still the era of uninhibited individualism. Everyone used the equipment that best suited his taste, and he dressed as he saw fit. There was no uniformity of blue jeans, white shirts, and stiff-molded straw hats as today. The old cowboys loved color, anything to relieve the drabness of backcountry workaday life. The rodeo was their holiday, the gala time when work, money making, and the serious side of life could be forgotten in pursuit of unlimited fun; it was the big, carefree vacation in town. They were determined to make the best of it. Like the Indians, the cowboys then shed their everyday raiment and dressed for the occasion. Silk shirts of any and all colors topped off by fluttering silk bandanas in contrasting shades blossomed out like the roses in spring. New Stetson hats in the most impressive styles available covered freshly barbered heads. Chaps of white and colored angora skins, or the plain leather variety decorated in every imaginable design with conchos and silver or nickel spots, covered legs that might be wearing anything from patched Levi's to fitted Pendleton wool pants. The best in finely made boots flashed their fancy stitching and decorative inlays from tops made long enough to set them off to the best advantage. Spurs and bits elaborate enough to catch a dim eye on a dark night sparkled in the sunlight. Beautiful Navajo blankets formed a bright background for the finest in saddle-making art. No two were quite alike. Each set the rider apart individually. Collectively, they presented a kaleidoscope of scintillating color that was romance on parade. And win, lose, or draw, they had a spontaneous gaiety that made light of all yesterdays and denied the existence of any tomorrows.

The activities were no less colorful. With a hundred unregimented cowboys and twice that many unpredictable animals in the field, anything could happen—and it usually did. It was not until a uniform set of rules was established, conformity in equipment regulated, and the precision made possible by chutes, starting gates, experienced judges, and timers properly developed, that rodeo settled into the neat orderliness of today.

Although some of the old Wild West shows used improvised bucking chutes, they were not employed in regular rodeos until up around 1918 or 1919. This date must be recognized as somewhat elastic, as the early rodeos seem to have kept no definite records of when and where in the United States such improvements first appeared.

The veteran rodeo producer Verne Elliott cites the 1919 rodeo at Fort Worth, Texas, as having been the first in his knowledge to use chutes. Foghorn Clancy wrote that shotgun chutes were used at Magdalena, New Mexico, in 1918, while the breakaway chute was in use elsewhere at that time. Colonel James Eskew, another early producer, puts the date at 1916. The colonel, however, gives no location for this 1916 chute. As he was operating a commercial show at about that time, his reference may have concerned a private affair rather than a regular rodeo. We know that Cheyenne, Wyoming, the great headliner of that period, was still saddling in the open until after 1915. This writer's more or less faulty memory is inclined to agree with Elliott and Clancy, as 1918–1920 saw the new method's initial appearance in several northern localities. The best supposition is that chutes were adopted simultaneously as individual innovations in various places at about the same time, starting about 1918 or 1919. At any rate, the following years saw them come into quite general use wherever rodeos were held. Pendleton seems to have been the last of the big-time places to follow the trend. It first installed chutes in 1939.

It was during the formative years, after the turn of the century, that rodeo molded itself into a pattern of standard events. Previously, it had rested mainly on the keystones of bronc riding and roping. Other features tagged along willy-nilly as local fancy or custom dictated. In the North, where bigger and stronger horses had developed a superior grade of riders, bronc busting held a leading position. Down in the Southwest, land of the great loop artists, roping was the big thing. The two sections built their first early rodeos around their favorite sports.

This regional superiority in the two crafts still holds true to a large extent, as the rodeo record books show. It stems from the unique demands each section has always imposed upon its cowboys, each forcing a perfection less needful elsewhere.

During the late 1890s, the Southwest went wild over local and regional contests for championship roping crowns. Such skillful performers as Ellison Carroll, John Lane, Blue Gentry, and Clay McGonigal spread their fame wide, shaping this ancient art of the snaky coils into a leading rodeo event for all time.

McGonigal's name, incidentally, became a byword throughout the Southwest. It is still with us in the expression "to do a McGonigal," meaning to perform a particularly skillful feat of roping. He once roped and tied a steer in 20 seconds at Tucson, Arizona. This was in 1901, the animal being given a 100-foot start in the open. He bettered this time by 1¼ seconds at Chicago in 1916, with only a 30-foot lead allowed the steer.

In comparing these old records with those of today, it must be remembered that the early contests lacked all the appurtenances and refinements of modern rodeos. Someone simply paced off a line out on the prairie at what was supposed to be the agreed distance, others shoved the animal out of the herd, and the roper went into action when the critter crossed the line with his tail cutting circles and his nose pointed toward anywhere else. Moreover, these were full-grown steers, not calves nor trough-fed dogies. Most were of the old half-wild, half-savage, half-human longhorn breed. They could run like deer, fight like cougars, dodge like jackrabbits, and scheme like a Comanche warrior in an enemy camp. Long, lean, and lithe as snakes, deadly with their four- to six-foot spread of scimiter-like horns and active as any ridge-running outlaw bronc, they could, and usually did, present problems seldom encountered by later generations of ropers. The only way they could be tied was to bust them at the end of a rope and put them down hard enough so that the fight was out of them until the piggin' string could be put on. As catty in mind and hoof as most longhorns were, this often took some doing.

At the same time, the men who downed them were invariably ordinary rangemen confined to their jobs. Roping was only one of the many tasks in an everyday run of affairs, which left little time or opportunity for extra practice. Competition was something to be set aside for an occasional holiday. Financial returns rested chiefly on winning personal bets. One can speculate on how records might have been different if these men had enjoyed the advantages common to professional ropers of later years.

Many spectators, unfortunately, looked at steer roping with a decidedly jaundiced eye. Their cries of brutality and cruelty in such rough handling of animals began to haunt the arenas. Civic organizations, stockgrowers associations, humane societies, and the like joined their voices in condemnation of the practice. This led in a short while to various state laws and individual rodeo rulings which prohibited the busting of steers at the end of a rope. Ensuing years saw the old-style steer roping pared down to where it is now seen at only nine Rodeo Cowboys Association (RCA) sponsored rodeos. Pendleton and Cheyenne are the principal ones, followed in a lesser degree by Lander, Wyoming; Prineville, Oregon; Safford, Arizona, and Claremore, Ada, Woodward, and McAlester, Oklahoma.

The elimination of this rugged event from so many of the country's rodeos was a hard blow to the roping fraternity. For a time it looked like the death of one of rangeland's foremost arts as a spectator sport. But thanks to the clear thinking of many rodeo managements and interested observers, a change was made to substitute a pair of ropers working together, their object being to catch the steer by head and heels and stretch him out to an easy, harmless fall. This gave the spectators all the thrill and excitement of watching riders chase and capture half a ton of fleeing wilderness, while eliminating little of the dash and skill necessary for such work, and imposing no particular hardship on the horned victim. The new style quickly won approval from both the contestants and public, restoring the ancient craft to general favor.

At the same time, calf roping was rapidly running up the scale in popularity. It was a natural for the cowboys, a direct step from the everyday branding corrals at home. It was work that they enjoyed and that displayed their efficiency at its best. And the public loved it. Half-grown calves scuttling in every direction and dodging like jackrabbits called for the ultimate in skill from both man and horse, while providing a highly exciting and dramatic event for the audience. As the calf had only to be caught and stopped, then thrown by hand while still on its feet, there could be no complaint of excessive cruelty from the tender hearted. As a matter of fact, it is usually the cowboy who gets the toughest end of the deal, having to jump to the ground, run down the rope, and wrestle a snaky, bull-headed, 400-pound chunk of contorting obstinacy onto its side before he can put on his tie.

By 1921, this type of contest was a leading event across the nation, overshadowing the dwindling steer roping and placing ahead of team roping. It now accounts for the greatest number of contestants and the largest amount of prize money in any single rodeo event.

Calf roping is also a performance which offers the horse almost as much chance for renown as it does the man. When back-of-the-chutes memories are being built around legendary ropers, no less honors are accorded to equine names.

Along with steer, team and calf roping, a fourth type of loop artistry, trick roping, has reached its highest point of perfection in the American West. Though this specialized craft is practiced to some extent by most cowboys and nearly all professional ropers, its execution as a fine art depends on the delicate finesse displayed by the few trained in its intricacies by countless months of patient and dogged effort. It is a skill that demands the hands of a surgeon, the temperament of a musician, the inborn precision of a target shooter, and the soul of a perfectionist. An exhibition performance rather than a competitive sport, it delights audiences ever eager for the legerdemain of the cowboy's magic rope.

How old the science of trick and fancy roping may be is anybody's guess. If it was present among old-world horsemen, it seems to have gone unrecorded by historians. Its earliest recognition by writers appears to be in a few stories of Spanish ranching in America, where very brief mention is made of ropes that behaved in strange and wonderous ways under the hands of certain *vaqueros.* Such items, undetailed as they were, strongly suggest the spinning loops and eccentric coils of present-day trick ropers. Authorities agree that the craft came north from Mexico.

The first actual trick roping that we find definitely recorded was brought to the United States by a Mexican named Vicenti Orespo. He made his debut with Buffalo Bill's Wild West Show about 1900, and is credited with having invented the act. The probability is that he simply worked up an improved routine copied from various tricks known to some of the old *vaqueros.* But be that as it may, his performance caught the public fancy immediately, winning him headline status during his several seasons with the Cody show.

Quick to sense audience reaction to the new act, other Wild West producers hurriedly developed fancy ropers of their own. By 1905 or 1906 no western rodeo was complete without its exponent of the tricky art. These experts invented and perfected a host of new innovations and elaborations which raised performances to the crowning height of audience appeal.

On a par with trick roping is the companion performance of trick riding. This is the cowboy's version of the old circus-ring act, enlarged to fit his high, wide, and handsome concept of proper entertainment. He saw plenty of virtue in performing acrobatics on the back of a running horse, but he wanted something better than the slow canter of a rosinback ordered around by the popping whip of a silk-hatted dude. Moreover, he felt himself running on a short rope when confined to a small sawdust ring. When the wider scope of rodeo arenas presented itself by around 1911–1912, he had developed a free-wheeling performance that took him off, over, under, and around his mount while racing at top speed the quarter-mile length of the grandstand. Here was something that fitted his imagination, something few lands had ever seen since the days of the ancient Scythians and Cossacks. Equipped with a newly designed saddle specially fashioned for his work and a horse trained to perfection, his skill and daring soon made him a star attraction wherever people gathered to see the cowboy at his best.

Closely akin to trick riders, and often from within their ranks, are those who ride the relay races. In this reenactment of the old pony express each contestant usually has three horses and one saddle. Only a combination of swift hands, steady nerves, and the courage for a headlong plunge into relay stations, dismounting almost in midair with the saddle already uncinched for removal, can insure a favorable position in the race.

It is only natural that many of the trick and relay riding experts should come from the bronc-riding group. The latter are at home on a horse under any circumstances and have launched as associated sports most of the more rugged events that make up rodeo routines.

Bronc riders, in fact, stand as one of the two great cornerstones of rodeo. Everyone knows "There was never a hoss that couldn't be rode and never a man that couldn't be throwed." Nothing so much interests the average cowboy and average outsider alike as to see the result of a hundred and fifty pound man pitting his skill and strength against a half ton of pure unadulterated hellishness. It was the ability of such men to break the wild mustangs to their bidding that made possible the development of the West.

Bareback riding goes back into the dawn of horse culture. Our Indians and pioneers resorted to this primitive method when the need arose and better means were lacking. Most ranch kids learn to ride bareback before they are strong enough to throw a saddle on a horse.

It is said that Tom Horn, the noted Arizona Indian scout, won early fame as a bareback rider in the 1880s. His favorite sport was to hang by his hands from the crossbar over the corral gate when the horses were being let out, then drop straddle of any likely mustang that passed beneath him. With only open country before them and no interference from behind, the outcome was entirely up to him and the horse.

Steer and bull riding also owes its origin to the spirit of fun in the early days of cowboy history. In fact, it might be said to date back to the old Comanche practice of jumping on the back of a fleeing buffalo from a running horse, and then riding the beast until it went down from repeated knife thrusts.

Steer riding moved swiftly from a common Sunday afternoon ranch sport to the rodeo arena. After 1900, it was a fairly common thing at most rodeos. It did not, however, get up into the big time as a major event until after the introduction of Brahma bulls, in 1920.

These unusual animals proved to be big and strong and exceptionally active. They were also filled to the horn tips with an unpredictable brand of nasty, vicious temper, their hearts dedicated to mayhem, murder, and madness. Here, reasoned a few knowing souls, should be something that would help the cowboys find out how tough they really were. The cowboys seemed willing to gamble a fair amount of hide and bones on the deal, so the hump-backed Brahmas began bursting out of the chutes all over the land.

Verne Elliott and his partner the late Ed McCarty are credited with having first introduced these big beasts into the rodeo circuit in 1920. Two years later, with Tex Austin, they took them to Madison Square Garden. Following years saw Brahmas become the standard mounts for bull riders from coast to coast. They even went overseas to London a few times.

But it's a rough game, suitable only to experienced top-hand riders. Not many women indulge in it. Fox Hastings, Tad Lucas and Ruby Roberts are the best known among the few whose talents lie in this direction. They served their apprenticeship in the less hazardous steer-riding field, graduating to the big bulls later.

Incidentally, not a few of the bulls have won distinction by their ability to take the conceit out of ambitious riders. One such was old

Bovolupus of the 1928–1930 period. He unseated every aspirant to fame for three years.

The bronc- and bull-riding ranks also furnish most of the bulldoggers, or steer wrestlers, as they are often called. This has been changed to steer decorating at Calgary since 1912, the animals there being tagged with a horn decoration instead of being thrown.

When and where bulldogging originated is a controversial question. It might perhaps be traced back to the old California custom of killing cattle intended for slaughter by riding up on them and stabbing them from horseback. Too, cowmen have no doubt thrown occasional critters by twisting their necks ever since cattle were first domesticated.

A case in point is the story of John Slaughter, cornered by a mad steer and about to be trampled to death. That was in 1879, soon after he established his Sulphur Springs Valley ranch in Arizona. The steer had him down and was about to finish him off when Billy Clayburne, one of his cowboys, came to the rescue. Clayburne galloped up from behind the steer and threw himself onto its head, twisting it down beside the nearly unconscious rancher.

As a sport, however, the most logical conclusion is that bulldogging is a more or less direct descendant of the old *vaquero* practice of upsetting unruly animals by tailing, called *el coleo*. Many early visitors to California described this method of standing a critter on its head. Josiah Gregg wrote about seeing the performance while at Santa Fe in 1839. It was a favorite way of taking the brassiness out of outlaw longhorns in early-day Texas.

Those old brush poppers were wild, mean, and bristling with independence. Their chief delight was to quit the bunch and take off for parts unknown, and woe be to anything that got in their way. Their long, sharp horns could rip the belly out of a horse before the rider knew what hit him. Americans soon learned the time-honored Mexican trick of falling in to the rear of such runaways and grabbing the exceptionally long tail peculiar to longhorns. A dally of the tail brush around the saddle horn, quickly followed by spurring the horse ahead and out at an angle would send the steer sprawling, usually ridding his mind of his antagonistic ideas.

Many of the early rodeos followed the Mexican custom of including *el coleo* in their list of events. Its last appearance in the better rodeos seems to have been at Denver in 1887. Thereafter, it was quite generally outlawed as a needlessly ruthless and brutal performance.

Stopping an animal, however, can be accomplished as easily by putting the front end down as by pulling the rear end up. Rodeo hands found that tailing could be fairly well duplicated by riding up alongside a steer, leaping from the saddle, and twisting the beast's neck until it came to a halt and finally went down. This was comparatively harmless to the animal, the cowboy being the chief sufferer if anything went wrong.

While steers, rather than the big bulls, are commonly used for this event, the former are fully as wild, often as mean, and usually more elusive. Crafty dodging and stiff necks often reward the cowboy with only a mouthful of dust for his trouble. An occasional aspirant has the rueful experience of seeing the steer lope happily away, perhaps shaking a little cowboy blood from one horn, while he himself waits for an ambulance.

The first recording of this event seems to be an item written in the *New York World* in 1886. The reporter said that Buck Taylor, then billed as King of the Cowboys with Buffalo Bill's Wild West Show, ". . . was able to stand in the path of any Mexican steer and turn it over by the horns." This was evidently more in the nature of a circus stunt than an example of actual bulldogging, as there is no further record of the craft until some years later.

The origin of bulldogging, as we know it, has been attributed to a number of different people. One was a Yakima Indian by the name of Alec (Owl Child) McCoy, cited in a 1939 Associated Press news item as having invented the stunt while working for Ben Snipes, the Yakima Valley's first cowman. Buffalo Vernon wrote in a magazine article that he had been the first to perfect it for a rodeo performance, around 1909. Several others have voiced similar claims from time to time. Probably it was brought forth more or less simultaneously in different parts of the country by individuals unknown to each other.

Tradition and the best of recorded evidence, however, would tend to give the honor of being first to present the act in public exhibition to Bill Pickett, the Texas Negro cowboy. Ed Foy, Sr., a pioneer cowman of Glendo, Wyoming, said he saw Pickett bulldog a steer in 1903. The veteran rodeo announcer, Foghorn Clancy, mentioned seeing him throw a steer in this manner at the Old Settlers' Reunion at Dublin, Texas, in 1905. Clancy referred to it as an act already well established as a rodeo feature at that time. Other old-timers appear to agree on 1903 as the start of Pickett's career and the birth of bulldogging.

We owe the name for this performance to Pickett's manner of throwing the animals. He would twist the animal's nose upward and then sink his teeth into its tender lip, hanging on until the steer went down, almost in the same way the specially trained dogs did in England's old bull baiting.

Pickett suffered a rather serious injury in 1907, while performing at the Jamestown Exposition. To keep the act going, a cowboy by the name of Lon Seeley substituted in his place, thus becoming the first definitely authenticated white cowboy to appear publicly in this field. Pickett, however, recovered to continue his career until stamped to death by an outlaw horse in 1935.

Seeley went on to enter the game as a steady performer. His success brought with it a growing number of cowboys eager to engage in such work. The act was appearing at Cheyenne and a few other places as early as 1908 or 1909. With the increasing interest in it as a sport, it was not long until there had to be a contest to see who was top hand. The years 1913–1915 found it being established as a regular contest on a time basis at most of the major rodeos. It was introduced as a contest event at Pendleton in 1913. Cheyenne incorporated it into the Frontier Days schedule at about the same time.

In bulldogging, as in roping, a good share of the contestant's success depends on the speed and knowledge of his horse. Without a mount that will put him in the right spot at the right time, practically without guidance, the best bulldogger in the world could never hope to place among the winners.

Mike Hastings is said to have once refused $3,500 for his famous bulldogging horse Stranger. And that was back in the 1920s, when dollars still had their old respectable size.

Hastings was, by the way, one of the greats in early bulldogging days. His wife Fox was one of the first women to engage in this rough sport, making her debut at Houston in 1924.

Few followed her example. Not many women had the strength or desire for such a rugged affair. Grayce Runyon and Lucyle Richardson were perhaps the best known.

Certain performers even got mechanized ideas and tried bulldogging from automobiles. What the writer believes to have been the first stunt of this kind took place during the Fourth of July Stampede at Cody, Wyoming, in 1916. The name of the bulldogger has passed into the limbo of forgotten things, but the car, a 1916 Studebaker, was driven by Cody's premier sportsman Jakie Schwoob. It was purely an exhibition affair. Any time that might have been kept was no doubt conveniently forgotten, as the steer did everything but climb the grandstand fence to dodge the fearsomely snorting vehicle. It was only after several runs that the steer was crowded into the rail and successfully thrown.

Tex Parker performed the same stunt at Magdalena, New Mexico, in 1918, with somewhat less difficulty. Others likely did the same thing in various places as the motor age came in.

In December, 1944, Master Sergeant Bill Roer of Phoenix, Arizona, bulldogged one from a jeep going twenty-five miles an hour at Karachi, India.

But stunts of this kind are rather like entering a mechanical dummy in a dance contest. Despite a certain amount of novelty, they have no place in rodeo. For rodeo is the realm of the horse, the old West.

And straight out of this West of a century ago comes the carefree, grinning bronc rider atop his hideful of concentrated hellishness. This might be called the oldest art of the cowboy. For not until untamed broncos were broken to his needs could he rope a maverick, gather a herd, drive his steers to market, or even ride into town for a fresh supply of "makin's."

The same holds true today: work cannot begin until the horses are ready for service. The foundations of all rodeos are the horses that have been selected for the salty individuals who view riding as the keystone of the West. With the opening of the chute gate, time slips back to when the wild mustang first felt something drop onto his back; and, perhaps remembering the habits of cougars, he loses no time in coming uncorked in a fight for freedom. The boys we see rocking against the skyline in every rodeo are the answer to the secrets of a rough, tough trade.

That they learned their lesson well is exemplified by some of the best riders the world has ever known, still following the pattern set by those who got rodeo off to a successful start back in the eighties and nineties.

Not a few of these old-timers continued on to furnish inspiration for later contestants and thrill-hungry spectators. Sam (Booger Red) Privett was still capable of turning in an excellent ride at Fort Worth, in 1925, when he was sixty-one years old. Starkey Teeples celebrated his fiftieth birthday by winning first money at Byron, Wyoming, in 1913. Jiddy Smith of Nevada was still going strong in local competition after knowing friends claimed he shaved some eight or ten years off his declared age of fifty-three.

Nor was this work confined solely to the male element. Women there were in plenty who could fan a bucker as well as any man. Although the shroud of convention kept them pretty well out of the public eye in early days, they were no novelty among their contemporaries.

Buffalo Bill added some cowgirls to his show in 1886, though they were used more as western atmosphere than exponents of the harsher acts. He, as well as other showmen, later recruited cow-country girls as actual performers in the arena. Most of the early lady bronc riders came up through this route to find their place in the sun as rodeos replaced the vanishing Wild West shows.

Rodeo in its formative years, however, bowed to the social mores in not including major events for women. Prairie Rose Henderson was the first of her sex to appear in a rodeo, making her debut at Cheyenne, in 1901. Others soon followed her example.

The only sidesaddle user in rodeo was Mrs. Riordan. She appeared at Cheyenne in 1912, making a beautiful ride but losing the contest to Rose Wenger aboard a regular astride outfit.

Thelma Warner was one of the very few women to work as a pickup rider. This was in the 1929 era, when she was reputed to be as adept at the job as any of the men.

To another rider, Bonnie McCarroll, might be attributed the banishment of the women's bronc-riding event at Pendleton's Roundup. She was killed by a horse in the 1929 championship contest. Following the unfortunate accident, the Roundup authorities decided to avoid any possibility of similar mishaps in the future.

Many of the horses which carried these champion riders to world renown earned for themselves reputations as brilliant as those claimed by the individuals astride them. Rodeo bucking horses are anything but stooges. The great majority are incorrigible buckers dedicated to the task of humiliating ambitious humans. Not a few are crafty schemers who profit by past experience to become truly educated artists in their profession.

Note the distinction commonly made between an outlaw and a killer horse. The former only objects to attempts at subjugation by man, going on the prod against whatever threatens to infringe on his freedom. The killer, on the other hand, will attack anything he considers a potential enemy, eagerly willing to bite, kick, strike, or stamp to death a thrown rider or anyone else within reach. Known killers are seldom used in rodeo.

It is the great outlaws, the squealing, bawling, sunfishing, pile-driving, hump-backed bundles of concentrated fury that have bucked their way into the select coterie of outstanding individuals.

Perhaps the most famous member of this unique and distinguished company was old Steamboat, a black gelding with three white stockings. His name derived from the peculiar whistling noise he emitted while bucking. Steamboat was born in 1897 on the Two Bar ranch in southern Wyoming. He proved to be such a bucking fiend that C. B. Irwin bought him for use in the Cheyenne Frontier Days rough string. He appeared in 1905, but no one succeeded in riding him until Dick Stanley of Portland, Oregon, accomplished the feat in 1908. Henry Webb rode him again in 1913. A few others managed to stay with him at different times, but none of them did anything to shrink his reputation. He died of an injury at the Salt Lake City rodeo in 1914.

Also from Wyoming was Eddie McCarty's K. C. Roan, a champion bucker through the 1916–1924 period. E. A. Scott, down at Anson, Texas, had one they called Bluejay, who held his own with all comers until ridden at Fort Worth in 1917. Another, Done Gone, starring with Tex Austin's rodeo at Albuquerque that same year, went on to win the vote for the hardest bucker in 1919.

Tipperary, featured at Belle Fourche, South Dakota, in 1918–1922, was equally bad. The rodeo management hung up a $500 prize for a qualifying ride on him as a special attraction. Yakima Canutt was the first to stay with him, making his ride in 1921.

Then there was the never-to-be-forgotten Midnight. Brought down from Canada in 1929, he was bought by Elliott and McCarty, with whose rodeo string he bucked his way to everlasting fame. He was the kind of horse whose spirit continues always to hover ghostlike over bucking chutes since his untimely death in 1936. So highly was this great horse respected by all who knew him that the boys made up a purse to buy a monument for his grave on the Elliott ranch at Johnstown, Colorado. Colorado's Senator Cris Cusack composed the following epitaph now engraved on the monument:

> Under the sod lies a great bucking horse.
> There was nary a cowboy he couldn't toss.
> His name was Midnight, his coat black as coal.
> If there is a horse heaven, please, God, rest his soul.

Occasionally a bucker noted for outstanding performances will suddenly reform, as if tired of the fanfare, and become a model saddle horse.

One such was a dappled iron-gray stud owned by William Brooks of Blackland, Texas. This animal was an actual man-killer, seldom ridden and ever vicious, until Jim Wood rode him to a finish at Forney, Texas, in 1896. He never tried to throw a rider again.

Another was Double Tough, owned by Bob Askin of Ismay, Montana. He was rated among the champion buckers until he suddenly quit without any apparent cause in 1926. The rest of his life, he remained perfectly gentle, the old, wild days seemingly forgotten.

The list of bucking horses, famous in one respect or another, could go on endlessly: Jack Dempsey, Will James, and Calgary Red; Mary's Lamb, Gentle Lizzy, and Dimples; Golden Rule, Starlight, and Hootchie Kootchie; I be Damn, You be Damn, and Damnfiknow. Many are remembered by their uniquely descriptive names sprung from the singular vocabulary of the West: Flying Devil, Gut Buster, and Dynamite; Skyrocket, Corkscrew, and Rocking Chair; Yellow Fever, Cholera Morbus, and Leprosay; Destruction, Widow Maker, Grave Digger, and Tombstone; Rock and Rye, Red Pepper, Gin Fizz, and Bad Whisky; Brenner Pass, Badger Mountain, South Dakota, and Powder River. Their names are legion.

In the infancy of rodeo, most of the stock necessary for contests was recruited from among suitable critters in the immediate vicinity. Owners of particularly bad horses just wanted to see how they would stack up against top riders, while almost any range cattle were wild enough to give the boys a run for their money. But succeeding years, stock improvement, and growing dollar consciousness forced rodeo managements to look farther afield for available animals of the proper caliber.

The natural outcome, in the early 1900s, was the birth of stock contracting by certain ranchers who had accumulated a special assortment of bad horses and tough cattle particularly suited for arena contests. These would be maintained, usually as a side line, for renting to nearby rodeos.

Nowadays, practically all rodeo stock is owned and supplied by various contractors who devote their spare time to seeking out the meanest bulls, the wildest steers, and the toughest outlaw broncs to be found in the West. These are maintained in the peak of condition and transported to and from a series of rodeos throughout the season. Most of such contractors are old-time western ranchers or retired rodeo hands operating from back-country ranches in various sections of the country.

Verne Elliott and Don Nesbitt of Platteville, Colorado; Ed McCarty and Charles Irwin of Cheyenne, Wyoming; Zack Mulhall and Homer Wilson of Oklahoma; Leo Moomaw and Tim Bernard of Tonasket, Washington; Leo Cremer of Big Timber, Montana; Colonel James Eskew of Waverly, New York, were among the pioneers in developing this industry.

Another form of contracting is practiced by the country's rodeo clowns. There is no contesting among this group; they rent their services for a flat fee. And while any one of these men may receive from $50 to $150 for an afternoon's work, don't let anybody get the idea they are being overpaid.

Rodeo clowns rival any funsters in the world as entertainment features; but that part of their work is largely superficial. Behind all the elaborate facade of foolishness lies their real purpose. This is to draw the attention of fighting-mad Brahma bulls away from thrown riders, to get injured contestants clear of proddy steers or pounding hoofs of outlaw broncs, and to be on hand in case of any accident in the arena. Most of them are expert bulldoggers, riders, and ropers in their own right; some are first-class matadors. Long experience has taught them what to expect under various circumstances and how to meet any of the many contingencies that might arise. Many a potentially serious accident has been turned into an amusing joke by the deft cleverness of an ever-present clown. Every season finds a few untimely graves cheated of their customers by these heroes in baggy pants.

But it is an exacting and hazardous business. Armed with only a scrap of cloth, an empty barrel, and his wits, the clown never hesitates in putting himself into the danger spot when a cowboy is down or in trouble. Many are injured. Broken bones are a commonplace. Death is always a possibility. Yet, true to the traditions of the horseback aristocracy, from which they invariably spring, no rodeo clown ever tries to dodge his responsibilities, come what may.

When rodeo was young, clowns were chiefly just a comedy relief meant to keep the crowd in good humor during dull moments. They were little altered from the popular circus buffoons whose heritage dates back to the court jesters of ancient Eastern warlords. Local boys with a bent for the ridiculous were usually pressed into service. With a trick mule and the unique ingenuity of a fun-loving cowboy, such individuals seldom failed to satisfy the age-old desire for amusement. Moreover, most of them were top hands in all phases of cowboy work before they were clowns. It was easy for them to enliven the scene at any opportune moment by roping an escaping animal in some exaggerated manner or mounting a salty bronc or steer for a wild ride across the arena in their funny costumes.

But rodeo soon began to come of age. Productions were expanded and more unseasoned contestants appeared yearly. The clowns, in their traditional fashion, were always in the center of things, offering simulated help and making comic rescues. Occasionally, they shielded the audience's holiday spirit from tragic reality. It was soon found that an experienced rodeo hand doubling as a clown could usually prevent the more serious aspects of accidents. Thus it was that such men gradually worked themselves into acknowledged necessities. With the advent of the savage Brahmas into rodeo, around 1920, the clowns took their rightful place as highly respected performers.

Red Sublette was one of the earliest members of this professional group. Backed by previous clown experience and an excellent bronc- and bull-riding reputation, he sprang into the limelight with his trick mule Sparkplug at Magdalena, New Mexico, in 1918. His success set the pattern for many who have clowned their way to fame in later years.

Rodeo sets itself apart from all other professional sports by confining its monetary returns to what each member actually wins in individual contests. Furthermore, this group has followed its own ideas about having a large percentage of these winnings consist of entry fees paid by the entrants themselves. Primarily, this arises from the horseman's ever-present willingness to back his honor and judgment with money, marbles, or chalk. Secondly, it is the fairest method and the one least subject to financial finagling.

Entry fees for individual rodeo events usually run from $10 to $100 each. This comes out of the cowboy's own pocket for the privilege of testing his skill and luck against the field. He furnishes his own equipment and pays all his own expenses. Up until 1951, he also took care of whatever doctor or hospital bills might result from accidents. This last item has in later years fortunately been alleviated by a blanket insurance plan negotiated by the Rodeo Cowboys Association, devised and paid for by the associated members, covering all RCA contestants as a group.

Practically all of today's rodeos are operated on a nonprofit basis by civic organizations. Prize moneys are apportioned in accordance with expected gate receipts and entry fees. Woe be to the cowboy who empties his purse for the chance to draw a winning bucker and then winds up in the hospital; or one who follows the circuit for half a season without pulling down a substantial prize. It is an arrangement unique in the history of professional sports. Each participant is a free individual. No one owns him, hires him, or supervises his activities, directs his thoughts, or receives his homage. He is the cavalier of all the ages—free, bold, and independent, relying at all times on his own nerve and ability to see him through. In most cases, he does an excellent job of it, this twentieth century spirit of America on horseback.

Perhaps one of the best jobs he has done was bringing order into his own house. When poor management, shady influences, and lack of uniform standards threatened to wreck American rodeo, in the mid-1920s, he joined with his fellows in forming the first organized group in cowboy history. This Rodeo Association of America, born in 1928, and later reorganized as the Rodeo Cowboys Association, in 1945, now stands as a shining emblem to the initiative and clear thinking of those who would preserve one of our greatest national heritages.

Recent years have shown that the cowboy fraternity is quite entitled to pride in the rule book it has written. The American public demonstrates its acclamation by an annual attendance of around 15,000,000 paid admissions at the approximately 675 RCA approved rodeos in this country.

How many more people attend the five or six hundred lesser affairs not affiliated with the RCA can only be a matter of conjecture. Authorities agree that if it were possible to determine the total attendance records of all rodeos, local community affairs, junior, collegiate, and amateur contests being held all over the nation, the attendance figure would stand somewhere near 25 or 30 million a year. It is an imposing figure when compared with the 16 to 17 million who pay each year to see that other top ranking sport, baseball.

All this is rodeo, the pageant of the Old West, the life that has changed little since the old days. The stagecoach and relay races revive the days of the Overland Mail and the pony express. Cutting horse competitions and stake races portray everyday ranch hands in their best form. In the wild horse race we see a roundup crew starting an ordinary day's work on almost any frosty morning. Chuckwagon races, wild-cow milking, steer branding, and the like symbolize the more prosaic side of cowboy life—if there is such a thing. Carefree holiday fun appears in the cowpony races, burro riding, rooster pulling, and various novelty contests. The Roman race, mounted upright on two horses, reincarnates the whole line of horseback men back to Greece's Golden Age.

Through it all rides the philosophical, fun-loving cowboy sportsman. It is his world and his work, a work that he does willingly and with ever-fresh enjoyment. In it he more or less unconsciously emphasizes all the traditions that have symbolized every generation of the horseback clan since Bellerophon first materialized out of the Turkestan mists astride the winged Pegasus.

Actually, the worst thing about this man on horseback, as everyone has discovered in all lands and all ages, is the fact that, once started talking about him, a person never knows when to stop.

Acknowledgments

I WISH TO acknowledge my immense indebtedness to all those men and women of arts and letters, past and present, whose works have yielded so many items of historical importance and pertinent detail, and to the friends and correspondents who generously helped me uncover dim trails and all-but-forgotten relics of the past.

For his great kindness in directing my research on the ancient horseman of southern Asia, I wish to thank Harold Lamb, historical novelist. I likewise extend my sincere thanks to the late Dr. Roy Chapman Andrews, archeologist and explorer, for information pertaining to Mongolia's early horsemen; to Colonel Paul H. Downing, consultant on equipage at Colonial Williamsburg, Virginia, for material on equipment used by colonial America's pioneers and in western Europe's cavalier period; to Jack H. Bishop, director of historical research in the Library of Congress, for background material on saddlery of America's colonial era and of medieval and Elizabethan England; to Eleanor L. Duncan, assistant curator at Colonial Williamsburg, for descriptive details of ladies' pillions; to Colonel V. D. Krijanovsky, former officer in the Czar of Russia's Royal Guards, for sharing his personal knowledge of riding gear in prerevolutionary Russia.

I am deeply grateful to the late Dr. Herbert E. Bolton, Spanish-American historian and professor of history at the University of California, for source material showing the evolution of riding gear in Spanish-America; to Ruth Mahood, curator of history at the Los Angeles County Museum, California, for description of the Larades saddle and riding customs of women in early Spanish California; to William G.

Reed, assistant librarian of the New Mexico Historical Society, for research assistance on Spanish-American saddles; to Dr. John C. Ewers, assistant curator of ethnology at the Smithsonian Institution, for first-hand information and research suggestions on early Indian saddles; to Barbara Kell, reference librarian of the Missouri Historical Society, for the valuable material from old fur company records and St. Louis saddle-maker advertisements; to Dorothy C. Barck, librarian of the New-York Historical Society, for pertinent data in Astor's fur company records; to the late Bernard De Voto and Stanley Vestal (Dr. Walter S. Campbell) of the University of Oklahoma, western historians, for information and research help on Indian saddles.

For detailed information on U.S. Cavalry gear, I wish to thank Major General John K. Herr, military historian of Washington, D.C., for allowing me to use his notes gleaned from the National Archives; Colonel Harry C. Larter, military historian of San Antonio, Texas, for enlightening me on many phases of old-time cavalry saddles; Edgar W. Lancaster, civilian executive officer of the U.S. Army Ordnance Department, for providing various obscure details about cavalry equipment; Milton F. Perry, assistant curator of the West Point Museum, for details on the Captain James Duncan saddle; Herbert E. Kahler, chief historian, and Harold L. Peterson of the National Park Service, Remington Kellogg, director of the U.S. National Museum, and T. R. Walker, curator of the Rock Island Arsenal Museum, for information and research suggestions on cavalry outfits.

I wish to thank Walter D. King, general manager of Hermann H. Heiser Saddlery Company, Denver, Colorado; Irene Simpson, director of Wells Fargo Bank History Room, San Francisco, California; A. R. Mortensen, executive secretary of the Utah State Historical Society, Salt Lake City, Utah; C. D. Hall, monument supervisor of the Sutter's Fort Monument, Sacramento, California; Raymond W. Settle and Lee M. Rice, western historians, for their kind and generous help in uncovering many little-known facts about equipment used by the Pony Express.

I owe gratitude for much valuable information on the development of saddles past and present to Lee M. Rice; L. H. Hamley, Hamley Saddlery Company, Pendleton, Oregon; Sam D. Myers, Myers Saddlery Company, El Paso, Texas; Charles E. Bohlman, Portland, Oregon; Alfred H. Cornish, Cornish Saddlery Company, Omaha, Nebraska; Victor Marden, formerly of the Victor Marden Saddlery Company, The Dalles, Oregon; C. E. Parr, of the Hermann H. Heiser Saddlery Company,

Denver, Colorado; H. R. Miller, H. R. Miller Saddlery Company, Kansas City, Missouri; Victor Alexander, Bona Allen Saddlery Company, Buford, Georgia; J. Frank Dobie, western historian; Randy Steffen, western artist and historian, and A. J. Moreno, Frustnow Saddlery Company, Miles City, Montana.

I am most grateful to Mike Swift, of the Rodeo Information Commission, Denver, Colorado, and to veteran rodeo producers Verne Elliott, Colonel James Eskew, and L. H. Hamley for research help and many background items governing rodeo, past and present, and the introduction of its various events.

For use of historical items loaned me from the company files, my sincere thanks to Thomas E. Thompson of the John B. Stetson Company, Philadelphia, Pennsylvania, and Bob Lippman of the Levi Strauss Company, San Francisco, California. For permission to use certain items from *Vaquero of the Brush Country* I extend my thanks to Little, Brown and Company of Boston. I likewise thank Senator Francis Case of South Dakota for permission to use the poem "Horseback Men" from Badger Clark's book of western poetry, *Sky Lines and Wood Smoke,* as well as the excerpt from *From Town.* Further thanks to Senator Wayne Morse of Oregon and Harris Ellsworth, former Oregon member of Congress, for help in securing historical material from the Library of Congress; to Eleanor Stephens of the Oregon State Library for help with research problems and for the loan of material for study; Vesta M. Mulligan, director of interlibrary loans at the Oregon State Library, for her unlimited efforts in searching out and obtaining for me the many out-of-print and little-known works relative to the history of the man on horseback; and Blanche Moen, reference librarian at the University of Minnesota, for the loan of rare books on the subject.

To the numerous friends and acquaintances who have so kindly furnished me with countless odd facts, bits and pieces of pertinent information, and items of interest, without which this story would be sadly incomplete, I offer my most grateful thanks. One and all have been cooperative and generous. It is owing to their unselfish encouragement, constructive suggestions, and helpful interest in my pursuit of the man on horseback that the completion of this book was made possible.

GRV

Bibliography

BOOKS

ABBOTT, E. C. (Teddy Blue). *We Pointed Them North,* Farrar & Rinehart, New York, 1939.

ADAIR, JAMES (Samuel C. Wiliams, ed.). *History of the American Indians,* Watauga Press, Johnson City, Tenn., 1930.

ADAMS, ANDY. *Log of a Cowboy,* Houghton Mifflin & Co., Boston, 1903.

ADAMS, JAMES TRUSLOW (ed.). *Album of American History,* 5 vols., Charles Scribner's Sons, New York, 1949.

ALLEN, JULES VERNE. *Cowboy Lore,* Naylor Printing Co., San Antonio, 1933.

ANDREWS, ROY CHAPMAN. *On the Trail of Ancient Man,* G. P. Putnam's Sons, New York, 1935.

ASHTON, PHILIP. *The Cowboy,* Charles Scribner's Sons, New York, 1924.

BAILEY, ROBERT G. *River of No Return,* Bailey-Blake Printing Co., Lewiston, Idaho, 1933.

BERBNER, JOHN B. *The Explorers of North America,* 1492–1806, Macmillan Co., New York, 1933.

BERENGER, RICHARD. *The History and Art of Horsemanship,* T. Davies & T. Cadell, London, 1771.

BERJEAU, PHILIBERT CHARLES. *The Horses of Antiquity, Middle Ages and Renaissance,* Dulau & Co., London, 1864.

BOLTON, HERBERT E. *Coronado,* Whittlesey House, New York, 1949.

———. *Rim of Christendom,* Macmillan Co., New York, 1936.

———. *Texas in the Middle Eighteenth Century,* University of California Press, Berkeley, 1915.

BRONSON, E. B. *Reminiscences of a Ranchman,* A. C. McClurg & Co., Chicago, 1910.

BROWN, MARK H. and FELTON, W. R. *The Frontier Years,* Henry Holt & Co., New York, 1955.

BURNS, WALTER NOBLE. *Tombstone,* Doubleday, Page & Co., Garden City, N.Y., 1927.

BURT, STRUTHERS. *Powder River,* Farrar & Rinehart, New York, 1938.

CALDWELL, TAYLOR. *The Earth Is the Lord's* (Novel), World Publishing Co., Cleveland, 1947.

CALVERT, A. F. *Spanish Arms and Armor,* John Lane Co., London and New York, 1901.

CARTER, WILLIAM H. *Horses, Saddles and Bridles,* Lord Baltimore Press, Baltimore, 1906.

CATLIN, GEORGE. *Letters and Notes on the Manners, Customs and Conditions of the North American Indians,* Privately published, London, 1841.

CAUGHEY, JOHN W. *California,* Prenctice-Hall, New York, 1938.

CHAPMAN, ARTHUR. *The Pony Express,* G. P. Putnam's Sons, New York, 1932.

CLANCY, FOGHORN (FREDERICK M.). *My Fifty Years in Rodeo,* Naylor Co., San Antonio, 1952.

CLARK, BADGER. *Sky Lines and Wood Smoke* (Verse) Chronicle Shop, Custer, S.D., 1935.

COOK, JAMES H. *Fifty Years on the Old Frontier,* Yale University Press, New Haven, 1923.

COOLIDGE, DALE. *Old California Cowboys,* E. P. Dutton & Co., New York, 1939.

DAVENPORT, HOMER. *My Quest of the Arab Horse,* B. W. Dodge & Co., New York, 1909.

DAVIS, WILLIAM S. *Life on a Medieval Barony,* Harper & Brothers, New York, 1923.

DE GARSAULT, FRANÇOIS. *L'art du Bourrelier et du Sellier,* Paris, 1774.

DENHARDT, ROBERT M. *The Horse of the Americas,* University of Oklahoma Press, Norman, 1947.

DEPEW, CHAUNCEY (ed.). *1795–1895: One Hundred Years of American Commerce,* Vol. 2, D. C. Haynes & Co., New York, 1895.

DE SMET, FATHER P. J. (Edward Dunigan, ed.). *De Smet's Oregon Missions and Travel over the Rocky Mountains, 1845–46,* New York, 1847.

DE VOTO, BERNARD (ed.). *The Journals of Lewis and Clark, 1804–06,* Riverside Press, Cambridge, Mass., 1953.

DIDEROT, DENIS. *Encyclopédie,* Paris, 1753.

DOBIE, FRANK. *The Longhorns,* Little, Brown & Co., Boston, 1941.

———. *A Vaquero of the Brush Country,* Little, Brown & Co., Boston, 1943.

———. (M. C. Boatright and H. H. Ransom, eds.). *Mustangs and Cowhorses,* Texas Folk-Lore Society, Austin, 1940.

DODGE, RICHARD I. *Hunting Grounds of the Great West,* London, Chatto & Windus, 1878.

DODGE, THEODORE A. *Riders of Many Lands,* Harper & Brothers, New York, 1894.

DREPPERD, CARL W. *Pioneer America,* Doubleday & Co., New York, 1949.

DWYER, FRANCIS. *On Seats and Saddles,* J. B. Lippincott, Philadelphia, 1869.

EARLE, ALICE M. *Stagecoach and Tavern Days,* Macmillan Co., New York.

Encyclopedia Americana.

Encyclopaedia Britannica.

Farnham, Thomas J. *Travels in the Great Western Prairies,* Killey & Lossing, Poughkeepsie, New York, 1841.

Farshler, Earle R. *The American Saddle Horse,* Standard Printing Co., Louisville, 1933.

Foster-Harris, William. *The Look of the Old West,* Viking Press, New York, 1955.

Frazer, Sir James G. *The Golden Bough,* Macmillan Co., New York, 1949.

Histoire civile et naturelle du royaume de Siam, Costard, Paris, 1771.

Garrard, Lewis H. *Wah-to-yah and the Taos Trail,* A. S. Barnes Co., New York, 1850.

Garrison, Myrtle. *The Romance and History of the California Ranchos,* Harr Wagner, San Francisco, 1935.

Graham, Robert B. C. *The Horses of the Conquest,* William Heinemann, Ltd., London, 1930.

Gregg, Josiah. *Commerce of the Prairies,* H. G. Langley Co., 1844.

Gregg, J. R. *Pioneer Days in Malheur County, Oregon,* private printing, 1950.

Haley, J. Evetts. *Charles Goodnight, Cowman and Plainsman,* Houghton Mifflin & Co., Boston, 1936.

Hartman, Gertrude. *Medieval Days and Ways,* Macmillan Co., New York, 1948.

Hasluck, Paul N. (ed.). *Saddlery and Harness Making,* McKay, London, 18 ? .

Hastings, Frank S. *A Ranchman's Recollections,* Breeder's Gazette, Chicago, 1921.

Herr, General John K. and Wallace, Edward S. *The Story of the U.S. Cavalry,* Little, Brown & Co., Boston, 1953.

Hitti, Philip. *History of the Arabs,* Princeton University Press, Princeton, 1946.

Howard, Joseph K. *Strange Empire,* William Morrow & Co., New York, 1952.

Hunter, J. Marvin (ed.). *Trail Drivers of Texas,* Cokesbury Press, Nashville, 1925.

Irving, Washington. *Astoria,* G. P. Putnam, New York, 1849.

———. *Captain Bonneville,* G. P. Putnam, New York, 1849.

Jackson, William H. *Picture Maker of the Old West,* Charles Scribner's Sons, New York, 1947.

James, Will. *Cowboys North and South,* Grosset & Dunlap, New York, 1948.

———. *Lone Cowboy, My Life Story,* Charles Scribner's Sons, New York, 1930.

Kurz, Rudolph F. (J. N. B. Hewitt, ed.). *A Journal of His Experiences Among the Fur Traders of the Upper Missouri River, 1846–52,* Government Printing Office, Washington, 1937.

Lake, Stuart. *Wyatt Earp,* Houghton Mifflin Co., Boston, 1931.

Lamb, Harold. *Tamerlane,* Robert M. McBride & Co., New York, 1928.

Lawrence, Walter R. *The Valley of Kashmir,* Oxford University Press, London, 1895.

Macauley, Thurston. *The Great Horse Omnibus,* Ziff-Davis Co., Chicago, 1949.

Maddox, William A. *Historical Carvings in Leather,* Naylor Co., San Antonio, 1940.

Maloney, Alice B. *Fur Brigade to the Bonaventura,* California Historical Society, San Francisco, 1945.

MARSHALL, EDISON. *Caravan to Xanadu* (Novel), Dell Publishing Co., New York, 1953.

MASON, VAN WYCK. *The Barbarians* (Novel), Pocket Books, Inc., New York, 1954.

McGOVERN, WILLIAM M. *The Early Empires of Central Asia,* University of North Carolina Press, Chapel Hill, 1939.

MILLER, FRANCIS TREVELYN (ed.). *The Photographic History of the Civil War,* Review of Reviews Co., New York, 1911.

MORA, JO. *Trail Dust and Saddle Leather,* Charles Scribner's Sons, New York, 1946.

———. *Californios,* Doubleday & Co., Garden City, N.Y., 1949.

OSGOOD, ERNEST S. *The Day of the Cattleman,* University of Minnesota Press, 1929.

PARKMAN, FRANCIS. *The Oregon Trail,* Little, Brown & Co., Boston, 1936.

PINKERTON, JOHN (ed.). *A General Collection of the Best and Most Interesting Voyages and Travels in All Parts of the World,* 17 vols., London, 1811.

———. *Travels of Pietro Della Valle in Persia, 1617.*

———. *Travels of Sir John Chardin, 1671.*

———. *Michael Syme's Embassy to Ava, India, 1795.*

———. *Voyages and Travels of Anthony Jenkinson from Russia to Bokhara, in 1557.*

———. *William Francklin's Tour from Bengal to Persia, 1786–1787.*

POPE, ARTHUR UPHAM. *A Survey of Persian Art,* Oxford University Press, New York, 1939.

POTTER, JACK. *Cattle Trails of the Old West,* Clayton, N.M., 1935.

POWERS, LAURA B. *Old Monterey,* San Carlos Press, San Francisco, 1934.

PRICE, CON. *Trails I Rode,* Trail's End Pub. Co., Pasadena, 1947.

RASWAN, CARL R. *Black Tents of Arabia,* Little, Brown & Co., Boston, 1935.

ROLLINSON, JOHN K. *Wyoming Cattle Trails,* Caxton Printers, Caldwell, Idaho, 1948.

SANDOZ, MARI. *The Buffalo Hunters,* Hastings House, New York, 1954.

SCHMITT, MARTIN and BROWN, DEE. *Trail Driving Days,* Charles Scribner's Sons, New York, 1952.

SETTLE, RAYMOND W. and MARY L. *Empire on Wheels,* Stanford University Press, 1949.

SHELLABARGER, SAMUEL *Captain from Castile* (Novel), Little, Brown & Co., Boston, 1945.

SHELLER, ROSCOE. *Ben Snipes,* Binfords & Mort, Portland, Ore., 1958.

SIRINGO, CHARLES A. *A Texas Cowboy,* J. S. Ogilvie Co., New York, 1886.

STONE, G. C. *A Glossary of the Construction, Decoration and Use of Arms and Armor,* Southworth Press, Portland, Me., 1934.

STONG, PHIL. *Horses and Americans,* Frederick A. Stokes Co., New York, 1939.

STREETER, FLOYD B. *Prairie Trails and Cowtowns,* Chapman & Grimes, Inc., Boston, 1936.

TAIT, GEORGE E. *The Saddle of Carlos Perez,* Westminster Press, Philadelphia, 1950.

THWAITES, REUBEN G. (ed.) *Early Western Travels, 1748–1846,* Arthur H. Clark & Co., Cleveland, 1906.

———. Brackenridge, H. M. *Journal of A Voyage up the Missouri River in 1811,* Vol. 6.

———. Bradbury, John. *A Journal of Travel on the Upper Missouri River in 1811,* Vol. 5.

———. Franchère, Gabriel. *A Journal of a Voyage to Northwest Coast of America in Year 1811* Vol. 6. Trans. & ed. J. U Huntington.

———. James, Edwin. *Major Stephen H. Long's Expedition to the Rocky Mountains in 1819–20,* Vols. 15–17.

———. Maximilian, Prince of Wied. *Travels in the Interior of North America, 1832–34,* Vols. 22–24.

———. Pattie, James C. *A Personal Narrative* (of Travels in the Southwest, 1924–26), Vol. 18.

———. Ross, Alexander. *The Fur Hunters,* Vol. 7.

———. Wyeth, Nathaniel. *Journal of an Expedition to the Rocky Mountains and Columbia River in 1834,* Vol. 21.

TRENHOLM, VIRGINIA, and CARLEY, MAURINE. *Wyoming Pageant,* Prairie Pub. Co., Casper, Wyo., 1946.

UNDERHILL, REUBEN L. *From Cowhides to Golden Fleece,* Stanford University Press, Stanford, 1946.

VESTAL, STANLEY. *Dodge City,* Harper & Brothers, New York, 1952.

———. *The Missouri,* Farrar & Rinehart, New York, 1945.

———. *Joe Meek,* Caxton Printers, Caldwell, Idaho, 1952.

WATERER, JOHN W. *Leather in Life, Art and Industry,* London, 1946.

WELLMAN, PAUL I. *Glory, God and Gold,* Doubleday & Co., New York, 1949.

———. *The Trampling Herd,* Carrick & Evans, New York, 1930.

WELLS, H. G. *The Outline of History,* Doubleday & Co., New York, 1949.

WESTERMEIER, CLIFFORD P. *Man, Beast, Dust,* World Press, Inc., 1947.

WEYBRIGHT, VICTOR and SELL, HENRY BLACKMAN. *Buffalo Bill and the Wild West,* Oxford University Press, 1955.

WINSHIP, G. F. *The Coronado Expedition,* 14th Annual Report, Bureau of American Ethnology, Washington, 1896.

WINTHROP, THEODORE (J. H. Williams, ed.). *The Canoe and the Saddle,* Tacoma, 1913.

WISE, HENRY A. *Los Gringos, or An Inside View of Mexico and California, with Wanderings in Peru, Chili, and Polynesia,* Baker & Scribner, New York, 1849.

WRIGHT, ROBERT M. *Dodge City,* Wichita Eagle Press, Wichita, 1913.

MAGAZINE ARTICLES

BARBOUR, WILLIAM R. "Buenos Aires and Its River of Silver," *National Geographic,* Oct. 1921.

BURT, STRUTHERS. "The Diary of a Dude Wrangler," *Saturday Evening Post* (serial) March–May 1924.

CARTER, WILLIAM H. "The Story of a Horse," *National Geographic,* Nov. 1923.

Casteret, Norbert. "Discovery of the Oldest Statue in the World," *National Geographic,* Aug. 1924.

Collins, G. E. P. "Seafarers of the South Celebes," *National Gegraphic,* Jan. 1945.

Cott, Hugh B. "Wonder Island of the Amazon Delta," *National Geographic,* Nov. 1938.

De Young, Joe. "The Tricks of a Rough, Tough Trade," *Western Horseman,* Sept. 1949.

Ewers, John C. "The Indian Buffalo Hunter's Saddle," *Western Horseman,* Sept. 1949.

Haines, Frances. "The Northward Spread of Horses Among the Plains Indians," *American Anthropologist,* Vol. XL, 1938.

Halliday, Dick. "Spurs an' Such," *Ace-High,* Aug. 1934.

Holmes, Kenneth. "Early-Day Indian Stockman," *Oregon Farmer,* Oct. 15, 1935.

Kingston, C. S. "Introduction of Cattle into the Pacific Northwest," *Oregon Historical Quarterly,* July 1923.

Latham, Sid. "Will Rogers Was Good at It Too," *True,* Aug. 1951.

Oliphant, James C. "Cattle Trails from the Pacific Northwest to Montana," *Agricultural History,* April 1933.

———. "The Cattle Trade on Pugent Sound," *Agricultural History,* April 1933.

Patrick, John. "Magyar Mirth and Melancholy," *National Geographic,* Jan. 1938.

Roth, Charles B. "The Cowboy's Pride and Joy," *True,* Aug. 1949.

Simpich, Frederick. "Life on the Argentine Pampas," *National Geographic,* Oct. 1933.

Terrett, Courtenay. "Miles City Saddles," *Western Horseman,* Sept. 1949.

Tschiffely, A. F. "The Crillo of South America," *Western Horseman,* Sept. 1949.

Vernam, Glenn R. "The Northwest's Riding Man," *Western Horseman,* June 1956.

———."Packing the Saddle Gun," *Outdoor Life,* Aug. 1933.

Vialles, Dr. André. "Camargue, the Cowboy Conutry of Southern Franch," *National Geographic,* July 1922.

Warwick, Adam. "Thousand Miles Along the Great Wall of China," *National Geographic,* Feb. 1923.

Wisler, Clark. "American Indian Saddles," *American Museum Journal,* Dec. 1916.

——— . "Riding Gear of the North American Indians," American Museum Anthropological Paper, Part I, Vol. 17, 1915.

CATALOGUES AND OTHER SOURCES

Military goods

Francis Bannerman Sons, New York (1913).

Saddlery

Allen-Bona, Inc., Buford, Ga.
DeCamp, Levoy & Co., Cincinnati, O. (1912).
Al Frustnow, Miles City, Mont. (1916).
Hamley Company, Pendleton, Ore. (1915–1934).
Harbison & Gathright, Louisville, Ky. (1875).
Victor Marden, The Dalles, Ore. (1914).
Miles City Saddlery Co., Miles City, Mont. (1914).
Miller, Stockman-Farmer, Denver, Colo. (1930–1953).
Sam D. Myers, El Paso, Tex. (1950).
E. G. Noble, Heppner, Ore. (1912).
Richardson Walsh Co., Sacramento, Calif. (1910).

Notes from company files

John B. Stetson, Philadelphia, Pa.
Levi Strauss Co., San Francisco, Calif.

Rodeo Annual

Chuck Walters, 1958 Rodeo Annual, Rodeo Information Commission, Denver, Colo.

LETTERS

Alexander Victor, Allen-Bona, Inc., Saddlery, Buford, Ga.
Andrews, Dr. Roy Chapman, archeologist; author, Colebrook, Conn.
Bishop, Jack R., Department of Historical Research, Library of Congress, Washington, D.C.
Bohlman, Charles E., pioneer saddlemaker and factory superintendent, 1894–1948. George Lawrence Saddle Co., Portland, Ore.
Bolton, Dr. Herbert E., professor of history, University of California, Berkeley.
Cornish, Alfred H., president, Cornish Saddlery Co., Omaha, Nebr.
De Voto, Bernard, author; historian, Cambridge, Mass.
Dobie, J. Frank, author; professor of history, University of Texas, Austin.
Downing, Col. Paul H., consultant of equipage at colonial Williamsburg, Va.
Duncan, Eleanor L., assistant curator, colonial Williamsburg, Va.
Elliott, Verne, pioneer rodeo producer and stock contractor, Platteville, Colo.
Eskew, Col. James, pioneer rodeo producer, Waverly, N.Y.
Ewers, Dr. John C., assistant curator of ethnology, Smithsonian Institution, Washington, D.C.
Hamley, L. H., president, The Hamley Co., Pendleton, Ore.
Herr, Maj. Gen. John K., military historian; author, Washington, D.C.
Kahler, Herbert E., chief historian, National Park Service, Washington, D.C.
Kell, Barbara, reference librarian, Missouri Historical Society, St. Louis, Mo.
Kellogg, Remington, director, U.S. National Museum, Washington, D.C.

King, Walter D., general manager, Hermann H. Heiser Saddlery Co., Denver, Colo.

Krijanovsky, Col. V. D., former officer in Czar of Russia's Royal Guards, West Scarboro, Me.

Lamb, Harold, author; historian, Beverly Hills, Calif.

Lancaster, Edgar W., civilian exeuctive officer of the U.S. Army Ordnance Dept., Washington, D.C.

Lapman, Bob, advertising manager, Levi Strauss Co., San Francisco, Calif.

Larter, Col. Harry C., military historian; author, San Antonio, Tex.

Mahood, Ruth, curator of history, Los Angeles County Museum, Los Angeles, Calif.

Marden, Victor, pioneer saddlemaker, Portland, Ore.

Miller, H. R., president, Miller Saddlery Co., Kansas City, Mo.

Moreno, A. J., president, Frustnow Saddlery Co., Miles City, Mont.

Mortensen, A. R., executive secretary, Utah State Historical Society, Salt Lake City, Utah.

Myers, Sam D., president, Myers Saddlery Co., El Paso, Texas.

Parr, C. E., Hermann H. Heiser Saddlery Co., Denver, Colo.

Perry, Milton F., assistant curator, West Point Museum, West Point, N.Y.

Peterson, Harold L., National Park Service, Washington, D.C.

Rice, Lee M., poineer saddlemaker; author; historian, San Leandro, Calif.

Simpson, Irene, director, Wells Fargo Bank History Room, San Francisco, Calif.

Swift, Mike, director, Rodeo Information Commission, Denver, Colo.

Thompson, Thomas E., assistant advertising manager, John B. Stetson Co., Philadelphia, Pa.

Walker, T. R., curator, Rock Island Arsenal Museum, U.S. Army Ordnance Department, Rock Island, Ill.

Index